Volume 2

 alba house
DIVISION OF THE SOCIETY OF ST. PAUL
STATEN ISLAND, N.Y. 10314

THE PSALMS

THEIR ORIGIN AND MEANING

Leopold Sabourin, S.J.

IMPRIMI POTEST:
R. A. F. Mackenzie, S.J.
Rector, Pontifical Biblical Institute

NIHIL OBSTAT:
Donald A. Panella, M.A., S.T.L., S.S.L.
Censor Librorum

IMPRIMATUR:
Joseph P. O'Brien, S.T.D.
Vicar General, New York

Library of Congress Catalog Card No. 71-77647

The nihil obstat, imprimi potest and imprimatur are official declarations that a book or pamphlet is free of doctrinal or moral error. No implication is contained therein that those who have granted the nihil obstat, imprimi potest or imprimatur agree with the contents, opinions or statements expressed.

© 1969 by the Society of St. Paul, 2187 Victory Blvd., Staten Island, N.Y. 10314

Designed, printed and bound in the U.S.A. by the Pauline Fathers and Brothers of the Society of St. Paul at Staten Island, New York as a part of their communications apostolate.

FOREWORD

Seper tehillim, the Book of Psalms, has had a privileged history, among all existing collections of prayer-texts. Some of its 150 numbers date from 1000 years before the Christian era; the collection was completed and "closed" probably in the fourth or third century B.C. All its contents, from the times of their respective creations down to the present day, have been in uninterrupted regular use, first in Jerusalem, then in Palestine, in the Near East, and now all over the world. First the Jewish people, then the Christian church in its worldwide expansion, have carried with them, as a precious ancestral heritage, this treasury of sacred song. If ever men could apply to themselves what one of them said about the heavens — "through all the earth their voice resounds, and to the ends of the world, their message" — surely those men were the psalmists of Israel.

Many other prayers, from many ancient cults and religions, are known to us, some of them even older than the psalms. But those texts are museum-pieces, relics of a dead past, addressed to divinities long since deserted by men and almost forgotten. No religious community of today uses an Egyptian hymn to the Sun-god, or Babylonian prayers to Marduk, or the Stoics' Hymn to Zeus, as expressions of modern faith and worship. But Israel's hymns and supplications to

YHWH are still a living language of prayer, used by millions in the modern world to address the One God whom they worship.

In this millennial tradition of the Psalter's use, successive generations and various cultures have had the problem of making the psalms accessible and comprehensive to their members, in the first place by translation into whatever language was their own. Already in pre-Christian times the text, along with the rest of the Hebrew scriptures, was rendered into Greek and into Aramaic, by the Jews themselves. Since then, such work has been continually repeated, as indeed it must ever be.

In the Catholic Church of today, there has been a marked revival of interest in the liturgy, a renewed understanding of the vital importance of meaningful and comprehensive public worship. This movement was sanctioned and powerfully promoted by Vatican Council II. Automatically, it has awakened among Catholics fresh interest in the psalms. All existing Christian liturgies, some of them very ancient, have given the psalms pride of place. They make up a large part of the prayer-texts used by the Church, they supply much of her dialogue with her Creator and Redeemer. Any revitalizing of the liturgy, therefore, necessarily involves a re-examination and *re-valuing* of the psalms. Even if (and this is a moot point) they are to have a smaller part in the liturgy of the future, to make intelligent changes we must first discover and understand why they have had such a predominant position in the liturgies of the past.

To make the psalms "accessible," therefore, to modern man, to help him to understand them as expressive of his needs and aspirations, is an important and not altogether an easy task. Much has been accomplished, much more remains to be done. For users of the English language, there is certainly room, and need, for new translations, perhaps still more for new commentaries, which will help pastors, preachers, catechists and liturgists, to experience for themselves the religious value of the psalms and to facilitate that experience for others.

It is to such a task that Father Sabourin has addressed himself in this book. He tells us that his purpose was "to present in readable form the best material now available on the biblical psalms." That means especially the results of modern literary and historical studies, which have so greatly enlarged our understanding of the historical setting and original function of the psalms. They have illuminated also the thought-world of the psalmists, and analyzed the beliefs and doctrines which they held and expressed.

In this book the author has digested and summarized the results of an immense amount of labor devoted to the text of the psalms, in modern times, mostly by Protestant and Catholic scholars. A glance at the Bibliography, limited to "works to which the present writer had direct access," will attest the thoroughness of his researches and his mastery of the vast field. The reader will see that the fundamental achievement of this "modern approach" has been the classification of the psalms in terms of their original functions, the *Gattungsforschung* pioneered by Hermann Gunkel and refined by his successors.

There is also the question of the Christian interpretation of the psalms. They are presented to us in the liturgy, enriched by a whole tradition, which starts with the quotations in the New Testament and continues through the patristic and mediaeval usage, in both Eastern and Western churches. Modern Christian interpreters cannot ignore the wealth of Christian signification which our predecessors have found in the Psalter. In the present work, this important question is discussed at the end of the third chapter.

One may hope and expect that Father Sabourin's devoted labors will make easier and more effective the work of many other popularizers of these inspired praises of God.

Rome   R. A. F. MacKenzie, S.J.

PREFACE

Not a detailed commentary but a substantial introduction to the Psalter and to each psalm will be found in this work. A special attention is paid to the original setting of the poems and to their essential message. As a rule, the more common or traditional opinion is first expressed, then other views are exposed and appraised. This explains that the introduction to Psalms 2, 18, 22, 51, 68, 73, 110, for example, is much more extensive than for other psalms rarely studied. The main purpose of the present work is in fact to present in readable form the best material now available on the biblical psalms. Too many sound results of scholarly investigations remain unnoticed by readers who would have the necessary preparation for understanding them. It is not enough to read about them in periodical "abstracts." They appear in their proper light when seen against the complex background of research. Impressions and convictions need to be tempered and matured against divergent opinion. Not a few commentaries of the psalms or introductions to them have been written, it would seem, to prove a thesis rather than to help the reader understand the text. It is hoped that the present work will offer to the clergy, to the theological students and to a qualified laity what they need at the present time to update their knowledge of a biblical book so widely used in the Jewish as well as in the Christian liturgy and so expressive of mankind's religious sentiment.

The fruits of serious biblical research have also been drawn upon in the general introduction which consists of the first three chapters. It will be noticed that several sections are devoted to the contribution of modern interpreters like Hermann Gunkel and Sigmund Mowinckel. New trends are also noted: that, for example, represented by the Myth and Ritual School, that also which results from the impact produced on psalm study by the discoveries of Ras-Shamra-Ugarit. The chapter entitled "The Beliefs of Piety" analyzes the main points of the teachings of the psalmists, exposes their biblical background and sets forth great themes of the religious thought of the Old Testament. Messianism in the Psalter receives proper attention, as does also the significance of the psalms for Christ and the Christian.

In 1953 was published *The Book of Psalms* in volume three of *The Holy Bible,* sponsored by the Episcopal Committee of the Confraternity of Christian Doctrine. This new Catholic edition of the Holy Bible follows the norms set down by Pope Pius XII in his encyclical *Divino Afflante Spiritu* (September 30, 1943). It is prepared by members of the Catholic Biblical Association of America, who were requested to translate the Sacred Scriptures "from the original languages or from the oldest extant form of the text, and to present the sense of the Biblical text in as correct a form as possible." In a short introduction to volume three (*Sapiential Books*) it is stated that the basic text used for the psalms was not the Massoretic (cf. §2a), "but one considered closer to the original inspired form, namely the Hebrew text underlying the new Latin Psalter of the Church, the *Liber Psalmorum* (Rome 1944 and 1945). Though the editors of the psalms retained full liberty to establish the reading of the original text on sound critical principles, the limited number of passages in which they actually departed [from the *Liber Psalmorum*] brings their translation into substantial conformity with the public prayer of the Church" (p.V). The Confraternity text [henceforth = *CV*] has been acclaimed as one of the best English translations of the psalms. It is incorporated in this book for the convenience of the readers. New evidence has often brought the present writer to propose in the commentary an alternative and hopefully a better translation of particular verses. The grounds for disagreement are always given, but the "textual notes" appended to the Confraternity edition are not reproduced (see *The Holy Bible,* vol. III, pp. 670-682).

Classification, an essential element in any knowledge, is especially relevant for the study of a book consisting of 150 poems. It is not surprising therefore that their classification in "types" has received special attention since the basic work of Hermann Gunkel (cf. §7a). The grouping of the psalms into their literary categories also facilitates exposition and adds to clarity. A numerical index (§34) will tell the reader where a given psalm is treated *ex professo* in this work. The special introduction which presents each category increases perceptiveness in regard to the individual compositions. Tedious repetitions of common features is also thus avoided without weakening information.

In the beginning of this century C. A. Briggs referred to the "vast amount of literature" devoted to the Psalms. How would he characterize the present situation? A complete bibliography extending from 1929 has been published in 1955 by J. J. Stamm in *Theologische Rundschau* 23 (1955), p. 1-68. A good survey, which gives due credit to Catholic authors, is that of J. Coppens in *Le Psautier* (Louvain, 1962), p. 1-71. Previously A. R. Johnson had done a similar work in *The Old Testament and Modern Study* (H. H. Rowley, edit.: Oxford, 1951), pp. 162-209.

The bibliography offered in the present book is extensive, although it includes only works to which the present writer had direct access. The majority of the authors mentioned are quoted or referred to in some instance, generally by a simple indication of the name and page (or simply the name, if it is a commentary or a short article). For practical reasons the bibliography follows the alphabetical order, but studies relevant to a given psalm or subject will be opportunely indicated. In the bibliography itself references to particularly relevant paragraphs (§ . . .) are appended to the main work of some prominent authors. A good bibliography of the ancient commentators, omitted here, will be found in G. Castellino, *Libro dei Salmi* (Roma, 1955) 34-38.

Items treated explicitly in one of the first three chapters or elsewhere are also referred to by indicating the paragraph and, in most cases, its sub-division, like §5b, 10d (the pages are given in the Contents). Readings like cf. Ps *52 or cf. *Ps 110:7 indicate that in the introduction to this particular psalm or verse, offered in the present work, the reader will find additional relevant material. The biblical texts are generally quoted from the Confraternity of Christian Doctrine edition (*CV*). In this edition the verse numeration of the psalms includes the headings; thus it can differ slightly from other English texts, for example the Revised Standard Version (*RSV;* see also §3a for the numeration of the psalms themselves).

From the unpublished chapter of thanks the present writer wishes to single out authors of studies which have proved particularly useful to him: M. Dahood, H.-J. Kraus, S. Mowinckel, R. Tournay (*BJ*), A. Weiser. He owes a special gratitude to an emeritus professor of Hebrew language, Father Louis Semkowski, S.J., who has reviewed the manuscript.

Pontifical Biblical Institute,
25 Via Pilotta, Rome.

LIST OF ABBREVIATIONS

ANEP	Ancient Near East in Pictures (J. B. Pritchard)
ANET	Ancient Near Eastern Texts (J. B. Pritchard)
AssSeign	Assemblées du Seigneur
BA	Biblical Archaeologist
BASOR	Bulletin of the American Schools of Oriental Research
Bib	Biblica
BibOr	Bibbia e Oriente
BiLeb	Bibel und Leben
BiLit	Bibel und Liturgie
BiViChr	Bible et Vie Chrétienne
BJ	Bible de Jérusalem [= R. Tournay-R. Schwab, *Les Psaumes*]
BZ	Biblische Zeitschrift
BZAW	Beihefte zum *ZAW*
CBQ	Catholic Biblical Quarterly
ColBibLat	Collectanea Biblica Latina (Roma)
CV	Confraternity Version [= text of the Confraternity of Christian Doctrine]
EncBib	Enciclopedia de la Biblia (Barcelona)
EstBib	Estudios Biblicos
EstE	Estudios Eclesiasticos
ETL	Ephemerides Theologicae Lovanienses
FRLANT	Forschungen zur Religion und Literatur d.Alten u.Neuen Testaments
Greg	Gregorianum
HUCA	Hebrew Union College Annual
IEJ	Israel Exploration Journal

JB	Jerusalem Bible
JBL	Journal of Biblical Literature
JEOL	Jaarbericht . . . ex Oriente Lux
JNES	Journal of Near Eastern Studies
JQR	Jewish Quarterly Review
JSS	Journal of Semitic Studies
JTS	Journal of Theological Studies
Liber Annuus	Studii Biblici Franciscani Liber Annuus (Jerusalem)
MT	Massoretic Text (cf. §2a)
MüTZ	Münchener Theologische Zeitschrift
NRT	Nouvelle Revue Théologique
OABA	Oxford Annotated Bible with the Apocrypha
OTS	Oudtestamentische Studien
PEQ	Palestine Exploration Quarterly
RB	Revue Biblique
RBibIt	Rivista Biblica [Italiana]
RQum	Revue de Qumran
RSR	Recherches de Science Religieuse
RSV	Revised Standard Version
ScEcc	Sciences Ecclésiastiques
SDB	Supplément au Dictionnaire de la Bible
TGl	Theologie und Glaube
TLZ	Theologische Literaturzeitung
TS	Theological Studies
TZBas	Theologische Zeitschrift (Basel)
VD	Verbum Domini
VT	Vetus Testamentum
ZAW	Zeitschrift für die Alttestamentliche Wissenschaft

CONTENTS

Volume I

Volume II

CHAPTER V.   LAMENTS, PSALMS OF CONFIDENCE, AND
THANKSGIVINGS: of the Individual 1

§20. *Laments of the individual* 1

(a) Literary structure 1
(b) Text and introduction: Pss 5-5, 6-8, 7-9, 13-12, 17-14, 22-17, 25-22, 26-25, 28-27, 31-29, 35-32, 36-35, 38-38, 39-40, 42-42, 43-43, 51-45, 54-51, 55-52, 56-54, 57-56, 59-58, 61-60, 63-62, 64-63, 69-64, 70-68, 71-69, 86-71, 88-73, 102-75, 109-78, 120-80, 130-82, 140-83, 141-84, 142-86, 143-87.

§21. *Psalms of confidence of the individual* 90

(a) General character 90
(b) Text and introduction: Pss 3-91, 4-92, 11-94, 16-96, 23-99, 27-102, 62-105, 121-107, 131-108.

§22. *Thanksgivings of the individual* 109

(a) Literary structure 110
(b) Text and introduction: Pss 9/10-112/113, 30-117, 32-119, 34-121, 40 (vv 2-12)-124, 41-127, 92-130, 107-133, 116-136, 138-138.

CHAPTER VI.   LAMENTS, PSALMS OF CONFIDENCE, AND
THANKSGIVINGS: of the COMMUNITY 141

§23. *Laments of the community* 141

(a) General character 141
(b) Text and introduction: Pss 12-143, 44-145, 58-148, 60-149, 74-151, 77-155, 79-157, 80-159, 82-162, 83-164, 85-165, 90-168, 94-170, 106-174, 108-178, 123-179, 126-180, 137-182.

§24. *Psalms of confidence of the community* 184

(a) General character 184
(b) Text and introduction: Pss 115-185, 125-187, 129-188.

§25. *Thanksgivings of the community* 189

(a) General character 189
(b) Text and introduction: Pss 65-190, 66-192, 67-195, 68-196, 118-203, 124-207.

CONTENTS

CHAPTER FIVE

LAMENTS
Psalms of Confidence, and Thanksgivings: of the Individual

According to the principles of the *Gattungsforschung* (cf. §7) great importance is attached to the original context of literary works. Prayers of or for the community generally originate from the cult and thus differ from compositions prompted by individual concerns. On the other hand, the three categories of the present family of psalms are related by a common interest: the situation of a man in distress. The lament and the expression of confidence accompany the crisis, while the thanksgiving describes its happy *dénouement*. That these three categories are in some way connected appears from their simultaneous presence in a few psalms (e.g. 22, 30, 31, 54, 56, 61).

§20. LAMENTS OF THE INDIVIDUAL

(a) The *structure* of these psalms generally includes the following elements:

1) *Introduction*: *Invocation of the name* (Yahweh or Elohim), followed by a cry for help (cf. 142:2), often in the imperative (cf. 5:2). This initial contact with God can be repeated or amplified. Like the hymn, writes A. Bentzen (I, p. 156), "the psalms of lamentation

have a *'primitive cell'* in a *cultic exclamation,* probably the *'honnēnī Yahweh'*, "Be gracious to me . . .," (51:3; 57:2; 86:3; cf. Lk 18:13), and probably the category has been called *tehinnā* ("supplication"; cf. the superscription of Ps 102)." When the supplication proper mixes with the invocation, or when the complaint and the motives support the cry for help, it is not always easy to isolate the invocation (cf. Ps 5).

2) *Main section* (*corpus supplicationis*). It includes several elements, not always presented in the same order. They often intermingle or appear in successive stages. One or another is likely to be abridged.

(aa) *The complaint.* It is not always announced as in Ps 142:3: "My complaint I pour out before him; before him I lay bare my distress," or as in the heading of Ps 102: "The prayer of an afflicted one when he is faint and pours out his anguish before the Lord." These exceptional formulations reveal one of the common *motives* of the complaint: to relieve the heart. There existed in Babylonia a collection of psalms entitled: "complaint to appease the heart" (cf. *SDB,* vol. I, c. 818f). But the complaint's main motive is to move God to act. Among these *Gebetserhörungsmotive the description of the man's distress* stands in first place. The danger of death is almost always involved, be it from natural causes (disease and calamities) or from human malice. So not the small *malaises* are the object of prayer but the dangers arising from the enemies of Life. Illness has a religious meaning: "for the biblical writer," writes G. Pidoux, "life was conceived as a power, of reduced strength in the sick and almost inexistent in the dead" (*Du Portique . . . ,* p. 72). It is not surprising that the sick man felt to be at the mercy of hostile forces, if God had turned away his face from him. Hence his wish to see again the face of God (31:17; 42:3), to enjoy again the community's fellowship (22: 26): "I am sleepless, and I moan; I am like a sparrow *alone* on the housetop" (102:8). It is in the complaint especially that the individual traits of the lament are revealed, as distinct from the hymn, much less personal. Not all the expressions of the complaint are to be understood literally, however, since the suppliant draws also from a common stock of conventional formulas and semitic overstatements (cf. Pss 22:15f; 38:6-9). People in distress will likely depend for help on fixed religious patterns, which in turn can be reflected in the description of the need (cf. H. Ringgren, *The Faith . . . ,* p. 62).

(bb) *The supplication.* It is a moving prayer requesting urgent help by people whom A. Gelin calls *"les tutoyeurs de Dieu,"* those who say *"tu"* to God. The familiar way of addressing God is also reflected in the frequent use of anthropomorphisms: "Listen to me!" "Open your ear!" "Look!" "Rouse yourself!" "Wake up!" "Hurry!" "Answer me!" "Save me!" "Return!" These repeated appeals, which generally spring from filial confidence, can also reflect moments of impatience: "How long, O Lord? . . . How long will you hide your face from me?" (Ps 13:2) But phrases like these also follow stereotyped patterns (see on *Ps 13). Some authors would propose that the Israelite prayer has been purified in a multiple-stage process: first, God was blamed, then the enemy; the prayers with a request were replaced by pure penitential prayers, as in Neh 9. But in all periods one or another of these elements is likely to predominate.

(cc) *Who are the suppliants?* Psalm 102 is "the prayer of an 'ānî, a "poor," an "afflicted" (see on §12a-c). Modern scholars show interest in classifying the laments according to the distress involved (cf. J. Coppens in *Le Psautier,* pp. 17, 21, 29, 49, 77). There are psalms of the sick (6, 13, 28, 31B, 39, 61, 69, 70, 102, 109; cf. Is 38:9-20), psalms of the accused (5, 7, 13, 17, 25, 28, 38, 39, 54-59, 86, 88, 102: cf. H. Schmidt, *Das Gebet* . . .), psalms of the persecuted (13, 22, 31, 42/43, 109, 142, 143). No real evidence can be produced to support Mowinckel's suggestion that the majority of the suppliants are victims of sorcery (cf. §12g). Studying "Theophanies in holy places in Hebrew Religion," J. Lindblom discovered in Ps 3:6 evidence of "an incubation-oracle imparted in an incubation-dream. Thus the psalm was recited in the morning after the incubation-sleep." In Ps 17, however, the "incubation" leads to a real theophany (v 15), expected by the suppliant at his awakening. So the poet "is here thinking of an awakening from an incubation-sleep" (cf. p. 104f). A similar explanation is proposed for Ps 63:3. The theory is not convincing and is evidently based on extra-biblical postulates, like Mary Hamilton's *Incubation or the Cure of Disease in Pagan Temples and Christian Churches* (London, 1906), quoted by Lindblom. Other problems connected with the supplication have been examined elsewhere: are the suppliants individuals or representatives of the community (the "I" and "We" psalms; cf. 12g and 23a); who are the "enemies" of the psalmists, who are the "evildoers"? (cf. §12g); what about the "imprecations" of the psalmists? (cf. §14d, *c.fi.*) *Bible de la Pléiade,* vol. II, p. 122, distinguished imprecations intended for (personal) "foes" (Pss 5, 35, 40, 41, 55, 58, 59, 69, 109, 140, 141) and imprecations pronounced against the enemies of the nations or of religion (Pss 14, 52, 59, 79, 83).

(dd) The expression of *trust in God* is rarely absent from the lament. When it predominates it becomes the main element of a special category of psalms, "the psalms of confidence." The motives of confidence vary: God's attributes and honor, the suppliant's urgent needs, his innocence (cf. *Pss 18 and 101) or penitence (cf. §12e). The worshipper's prayer often includes the vow to offer a sacrifice (Pss 22:26; 61:9; cf. §8b).

3) There is no fixed *conclusion* of the lament, although it will generally end with a *blessing* (cf. 5:13; 26:12; 28:9), with a renewed expression of *trust* (cf. 17:15; 140:14), or with a thanksgiving (7: 18; 13:6; 109:30). It is likely that the laments with a thanksgiving conclusion were written soon after the prayer had been heard, when the psalmist's feelings were still alive with the bitter experience (cf. Ps 31). The same can be said of those supplications ending on a tone of triumph (cf. Ps 6:9-11). Another explanation is that the thanksgiving followed the *Heilsorakel,* in which the suppliant had received the assurance that his prayer was heard (see §8e). In some psalms a direct answer from God seems to be expected: "My soul trusts in his word. My soul waits for the Lord more than sentinels wait for the dawn" (Ps 130:5f); "Say to my soul: I am your salvation" (Ps 35:3). If God listens the oracle follows (cf. Pss 6:9f; 22:25; 28:6; 34:7; 66:19). Some authors believe that the psalmic oracle is a simple literary device while others claim it represents a real divine answer made known through direct revelation or ritual consultation. Several psalms seem to have been composed before the peril (17, 25, 38, 39, 42/43, 51, 55, 59, 61, 70, 109, 130, 141, 142, 143); others would have been written between the prayer and the rescue (5, 7, 35, 69, 71, 86, 102), while a third group of psalms are rather reflections on a past danger averted with God's help (6, 13, 22, 26, 28, 31, 54, 56, 57, 63, 64, 120, 140). A. Bentzen writes: "The psalms of lamentation have been very much imitated by *the prophets,* especially Jeremiah (cf. Is 50:4; 59:12ff; 64:5-7 . . .). The Jeremianic lamentations are found in the chapters 11-20" (I, p. 156). Other authors will prefer to give the priority to Jeremiah (on P. E. Bonnard's *Le Psautier selon Jérémie,* cf. §5d and *Ps 6).

(b) The Laments of the individual are the following: Pss 5, 6, 7, 13, 17, (22), 25, 26, 28, 31, 35, (36), 38, 39, 42/43, 51, 54, 55, 56, 57, 59, 61, (63), 64, 69, 70 (= 40:14-18), 71, 86, 88, 102, 109, 120, 130, 140, 141, 142, 143. [The brackets indicate the psalms not as firmly classified as the others.]

PSALM 5

Prayer for Divine Help

1 *For the leader; with wind instruments. A psalm of David.*

I

2 Hearken to my words, O Lord,
   attend to my sighing.

Ps 3:5

3 Heed my call for help,
   my king and my God!

Pss 44:5; 84:4

4 To you I pray, O Lord;
   at dawn you hear my voice;
   at dawn I bring my plea expectantly before you.

Pss 3:6; 17:15; 30:6 Is 33:2; Wis 16:28

II

5 For you, O God, delight not in wickedness;
   no evil man remains with you;

Hb 1:13

6   the arrogant may not stand in your sight.
   You hate all evildoers;

7   you destroy all who speak falsehood;
   The bloodthirsty and the deceitful
      the Lord abhors.

Pss 34:17; 139:19f Prv 6:17ff

Wis 14:9; Ps 11:5

III

8 But I, because of your abundant kindness,
   will enter your house;
   I will worship at your holy temple
9   in fear of you, O Lord;
      make straight your way before me.
   Because of my enemies, guide me in your justice;
      make straight your way before me.

Dn 6:11; Ps 28:2 Ps 138:2

Is 26:7; Ps 27:1

IV

10 For in their mouth there is no sincerity;
   their heart teems with treacheries.

Jer 5:16; Rm 3:13		Their throat is an open grave;
		they flatter with their tongue.
	11	Punish them, O God;
Prv 14:32; 26:27		let them fall by their own devices;
Pss 7:16f; 36:13		For their many sins, cast them out
Jb 15:25; 17:18		because they have rebelled against you.
	V	
	12	But let all who take refuge in you
Is 61:10; Hb 3:18		be glad and exult forever.
Hb 3:18		Protect them, that you may be the joy
Is 56:6; Ps 69:37		of those who love your name.
Pss 3:4; 119:132	13	For you, O Lord, bless the just man;
		you surround him with the shield of your good will.

This individual lament seems to have been uttered in connection with the *morning* sacrifice (vv 4, 8; cf. 2 Kgs 3:20; cf. below). After the opening cry to God (vv 2-4), the psalmist reflects on the condition of admittance to the divine presence (5-7), as is usually done in the so-called "psalms of innocence" (cf. §12e). By admitting the defective spelling of the 1st person (cp. Ps 16:2) and a change of vowels, "you hate all evildoers," in verse 6, becomes "I hate all evildoers." This last statement, Dahood writes, "appears to be a *terminus technicus* employed in the formula of repudiation of false gods, when one was accused of idolatry" (cp. *Ps 31:7). Although admitted in God's presence, the suppliant still asks for God's guidance before invoking divine judgment on the enemies (cf. §12g), lest he deviate, like them, from sincerity and truthfulness (vv 8-9). The Lord is then petitioned to "punish" the treacherous and "cast out" the sinners, that God's judgment be manifested against those who rebel against him (10-11). In the last two verses the reassured psalmist includes all just men in his jubilant hymn to God who protects and blesses the righteous.

Quite obviously the suppliant of the psalm is a man falsely accused. "At dawn I will draw up my case" (v 4), he says, according to Dahood's translation (cf. Ps 50:2). His accusers are of course those "who speak falsehood" (v 7). That they accused the psalmist of idolatry has been indicated above. This assumption would find support also in Dahood's suggestion that in verse 7 *'iš dāmîm* (vocalization doubtful) be translated not "a man of blood" but "a man of idols" (cf. *Ps 26:9), the verb root being *dāmāh,* to be similar (cf. the latin *simulacrum,* used to designate an idol). In the same line of thought, the next word *mirmāh* would not mean "deceit(ful)" but "figurine," as in Jer 5:27: "Like a cage full of birds, their houses are full of figurines (*mirmāh*)" (cf. 9:5). Read then in Ps 5:7b: "The man of idols and figurines Yahweh detests." The detractors are mentioned again in verse 10b: "their throats are yawning graves; they make their tongues so smooth (*hlq*) (*JB*). If Ugaritic *ḥālāq,* "to die, perish," applies here, as Dahood thinks, then good parallels certainly follow: "A grave wide-open is their throat, with their tongue they bring death."

When, in verse 5, the psalmist says: "At dawn you hear my voice," it may be simply because he usually addresses his prayers in the morning (Ps 88:14). Yet there is evidence that dawn or morning (cf. J. B. Bauer, J. Ziegler) were considered as the most auspicious time for prayer: "O Lord, be our strength every morning" (Is 33:2); "[The favors of the Lord] are renewed each morning, so great is his faithfulness" (Lam 3:23). The same theme occurs in several psalms: the kindness of the Lord is expected mostly in the morning (58:17; 90:14). God will help the holy city at the break of dawn (46:6; cf. 101:8), a probable allusion to the angel of the Lord's intervention against Sennacherib's army: "And when he arose early in the morning, he saw all the bodies of the dead" (2 Kgs 19:35). One psalmist says: "My soul waits for the Lord more than sentinels wait for the dawn" (130:6). There may be an allusion to the "resurrection" theme when the psalmists speak of awakening in the presence of the Lord (3:4; 17:15; see §14d; cf. also R. Tournay's remark about *Ps 72:16). Much indicates, thinks J. Lindblom, that in Ps 17:15 "the poet is here thinking of an awakening from an incubation-sleep" ("Theophanies . . . ," p. 105). "It might perhaps be objected, he adds, that the only word 'awake' is insufficient for characterizing the Psalm as a ritual preparation for an incubation-sleep. But what we do not find in the text was, of course, completed by the *Sitz im Leben* of the Psalm, recited as it was as a liturgical introduction to the following ritual act." It is more likely that the morning, when awakening occurred, was simply considered by popular conviction as the time when God used to intervene for the benefit of his worshippers (cf. *ZAW* 59, 1942/43, p. 1ff; see also on *Ps 90; on the Lord and the night, see *Ps 104:20f and Ps 74:16).

PSALM 6

Prayer in Time of Distress

Ps 12:1

1 *For the leader; with stringed instruments, "Upon the eighth."*
  A psalm of David.

        I

Jer 10:24; Ps
38:2

2 O Lord, reprove me not in your anger,
        nor chastise me in your wrath.

Pss 4:2; 9:14;
31:10
Jer 17:14

3 Have pity on me, O Lord, for I am languishing;
        heal me, O Lord, for my body is in terror;

4 My soul, too, is utterly terrified;

Lam 5:20; Ps
13:2ff

        but you, O Lord, how long ...?

        II

Ps 16:10

5 Return, O Lord, save my life;
        rescue me because of your kindness,

Is 38:18; Ps
88:11f
Jb 10:21; Ps
115:17

6 For among the dead no one remembers you;
        in the nether world who gives you thanks?

        III

Jer 45:3; Ps
38:9

7 I am wearied with sighing;
        every night I flood my bed with weeping;
        I drench my couch with my tears.

Jb 17:7

8 My eyes are dimmed with sorrow;
        they have aged because of all my foes.

        IV

Ps 119:115;
Mt 7:23

9 Depart from me, all evildoers,
        for the Lord has heard the sound of my weeping;

10 The Lord has heard my plea;
        the Lord has accepted my prayer.

Pss 35:4; 40:
15

11 All my enemies shall be put to shame in utter terror;
        they shall fall back in sudden shame.

This lament is one of the seven "penitential" psalms (6, 32, 38, 51, 102, 130, 143; cf. §12e), although in it the suppliant's sinfulness is only implied by the statement on divine wrath (v 2), seemingly justified. In fact, whereas other suffering psalmists confess their sin (Pss 32:1, 25; 38:4ff, 19; 39:9; 51:6), this suppliant refrains both from proclaiming, like others, his innocence (cf. Pss 7:4-10; 26:1f) and from confessing his guilt. He seems to solicit, from the first, a "paternal" punishment (cf. Jb 33:19-30; Prv 3:11f). The formula, "reprove me not in your anger" (v 2), is conventional; it recurs in Ps 38:2 and probably derives from Jeremiah: "Punish us, O Lord, but with equity, not in anger, lest you have us dwindle away" (10:24). Then the prophet suggests to God: "Pour out your wrath on the nations that know you not" (v 25; on God's wrath, cf. §11h).

Taken literally words like "I am languishing," "heal me," and the allusion to threatening "death" point to physical illness. The disease is aggravated by mental distress: the suppliant is convinced that God is angry against him. Yet all that is an ordeal of the past. Now that God has heard his plea (v 10) he doesn't dread any more the triumph of his enemies, for they shall be put to shame in utter terror (v 11). Among the motives put forth in his prayer, the psalmist had listed the following: "For among the dead no one remembers you; in the nether world who gives you thanks?" (v 6). The dead are unable to share in the praise of Yahweh, a characteristic aspect of Israel's worship (cf. §14d). If the suppliant dies God will have failed to manifest "his providential rule" (a favorite Weiser expression) in his life and the dead man will be in a hopeless state, severed body and soul from his lifeline, God's grace.

In his *Le psautier selon Jérémie*, P. E. Bonnard studies 33 psalms supposedly influenced by Jeremiah (cf. §5d). So Ps 6 would belong, with two other penitentials (38 and 51) to such a "Psalter according to Jeremiah." Bonnard would characterize Ps 6 as a post-exilic composition in the "anthological" style (cf. *Ps 33). The borrowings, mainly from Jeremiah, have been admitted also by Podechard, while Kissane remains unimpressed: "The supposed borrowings are mere commonplaces which any writer might have used!" Coppens reads in Pss 6 and 41 two formulas of prayers for the sick, presumably older than the Book of Jeremiah. Such literary forms, as individual complaints, were certainly known to the prophet.

PSALM 7

An Appeal to the Divine Judge

2 Sm 18:21   1   *A plaintive song of David, which he sang to the Lord because of Chus the Benjaminite.*

I

2   O Lord, my God, in you I take refuge;

Ps 31:16		save me from all my pursuers and rescue me,
Ps 16:12	3	Lest I become like the lion's prey,
		to be torn to pieces, with no one to rescue me.
		II
	4	O Lord, my God, if I am at fault in this,
		if there is guilt on my hands,
1 Sm 24:11; 26:9 Ex 21:23ff	5	If I have repaid my friend with evil,
		I who spared those who without cause were my foes —
	6	Let the enemy pursue and overtake me;
Pss 22:16. 30; 44:26 Gn 49:6; Lam 2:11		let him trample my life to the ground,
		and lay my glory in the dust.
		III
	7	Rise up, O Lord, in your anger;
Ps 68:2		rise against the fury of my foes;
		wake to the judgment you have decreed.
Am 3:9; Ps 82:1 Ps 68:19	8	Let the assembly of the peoples surround you
		above them on high be enthroned.
Pss 9:5; 96:10	9	[The Lord judges the nations.]
Pss 26:1; 43:1		Do me justice, O Lord, because I am just,
1 Sm 26:23		and because of the innocence that is mine.
	10	Let the malice of the wicked come to an end,
Pss 26:2; 139:23 Jer 11:20; 12:3; 17:10 Prv 15:3; Rm 8:27 Wis 5:16		but sustain the just,
		O searcher of heart and soul, O just God.
		IV
	11	A shield before me is God,
Pss 3:9; 17:7		who saves the upright of heart;
Ps 9:5	12	A just judge is God,
Ex 34:6f		a God who punishes day by day.
	13	Unless they be converted, God will sharpen his sword;
Pss 11:2; 37:14		he will bend and aim his bow,
	14	Prepare his deadly weapons against them,
		and use fiery darts for arrows.
		V
Jb 15:35; Is 59:4	15	He who conceived iniquity and was pregnant with mischief,
		brings forth failure.
Prv 26:27; Jb 4:8	16	He has opened a hole, he has dug it deep
		but he falls into the pit which he has made.
Eccl 10:8; Ps 5:11	17	His mischief shall recoil upon his own head;

Sir 27:26; Ps 9:16f
Pss 27:6; 28:7; Dt 32:8
Gn 14:19; Is 14:14

upon the crown of his head his violence shall rebound.

18 I will give thanks to the Lord for his justice,

and sing praise to the name of the Lord Most High.

In spite of textual and literary problems, the unity of this psalm is to be maintained. In it a man pursued by an enemy takes refuge in God, and, in the temple, submits to "an oath of exculpation" (vv 4-6) that will establish his innocence and confound his adversary (cf. 1 Kgs 8:31f), presumably a colleague who has betrayed him. The faults he mentions could reflect, according to one interpretation, the false accusations levied against him. Here, as in Job 31, these conditional statements are equivalent to "negative confessions," a literary genre known in the Near-East literature (cf. *Ps 101). Having cleared his conscience, the suppliant now invokes boldly God's judgment against his foes and the wicked. It belongs to the cultic tradition to consider God as the Holy One (cf. §10d), the just judge, enthroned on high to pass judgment on the nations or on the wicked (cf. vv 8, 10, 12). When writing that the wicked "falls into the pit which he has made " (v 16) and the like (v 17; cf. Ps 5:11), the psalmist may allude to a legal maxim applied to slanderous accusers, but in speaking thus he also reveals that sin contains in itself its own judgment, to manifest God's righteousness (cf. §12e).

Other authors, like *BJ,* believe, that verses 4-5 reflect *lex talionis* (§14d), "the tit for tat law" (Ex 21:23f). Verse 5 would then express a regret and, according to Driver, it should read: ". . . and I have rescued him that was for no reason mine enemy," that is: "If I have been so foolish as to requite a friend with evil or to do an enemy a good turn, may I be destroyed!". "The passage, he adds, has been misunderstood owing to its un-Christian sentiment, which, however, is not unparalleled in the Psalter" (p. 151; cf. §14d, *c.fi.*). The same line of thought is followed by Kissane, who translates: "If I have done evil to my friend, and delivered one who had assailed me without cause," and comments: "There is only one charge — that he placated his enemy at the expense of his friend. If the psalm is Davidic, one can understand that he incurred the enmity of many of his friends when he spared the life of Saul (cf. 1 Sm 24:11; 26:18)."

The beginning of v 13 does not make much sense in the *MT. BJ* finds it necessary to supplement "the enemy" to the text. "When the enemy sharpens his sword . . ." would follow on v 6. But Dahood reminds us that *lē'* can mean "the Strong One," "the Victor." By vocalizing *'im lē' yāšūb,* verse 13 could sound like this: "O that the Victor would again sharpen his sword, draw and aim the bow!" (see *Ps 18:15) Other divine appellatives appear in verse 11: "My Suzerain is the Most High God, the Savior of the upright of heart" (see on *Ps 3:4 and *Ps 18:42). The first hemistich of verse 9 is probably a gloss (cf. Ps 96:10, Is 3:13) stressing that the "nations" (perhaps substituted to the "gods"; cf. *Ps 96:7) stand as defendants before God's tribunal, not as witnesses (cf. *BJ*). J. Leveen has discussed omissions from the *MT* in verses 7, 9, 10, 12, 13. In verse 12 he retrieves a whole hemistich (cf. §6a) with the help of the Septuagint: "God is a righteous judge, *Mighty and slow to anger:* Yet a god who is also angry every day; *Yea, his anger will not turn back.*"

PSALM 13 (12)

Prayer of One in Sorrow

1 *For the leader. A psalm of David.*

I

<table>
<tr><td>Pss 6:4; 62:4;
74:10</td><td>2</td><td>How long, O Lord? Will you utterly forget me?</td></tr>
<tr><td>Lam 5:20; Ps
10:11</td><td></td><td>How long will you hide your face from me?</td></tr>
<tr><td>Pss 27:9; 44:
25</td><td>3</td><td>How long shall I harbor sorrow in my soul,
grief in my heart day after day?</td></tr>
<tr><td>Ps 25:2</td><td></td><td>How long will my enemy triumph over me?</td></tr>
<tr><td></td><td>4</td><td>Look, answer me, O Lord, my God!</td></tr>
</table>

II

<table>
<tr><td>Jer 51:39, 57</td><td></td><td>Give light to my eyes that I may not sleep in death</td></tr>
<tr><td></td><td>5</td><td>lest my enemy say, "I have overcome him";</td></tr>
<tr><td></td><td></td><td>Lest my foes rejoice at my downfall</td></tr>
<tr><td></td><td>6</td><td>though I trusted in your kindness.</td></tr>
<tr><td></td><td></td><td>Let my heart rejoice in your salvation;</td></tr>
<tr><td>Ps 7:18</td><td></td><td>let me sing of the Lord, "He has been good to me."</td></tr>
</table>

Both in the complaint (vv 2, 3) and in the supplication (4, 5) of this lament the thought goes first to God, then to the sick man and finally to the threatening enemy. There exist Babylonian parallels (cf. §9b) for the typical lament "how long?" or "Until when?", and for the idea, common in ancient cult tradition, that if the divine eye or face beholds the suppliant, his prayer has been answered (cf. E. Baumann, *ZAW* 61, pp. 125-131). It seems apposite to quote here extracts from the "prayer of lamentation to Ishtar," the goddess of valor and of war (cf. *ANET,* p. 383ff):

"O deity of men, goddess of women, whose designs no
    one can conceive,
Where thou dost look, one who is dead lives; one who
    is sick rises up;
The erring one who sees thy face goes aright.
I have cried to thee, suffering, wearied, and distressed,
    as thy servant.
See me O my Lady; accept my prayers.
Faithfully look upon me and hear my supplication . . .
How long, O my Lady, shall my adversaries be looking upon me,
In lying and untruth shall they plan evil against me,
Shall my pursuers and those who exult over me rage against me?
How long, O my Lady, shall the crippled and weak seek me out? . . .
Faithfully look upon me and accept my supplication.
How long, O my Lady, wilt thou be infuriated so that
    thy face is turned away?
How long, O my Lady, wilt thou be infuriated so that
    thy spirit is enraged?
Turn thy neck which thou hast set against me; set thy
    face [toward] good favor.

Could the "enemy" mentioned in verses 3 and 5 be "the Enemy," Death personified. It is a fact, recalled by W. H. Brownlee ("Le livre grec . . . ," p. 167), that death in the Old Testament was not always considered merely as a physical event. It was often looked upon as a Power (cf. Jer 9:20; 2 Sm 22:5f), comparable to god *Mot* in Ugaritic literature and to the Angel of death of more recent rabbinical writings (cf. 1 Par 21:15). People afflicted by illness or caught in a peril were thought to be already in the power of Death or of Sheol. Brownlee then quotes Jon 2:2-9; Pss 16:10; 49:5; 71:20; 68:13; 116:3, 4, 8 as passages anticipating the later doctrine of resurrection (cf. §14d), by their affirmation of the power of the Lord to triumph over the powers of Death. Can it be, as Dahood suggests, that the psalmist's prayer to

God is in fact: "Grant me immortality"? In verse 4 the phrase "Give light to my eyes" could mean "Restore my health" (cf. Ps 38:11) or "grant me immortality." "To see the light," Dahood believes, is idiomatic for "to enjoy immortality" (cf. Ps 36:9f). Other authors would agree with Weiser that "Give light to my eyes" is a prayer for the renewal of a faith that will attract divine grace (cf. v 6). If the enemy in the psalm is Death only, then the presence of *ṣāray,* "my foes" (governing a plural verb) in verse 5b has to be explained. The term, Dahood says, is a *plurale majestatis.* It means "the Adversary" and stands for *Mot,* "the psalmist's archrival" (cf. also J. Zandee, *Death as an enemy . . .*).

PSALM 17 (16)

Prayer against Persecutors

1   *A prayer of David.*

I

Hear, O Lord, a just suit;
  attend to my outcry;
  hearken to my prayer from lips without deceit.

2   From you let my judgment come;
  your eyes behold what is right.

3   Though you test my heart, searching it in the night,
  though you try me with fire, you shall find no malice in me.

4   My mouth has not transgressed after the manner of man;
  according to the words of your lips I have kept
  the ways of the law.

5   My steps have been steadfast in your paths,
  my feet have not faltered.

II

6   I call upon you, for you will answer me, O God;
  incline your ear to me; hear my word.

7   Show your wondrous kindness,
  O savior of those who flee
  from their foes to refuge at your right hand.

8   Keep me as the apple of your eye;
  hide me in the shadow of your wings

9   from the wicked who use violence against me.

Is 50:10; Ps 7:10
Jb 7:18; Wis 3:6
Prv 23:12; Ps 26:2

Jb 23:11f; Ps 18:37
Ps 119:133

Ps 31:22
Ps 7:11; 18:3
Ps 25:20

Is 31:5; Dt 32:11
Ps 36:8

III

Ps 22:13		My ravenous enemies beset me;
Ps 73:7	10	they shut up their cruel hearts,
Pss 12:5; 73:8		their mouths speak proudly.
	11	Their steps even now surround me;
		crouching to the ground, they fix their gaze,
Pss 7:3; 10:9; 22:14	12	Like lions hungry for prey,
Jb 4:10; Ps 57:5		like young lions lurking in hiding.

IV

Hb 3:14; Ez 21:14	13	Rise, O Lord, confront them and cast them down;
Is 34:6; 66:16		rescue me by your sword from the wicked,
Jer 12:12; 47:6	14	by your hand, O Lord, from mortal men:
Rev 19:15		From mortal men whose portion in life is in this world,
		where with your treasures you fill their bellies.
Ps 73:12		Their sons are enriched
		and bequeath their abundance to their little ones.
Nm 12:8; Ps 11:7	15	But I in justice shall behold your face;
Ps 5:4; Dn 12:2		on waking, I shall be content in your presence.

Here, as in Ps 7, the supplication is preceded by a negative declaration, denying the false charges brought against the accused (vv 1-5). It is God, the savior (*môšíʿa,* v 7; cf. §11d), present on the Ark, who is asked to protect the suppliant against the wicked, violent, cruel, ravenous enemies, lying in wait like lions (6-12). Then the prayer for rescue takes a tone of vindictiveness (cf. §14d) to ask (vv 13-14), according to Weiser, that the wicked be destroyed "by means of a mysterious food secretly stored up by God for future retribution, whereby they as well as their children and grandchildren shall be satiated" (other interpretations below!). As for the psalmist he will be satiated with beholding the divine form (*tᵉmûnâh:* v 15).

As in Ps 5, so here also, Dahood believes the psalmist has been falsely accused of worshipping idols. This assumption is confirmed by reading in verse 3: "Test me with fire, you will find no idolatry (*zimmātî*) in me." In verse 4 the accused would besides proclaim: "My mouth has not transgressed against the work of your hands" (reading here *'ādēm* instead of *MT 'ādām, 'ādēm* being "the contracted Northern dual of *'ad,* 'hand,' a by-form of *yad*"; see Dahood, p. 95). Other psalms speak of the wicked who "consider not the deeds of the Lord nor the works of his hands" (28:5). One psalmist tells God:

"I meditate on your works; your exploits I ponder" (77:13). On the metaphor of "the shadow of the wings" (v 8), see §11b.

The obscurity of verse 14 has given rise to various interpretations. Two have been mentioned (*CV* and Weiser); three others are reflected in the following translations of (1) Pautrel, (2) *JB*, (3) Leveen:

(1) Anathematiza occidentes amicum tuum Domine,
dele de terra partem eorum in vita.
Et selectos tuos replebis, venter eorum sàturabitur,
et filii tradent reliquias suas parvulis suis.

(2) Rescue my soul from the wicked with your sword,
with your hand, Yahweh, rescue me from men,
from the sort of men whose lot is here and now.
Cram their bellies from your stores,
give them all the sons that they could wish for,
let them have a surplus to leave their children!

(3) They that are perfect in thy ways will praise thee, O Lord:
As for the perfect of this world, their portion is in this life;
And for thy saints, thou wilt fill their belly,
They will be satisfied with children,
And shall leave their substance to their offspring.

In Dahood's translation, the psalmist then prophesies: "At my vindication I will gaze upon your face; At the resurrection I will be saturated with your being" (v 15). "At the resurrection," it is commented, seems to be the plain sense of *beḥāqîṣ*, when one compares it with the eschatological passage Is 26:19, "But your dead will live, their bodies will rise. Arise (*ḥāqîṣû*) and sing, O you who dwell in the slime!", and Dn 12:2, "And many of those who sleep in the land of slime will arise (*yaqîṣû*), some to everlasting life, and others to everlasting reproach and contempt".... "In Ps 16:10f; 49:16; 73:23f, Dahood writes, the psalmists express their conviction that they will be accorded the grace of assumption that was bestowed upon Enoch and Elijah." E. Podechard and others (cf. *BJ*) would reduce the psalmist's perspective: on waking he will be admitted again, so he hopes, in God's presence and will participate in the temple liturgy. In

F. Asensio's view, however, this is not enough: what the psalmist tries to express is the hope for the just that after awakening from the sleep of death he will enjoy beatific vision (see also §14d and on Ps 17:15; cf. *Ps 5:4, and *RB* 1949, p. 489ff).

PSALM 22 (21)

Passion and Triumph of the Messiah

1 *For the leader; according to "The hind of the dawn." A psalm of David.*

A

Is 52:13-53:12

I

Is 49:14; 54:7; 62:4
Ps 10:1; Mt 27:46
Sir 2:10

2 My God, my God, why have you forsaken me,
  far from my prayer, from the words of my cry?
3 O my God, I cry out by day, and you answer not;
  by night, and there is no relief for me.

Is 59:11

Is 57:15; Ps 114:2
Hb 3:3; Jer 17:14

4 Yet you are enthroned in the holy place,
  O glory of Israel!
5 In you our fathers trusted;
  they trusted, and you delivered them.
6 To you they cried, and they escaped;

Ps 25:3

  in you they trusted, and they were not put to shame.
7 But I am a worm, not a man;

Is 53:3

  the scorn of men, despised by the people.
8 All who see me scoff at me;

Ps 64:9; Mt 27:39
Wis 2:18f; Mt 27:39

  they mock me with parted lips, they wag their heads:
9 "He relied on the Lord; let him deliver him,
  let him rescue him, if he loves him."

Jgs 16:17f; Jer 1:5
Is 44:2; 49:1

10 You have been my guide since I was first formed,
  my security at my mother's breast.

Gn 50:23; Jb 3:12
Is 46:3; Ps 71:6
Pss 110:3; 139:13

11 To you I was committed at birth,
  From my mother's womb you are my God.
12 Be not far from me, for I am in distress;
  be near, for I have no one to help me.

II

Ps 17:9; Dt 32:14
Am 4:1; Ex 39:18

13 Many bullocks surround me;
  the strong bulls of Basan encircle me.

14 They open their mouths against me
Ez 22:25; Ps
17:12
    like ravening and roaring lions.
15 I am like water poured out;
Is 53:5
    all my bones are racked.
My heart has become like wax
    melting away within my bosom.
16 My throat is dried up like baked clay,
    my tongue cleaves to my jaws;
Ps 7:6
    to the dust of death you have brought me down.
17 Indeed, many dogs surround me,
    a pack of evildoers closes in upon me;
Is 53:5
They have pierced my hands and my feet;
18   I can count all my bones.
Is 49:7
They look on and gloat over me;
Jn 19:24; Mt
27:35
19   they divide my garments among them,
    and for my vesture they cast lots.

III

20 But you, O Lord, be not far from me;
    O my help, hasten to aid me.
21 Rescue my soul from the sword,
Pss 35:17; 59:
7
    my loneliness from the grip of the dog.
Pss 17:12; 57:
5
22 Save me from the lion's mouth;
Ps 68:31; 2
Tm 4:17
    from the horns of the wild bulls, my wretched life.

B

I

Ps 7:18; Heb
2:12
23 I will proclaim your name to my brethren;
    in the midst of the assembly I will praise you:
2 Sm 22:50;
Ps 35:18
24 "You who fear the Lord, praise him;
    all you descendants of Jacob, give glory to him;
Ps 53:10
    revere him, all you descendants of Israel!
25 For he has not spurned nor disdained
    the wretched man in his misery,
Nor did he turn his face away from him,
    but when he cried out to him, he heard him."
26 So by your gift will I utter praise in the vast assembly;
    I will fulfill my vows before those who fear him.
Jon 2:10; Ps
50:14
Dt 14:29; Is
25:6; 55:1
Ps 63:6
27 The lowly shall eat their fill;
    they who seek the Lord shall praise him:

Ps 69:33		May your hearts be ever merry!"
		II
Is 45:22; 52: 10	28	All the ends of the earth
Tb 13:13f		shall remember and turn to the Lord;
		All the families of the nations
Is 53:12		shall bow down before him.
	29	For dominion is the Lord's,
		and he rules the nations.
	30	To him alone shall bow down
Zech 14:9; Dn 12:2		all who sleep in the earth;
		Before him shall bend
Ps 7:6		all who go down into the dust.
		III
		And to him my soul shall live;
	31	my descendants shall serve him.
Is 41:20; Ps 48:14		Let the coming generation be told of the Lord
Pss 71:18; 78: 6	32	that they may proclaim to a people yet to be born
Ps 97: 8		the justice he has shown.

An extensive commentary would be appropriate for this important messianic psalm (cf. §16a), recited on the cross by Jesus (cf. Mt 27: 46) and quoted in the Passion narrative (cf. Jn 19:24). The lament (vv 1-22) is followed by a thanksgiving (23-32), which may have been added when the worshipper obtained the assurance that his prayer had been heard. Some scholars believe, perhaps correctly, that the original psalm consisted of two sections: a lament (2-22) and a thanksgiving (23-27), both written out after the terrible experience had been lived through. Verses 28-32, they say, differ in style and subject-matter from what precedes. According to E. Podechard (p. 108), they would have been added later for use in the temple. In these verses the theme of the conversion of the nations is used to glorify the Lord, as in Ps 102:19-23. More precisely, writes A. Gelin, these verses, added about the end of the fourth century B.C., interpreted the whole psalm as concerning the future in a messianic sense.

The physical illness alluded to in the metaphors of verses 15-16 was aggravated by the sufferer's mental anguish at feeling himself forsaken by God. Figurative speech is also used by the poet when he describes his enemies as bulls, dogs or lions (vv 13, 14, 21, 22). The suppliant seeks comfort in recalling the saving deeds wrought for his people by God "enthroned on the praises of Israel (*yôshēb t^ehillôt yiśraēl*)" (vv 4-6), a peculiar designation of God ·"who is enthroned on the cherubim" (1 Sm 4:4; see below). He, on the contrary, feels to be put to shame, mocked, trampled underfoot, like a worm, by his adversaries (7-9). Is he not hoping for God in vain? The real sting of his suffering, Weiser believes, is the strain on his faith.

After a brief comforting recollection of his providential origin (10-11), the suppliant resumes his complaint (12-19) in terms even more pathetic. Fierce animals, his foes, surround him, his body disintegrates and he feels that God himself, his creator, has brought him down to the dust of death. But despite his extreme anxiety and suffering this great afflicted does not in his final prayer (20-22) call the judgment of God on his enemies but only asks to be delivered from their grip.

Somehow the suppliant's prayer has been heard and he is now participating in a communal thanksgiving service (23-27) where he recounts his experience, praises the Lord and invites the poor to share in the sacrificial banquet. The last part of the psalm (28-32), as it appears in our Psalter, is eschatological in character, and foresees the establishment of the kingdom of God. The first phase of eschatology has been realized with the advent of the messianic King, who through his death and resurrection brought salvation to the whole world (cf. §15).

It is noteworthy that the "just one" (*ḥāsîd;* cf. Ps. 4:4) of this psalm makes no mention of his rights or of his sins and does not curse his adversaries. As both Gelin and Martin-Achard have pointed out, the original suppliant has been magnified by the liturgical use of the poem into an eschatological and oecumenical figure. So much so that some commentators, like G. Beer, have thought that the real subject of the psalm is "the people of Yahweh." It is not said of this suffering *ḥāsîd* (cf. §12c) that he saved "many" *by his "sacrifice,"* like the suffering servant of Isaiah 53 (cf. §15a), whose vicarious role is stressed throughout the whole poem (Is 52:13-53:12). Yet the conceptual pattern of Ps 22 follows the Deutero-Isaian thought-pattern: from failure and suffering to reinstatement and glory. Verbal reminiscences of Ps 22 did affect the Gospel narratives of our Lord's Passion (cf. J. Scheifler's + H. Gese's studies). The conclusion is not that the prophecy has brought about the "creation" of these narratives. It is rather that the evangelists have chosen to narrate those incidents of the Passion which were significant to the faith, the episodes namely that Old Testament prophecy was seen to have foretold (A. Gelin). The quotation of Ps 22 on the cross indicates that Jesus wanted to share the particular experience which God forced Israel to endure and which is echoed generally in the psalms of lamentation: the bitter experience of those who feel forsaken by God after having cast themselves entirely in his care and mercy (cf. G .von Rad, II, p. 377). Patristic writers, both from the East and from the West, have read in Ps 22:10a a prophecy concerning the special character of the birth of Christ (cf. J. A. de Aldana). The verse was associated with an ancient belief of the Church: *virginitas in partu*. The relevance of the association is more apparent in Dahood's translation: "Yet *you brought me forth from the womb,* made me tranquil on my mother's breast."

Other remarks on the psalm concern philology rather than theology. Dahood reads in verse 4: "While you sit upon the holy throne (*qādōš yōšeb*), the Glory of Israel." *Qādōš,* "holy," becomes, by metonymy, the name of the throne itself, as in Ps 114:2: "Judah became his holy throne, Israel his kingdom" (cf. Ps 11:4). The same author translates verse 12: "Stay not far from me, for the adversaries (*ṣārāh*) are near, for there is none to help." *Sārāh* ("distress" in *CV*) would be here "an abstract form with a concrete meaning" (cf. Ps 13:5). The much-contested *k'ry* in verse 17 can have the meaning "to pierce" or "to dig" (cf. Gn 30:8; 49:11). *JB* notes that the Passion narratives do not use the verse and it translates verse 17c = 16c (followed by 16c = 15c): "They tie me hand and foot and leave my lying in the dust of death."

The interpretation of verse 21 also is renewed in *The Anchor Bible*: "Rescue my neck (*napši*) from the sword, my face from the blade of the ax." *Nefeš* (*CV*: "soul") does in fact mean "neck" in some biblical contexts (cf. Nb 11:6; Jb 7:15; Jon 2:6; Pss 69:2; 105:18) and the original meaning of Akkadian *napištu* is "throat." The *MT* of verse 21b offering a poor meaning, it is tempting to accept Dahood's interpretation, in which *yᵉḥīdātī* ("my loneliness" in *CV*) would mean "my face." Compare with Is 40:5: "And the glory of Yahweh shall be revealed, and all flesh shall see his face (*yaḥdāw*)" (cf. *CBQ* 1958, pp. 46-49). In Ps 63:11 *yᵉdē ḥāreb* probably means "the edges of the sword," and sufficient evidence shows that consonantal *klb* "is a by-form of *kēlappōt,* 'ax,' which occurs in Ps 74:6." Both *kᵉlōb* and *kēlūp,* "ax," are found in late Hebrew, Dahood adds (quoting G. Dalman, *Aramäisch-Neuhebräisches Wörterbuch,* Frankfurt a.M., 1897, p. 187ff), while Aramaic has *kūlbā,* "ax." "[Rescue] my face from the blade of the ax" offers certainly a better parallel to "[Rescue] my neck from the sword" than "[Rescue] my loneliness from the grip of the dog (*miyyad-keleb*)."

More remarks on the text of this important psalm seems appropriate. Dahood proposes to read in verse 29: "For truly is Yahweh the king, and the ruler over the nations." The *lamedh* of *lyhwh* ("to the Lord") is here parsed as "emphatic *lamedh*" and its meaning expressed by "truly." A good parallel is quoted: *ki lyhwh mᵉgānēnū* (*MT māginnēnū*) *wᵉlīqdōš yiśrā'ēl malkēnū,* "For truly Yahweh himself is our Suzerain, the Holy One of Israel is himself our King." As for *mᵉlūkāh* (*CV,* "kingdom") in our verse "it traces a semantic development much like that of Hebrew-Phoenician abstract *mmlkt,* "royalty, kingdom," which frequently denotes concretely, "king." The biblical texts supplied as examples do not seem too convincing. Another instance of *lē'* (for *MT lō'*), meaning "the Victor" (cf. on *Ps 7:13), is offered by the last stich of verse 30, where instead of "and to him my soul shall live" Dahood reads: "For the Victor himself restores to life." Of the many examples cited, one is particularly striking:

"For he is the Victor from the East and from the West;
he is the Victor from the desert to the mountains" (Ps 75:7).

PSALM 25 (24)

Prayer for Guidance and Help

1 *Of David.*

I

<table>
<tr><td>Pss 86:4; 143:
6-8</td><td>To you I lift up my soul,</td></tr>
<tr><td></td><td>2 O Lord, my God.</td></tr>
<tr><td>Dn 3:40</td><td>In you I trust; let me not be put to shame</td></tr>
<tr><td>Ps 13:5</td><td>let not my enemies exult over me.</td></tr>
<tr><td>Is 50:7; Ps 22:
6</td><td>3 No one who waits for you shall be put to shame;</td></tr>
<tr><td>Pss 40:15; 73:
27</td><td>those shall be put to shame who heedlessly break faith.</td></tr>
</table>

Pss 23:3; 27:11
Pss 86:11; 143:8
Ps 27:11; Jn 16:13
Pss 18:47; 27:1

4 Your ways, O Lord, make known to me;
 teach me your paths.

5 Guide me in your truth and teach me,
 for you are my savior,
 and for you I wait all the day.

6 Remember that your compassion, O Lord,

Sir 51:8

 and your kindness are from of old.

Is 43:25; 64:8

7 The sins of my youth and my frailties remember not;

Jb 13:26

 in your kindness remember me,
 because of your goodness, O Lord.

II

8 Good and upright is the Lord;
 thus he shows sinners the way.

9 He guides the humble to justice,
 he teaches the humble his way.

Pss 26:3; 40:11f
Dt 4:40; 33:9;
Tb 3:2
Ba 2:14ff

10 All the paths of the Lord are kindness and constancy
 toward those who keep his covenant and his decrees.

Ps 19:14

11 For your name's sake, O Lord,
 you will pardon my guilt, great as it is.

12 When a man fears the Lord,
 he shows him the way he should choose.

13 He abides in prosperity,

Is 57:13; 60:21; Mt 5:4
Prv 3:32; Jb 29:3
Ex 33:11; Jr 16:21; Os 6:6
Pss 119:148; 121:1
Pss 123:2; 141:8

 and his descendants inherit the land.

14 The friendship of the Lord is with those who fear him,
 and his covenant, for their instruction.

15 My eyes are ever toward the Lord,
 for he will free my feet from the snare.

III

Pss 11:4; 33:18; 86:16
Pss 35:10; 40:18; 69:30

16 Look toward me, and have pity on me,
 for I am alone and afflicted.

17 Relieve the troubles of my heart,
 and bring me out of my distress.

18 Put an end to my affliction and my suffering,
 and take away all my sins.

19 Behold, my enemies are many,

Pss 18:41; 38:20
Ps 17:7

 and they hate me violently.

20 Preserve my life, and rescue me;

Ps 16:1

 let me not be put to shame, for I take refuge in you.

21 Let integrity and uprightness preserve me,
        because I wait for you, O Lord.

Fss 19:15; 44:   22 Redeem Israel, O God,
27
Ps 130:8   from all its distress!

This rather peaceful lament of a pensive and solitary soul is laid down in an alphabetical psalm (cf. §6d) consisting of three almost equal stanzas. The psalmist is deeply convinced that it is a grace to follow always the path of the Lord, so he prays "God of his salvation" to make him walk in his truthfulness (v 5). Twice in the psalm (vv 7, 18) he asks to be forgiven his sins, especially those of his youth (cf. §12e). By the grace of God, who "shows sinners the way" (v 8), he has abandoned his evil ways. Wisdom concepts are represented even better in the second stanza, which contains a remarkable formulation of a basic *Heilsgeschichte* principle: "All the paths of the Lord are kindness (*ḥesed*) and constancy (*'emet;* cf. Ex 34:6: "kindness and fidelity; cf. §11f). This should apply also to the psalmist in distress, if only his sins are forgiven (16-21). The concluding verse does not fit in the alphabetical structure. It was apparently added later, when the psalm was adopted by the cult community.

The text of the psalm presents few problems. Instead of "guide me in your truth" (v 5) Dahood reads "make me walk faithful to you" (literally: "in fidelity to you"). If the psalmist's "great" sin (v 11; cf. Ps 19:14) and the sins of his youth (v 7) refer to idolatry, as it is certainly possible, then comparison can be made with Ps 86:11: "Teach me, O Lord, your way that I may walk in your truth (*ba'amit-tekā*); direct my heart that it may fear your name." Here, says Dahood, *ba'amittekā* is employed "in the context of a profession of faith in Yahweh and a repudiation of the pagan deities" (cf. Ps 26:3). In verse 14, *CV* reads, correctly it seems, *sod* as meaning "friendship," which stands parallel to *bᵉrît,* "covenant." That these two notions were associated comes out clearly in the three occurrences of the expression *'dy' wṭbt',* 'the treaty and the friendship," in the Aramaic treaty texts of Sefire (cf. W. L. Moran, "A Note on the Treaty Terminology of the Sefire Stelas," *JNES* 22, 1963, pp. 173-6). Dahood also recalls on verse 21 that "integrity and uprightness" are "personified as two messengers sent by God to accompany and protect the psalmist." "Light and fidelity," "kindness and truth," "goodness and kindness" are similarly presented in other psalms (23:6; 43:3; 57:11; 62:8; cf. §11ef).

PSALM 26 (25)

Prayer of an Innocent Man

1 *Of David.*

I

Ps 7:9   Do me justice, O Lord! for I have walked in integrity,
and in the Lord I trust without wavering.

Pss 7:10; 17:3;   2 Search me, O Lord, and try me;
81:8   test my soul and my heart.

II

Pss 30:8; 73:1   3 For your kindness is before my eyes,

Pss 25:10; 85:   and I walk in your truth.
11; 89:15
Ps 28:3   4 I stay not with worthless men,
nor do I consort with hypocrites.

5 I hate the assembly of evildoers,
and with the wicked I will not stay.

Dt 21:6ff; Pss   6 I wash my hands in innocence,
73.13   and I go around your altar, O Lord,

7 Giving voice to my thanks,

Ps 40:6   and recounting all your wondrous deeds.

8 O Lord, I love the house in which you dwell,

Ex 24:16   the tenting-place of your glory.

III

Ps 43:1   9 Gather not my soul with those of sinners,

Pss 28:3; 84:   nor with men of blood my life.
11
10 On their hands are crimes,
and their right hands are full of bribes.

Ps 101:2   11 But I walk in integrity;

Nm 35:19; Ps   redeem me, and have pity on me.
9:13
Pss 27:11; 94:   12 My foot stands on level ground;
18   in the assemblies I will bless the Lord.

Falsely accused in the name of the sacral law, an innocent man willingly submits to an oath of exculpation (cf. *Pss 7, 26) and other purification ceremonies (cf. Dt 21:6; Ps 73:13), which includes negative confessions (vv 1-8; cf. *Ps 101). Yet he admits his fallibility and asks for moral preservation and even redemption (9-12). Some expressions in the psalm do in fact point to a "supplication": "Do me justice!" (v

3), "Gather not my soul with those of sinners" (v 9), "Redeem me, and have pity on me" (v 11). Not all commentators, as will be seen, admit that the psalm is a lament, since it is not clear what the psalmist is complaining about. But in Dahood's translation of verse 3 recurs the expression "to walk faithful to you" (cf. Ps 25:5). Here again this is taken to indicate that the psalmist has been accused of idol-worship (see on Pss 5:6f; 17:3; 19:14; 31:7). Other verses of Ps 26 would point to the same accusation. When, for example, the psalmist says, "I have washed my hands in innocence," his statement is that he has kept himself free of the sin of idolatry, "if the cognate expression of Ps 24:4 is exegetically relevant": "the clean of hands and the pure of heart, who has not raised his mind to an idol." The "sinners" and the "men of blood" (see on Ps 5:8) of verse 9 are "polytheists" and "men of idols" (cf. Ps 139:19). On their (left) hand are "idols" (*zimmāh;* see on *Ps 17:3) while their right hand is full of "bribes." M. H. Pope denies, however, that *zimmāh* means "idols" that could be held in the hand; it is a general term for wickedness, especially of a sexual nature, and can be used metaphorically for idolatry (*JBL* 1966, p. 458). It is claimed by some authors (cf. *ZAW* 1963, p. 91f) that *miškan* (v 8; tabernacle, *habitaculum*) is a Canaanite loanword in the cultic language of Jerusalem. As used for God's dwelling during the wilderness period (cf. Ex 26:1, 6f) the word could well be rendered "tent-shrine" (cf. *HUCA* 1961, p. 92).

A different interpretation of the psalm has been proposed by E. Vogt. A "protestation of innocence" (*Unschuldsbeteüerung*), he writes, need not be associated with laments (*Klagelieder*). It is in fact true, as we shall see, that such declarations belong also to the "liturgies of entry," as reflected in Pss 15 and 24 (cf. §32). It is Vogt's opinion that Ps 26 reflects the *Torliturgie* of a pilgrim. But it is not the priest's monition that is heard here, but the voice of the pilgrim, who declares that he has fulfilled all the conditions of admittance to the sanctuary. Yet he experiences sacred fear before the majesty and the holiness of God and his temple. This mixed feeling of joy and fear would explain that this innocent man prays for "justice" and "redemption." As Briggs writes (I, p. 230), "this profession of integrity is not so inappropriate as many moderns think. It is not self-righteousness. It is not so much self-conscious, as conscious of the divine presence and the requirements to invoke it." L. A. Snijders, for his part, observes that an affirmation of innocence is not a profession of absolute guiltlessness (cf. §12e). Its purpose is to destroy unfounded suspicions. If this is true, then Ps 26 could very well reflect a series of false accusations and be the lament of an accused. In connection with his category of "national psalms of lamentation" Mowinckel (I, 207) cites Pss 5, 7, 12, 26 to illustrate the following remark: "Even in the I-psalms where an individual is speaking on behalf of the congregation, we are often assured that he is 'guiltless,' 'has not transgressed thy commandments,' and that therefore the enemies 'hate him without cause' or even because of his piety" (cf. Ps 69:10).

PSALM 28 (27)

Petition and Thanksgiving

1 *Of David.*

I

To you, O Lord, I call;

Pss 18:3; 31:3   O my Rock, be not deaf to me,

Lest, if you heed me not,

Pss 30:4; 88:11f   I become one of those going down into the pit.

Dn 6:11   2 Hear the sound of my pleading, when I cry to you,

1 Kgs 8:44; Ps 5:8   lifting up my hands toward your holy shrine.

Pss 14:4; 53:5   3 Drag me not away with the wicked,

     with those who do wrong,

Ps 43:1   Who speak civilly to their neighbors

Prv 26:23ff   though evil is in their hearts.

Ps 26:4

2 Sm 3:39; Jer 50:29   4 Repay them for their deeds,

     for the evil of their doings.

For the work of their hands repay them;

give them their deserts.

5 Because they consider not

Is 5:12   the deeds of the Lord nor the work of his hands,

     may he tear them down and not build them up.

II

6 Blessed be the Lord,

     for he has heard the sound of my pleading;

Ps 33:20   7 the Lord is my strength and my shield.

In him my heart trusts, and I find help;

Pss 27:6; 57:9f
then my heart exults, and with my song

I give him thanks.

III

Ps 68:36
8 The Lord is the strength of his people,
the saving refuge of his anointed.

Ps 33:12
9 Save your people, and bless your inheritance;
feed them, and carry them forever!

In this lament, as in Ps 26, the psalmist insists that he had nothing to do with evildoers (cf. Ps 43:1): perhaps an anticipation of a judgment of God expected in the cult. By means of the blessing and the curse, Weiser thinks, the members of the covenant community meant to express and even to effect their separation from the unworthy elements in their midst (cf. Dt 27:11ff). In the second part of the psalm (vv 6-9), the suppliant, convinced that the Lord has heard him, formulates his thanksgiving (cf. *Ps 6). His assurance, the mention of the "anointed" and the people, the *Heilsgeschichte* theme, all these elements indicate that his personal prayer was formulated in the framework of a communal cult celebration. "Psalm 28 is, in all probability, a psalm referring to the king's sickness, although it may be uncertain whether this psalm was originally made for this definite occasion or whether an older psalm has been adapted" (Mowinckel, I, p. 74). A psalm mentioning the king would have a pre-exilic origin. The welfare of the king was of course a concern for the whole people. This is reflected in verse 8: "The Lord is the strength of his people, the saving refuge of his anointed," as it is in King Hezekiah's hymn of thanksgiving (Is 38:9-20). A peril is threatening the "anointed" (cf. §15c) and the people, but it is neither specified nor past. These two elements combined suggest to Mowinckel (I, p. 219f) that Ps 28, like Pss 61 and 63, is at once "a royal psalm" and a "protective psalm" (cf. *Ps 103), this last type being related to the "national psalms of lamentation."

Dahood's translation of verse 8 runs as follows: "Yahweh is our stronghold and our refuge, the Savior of his anointed is he." In the phrase *yhwh 'ōz* (see on Ps 8:3) *lāmō umā'ôz* ("refuge"), the word *lāmō* must mean "for us" (cf. *lānū* in Ps 46:2) as in Pss 44:11; 64:5; 80:7; Is 26:16; 44:7; Jb 22:17. In Is 53:8 *lāmō* would mean "by us," not without theological implications: "for the crime of his people he was smitten *by us*." The "Savior" translates *yᵉšū'ōt*, here as in Pss 42:6, 12; 43:5: it is an abstract plural ("salvations") with a concrete meaning.

PSALM 31 (30)

Prayer in Distress and Thanksgiving for Escape

1 *For the leader. A psalm of David.*

I

Pss 27:1; 37: 39
Pss 34:6; 69:7

2 In you, O Lord, I take refuge;
    let me never be put to shame.

Pss 71:2; 143: 1, 11

In your justice rescue me,

3   incline your ear to me,

Pss 38:23; 40: 14
Is 30:29; 44: 8; Ps 28:1
Pss 42:10; 48: 4
Ps 18:2

    make haste to deliver me!
Be my rock of refuge,
    a stronghold to give me safety.

Pss 23:3; 27: 11; 32:8
Pss 91:3; 124: 7; 140:6

4 You are my rock and my fortress;
    for your name's sake you will lead and guide me.

5 You will free me from the snare they set for me,
    for you are my refuge.

Lk 23:46; Acts 7:59
Pss 26:11; 34: 23

6 Into your hands I commend my spirit;
    you will redeem me, O Lord, O faithful God.

7 You hate those who worship vain idols,
    but my trust is in the Lord.

8 I will rejoice and be glad of your kindness,
    when you have seen my affliction
    and watched over me in my distress,

9 Not shutting me up in the grip of the enemy
    but enabling me to move about at large.

II

Pss 6:3; 30: 11; 56:2

10 Have pity on me, O Lord, for I am in distress;
    with sorrow my eye is consumed; my soul also, and my
                      body.

11 For my life is spent with grief
    and my years with sighing;
My strength has failed through affliction,

and my bones are consumed.

Jb 12:4ff; 19:
13f
Jer 20:10; Ps
38:12

12 For all my foes I am an object of reproach,
    a laughingstock to my neighbors, and a dread to my
                                                      friends;
    they who see me abroad flee from me.

13 I am forgotten like the unremembered dead;
    I am like a dish that is broken.

14 I hear the whispers of the crowd, that frighten me
                                        from every side,
    as they consult together against me, plotting
                                        to take my life.

Is 25:1

15 But my trust is in you, O Lord;
    I say, "You are my God."

Wis 7:16

16 In your hands is my destiny; rescue me
    from the clutches of my enemies and my persecutors.

Nm 6:25; Ps
4:7; 67:2

17 Let your face shine upon your servants;
    save me in your kindness.

18 O Lord, let me not be put to shame, for I call upon you;
    let the wicked be put to shame; let them be reduced
                                        to silence in the nether world.

Pss 12:3f; 55:
22f

19 Let dumbness strike their lying lips
    that speak insolence against the just in pride and scorn.

III

20 How great is the goodness, O Lord,
    which you have in store for those who fear you,

Pss 33:18; 34:
10

    And which, toward those who take refuge in you,
    you show in the sight of men;

Rev 7:15f

21 You hide them in the shelter of your presence
    from the plottings of men;
    You screen them within your abode

Jb 5:21; Sir
51:3
Pss 4:4; 16:7

    from the strife of tongues.

22 Blessed be the Lord whose wondrous kindness

Is 26:1; Ps 60:
11

    he has shown me in a fortified city.

23 Once I said in my anguish,

Jon 2:5; Ps
32:8
Ps 33:13f

    "I am cut off from your sight";
    Yet you heard the sound of my pleading
    when I cried out to you.

Pss 30:5; 32:6

24 Love the Lord, all you his faithful ones!

The Lord keeps those who are constant,
but more than requites those who act proudly.
25 Take courage and be stouthearted,
all you who hope in the Lord.

Here again a thanksgiving (vv 20-25) is added to the lament. Not a few elements in the psalm seem to indicate that the supplication was recited amidst the cult community after it had been answered (cf. v 21). The abundance of stereotyped forms in the psalm points to an exceptional familiarity of the author with the traditional vocabulary of the lament. The man seems to have been ill (vv 10, 11, 13), certainly he was persecuted (9, 12, 14, 16) and he worried a lot about his reputation (12, 14, 19, 21). "Into your hands I commend my spirit" (v 6): this phrase, immortalized on the Cross (Lk 23:46; cf. Acts 7:59) was formulated, it seems, by the psalmist in the temple, where he had sought refuge from his enemies and from his affliction (vv 1-9). Abandoned, as he thinks, by his friends, he seeks relief in lament and prayer, opening his burdened heart to the Lord and expressing his ardent trust in God (vv 10-19). In the thanksgiving section (20-25) the psalmist lauds above all else God's kindness and seems to recall that his faith wavered during his ordeal (v 23). Now he leaves his isolation for a fellowship with the community (24-25). The phrase: "in your justice ($s^e d\bar{a}q\hat{a}h$) rescue me" (v 2) is one of several psalms' formulations which bring out the saving aspect of God's justice (cf. §11e).

The *lamedh,* supposedly a kind of grammatical *passepartout* in Ugaritic, proves handy also in Hebrew. In Ps 31:2f the *lamedh vocativum* appears again (cf. Ps 33:1) in *The Anchor Bible* to introduce a series of divine names: "O Eternal One," "O mountain of refuge," "O fortified citadel"! Its presence does not seem equally compelling in all the cases enumerated by Dahood in the commentary of Ps 3:9. But it is well to note this: "The bearing of the Ras Shamra tablets on biblical philology is most widely felt in the study and interpretation of prepositions" (on Ps 31:10). The *MT śānē'tî,* "I hate," seems acceptable in verse 7, as "a *terminus technicus used* in the formal repudiation of idolatry or charges of idolatry" (cf. *Ps 5:6). Thus, notes Dahood, the psalmist repudiates a sin which among the Israelites was believed to be one of the chief causes of sickness or other misfortunes. The repudiation of false gods was one of the primary duties of the members of the covenant (cf. Dt 13:7-12; 17:2-5).

The dense consonantal Hebrew phrase *ydmw lš'l* (v 18), "let them [the wicked] be reduced to silence in the nether world" (*CV*) becomes in *The Anchor Bible*: "Let the wicked be humiliated, *hurled into Sheol!*" On the strength of Ex 15:16, *yuddūm* (encl. *mem*) *kā'eben*, "they were hurled like a stone" (cf. Neh 9:11), one is justified, writes Dahood, in vocalizing *yuddūm liše'ōl*, from the verb *nādāh*, "to hurl, cast," well known from Akkadian and fully attested in Ugaritic. The final *m* is *mem encliticum*, "a stylistic balance that recurs in Ps 109:13, 15; Jb 29; 36:15" (*Psalms I*, p. 34; cf. Dahood's art. of *Bib* 1956, p. 338ff; cf. on *Ps 18). The Septuagint's *katachteíêsen*, "they are driven down," evinces a similar understanding of the phrase, Dahood adds, "while Ps 55:16 and Ez 31:16 express equally unholy sentiments" (cf. §14d on "imprecations," *c.fi.*). Another phrase, *be'îr māṣōr* (*CV* "in a fortified city"), difficult in the context, receives a plausible interpretation as read by Dahood: "Praise to Yahweh, for he has shown me wondrous kindness *from the fortified city*" (v 22). The preposition *b* often denotes "from" in Hebrew poetry, and "the fortified city" would be "a poetic name for the heavenly abode of Yahweh" (cf. Pss 18:7; 74:20).

PSALM 35 (34)

Prayer for Help against Unjust Enemies

1   *Of David.*

I

Pss 24:10; 43: 1; 44:10

Fight, O Lord, against those who fight me;
war against those who make war upon me.

2   Take up the shield and buckler,
and rise up in my defense.

3   Brandish the lance, and block the way
in the face of my pursuers;
Say to my soul,

Pss 27:1; 38: 23

"I am your salvation."

Ps 38:13

4   Let those be put to shame and disgraced
who seek my life;

Let those be turned back and confounded
who plot evil against me.

Pss 1:4; 58:
10; 83:14
Pss 83:16; 91:
11
Jer 23:12
5 Let them be like chaff before the wind,
with the angel of the Lord driving them on.

6 Let their way be dark and slippery,
with the angel of the Lord pursuing them.

II

Jb 18:18; Ps
31:5
Jer 18:20; Ps
38:20f
7 For without cause they set their snare for me,
without cause they dug a pit against my life.

8 Let ruin come upon them unawares,

Pss 5:11; 9:
16f; 37:15
and let the snare they have set catch them;
into the pit they have dug let them fall.

Pss 33:1; 40:
17
9 But I will rejoice in the Lord,
I will be joyful because of his salvation.

10 All my being shall say,

Ps 71:19; Mal
1:5
"O Lord, who is like you,
The rescuer of the afflicted man from those too strong
for him,

Pss 40:18; 68:
6
Ps 27:12
of the afflicted and the needy from their despoilers?"

11 Unjust witnesses have risen up;

Jer 18:20
things I knew not of, they lay to my charge.

Ps 38:20f
12 They have repaid me evil for good,
bringing bereavement to my soul.

III

13 But I, when they were ill, put on sackcloth;
I afflicted myself with fasting
and poured forth prayers within my bosom.

14 As though it were a friend of mine, or a brother,
I went about;

Ps 38:7
like one bewailing a mother, I was bowed down in
mourning.

15 Yet when I stumbled they were glad and gathered together;
they gathered together striking me unawares.
They tore at me without ceasing;

Pss 31:12; 40:
16
16 they put me to the test; they mocked me,
gnashing their teeth at me.

IV

Ps 13:2f
17 O Lord, how long will you look on?

Pss 17:12; 57:5   Save me from the roaring beast; from the lions, my
                                              only life.

Pss 22:23; 40:10   18   I will give you thanks in the vast assembly,
            in the mighty throng I will praise you.

Lam 3:52; Ps 30:2   19   Let not my unprovoked enemies rejoice over me;
Sir 27:22   let not my undeserved foes wink knowingly.

           20   For civil words they speak not,

Pss 29:11; 37:11   but against the peaceful in the land
            they fashion treacherous speech.

           21   And they open wide their mouths against me.

Lam 2:16   saying, "Aha, aha! We saw him with our own eyes!"

Hb 1:13   22   You, O Lord, have seen; be not silent;
            Lord, be not far from me!

           23   Awake, and be vigilant in my defense;
            in my cause, my God and my Lord.

Ps 7:9   24   Do me justice, because you are just, O Lord;
            my God, let them not rejoice over me.

           25   Let them not say in their hearts, "Aha! This is what
                                       we wanted!"
            Let them not say, "We have swallowed him up!"

Dn 3:44; Pss 25:3; 40:15   26   Let all be put to shame and confounded
            who are glad at my misfortune.
            Let those be clothed with shame and disgrace
            who glory over me.

Ps 48:12   27   But let those shout for joy and be glad
            who favor my just cause;

Pss 34:4; 40:17   And may they ever say, "The Lord be glorified;
            he wills the prosperity of his servant!"

Pss 33:5; 36:7   28   Then my tongue shall recount your justice,
Ps 71:15   your praise, all the day.

This is the lament of a man persecuted by enemies and former friends alike. "Unjust witnesses" have testified against him, they have repaid him evil for good. When they were ill he had compassion on them (11-14). They are "unprovoked enemies," "undeserved foes" (v 19). Using metaphorical language he calls on God to stand against them like a warrior (cf. §13d), to let his angel execute his judgment (1-6). Better yet, let evil produce its own punishment (cf. §12e): "Let the snare they have set catch them; into the pit they have dug let them fall" (v 8; cf. Pss 7:16; 54:7; 57:7; Prv 26:27; Sir 10:8), and thus will the Lord be glorified (v 27). Between bursts of imprecations (cf. §14d) he manages twice to anticipate the victory God's help will provide: "I will rejoice in the Lord" (v 9); "I will give you thanks in the vast assembly" (v 18; cf. Ps 22:26). The final word of his passionate soul is also one of hope: "my tongue shall recount your justice" (ṣedeq; cf. §11e).

Dahood proposes to read in verse 6: "Let their destiny be Darkness and Destruction, with the angel of Yahweh pursuing them." "Darkness," "Destruction," he writes, are poetic names for the underworld. The first expression is used as such in 1 Sm 2:9; Ps 88:13; Jb 22:11, etc., while "Destruction" would stem from ḥlq, "to perish" (cf. Pss 5:10; 73:18). Jer 23:12 can be read in the same way: "And so their way shall be like Perdition to them; they shall be thrust into Darkness and fall into it." "Dark and slippery," however, are also appropriate expressions for describing the way to Sheol (cf. §14d). Mowinckel observes (II, p. 87) that "the quiet in the land" (v 20), a hapax legomenon, "does not mean a special social milieu, nor a special pious tendency or pious milieu, but is a poetical term for the congregation or people itself, which wants to live in peace with its neighbors and oppressors . . . ." This could be correct but Dahood translates rigʿē ʾāreṣ as "the oppressed in the land": "For they do not speak of peace, but attack the oppressed in the land" (see on *Ps 30:6).

PSALM 36 (35)

Human Wickedness and Divine Providence

Pss 18:1; 35: 27
Ps 89:4, 21

1 For the leader. Of David, the servant of the Lord.

I

Jer 19:9; Eccl 9:3
Prv 11:20; Rom 3:18
Ps 10:4

2 Sin speaks to the wicked man in his heart;
      there is no dread of God before his eyes,

3 For he beguiles himself with the thought

Pss 10:13; 69: 5

      that his guilt will not be found out or hated.

4 The words of his mouth are empty and false;

Jer 4:22; Ps 32:9
Mi 2:1

      he has ceased to understand how to do good.

5 He plans wickedness in his bed;

Is 65:2

      he sets out on a way that is not good,
            with no repugnance for evil.

II

Pss 57:11;
103:11

6   O Lord, your kindness reaches to heaven;
        your faithfulness, to the clouds.

7   Your justice is like the mountains of God;

Pss 35:28; 40:
10f

        your judgments, like the mighty deep;
        man and beast you save, O Lord.

8   How precious is your kindness, O God!

Pss 17:8; 57:2;
Mt 23:37

        The children of men take refuge in the shadow
                                            of your wings.

Pss 63:6; 65:5

9   They have their fill of the prime gifts of your house;

Prv 13:14; 14:
27; 16:22
Is 55:1; Jer 2:
13; 17:13
Jb 3:16; 29:3;
Jn 4:14

        from your delightful stream you give them to drink.

10 For with you is the fountain of life,
        and in your light we see light.

III

Ps 9:11

11 Keep up your kindness toward your friends,
        your just defense of the upright of heart.

12 Let not the foot of the proud overtake me
        nor the hand of the wicked disquiet me.

13 See how the evildoers have fallen;

Is 22:17; Ps 5:
11

        they have thrust down and cannot rise.

Hans Schmidt divides the poem into two psalms: a prophetic word (vv 1-5 and 13) and a cultic hymn (6-12). But with Kraus, Weiser and others, it is better to maintain the unity of the psalm. The solution of *one* problem is sought: how to reconcile the reality of sin with the belief in God? The first part, sapiential in tone, describes the state of a man subject to evil (2-5). For him the voice of sin has replaced the word of God and there is no remedy to his delusion and hardness of heart. The best answer to human wickedness is the expression of faith in God's providence (6-10; cf. §11b). The worshippers "feast on the fat of the temple" in sacrificial meals symbolizing communion with God, fountain of life and light. But such a faith is also a gift and the psalmist asks for the grace to resist temptation: "Let not the foot of the proud overtake me nor the hand of the wicked disquiet me" (v 12). The peculiar form of the wording in the last verse (v 13), Weiser believes, seems to point to a judgment on the sinner, executed by means of a ritual act in the cult of the covenant. If this is true, the verse provides the *raison d'être* of the whole psalm, which,

Mowinckel (II, p. 13) notes, is written "with all the traditional elements but with a rich and free formulation."

It is natural to assume that deep truths lie in the background of verse 10: "For with you is the fountain of life, and in your light we see light" (*CV*). To let the text yield a more satisfactory interpretation Dahood proposes "a distinction between the homographs *'wr* (*'ōr*), 'light,' and *'wr* (*'ūr*), 'field.'" In Ps 56:14 it would be possible to read: "to walk before God in the field of life (*be'ūr hahayyīm*)," in parallel with Ps 116:9: "I shall walk before Yahweh in the fields of life (*be'arṣōt hahayyīm*)." In the poetic passages, it is argued, exists the motif of the *Elysian fields*, "the abode of the blessed after death." Some texts have to be understood accordingly:

Ps 36:10: "Truly with you is the fountain of life,
              in your field we shall see the light."

Is 26:19: "Your dead shall live, their bodies will rise;
              those who dwell in the dust will awake
                    and sing for joy:
              For your dew is the dew of the fields,
              but the land of the Shades will be parched."

Jb 33:30: "All these things God does,
              twice or thrice over with a man,
              To turn back his soul from the pit,
              that he might be resplendent in the field of life."

It is worth noticing that in *'ūr kaśdîm*, "Ur Chaldaeorum" (Gn 11: 28, 31; 15:7; Neh 9:7), *'ūr* is always translated in the Septuagint by *chōra*, "land, region." Could it be that Abraham's homeland is not, after all, specified the way it was hitherto thought? Be it what it may, the teaching of Ps 36:10b would then be the following: "in your field we shall see the light," i.e., "the light of your face in the beatific vision" (cf. Ps 17:15). In Is 53:11, adds Dahood, the LXX reading has found confirmation in the Qumran text (1QIs^a): *yir'eh 'ōr*, "he shall see the light," i.e., "the suffering servant will be rewarded with immortality for his vicarious suffering." Not unrelated with the "Elysian fields" is the theme *sedāqāh* = "meadow," which will be examined in connection with *Ps 143:10f.

PSALM 38 (37)

Prayer of an Afflicted Sinner

Ps 70:1; Lv 5:
12

1 *A psalm of David. For remembrance.*

I

Pss 6:2; 27:9;
74:1

2 O Lord, in your anger punish me not,
in your wrath chastise me not;

Dt 32:23; Ex
5:16
Jb 6:4; Lam
3:12f
Pss 34:20; 66:
10ff
Is 1:6; 53:2

3 For your arrows have sunk deep in me,
and your hand has come down upon me.

4 There is no health in my flesh because of your indignation;
there is no wholeness in my bones because of my sin,

Ps 32:4

5 For my iniquities have overwhelmed me;

Is 53:6; Ezr 9:
6

they are like a heavy burden, beyond my strength.

II

Is 53:5; Jer
30:12
Ps 69:6

6 Noisome and festering are my sores
because of my folly,

7 I am stooped and bowed down profoundly;

Jb 30:28

all the day I go in mourning,

8 For my loins are filled with burning pains;
there is no health in my flesh.

Pss 39:3; 44:
25
Jb 3:24

9 I am numbed and severely crushed;
I roar with anguish of heart.

10 O Lord, all my desire is before you;
from you my groaning is not hid.

11 My heart throbs; my strength forsakes me;
the very light of my eyes has failed me.

Pss 31:12; 44:
14

12 My friends and my companions stand back
because of my affliction;
my neighbors stand afar off.

Pss 35:4; 40:
15; 57:7

13 Men lay snares for me seeking my life;
they look to my misfortune, they speak of ruin,
treachery they talk of all the day.

III

14 But I am like a deaf man, hearing not,

Is 53:7; Ps 39:
3

like a dumb man who opens not his mouth.

15 I am become like a man who neither hears
nor has in his mouth a retort.

16 Because for you, O Lord, I wait;

you, O Lord my God, will answer

Pss 30:2; 35: 19
Ps 66:9

17 When I say, "Let them not be glad on my account
who, when my foot slips, glory over me."

IV

18 For I am very near to falling,

Ps 51:5

and my grief is with me always.

19 Indeed, I acknowledge my guilt;

Ps 32:5

I grieve over my sin.

20 But my undeserved enemies are strong;

Pss 35:12ff; 59:4f

many are my foes without cause.

21 Those who repay evil for good

Ps 109:4

harass me for pursuing good.

22 Forsake me not, O Lord;

my God, be not far from me!

Pss 31:3; 40: 14
Pss 35:3; 42: 12; Is 25:9

23 Make haste to help me,
O Lord my salvation!

This is another penitential psalm (cf. *Ps 6). The heading "for remembrance" probably alludes to the "memorial sacrifice" (cf. Lv 2:2, 9, 16; 5:12; Is 66:3). The psalm has an alphabetic structure (22 verses, heading omitted) without the alphabetic acrostic. "The 22-verse structure is a literary convention which characterizes laments" (Dahood). In fact chapters 1, 2, 4, 5 of the Book of Lamentations have 22 verses. Whereas in Ps 6, which opens in much the same way, the psalmist does not confess or deny his guilt, the suppliant of Ps 38 feels overwhelmed by his iniquities (vv 4, 5) and openly acknowledges his guilt (v 19), although he also (cf. Ps 35:12) is repaid evil for good (vv 20f).

The disease mentioned in verses 6-11 is of a sort (perhaps leprosy) that was especially considered a punishment for sin (vv 2-4; cf. Ps 91: 5) and for that reason also, the sufferer's friends turn away from him (v 12). Taking into account the psalm's Canaanite background, the illness could also be identified as pestilence. The divine "arrows" of verse 3 would reflect a theme associated with the "Canaanite god of pestilence," called "Resheph the archer" (Ugar. text 1001:3, Gordon, p. 214) or "Resheph of the arrow" (4th century Phoenician inscription). The theme, Dahood suggests, "has been adopted by Hebrew poets to express the belief that illness comes from Yahweh" (cf. Dt 32:23f; Jb 6:4; 16:12f). More probably perhaps, little can be known of the nature of the illness: its description is couched in a rich display of conventional imagery and hyperbolic semitisms (cf. Ezr 9:6). "Your arrows have sunk deep in me" is, according to *BJ*, anthropomorphic language to designate God sent trials: Dt 32:23; Ex 5:16; Lam 3:12f; Jb 6:4.

Like the man of Ps 39 (vv 2, 3, 10) and like the suffering servant (Is 53:7), the character of Ps 38 bears patiently his terrible lot, opens not his mouth (vv 14-15), and refrains from hurling imprecations at his enemies. He breaks his silence only to say: "Forsake me not, O Lord; my God, be not far from me! Make haste to help me, O Lord my salvation!" (vv 22f) The psalm adapts itself easily for recitation in the Church's choral office on Good Friday. So much so that some Greek manuscripts and versions add: "They have rejected me, the loved one, like a hideous corpse" (cf. Is 14:19), an allusion to the crucified Christ; the Coptic version, still more explicitly: "They have nailed my flesh" (*JB*).

PSALM 39 (38)

The Brevity and Vanity of Life

Pss 62:1; 77:1	1	*For the leader, for Idithun. A psalm of David.*

I

2 I said, "I will watch my ways,
          so as not to sin with my tongue;
          I will set a curb on my mouth."
    While the wicked man was before me

Is 53:7; Ps 38: 9, 14

3   I kept dumb and silent;
          I refrained from rash speech.
    But my grief was stirred up;

Jer 20:9

4   hot grew my heart within me;
          in my thoughts, a fire blazed forth.
    I spoke out with my tongue:

II

5 Let me know, O Lord, my end
          and what is the number of my days,

Ps 49:13

          that I may learn how frail I am.

6 A short span you have made my days,

Is 40:7; Wis 2:1
Jb 7:6, 16

          and my life is as nought before you;
          only a breath is any human existence.

Pss 78:39;
144:4
Eccl 2:22; 6:2
7 A phantom only, man goes his ways;
    like vapor only are his restless pursuits;
    he heaps up stores, and knows not who will use them.

III

8 And now, for what do I wait, O Lord?
    in you is my hope.

Ps 51:3ff
9 From all my sins deliver me;
    a fool's taunt let me not suffer.

IV

10 I was speechless and opened not my mouth,
    because it was your doing;

Pss 32:4; 41:5
11 Take away your scourge from me;
    at the blow of your hand I wasted away.

12 With rebukes for guilt you chasten man;
    you dissolve like a cobweb all that is dear to him;
    only a breath is any man.

13 Hear my prayer, O Lord;
    to my cry give ear;
    to my weeping be not deaf!

Lv 25:23; Ez
16:3
1 Pt 2:11
For I am but a wayfarer before you,
    a pilgrim like all my fathers.

Jb 10:20
14 Turn your gaze from me, that I may find respite
    ere I depart and be no more.

In this, as in the preceding psalm, a man confesses to be justly afflicted by God (v 10) on account of his sins (vv 9, 12) and also endeavors to control his tongue (vv 2, 3, 10). Yet he cannot refrain from applying to himself what Ecclesiastes teaches about the brevity and vanity of life (vv 5-7). Having reduced himself to a "phantom," a "vapor," he is in good standing to set his hope in God alone (v 8). While psalmists generally say to God "turn toward me" (cf. 86:16), this "pilgrim" (v 13) entreats the Lord: "Turn your gaze from me, that I may find respite ere I depart and be no more" (v 14). *BJ* describes Ps 39 as an elegy similar to Ps 88. Since one kind of illness was often considered as a divine scourge (v 11; cf. Nb 12:9f), it can almost be assumed that the suppliant of Ps 39 had a "stroke" of leprosy (cf. Lv 13:2f). Commentators A. Maillot and A. Lelièvre consider Ps 39 as singularly "original," a sort of unconscious answer to Ps 37. The psalmist does not pretend to propose a teaching but tries to express his torment to the Lord.

PSALM 42 (41)

Desire for God and His Temple

1 *For the leader. A maśkîl of the sons of Core.*

I

Pss 25:1; 63:2

2 As the hind longs for the running waters,
　　so my soul longs for you, O God.

Is 26:9; Jos 3:10

Hos 2:1; Jl 2:17

3 Athirst is my soul for God, the living God.
　　When shall I go and behold the face of God?

Mal 2:17; Ex 23:17

Pss 11:7; 102:10

4 My tears are my food day and night,
　　as they say to me day after day, "Where is your God?"

Mi 7:10; Ps 71:11

5 Those times I recall,
　　now that I pour out my soul within me,
When I went with the throng
　　and led them in procession to the house of God,
Amid loud cries of joy and thanksgiving,
　　with the multitude keeping festival.

Lam 3:20

6 Why are you so downcast, O my soul?
　　why do you sigh within me?
Hope in God! For I shall again be thanking him,
　　in the presence of my savior and my God.

II

7 Within me my soul is downcast;
　　so will I remember you
From the land of the Jordan and of Hermon,
　　from Mount Misar.

8 Deep calls unto deep
　　in the roar of your cataracts;

Pss 18:5; 69:15; 88:8
Jon 2:4

All your breakers and your billows
　　pass over me.

9 By day the Lord bestows his grace,
　　and at night I have his song,
　　a prayer to my living God.

Pss 31:3; 62:7f

10 I sing to God, my Rock:
　　"Why do you forget me?"

Ps 38:7

Why must I go about in mourning,
　　with the enemy oppressing me?"

Pss 40:16; 44:15

11 It crushes my bones that my foes mock me,

Mi 7:10; Jl 2:
17

            as they say to me day after day, "Where is your God?"

12 Why are you so downcast, O my soul?
      Why do you sigh within me?

PSALM 43 (42)

III

Pss 7:9; 28:3;
60:12

1 Do me justice, O God, and fight my fight
     against a faithless people;
     from the deceitful and impious man rescue me.

Pss 18:2; 28:
7; 59:17

2 For you, O God, are my strength.
     Why do you keep me so far away?
     Why must I go about in mourning,
       with the enemy oppressing me?

Pss 36:10; 56:
14

3 Send forth your light and your fidelity;
     they shall lead me on
  And bring me to your holy mountain,

Is 1:12

     to your dwelling-place.

4 Then will I go in to the altar of God,
     the God of my gladness and joy;

Pss 33:2f; 71:
22

     Then will I give you thanks upon the harp,
     O God, my God!

5 Why are you so downcast, O my soul?
     Why do you sigh within me?
     Hope in God! For I shall again be thanking him,

Pss 42:15; 51:
16

     in the presence of my savior and my God.

These two psalms (42 and 43) form one poem, of which the third stanza is Ps 43. This is indicated by the uniform subject-matter and by the recurrence of an identical refrain (42:6, 12; 43:5). In fine lyrical style the psalmist describes his homesickness caused by his being away from the temple, where he held a leading role in the liturgy (42:5). He is exiled in Northern Palestine, where cataracts roar down the Hermon (vv 7-8). But he finds renewed courage in his faith and he hears a voice saying: Hope in God! (v 12) The question, "Where is your God?", is one which characterizes the nature of disbelief in God in biblical times (see §10a). Psalm 43 is alluded to at the Mass by the priest who is about to go to the altar of God.

    Mowinckel lists Ps 42-43 among those "I"-psalms, which, although apparently quite personal, are in reality national (congregational) psalms (I, p. 219). And he is careful to note: "Even if psalms like 23 or 51 or 42-43 are expressions of personal experiences and feelings and of a quite personal piety, we should not be justified in concluding that the psalms in question were not written to be used in the cult" (II, p. 20). And a note tries to explain how this can be adapted to the poet's situation: "During the monarchy cultic acts might be performed in any holy place; or any place might for the special occasion be sanctified for an act of Sacrifice, see 1 Sm 14:33f." Gunkel's deduction (*Einleitung...*, p. 262), he adds, that Pss 42-43, 55, 61 and 120 were composed "in the exile" is a deduction based on erroneous exegesis; the passages prove only that the psalm in question (i.e., 42-43) was composed for use somewhere away from Yahweh's city and temple.

If *'ālay* in Ps 42:6 means "before me," then v 6a (cf. v 12 and Ps 43:5) can be translated: "Why are you so sad, O my soul? And why do you sigh *before me?*" Twice in Ps 42 (vv 6, 12) and once in Ps 43 (v 5) occurs the phrase *yᵉšû'ôt pānay wē'lōhay* (litt.: "the salvations of my face and my God"). Some commentators read in *yᵉšû'ôt* the divine name "Savior" (cf. §11d), morphologically explained as an abstract *plurale majestatis* with a concrete meaning (see on *Ps 28:8). Furthermore, *pānay* can be rendered "my Presence," Dahood thinks, and thus the psalmist would tell his soul in Ps 42: 12b: "Wait for God, for I shall still praise him, my Savior, my Presence, and my God." The "Presence" is in fact what preserves the Covenant. The Covenant is severed when God withdraws (Hos 5:6; Ez 10:2ff). A. Weiser reads Ps 42:3b as "When may I come and appear before the face of God?", giving a liturgical ring to the poet's visit to the sanctuary (cf. Ps 118:19; Is 1:12).

The geographical position of the poet is rather confusingly stated in Ps 42:7b: "From the land of the Jordan and of Hermon, from Mount Misar." G. Dalman thought he could identify Misar as a small hill N-E of Banyas of the Hermon slopes (cf. *Palästina Jahrbuch,* Berlin, 5, 1909, p. 101ff). The problem of identification is eliminated if the whole psalm is understood figuratively, that is, Dahood writes, as the biblical version of "The Dark Night of the Soul." The psalmist, who had enjoyed God's consoling grace, finds himself in a state of extreme desolation because God has withdrawn his spiritual favors. He compares his wretchedness to the cheerless existence of Sheol." Sheol, in fact, is what is described in verses 7-8, according to Dahood:

My soul before me is very sad
    because I remember you,
From the land of descent and of nets,
    from the mountains at the rim;
Where deep calls to deep,
    at the peal of your thunderbolts;
And all your breakers and your billows
    pass over me.

This interpretation has a better chance of being true, of course, if personified Death is close at hand, as verse 10 would affirm it: "My prayer to my living God: I shall say: O El, my Rock, why have you forgotten me? Why must I go in gloom because of harassment by the Foe, because of the Assassin within my bones?" In that context "my Rock" is doubly relevant, for "Sheol was considered a vast quagmire with no firm footing" (Ps 69:3). Similar imagery, adds Dahood, is used in Ps 61:3 (his translation): "From the edge of the nether world I called to you when my courage failed. Onto a lofty rock you led me from it" (see on Sheol: §14d).

PSALM 51 (50)

The Miserere: Prayer of Repentance

2 Sm 12   1-2   *For the leader. A psalm of David, when Nathan the prophet came to him after his sin with Bethsabee.*

A

Pss 41:11; 56:2   3 Have mercy on me, O God, in your goodness;
          in the greatness of your compassion wipe out my offense.

          4 Thoroughly wash me from my guilt
Pss 39:9; 65:4   and of my sin cleanse me.

B

I

          5 For I acknowledge my offense,
Is 59:12   and my sin is before me always:
          6 "Against you only have I sinned,
         and done what is evil in your sight" —
Rm 3:4   That you may be justified in your sentence,
         vindicated when you condemn.

Gn 8:21; Jb
14:4
Pss 58:4; 103:
14; Rm 5:12ff
Pss 19:8, 13;
104:24
Jb 11:6; Prv
2:6

7 Indeed, in guilt was I born,
  and in sin my mother conceived me;
8 Behold, you are pleased with sincerity of heart,
  and in my inmost being you teach me wisdom.

II

Ex 12:22; Lv
14:4
Nm 19:18; Is
1:18
Ez 36:25; Jb
9:30
Is 38:13; 57:
15
Is 59:2

9 Cleanse me of sin with hyssop, that I may be purified;
  wash me, and I shall be whiter than snow.
10 Let me hear the sounds of joy and gladness;
  the bones you have crushed shall rejoice.
11 Turn away your face from my sins,
  and blot out all my guilt.

III

Ez 11:19; 18:
31; 36:25
Is 57:15; 65:
17
Is 143:10

Wis 1:5; 9:17

Ez 18:23

Is 57:15f; Jdt
16:17

12 A clean heart create for me, O God,
  and a steadfast spirit renew within me.
13 Cast me not out from your presence,
  and your holy spirit take not from me.
14 Give me back the joy of your salvation,
  and a willing spirit sustain in me.

IV

15 I will teach transgressors your ways,
  and sinners shall return to you.

2 Sm 12:9f

Pss 43:5; 62:
2

16 Free me from blood guilt, O God, my saving God;
  then my tongue shall revel in your justice.
17 O Lord, open my lips,
  and my mouth shall proclaim your praise.

Pss 40:7; 50:
8ff

18 For you are not pleased with sacrifices;
  should I offer a holocaust, you would not accept it.

Is 57:15

Is 66:2; Dn 3:
39

19 My sacrifice, O God, is a contrite spirit;
  a heart contrite and humbled, O God, you will not spurn.

C

Ps 69:36f; Ez
36:33
Is 58:12; Jer
30:18
Pss 4:6; 20:4

20 Be bountiful, O Lord, to Sion in your kindness
  by rebuilding the walls of Jerusalem;
21 Then shall you be pleased with due sacrifices,
  burnt offerings and holocausts;
  then shall they offer up bullocks on your altar.

The *Miserere* is quite a common feature in the Jewish as well as in the Christian penitential liturgy. Rightly so, since it describes, in moving terms, a true conception of penitence. After calling on the mercy of God (vv 3-4) the psalmist confesses his sin (5-8), then asks to be purified, renovated and cured (vv 9-14). Finally he promises to give thanks and to work for the conversion of sinners (15-21). The prayer of the *Miserere* reaches the depths of human nature itself and thus it belongs to all men. As such it was easily received in the Jewish and Christian communities as a collective lament and supplication.

The title (vv 1-2) ascribes the psalm to David, "when Nathan the prophet came to him after his sin with Bethsabee." But there is nothing in the psalm itself which directly supports this attribution, while some indications contradict it. The last two verses (20-21) point to the period which preceded the building of the second temple (520-515 B.C.) or of the Jerusalem walls (445 B.C.). But if, as it seems, they are later additions, the original psalm can be pre-exilic.

Not a few instructive statements on penitence are clearly expressed in the psalm: sins must be confessed; sin is primarily an offense of God; sin has deep roots in our human nature; contrition has more value than the offering of sacrifices; the grace of God is needed for conversion and for renewal of the heart and spirit. Our penitent does not say to God as the suppliant of Ps 32, "Forgive me because I confess my sin" (v 5), but "Purify me, because I am defiled" (v 9), an attitude founded on deeper humility. Nothing indicates that the man was a public sinner, but he has a deep sense of his innate corruption (cf. §12e). Remarkably the afflicted man is mainly concerned with moral cure, although physical cure may be hinted at in the phrase "the bones you have crushed shall rejoice" (v 10). Deliverance from physical peril could be prayed for if verse 16a is thus understood: "Save me from [premature] death, God my savior" (cf. *JB* and Ps 30:10; Prv 1:18). Psalm 51 shows affinities with Pss 6, 38, 40, but in contrast with these no other enemy is mentioned than sin, guilt and perhaps death. Not conversion only or even purification is enough for our psalmist; sinners must be regenerated if future sins are to be avoided (v 12), because the remedy must reach as deep as the root of the evil. In the prophets (cf. Jr 24:7; Ez 36:26) God took the initiative to renovate interiorly. Here the penitent asks for it. It will be the work of the "holy spirit" (v 13), source of moral life for the individual (cf. Ps 143:10) and the community (cf. Is 63:11).

In the last section of the psalm (vv 15-21) the penitent promises a thanksgiving, an essential duty of the biblical man visited by God. His cure itself will be a teaching which his word will confirm (vv 15-17). The psalmists often mention a sacrificial oblation in the ritual of thanksgiving (cf. Ps 66:13ff). The difficult passage, "for you are not pleased with sacrifices; should I offer a holocaust, you would not accept it," can be explained, like some prophetic sayings, as a "dialectical negation," in which "though the expression of condemnation is unconditional, it should be taken in a relative sense" (R. de Vaux, *Ancient Israel,* p. 454; cf. *VT* 1954, p. 385ff). Here it would mean: I prefer the sacrifice of a contrite spirit to ritual sacrifices. If verses 20-21 were added to the psalm after the exile, a ritually minded scribe would have attenuated the previous statement by his restricting observation. Apart from these two verses a *terminus a quo* (c. 800 B.C.) for the composition of the psalm seems implied in the teaching of the prophets: verses 12-14, on the purity of heart and on obedience, would reflect Jer 24:7; 31:33; Ez 11:19; 36:25ff, while verses 18-19, on the relative value of sacrifice, remind of Am 5:22; Is 1:11; Mi 6:7; Jer 6:20.

Psalm 51 testifies, writes Mowinckel (II, 17), to true personal piety, and was evidently written "by an individual who has grasped something very essential in the relationship between God and man. However, this does not prove that the reason for his prayer and confession of sin need be of a private nature." If the last two verses are to be included in the original composition, he adds, "it is more natural to to think of a person in a condition much like that of Nehemiah when rebuilding the walls of Jerusalem, and of the hostility to which he was exposed on the part of political antagonists. And on the merits of the case the psalm will then have to be ranked among the public psalms, in which the whole congregation joins with the worshipper, while he officiates as the public religious spokesman of the congregation in a matter concerning them all." But perhaps the allusion to rebuilding the walls (vv 20-21) is too vague to warrant a personal connection with Nehemiah and Mowinckel's reasoning seems to miss the essential message of the psalm: the seriousness and significance of personal sin. Various elements of the psalm are eschatological in character, R. Press believes, and would reflect the exilic period, when sacrifices could not be offered, while the future was envisaged in a cultic setting (cf. Ez 40-48). These eschatological realities include the "Holy Spirit" (v 13; cf. Jl 3:1ff; Ti 3:5; Acts 2:16), "blood" (v 16; cf. Ez 38:22), and "clean heart" (v 12; cf. Ez 36:16ff; 29ff). The "hyssop," mentioned in verse 9, is "a small bush whose many woody twigs made a natural sprinkler. It was prescribed in the Mosaic Law as an instrument for scattering sacrificial blood or lustral water on persons to be ritually cleansed. Cf. Ex 12:22; Lv 14:4; Nm 19: 18. These ceremonies were mere symbols of purification; here the psalmist prays that God may effectively 'un-sin' him, as the Hebrew literally means" (*CV*).

Verse 7 is obviously important for Old Testament "hamartiology," theology of sin. The *Jerusalem Bible* translates it: "You know I was born guilty, a sinner from the moment of conception," and adds the comment: "Man is born in a state of impurity (Jb 14:4; cf. Prv 20:9), which is an implicit recognition of his tendency to evil (Gn 8:21). This basic impurity is here pleaded as a mitigating circumstance (cf. 1 Kgs 8:46), which God should take into account. The doctrine of original sin will be proposed explicitly (Rm 5:12-21) in connection with the revelation of redemption by Jesus Christ." Mowinckel's translation of the verse, as it appears in Ap-Thomas' text, runs as follows:

'Twas stained with sin that I was born.
Sinful I was conceived in my mother's womb.

Neither any sinful disorder on the part of the genitors, nor impurity in the conception, nor the doctrine of "original sin" are implied in this statement, comments Mowinckel. Rather "it is the strongest possible expression on the part of the author of the consciousness that as a weak and frail man he has never been without sin — from his very birth he has given offense in some thing or other. We must consider this against the background of the idea of unconscious sinning, which may happen to anybody at any moment" (cf. §12e). The commentator does not say what he means by "unconscious sinning." Would it be something approaching "the doctrine of original sin"? A. Feuillet believes that the affirmation in the verse of a native state of degeneracy affecting all men is a "serious preparation" for the Pauline doctrine of original sin, especially in view of the general context of the Old Testament. Yet neither explicitly nor implicitly does the verse affirm any connection between "the child's sin" and the Fall in paradise.

Only by reading the verse in the light of the New Testament can this connection be seen and a meaning given, deeper and fuller than that perceived by the inspired writer.

According to E. Beaucamp's interpretation, the conceptual pattern of the first part of the psalm, in its primitive state at least, ran as follows: "Forgive me" (vv 3-4) . . . because I have sinned (vv 5-6a) . . . that you may be justified (v 6b). It is God's saving justice (cf. §11e) which is here in cause and not the vindication of any punishment, as the *CV* text implies. This problem will be examined more fully in connection with Ps 143:1, but the meaning of verse 6b seems to be the following: "That you appear as just in your word and blameless in your judgment." The "word of God" here alludes generally to the often proclaimed disposition of God toward mercy (cf. Ex 34:6). When God punishes, it is to cure and thus is he blameless in his judgments, since they follow the path of mercy. Besides, as Lyonnet has pointed out, St. Paul, in Rm 3:5, gave to "David's confession" the traditional Jewish meaning of the "confessions of sins": in addition to repentance and humility the penitent expresses faith in God who fulfills *exactly* his promises of salvation.

In a recent study, A. Caquot again proposes that Ps 51 be interpreted as a collective lament of the exile period. The psalmist hopes that the sufferings of the exiled community will be accepted as a sacrifice worthy of God's pardon (vv 18f). His views are similar to those of Isaiah 53, interpreted collectively (see §15a and O. Kaiser, *Der königliche Knecht,* Göttingen, 1959). Verse 7 would refer to guilty Jerusalem (cf. Ez 16:1ff; 23:25), while the 'crushed bones' of verse 10 and the 'blood guilt' of verse 16 would allude to other themes of the exile prophets, mainly Ezekiel (cf. 7:23; 9:9; 37:1-14).

Dahood, however, solves otherwise the "blood-guilt" problem of verse 16a. He reads: "Deliver me *from the tears of death,* O God, my God," pointing *dammīm,* from *dāmam,* "to weep": cf. *Psalms,* I, p. 24 (on Ps 4:5: "upon your beds weep"!) and (*CBQ,* 1960, pp. 400-3): "Just as *māwet,* 'death,' can also denote 'the place of death, namely, Sheol' (e.g., Ps 6:6), so *dammīm* may have come to signify the place of tears par excellence . . . The connection between *dammīm,* 'tears,' and the nether world has been preserved in a misunderstood verse of Sir 9:9: "Lest you permit your heart to succumb to her, and in tears you descend to the Pit" (*Psalms,* II, p. 8).

PSALM 54 (53)

Confident Prayer in Great Peril

1 Sm 23:19f;
26:1

1 *For the leader; with stringed instruments. A maśkil of David,*
2 *when the Ziphites went and said to Saul, "David is hiding among us."*

I

3 O God, by your name save me,
    and by your might defend my cause.
4 O God, hear my prayer;
    hearken to the words of my mouth.
5 For haughty men have risen up against me,

Pss 40:15; 59:
4
Ps 86:14

    and fierce men seek my life;
    they set not God before their eyes.

II

Pss 33:20; 46:
2

6 Behold, God is my helper;
    the Lord sustains my life.
7 Turn back the evil upon my foes;
    in your faithfulness destroy them.

Pss 27:6; 66:
15

8 Freely will I offer you sacrifice;
    I will praise your name, O Lord, for its goodness,
9 Because from all distress you have rescued me,
    and my eyes look down upon my enemies.

Having been rescued from his distress (v 9) this persecuted man praises the name of the Lord and prepares to offer a sacrifice. Supplication is, however, the main theme of the psalm. The suppliant's cruel (*'ārîsîm*) enemies are called "strangers" (*zārîm*), mainly, it seems, because they are ungodly (v 5), while for the psalmist "God is my helper" (v 6). It seems that the suppliant had recourse both to a human court of justice (v 3) and to God's judgment (v 7) against his enemies. He wishes that they be destroyed, thus revealing the imperfection of his own religious sentiments.

The vow (cf. v 8) being by its very nature a personal matter, it is found mainly in the "I"-psalms (cf. §23a). Of these, writes Mowinckel (I, p. 217), "a great many . . . are actually collective psalms in which an individual is speaking on behalf of the congregation. "Ps 54 is one of these. Votive sacrifices are also mentioned in one at least of the collective thanksgivings (Ps 66). If the psalmist anticipates his rescue (v 9), it could be after learning somehow in the cult (see on *Ps 6) that his petition has been granted. The quotation in the heading, "David is hiding among us" (1 Sm 23:19), was apparently suggested by the similarity between "fierce men *seek my life*" (v 5) and 1 Sm 23:15: "And David was afraid because Saul had come out *to seek his life.*"

PSALM 55 (54)

Complaint against Enemies and a Disloyal Companion

1   *For the leader; with stringed instruments. A maśkil of David.*

I

2   Hearken, O God, to my prayer;
    turn not away from my pleading;
3   give heed to me, and answer me.
I rock with grief, and am troubled
4   at the voice of the enemy and the clamor of the wicked.
For they bring down evil upon me,

Ps 31:16
    and with fury they persecute me.
5   My heart quakes within me;

Jb 4:14
    the terror of death has fallen upon me.
6   Fear and trembling come upon me,

Ez 7:18
    and horror overwhelms me,

Ps 11:1
7   And I say, "Had I but wings like a dove,
I would fly away and be at rest.
8   Far away I would flee;

Jer 9:1; Ap 12:6
    I would lodge in the wilderness.
9   I would hasten to find shelter
    from the violent storm and the tempest."

II

Gn 11:1-9
10   Engulf them, O Lord; divide their counsels,

Ez 22:2; So 3:1
    for in the city I see violence and strife;

Pss 35:17; 58: 7; 59:7
11   day and night they prowl about upon its walls.
Evil and mischief are in its midst;
12   [treachery is in its midst;]

Jer 6:6; Hb 1:3

      oppression and fraud never depart from its streets.

13 If an enemy had reviled me,
    I could have borne it;
    If he who hates me had vaunted himself against me,
    I might have hidden from him.

14 But you, my other self,

Pss 41:10; 44:14; 69:9
Jer 9:3

    my companion and my bosom friend!

15 You, whose comradeship I enjoyed;
    at whose side I walked in procession in the house of God!

III

Jb 15:32

16 Let death surprise them;

Is 5:14; Prv 1:12
Nm 16:31ff;
Ps 9:18

    let them go down alive to the nether world,
    for evil is in their dwellings, in their very midst.

17 But I will call upon God,
    and the Lord will save me.

Dn 6:11

18 In the evening, and at dawn, and at noon,
    I will grieve and moan,
    and he will hear my voice.

Ps 46:10

19 He will give me freedom and peace

Hos 13:14; Ps 37:11

    from those who war against me,
    for many there are who oppose me.

20 God will hear me and will humble them

Ps 45:7; 74.12

    from his eternal throne;
    For improvement is not in them,

Jer 44:10

    nor do they fear God.

21 Each one lays hands on his associates,

Mal 2:10

    and violates his pact.

22 Softer than butter is his speech,

Pss 12:3; 31:19; 36:2
Ps 57:5

    but war is in his heart;
    His words are smoother than oil,

Jer 9:2, 7;
Prv 12:18

    but they are drawn swords.

23 Cast your care upon the Lord,

1 Pt 5:7

    and he will support you;

Pss 41:4; 73:23
Pss 36:13; 59:12

    never will he permit the just man to be disturbed.

24 And you, O God, will bring them down
    into the pit of destruction;

Ps 37:2; Jb 15.32
Pss 2:12; 33:21; 56:5

    Men of blood and deceit shall not live out half their days.
    But I trust in you, O Lord.

This suppliant also suffers persecution and the disorderly expression of his thoughts seems to reflect his restlessness. It is possible to read in the text allusions to at least two theologically significant events related in the Bible: the confusion of tongues round the tower of Babel (v 10; cf. Gn 11:1-9) and the punishment of Core and his company (v 16; cf. Nm 16:31ff). In the psalmist's sensitive soul two diverse sentiments alternately emerge: human vindictiveness and God inspired trust in the Lord.

Frail indications suggest to B. D. Eerdmans (*OTS* IV, 1947) a very precise setting in life of the psalm: its author was a trader who resolved to make a trip "to an oasis east of Palestine" (v 8). There he met a fellowman (v 14) who lived in the Jewish colony of "the Arabian city." A plot against the visitor was laid "in the house of Elohim" (v 15). "The psalm is an early instance of the perils of travelling Israelites visiting foreign cities. A "realistic picture of the Bedouins" features in verses 21ff; by the grace of God the psalmist escaped from their hands! (p. 284ff). This interpretation, it would seem, results from scanty evidence worked up by a fruitful imagination.

PSALM 56 (55)

Trust in God, the Helper in Need

1 Sm 21:10	1	*For the leader; according to Jonath ... rehokim. A miktam of David, when the Philistines held him in Geth.*
		I
Pss 31:10; 57:2	2	Have pity on me, O God, for men trample upon me; all the day they press their attack against me.
Pss 57:4; 62:4	3	My adversaries trample upon me all the day; yes, many fight against me.
1 Sm 21:12	4	O Most High, when I begin to fear, in you will I trust.
	5	In God, in whose promise I glory, in God I trust without fear;
1 Sm 30:6; Ps 118:6 Heb 13:6		what can flesh do against me?
		II
	6	All the day they molest me in my efforts; their every thought is of evil against me.
	7	They gather together in hiding,

they watch my steps.

As they have waited for my life,

8   because of their wickedness keep them in view:

Is 14:6; Ps
59:14
    in your wrath bring down the peoples, O God.

9 My wanderings you have counted;

Pss 37:29;
139:16
Jb 19:23
    my tears are stored in your flask;

    are they not recorded in your book?

10 Then do my enemies turn back,

Jn 18:6
    when I call upon you;

Gn 31:42; Ps
20:7
    now I know that God is with me.

11 In God, in whose promise I glory,

12   in God I trust without fear;

    what can flesh do against me?

III

13 I am bound, O God, by vows to you;

Pss 50:14; 61:
6, 9
    your thank offerings I will fulfill.

14 For you have rescued me from death,

    my feet, too, from stumbling;

Jb 33:30; Ps
27:13
    that I may walk before God in the light of the living.

This psalm is one of the laments pronounced after the prayer had been answered (v 14; cf. §20a). During the peril this persecuted man also had promised by vow to offer a thanksgiving sacrifice (vv 13f). Diverse metaphors illustrate that the sufferings of the just are not lost (v 9): his wanderings are counted by God, his tears stored in a divine flask and everything is recorded in the book of life (cf. §14d). In connection with *Ps 36, it has been suggested that Ps 56:14 could allude to the rescue from Sheol: "For you have rescued me from Death, my feet, too, from stumbling; to walk before God in the field of life" (cf. Ps 96:9). Whatever happens to the psalmist in this life, the final word is not with the powers of evil and of darkness, but with the word of life and of light.

The heading refers the psalm to the incident in David's life "when the Philistines held him in Gath." A subtle verbal affiinity could have suggested the allusion: the root *hll*, occurring in the refrain (vv 5, 11), with the meaning "to praise" (*CV*, "I glory"), had been used in 1 Sm 21:13: "And David feigned himself mad (*wayyithōlēl*) in their hands." Also in both Ps 56:4 and in 1 Sm 21:12 the idea of fear (with the same verb) is present (cf. vv 5 and 12).

PSALM 57 (56)

Confident Prayer for Deliverance

1 Sm 22:1;
24:1-3
Dt 9:26; Ps
142:1

1 *For the leader. (Do not destroy!) A miktam of David, when*
he fled away from Saul into the cave.

I

Pss 56:2; 86:
16
Pss 46:2; 62:
8f
Dt 32:11; Is 3:
15
Pss 46:2; 61:
5; 91:4
Pss 7:18; 83:
19

2 Have pity on me, O God; have pity on me,
    for in you I take refuge.
  In the shadow of your wings I take refuge,
    till harm pass by.

Ps 18:17

3 I call to God, the Most High,
    to God, my benefactor.

4 May he send from heaven and save me;

Pss 56:3; 62:4

    may he make those a reproach who trample upon me

Pss 61:8; 86:
15; 89:15
Pss 7:3; 10:9;
17:12
Pss 27:2; 58:
7; 77:7
Prv 30:14

    may God send his kindness and his faithfulness.

5 I lie prostrate in the midst of lions
    which devour men;
  Their teeth are spears and arrows,
    their tongue is a sharp sword.

Pss 55:22; 64:
4
1 Chr 29:11;
Nm 14:21
Is 6:3; 33:10;
Hb 2:14

6 Be exalted above the heavens, O God;
    above all the earth be your glory!

II

Pss 38:13; 64:
6

7 They have prepared a net for my feet;
    they have bowed me down;

Jb 18:8-10

  They have dug a pit before me,

Pss 5:11; 37:
15; 59:13
Ps 108:2ff

    but they fall into it.

8 My heart is steadfast, O God; my heart is steadfast;

Ps 7:18

    I will sing and chant praise

9 Awake, O my soul; awake, lyre and harp!

Jb 3:9; 38:12;
Ps 139:9

    I will wake the dawn.

10 I will give thanks to you among the peoples, O Lord,

Pss 28:7; 66:4

    I will chant your praise among the nations,

Pss 36:6; 73:
1; 103:11

11 For your kindness towers to the heavens,
    and your faithfulness to the skies.

Pss 8:2; 72:19

12 Be exalted above the heavens, O God;
    above all the earth be your glory!

This psalmist opens his supplication with the same words as in the preceding psalm. Dahood believes, moreover, that the composition "is of a piece with the royal psalms 54, 56, 58, 59," "is the lament of a king, harassed by malicious slanderers." In the present psalm this would be indicated by the presence of the words "Do not destroy!" in the superscription, "evidently connected with the prayer of Moses in Dt 9:26, so that the liturgist responsible for the psalm heading must have ascribed this lament to the king or to a religious leader of Israel." It remains more probable, in my opinion, that the psalm is an individual lament, just as Pss 54, 56, 59 and the others.

Perhaps the suppliant can be more precisely identified, even though the traditional phrases and images of a general character tend to blur the *Sitz im Leben*. The enemies are compared to bloodthirsty lions, armed with the sharp sword of their malicious tongue (v 5), who go hunting with net and pit (v 6). This conventional picture well suits the situation of victims of false accusations, H. Schmidt believes: cf. Pss 7:3, 16; 17:11f.; 27:2f.; 31:5; 35:7, etc. It seems, he explains, that the accused is in the temple for the night, with his adversaries (v 5; cf. Pss 3:6; 4:9; 5:4; 17:3), all waiting for God's judgment, which will decide where the guilt is. In one of the five apocryphal Psalms of David, known from Syrian manuscripts, a suppliant says: "I went to rest and slept, and dreamt, and help came to my rescue" (III:10; cf. *ZAW* 48, 1930, p. 10). After a night of "ordeal-incubation" (cf. 17:3), writes Kraus, comes, in the morning, the saving verdict of God (cf. Ps 130:5-6; see on *Ps 5:5).

Several noteworthy textual annotations are proposed in Dahood's commentary (II, pp. 51-53). Verse 3 he reads as follows: "I call to God, Most High, to the Avenger El, Most High." *Gōmēr 'ēl* is found elsewhere as a divine title (cf. Ps 7:10: "Avenge the treachery of the wicked . . .," and *art. cit.*), and is alluded to in verse 7: "May they fall into it." The title "Most High" recurs by reading *'ēli* (root *'ālâh*, "go up"), instead of MT *'ālāy*, "on me." Other possible examples would be Pss 7:9; 13:6; 16:5-6; 32:5; 1 Sm 2:10; Lam 3:61 (cf. Dahood I, p. 45, and *art. cit.*).

"Kindness and fidelity," Dahood writes (cf. v 4), "are personified as two attendants to lead the poet to safety . . . . Since in Canaanite mythology the gods or dignitaries are often accompanied by two attendants, the present personification may tell us something about the identity of the suppliant. According to Philo of Byblos (see Eusebius, *Praeparatio Evangelica,* I, 10, 13), 'justice' and 'rectitude' were gods in the Phoenician pantheon. We may infer that 'kindness' and 'fidelity' also belonged to the larger Canaanite pantheon, but in Hebrew theology they were demythologized and reduced to attendants of Yahweh" (see also on *Ps 25).

The commentator of "Anchor Bible" also discovers three cases of "double-duty prepositions" (see on *Ps 33) in Ps 57: in verse 4, "He will send *from* (*min*) heaven to save me *from* the taunts (read *ḥārēp*) of those who hound me"; in verse 5 (*transeat!*); and in verse 7, to be read: "They spread a net *for* (preposition *l*) my feet, a noose *for* my neck! They dug a pit for my face, may they fall in it!" Consonantal *kpp* (*CV*, "to bow down") is identified with Akkadian *kippu* (m), "noose, snare." *Nefeš* can mean "neck" (see on *Ps 22:21) and this sense seems to me recommended here also. The metaphor "noose" is used elsewhere in the context of nets, pits, and traps (cf. Job 18: 8-10). Continuity in metaphors does not seem, however, to require reading "for my face" instead of the more natural "before me" (*le-pānay*).

The particular situation described *supra* could help to explain that Ps 57 combines a lament (vv 1-6) and a thanksgiving (7-11), linked together by a refrain (vv 5 and 11). The two parts belong together, even though verses 7-11 reappear in Ps 108 with slight variations. Their juxtaposition, Weiser thinks, "is probably to be accounted for by the fact that the psalm was recited at a thanksgiving service where the lamentation and petition took the place of the otherwise customary 'narrative' of the deliverance of the worshipper."

PSALM 59 (58)

Against Bloodthirsty Enemies

1 Sm 19:11   1 *For the leader. (Do not destroy!) A miktam of David when Saul sent men to watch his house and put him to death.*
             I
             2 Rescue me from my enemies, O my God;
                   from my adversaries defend me.

Pss 53:5; 64:3   3 Rescue me from evildoers;

from bloodthirsty men save me.

Pss 54:5; 63:
10
4 For behold, they lie in wait for my life;
  mighty men come together against me.

Pss 38:20f; 69:
11f
Not for any offense or sin of mine, O Lord;
5 for no guilt of mine they hurry to take up arms.
Rouse yourself to see it, and aid me,

Pss 24:10; 41:
14; 68:36
Is 26:21; Ps
9:6
Is 26:10
  for you are the Lord of hosts, the God of Israel.
6 Arise; punish all the nations;
  have no pity on any worthless traitors.

Pss 22:21; 55:
11; 59:16
7 Each evening they return, they snarl like dogs
  and prowl about the city.

8 Though they bay with their mouths,
  and blasphemies are on their lips —
  "Who is there to listen?"

Wis 4:18
9 You, O Lord, laugh at them;
Pss 2:4; 37:13
  you deride all the nations.

Pss 46:2; 84:
10
Ps 18:3
10 O my strength! for you I watch;
  for you, O God, are my stronghold,

11   my gracious God!

II
May God come to my aid;
  may he show me the fall of my foes.

12 O God, slay them, lest they beguile my people;
Ps 55:24
  shake them by your power, and bring them down,
  O Lord our shield!

Prv 12:13; 18:·
7
13 By the sin of their mouths and the word of their lips
  let them be caught in their arrogance,
Jer 18:18; Pss
57:7; 64:9
Pss 56:8; 69:
25
Ez 5:13; 6:12
  for the lies they have told under oath.
14 Consume them in wrath; consume, till they are no more;
  that men may know that God is the ruler of Jacob,
Pss 24:6; 46:
11
Is 56:11
  yes, to the ends of the earth.
15 Each evening they return, they snarl like dogs
  and prowl about the city;

Ps 22:21
16 They wander about as scavengers;
  if they are not filled, they howl.

Pss 43:2; 118:
14
Pss 5:4; 46:6;
90:14
Ps 31:3f
17 But I will sing of your strength
  and revel at dawn in your kindness;
  You have been my stronghold,

my refuge in the day of distress.

18 O my strength! your praise will I sing;

Pss 48:4; 114:
2

for you, O God, are my stronghold,

my gracious God!

The two symmetrical parts of this psalm end with a similar refrain (vv 10, 18) and the two half-parts open with an identical reference to the "enemies": "Each evening they return, they snarl like dogs and prowl about the city" (vv 7, 15). The suppliant claims to be innocent, but his "enemies" or "adversaries" are mighty bloodthirsty evildoers. As in other "laments" (Pss 7:7; 17:13; 35:23f) and other psalms (44:24, 27; 10:12), God is called upon to "rouse" himself, to "awake," to "visit," that is, to punish all the nations (vv 5-6). This language, Weiser thinks, reflects the expectation of a cult theophany (cf. §13d), in which the just is vindicated and the enemies confounded. Communal liturgical use of the psalm has broadened its scope to include a prayer for a judgment on all nations (vv 6, 9).

Where in a psalm God is represented as intervening against the nations, as in verses 6, 9 (cf. Pss 7:7f; 56:8), the indication points, writes Mowinckel (I, p. 226) to a national lament, in which the speaker is the king of the people or one of the leading men of the congregation, such as the High Priest, or the governor, or the chairman of the council (the "prince" of Ezekiel 45). In the historical event referred to by the heading of Ps 59, Saul attempted in the *morning* to kill David who had fled during the *night* (1 Sm 19:11f). The association of the incident with the psalm could have been suggested (cf. *BJ*) by the use of a night-morning contrast (vv 7, 15, 17) and of the innocence motif (v 4; cf. 1 Sm 19:4) or by the mention of stray dogs (vv 7, 15; cf. 1 Sm 24:14).

PSALM 61 (60)

Prayer of the King in Exile

1 *For the leader; with stringed instruments. Of David.*

I

2 Hear, O God, my cry;

Ps 17:1

listen to my prayer!

Ps 71:20

3 From the earth's end I call to you

as my heart grows faint.

Pss 11:1; 18: 34 You will set me high upon a rock; you will give me rest,

4   for you are my refuge,

Prv 18:10   a tower of strength against the enemy.

Ps 27:4f 5 Oh, that I might lodge in your tent forever,

Ru 2:12; Pss 17:8; 57:2   take refuge in the shelter of your wings!

II

Ps 20:4 6 You indeed, O God, have accepted my vows;

Ps 16:6; Mal 3:17   you granted me the heritage of those who fear your name.

7   Add to the days of the king's life;

Ps 21:5   let his years be many generations;

2 Sm 7:16; Lk 1:32f Prv 20:28; Ps 57:4 Pss 7:18; 21: 14; 86:12 Pss 56:13; 65: 2 8 Let him sit enthroned before God forever;

bid kindness and faithfulness preserve him.

9   So will I sing the praises of your name forever,

fulfilling my vows day by day.

The main trial of this suppliant is to be away from the temple (v 5), as for the psalmist of Ps 42/43, but it is not said that the sufferer of Ps 61 has been exiled or that he was a temple official. The phrase "from the earth's end" (v 3) does not necessarily point to the diaspora; it is probably a metaphor expressing how far the psalmist feels to be from the temple. The second stanza (vv 6-9) is mainly concerned with the fulfillment of vows (cf. Pss 54:8; 56:13f). Does the suppliant simply imagine himself back in the temple? Weiser believes that the recital of Ps 61 took place after the petition had been granted. Its author attends the ceremony of the covenant community of Yahweh, at which the "lots" of land were distributed amongst the members of the covenant (§13c), that is, among "those who fear thy name" (v 6). In that context it is natural that a prayer would be said for the king (v 7), the guarantor of the observance laid out by the sacral law.

In both Ps 61 and Ps 63, Mowinckel believes (I, p. 226), it is a king who prays (see on *Ps 28). In Ps 63 he "appears in the Temple to offer up sacrifices and prayers for help against the threatening enemies." "Ps 61, too, must be understood in a similar way, as a prayer accompanying the offering before the battle, far away from that capital and Temple which the king hopes to see again before long." In verse 8 it is said of the king: "bid kindness and faithfulness preserve him." These personified divine attributes (cf. §11e) will accompany the messianic king (Pss 85:10f; 89:14, 24), as they protect the king (Prv 20:28) or the faithful Levite (Ps 40:11; cf. *JB*).

The peculiar significance of the divine name, "the Rock" (v 3), has been explained in connection with Ps 42:10 (cf. §11c). Dahood's translation of Ps 61:3 has been quoted: "From the edge of the nether world I called to you when my courage failed. Onto a lofty rock you led me from it." To understand that "from the edge of the nether world" (= Sheol) translates *miqᵉṣēh hā'āreṣ* (*CV*: "from the earth's end"), it must be admitted that *'ereṣ* can mean "land," "earth" and also "nether world" (see on *Ps 18:8).

PSALM 63 (62)

Ardent Longing for God

1 Sm 22-24	1	*A psalm of David, when he was in the wilderness of Juda.*
		I
	2	O God, you are my God whom I seek;
Pss 25:1; 42:3		for you my flesh pines and soul thirsts
Ez 19:13		like the earth, parched, lifeless and without water.
Jb 22:26	3	Thus have I gazed toward you in the sanctuary
		to see your power and your glory,
	4	For your kindness is a greater good than life;
		my lips shall glorify you.
		II
	5	Thus will I bless you while I live;
		lifting up my hands, I will call upon your name.
Pss 22:27; 23:5	6	As with the riches of a banquet shall my soul be satisfied,
Pss 65:5; 69:33		and with exultant lips my mouth shall praise you.
	7	I will remember you upon my couch,
Pss 1:2; 77:7		and through the night-watches I will meditate on you:
	8	That you are my help,
Pss 17:8; 61:5; 91:1		and in the shadow of your wings I shout for joy.
Dt 10:20; 11:22	9	My soul clings fast to you;
		your right hand upholds me.
		III
Ps 59:4	10	But they shall be destroyed who seek my life,
Ez 26:20; 32:18		they shall go into the depths of the earth;
Pss 68:23; 69:16	11	They shall be delivered over to the sword,

Is 18:6; Jer 7:
33
and shall be the prey of jackals.

12 The king, however, shall rejoice in God;

everyone who swears by him shall glory,

Pss 62:5; 120:
2
but the mouths of those who speak falsely shall be stopped.

Supporters of the view that a great many psalms have been written in relation to the covenant celebration before the sacred Ark find in this poem elements of such a ceremony: for example, an allusion to the cherubim (v 8) and the prayer for the king (v 12). Whereas Weiser calls our psalm a hymn (see on *Ps 120), H. Schmidt believes it is a thanksgiving prayer (*Dankgebet*) and he reads its verses in the following order: 2, 3, 7, 8, 9, 5, 6, 4, 10, 11, 12b, 12a (p. 118). Mowinckel (II, p. 220) thinks Pss 28, 61, 63 are royal psalms, because the king is mentioned, respectively in verses 8, 7, and 12. It is, however, preferable to identify Ps 63 as a lament even if one reads in verse 8 "thou hast been my help" (*RSV, JB*) and not, "you are my help" (*CV*, Osty). Podechard reads the past tense and explains that the suppliant is a temple singer who recalls the time which preceded his unjust expulsion from his functions in the temple (cf. Ps 42/43). Weiser questions the way authors turn psalms into laments by translating perfect tenses as if they were presents (see on *Ps 120). For Kraus also the psalm is a lament: the suppliant has taken refuge in the temple and from there, he hopes, God's judgment will strike his enemies. In v 12 it is not clear whether "who swears by him" refers to God (Jer 12:16; Dt 6:13) or to the king. At any rate the original text presumably stated that God would declare blameless those who swore by him (Dn 13:42, 60). For the meaning of "the depths of the earth," cf. Nm 16:31ff, *Ps 18:8, *Ps 61:3 and §14d.

PSALM 64 (63)

Treacherous Conspirators Punished by God

1 *For the leader. A psalm of David.*

    I

2 Hear, O God, my voice in my lament;

    from the dread enemy preserve my life.

3 Shelter me against the council of malefactors,

Pss 59:3; 92:
10
against the tumult of evildoers,

Prv 30:14; Ps 57:5 Jer 9:2	4	Who sharpen their tongues like swords, who aim like arrows their bitter words,
Prv 1:11	5	Shooting from ambush at the innocent man, suddenly shooting at him without fear.
	6	They resolve on their wicked plan;
Pss 57:7; 119:110		they conspire to set snares, saying, "Who will see us?"
	7	They devise a wicked scheme, and conceal the scheme they have devised;
Prv 6:14; Eccl 7:24		deep are the thoughts of each heart.
		II
Dt 32:42; Ps 35:1ff Ps 38:3	8	But God shoots his arrows at them; suddenly they are struck.
Pss 5:11; 59:13; 69:23 Ps 22:8	9	He brings them down by their own tongues; all who see them nod their heads.
	10	And all men fear and proclaim the work of God, and ponder what he has done.
Pss 62:8f; 71:7 Ps 44:9	11	The just man is glad in the Lord and takes refuge in him; in him glory all the upright of heart.

The psalmist, whose very life is threatened, implores God to shelter him from evildoers who "shoot from ambush at the innocent man" (v 5). Their tongues are like swords, their words like arrows. Although little can be drawn from these and other stereotyped metaphors, it would seem that he also is falsely accused before a tribunal. The judgment of God will pursue his enemies and, as is often the case in the psalms (cf. Ps 35:8; §12e) their sin will produce its own punishment: "He brings them down by their own tongues" (v 9; on God's "arrows" cf. *Ps 38:3).

PSALM 69 (68)

A Cry of Anguish in Great Distress

Ps 45:1	1	*For the leader; according to "Lilies." Of David.* I
Pss 42:8; 88:8	2	Save me, O God,
Is 28:2; Jon 2:6 Jb 22:11		for the waters threaten my life;
	3	I am sunk in the abysmal swamp

Pss 40:3; 69: 15; 94:18		where there is no foothold;
		I have reached the watery depths;
		the flood overwhelms me.
	4	I am wearied with calling,
Is 38:14		my throat is parched;
		My eyes have failed
		with looking for my God.
Lam 3:52	5	Those outnumber the hairs of my head
Ps 25:19; Jn 15:25		who hate me without cause.
		Too many for my strength
Ps 38:20f		are they who wrongfully are my enemies.
		Must I restore what I did not steal?
	II	
Ps 38:6	6	O God, you know my folly,
Pss 36:3; 90:8		and my faults are not hid from you.
Is 45:17; Ps 34:6	7	Let not those who wait for you be put to shame through me,
		O Lord, God of hosts.
Jer 15:15ff		Let not those who seek you blush for me,
		O God of Israel.
	8	Since for your sake I bear insult,
		and shame covers my face.
	9	I have become an outcast to my brothers,
Jb 19:13f; Ps 55:4		a stranger to my mother's sons.
Jn 2:17; Rm 15:3	10	Because zeal for your house consumes me,
Jer 15:15		and the insults of those who blaspheme you fall upon me.
	11	I humbled myself with fasting,
Pss 59:4f; 109:5		and this was made a reproach to me.
	12	I made a sackcloth my garment,
		and I became a byword for them.
Lam 3:4	13	They who sit at the gate gossip about me,
Jb 30:9; Pss 44:15; 70:4		and drunkards make me the butt of their songs.
	III	
	14	But I pray to you, O Lord,
Is 49:8		for the time of your favor, O God!
		In your great kindness answer me
		with your constant help.
Ps 26:12	15	Rescue me out of the mire; may I not sink!
		may I be rescued from my foes,
Pss 18:5; 42: 8; 88:8		and from the watery depths.

16 Let not the flood-waters overwhelm me,
nor the abyss swallow me up,

Pss 40:3; 88:5   nor the pit close its mouth over me.

17 Answer me, O Lord, for bounteous is your kindness;
in your great mercy turn toward me.

Pss 44:25; 88:15   18 Hide not your face from your servant;
in my distress, make haste to answer me.

Pss 55:19; 71:23
Prv 23:14; Ps 19:15   19 Come and ransom my life;
as an answer for my enemies, redeem me.

20 You know my reproach, my shame and my ignominy;
before you are all my foes.

21 Insult has broken my heart, and I am weak,
I looked for sympathy, but there was none;

Lam 1:2; Mt 26:40
Lam 3:15   for comforters, and I found none.

22 Rather they put gall in my food,

Mt 27:34, 48; Jn 19:28   and in my thirst they gave me vinegar to drink.

IV

Pss 23:5; 64:9; 141:10
Rm 11:9f   23 Let their own table be a snare before them,
and a net for their friends.

24 Let their eyes grow dim so that they cannot see,
and keep their backs always feeble.

Pss 59:14; 75:9   25 Pour out your wrath upon them;
let the fury of your anger overtake them.

26 Let their encampment become desolate;

Acts 1:20   in their tents let there be no one to dwell.

27 For they kept after him whom you smote,

Is 53:4; Ps 129:3   and added to the pain of him you wounded.

28 Heap guilt upon their guilt,
and let them not attain to your reward.

Ex 32:32; Dn 12:1
Ps 56:9; Is 4:3; Rev 3:5   29 May they be erased from the book of the living,
and not be recorded with the just!

V

Ps 25:16   30 But I am afflicted and in pain;
let your saving help, O God, protect me.

31 I will praise the name of God in song,
and I will glorify him in thanksgiving;

1 Sm 15:22   32 This will please the Lord more than oxen

Pss 50:14. 23; 107:22   or bullocks with horns and divided hooves:

33 "See, you lowly ones, and be glad;

Pss 22:27; 78:19	you who seek God, may your hearts be merry!
Ps 68:6	34 For the Lord hears the poor,
Ps 107:14	and his own who are in bonds he spurns not.
	35 Let the heavens and the earth praise him,
	the seas and whatever moves in them!"
Ps 51:20f; Ez 36:10	36 For God will save Zion
Is 44:26; 61:4	and rebuild the cities of Judah.
	37 They shall dwell in the land and own it,
Pss 34:23; 47:5; 74:2	and the descendants of his servants shall inherit it,
Is 65:9, 23; Ps 5:12	and those who love his name shall inhabit it.

The use of this psalm in the early Christian tradition (see §16a) indicates that parts of it at least were considered as having a messianic import. One must be careful, however, not to apply the whole psalm to Christ, who was without sin (comp. v 6; cf. §16c) and who asked God to forgive (Lk 23:34) his enemies, not to punish them (comp. vv 23-29 of the psalm). Various metaphors designating deep waters are used here as elsewhere (cf. Ps 88:7, 18) to describe the suppliant's deep calamity (cf. below). Although admitting some faults (v 6) the man claims to have been zealous for the house of God and to have practiced penance (10-12). For that reason he is rejected by his own and mocked by drunkards (vv 9, 13). His presence was a condemnation of their vices and perhaps his words provoked their anger. He could certainly have been violent in his speech if we may judge from the collection of curses he has in store for his enemies (vv 23-29). The fact that he "broke down" (v 21) explains but does not justify recourse to such imprecations (cf. §14d). A better spirit moves him when in the next verses (30-35) his prayer turns to the praise of God. The last two verses may be an addition in which is foreseen the future restoration of Israel after the Babylonian exile.

The psalmist expresses the following wish with regard to his enemies: "Let their own table be a snare before them, and a net for their friends" (v 23). E. Vogt explains that a "table" could look like a "snare": when the fowler's trap or clap-net was set, its two semi-circular flaps open, it looked like a table set for friends (cf. Ps 124: 7). Dahood, however, translates the verse: "May their table before them be a trap and even their allies a snare" (on Ps 7:5). He quotes Ex 34:12 as a parallel and adds: the association of "ally" and "sharing one's table" recurs in Ps 41:10, which he translates: "Even my colleague in whom I trusted, he who ate my bread spun slanderous tales about me."

The Jerusalem Bible reads in verse 1 [= 2: *CV*]. "Save me, God! The water is already up to my neck." It is true (cf. *Ps 22:21) that *nefeš* may have meant originally "neck" or "throat." If the expression "the water(s)" is taken metaphorically only, then *nefeš* was likely understood as meaning "soul." But "the water(s)," "the abysmal swamp," "the watery depths," "the flood" (vv 2-3), "the mire," "the floodwaters," "the abyss," "the pit" (vv 15-16) presumably refer also to the primeval watery chaos subdued by God (see §11a) and to Sheol considered as a location (cf. §14d). In that sense the psalmist may have imagined himself submerged (up to the neck!) by the enemy powers, mainly death and the nether world (cf. Jon 2:3-10).

PSALM 70 (69)

Prayer for Divine Help

Ps 38:1	1	*For the leader; of David. For remembrance.*
	2	Deign, O God, to rescue me;
Ps 40:14		O Lord, make haste to help me.
Pss 53:6; 71:13	3	Let them be put to shame and confounded
		who seek my life.
		Let them be turned back in disgrace
		who desire my ruin.
	4	Let them retire in their shame
Pss 69:13; 109:25		who say to me, "Aha, aha!"
	5	But may all who seek you
Pss 40:17; 75:10		exult and be glad in you,
		And may those who love your salvation
Pss 69:31; 72:19		say ever, "God be glorified!"
	6	But I am afflicted and poor;
		O God, hasten to me!
		You are my help and my deliverer;
		O Lord, hold not back!

This short psalm is a lament almost identical with Ps 40:14-18 (see §22b).

PSALM 71 (70)

Humble Prayer in Time of Old Age

I

1 In you, O Lord, I take refuge;
  let me never be put to shame.

Ps 69:7

2 In your justice rescue me, and deliver me;
  incline your ear to me, and save me.

Pss 31:2; 143:
1, 11

3 Be my rock of refuge,
  a stronghold to give me safety,
  for you are my rock and my fortress.

Pss 18:3; 62:
7; 75:6
Ps 31:3

4 O my God, rescue me from the hand of the wicked,
  from the grasp of the criminal and the violent.

5 For you are my hope, O Lord;
  my trust, O God, from my youth.

6 On you I depend from birth;
  from my mother's womb you are my strength;
  constant has been my hope in you.

Is 44:2; Jer 1:
5
Pss 22:10;
139:13
Ps 39:8

7 A portent I am to many,
  but you are my strong refuge!

Dt 28:46; Is
52:14
Pss 64:11; 73:
28
Jer 17:14

8 My mouth shall be filled with your praise,
  with your glory day by day.

II

9 Cast me not off in my old age;
  as my strength fails, forsake me not.

10 For my enemies speak against me,
  and they who keep watch against my life
                take counsel together.

Ps 37:12

11 They say, "God has forsaken him;
  pursue and seize him,
  for there is no one to rescue him."

Ps 22:1, 9

Ps 42:4

12 O God, be not far from me;
  my God, make haste to help me.

Pss 22:12, 20

13 Let them be put to shame and consumed who attack my life;
  let them be wrapped in ignominy and disgrace
                who seek to harm me.

Pss 35:4; 40:
15
Pss 70:3; 83:
17f

14 But I will always hope

and praise you ever more and more.

15 My mouth shall declare your justice,

Ps 35:28
day by day your salvation,

though I know not their extent.

Pss 66:3f; 72:
18
16 I will treat of the mighty works of the Lord;

O God, I will tell of your singular justice.

III

Jer 2:1f; Hos
2:17
Is 46:3; Ps
129:1f
Hos 7:9; Is
46:4
17 O God, you have taught me from my youth,

and till the present I proclaim your wondrous deeds;

18 And now that I am old and gray,

O God, forsake me not

Is 51:9
Till I proclaim your strength

Pss 22:31; 48:
14; 78:6
to every generation that is to come.

19 Your power and your justice,

O God, reach to heaven.

You have done great things;

Ex 15:11; Pss
35:10; 77:14
O God, who is like you?

20 Though you have made me feel many bitter afflictions,

you will again revive me;

Pss 61:3; 69:
3; 77:17
from the depths of the earth you will once more raise me.

21 Renew your benefits toward me,

and comfort me over and over.

Pss 43:4; 92:4
22 So will I give you thanks with music on the lyre,

for your faithfulness, O my God!

I will sing your praises with the harp,

Is 1:4; 10:20;
Ps 68:36
O Holy One of Israel!

23 My lips shall shout for joy

as I sing your praises;

Pss 69:19; 74:
2
24 My soul also, which you have redeemed,

and my tongue day by day shall discourse on your justice:

How shamed and how disgraced

are those who sought to harm me!

Persecuted in his old age (v 9) this man knows by experience (v 17) that God does not forsake anyone who trusts in Him. Consequently he firmly hopes to be rescued, delivered (2-4), revived by God (v 20). Self-control and faith prevent him from cursing his enemies. The numerous clichés of the psalm point to an unusual use of the traditional psalmic vocabulary and perhaps also to the closer connection of the poem with a particular cult ceremony.

Mowinckel lists Ps 71 among the "I"-psalms of the "protective" type (I, p. 220). In these "I"-psalms the speaker represents the community (cf. *Ps 129), the distress is not acute or the danger is only threatening. In Ps 71 it seems to be over: "How shamed and how disgraced are those who sought to harm me!" (v 24) In our category of individual laments Pss 7, 26, 28, 36, 54, 57, 61, 63, 64, 86, 140 are also listed by Mowinckel as "protective psalms."

PSALM 86 (85)

Prayer in Time of Distress

1 *A prayer of David.*

I

Incline your ear, O Lord; answer me,
    for I am afflicted and poor.

2 Keep my life, for I am devoted to you;

Ps 79:2   save your servant who trusts in you.

3 You are my God; have pity on me, O Lord,
    for to you I call all the day.

4 Gladden the soul of your servant,

Lam 3:41; Ps   for to you, O Lord, I lift up my soul;
25:1
Jl 2:13   5 For you, O Lord, are good and forgiving,

Pss 26:3; 106:   abounding in kindness to all who call upon you.
1; 107:1
             6 Hearken, O Lord, to my prayer
    and attend to the sound of my pleading.

7 In the day of my distress I call upon you,
    for you will answer me.

II

Pss 29:1; 58: 8 There is none like you among the gods, O Lord,
1; 89:7
Ex 15:11; Dt   and there are no works like yours.
4:7
Jer 10:6   9 All the nations you have made shall come

Zech 14:16   and worship you, O Lord,

Pss 76:11; 96:   and glorify your name.
3ff
Pss 78:4; 92:6 10 For you are great, and you do wondrous deeds;
    you alone are God.

III

Pss 25:4; 78: 72 11 Teach me, O Lord, your way

Ps 25:5   that I may walk in your truth;

                   direct my heart that it may fear your name.

Pss 66:4; 92:2 12 I will give thanks to you, O Lord my God,

                   with all my heart,

Pss 9:3; 72:19   and I will glorify your name forever.

              13 Great has been your kindness toward me;

Dt 32:22; Ps 30:4   you have rescued me from the depths of the nether world.

              14 O God, the haughty have risen up against me,

                   and the company of fierce men seeks my life,

Ps 54:5   nor do they set you before their eyes.

Pss 103:8; 145:8 15 But you, O Lord, are a God merciful and gracious,

Ex 34:6; Neh 9:17; Ps 57:4   slow to anger, abounding in kindness and fidelity.

Pss 25:16; 57: 2 16 Turn toward me, and have pity on me;

                   give your strength to your servant,

Wis 9:5   and save the son of your handmaid.

              17 Grant me a proof of your favor,

                   that my enemies may see, to their confusion,

                   that you, O Lord, have helped and comforted me.

Weiser maintains the originality of this psalm in spite of adverse opinions. It is certainly instructive to follow his reasoning. "The numerous borrowings from kindred passages in other psalms and the lack of straightforward development of thought lead most commentators to regard it as a late example of psalmody compiled from earlier prototypes and showing little importance or originality; but this view is hardly justified. First of all, the peculiar character of the individual laments does not lie in the originality of each example, but in the fact that their form and thoughts are both typical and generally valid, a fact which is to be accounted for by their association with the cultus. Moreover, we are not justified in regarding the affinity of the psalm with other songs as the result of borrowing from other literature in order to mask the author's own incompetence. On the contrary, we are here dealing with a liturgical style which is deliberately used to incorporate the personal concern of the worshipper in the larger context of the worship of the cult community and of the speech-forms and thought-forms proper to it" (p. 576). In a cultic setting it is not difficult to understand that three diverse literary types can appear together: a supplication (vv 1-7), a hymn of praise (vv 8-11) and a thanksgiving (12-14). This "anticipated" thanksgiving is followed by another supplication (15-17). Yet, according to *BJ,* the psalm is a recent anthology showing poor literary unity. It would reflect the piety of the *ḥasîdîm,* well represented in the Maccabean period (cf. §12c).

When the psalmist tells God in verse 17: "Grant me a proof (*'ôt*) of your favor," he is praying, suggests Mowinckel, for a "token for good." Ps 51:8 would allude to previous "omens and signs" which the priest (or the cult prophet; cf. §8e) has interpreted for the suppliant. Taken literally the verse can in fact allude to teaching revealed in dark and secret places. It would seem that the psalmist, God's servant (v 2), is especially concerned with renouncing idolatry. Commenting upon the expression "faithful to you" of *Ps 25:5, Dahood draws comparisons from verses 7, 10 and 11 of Ps 86. In this last verse he reads: "Teach me, O Yahweh, your way, that I might walk *faithful to you*" (cf. *Ps 26:3).

PSALM 88 (87)

Lament and Prayer in Affliction

Ps 53:1	1	*A song; a psalm of the sons of Core. For the leader; according to Mahalath. For singing; a maśkîl of Heman the Ezrahite.*
		I
	2	O Lord, my God, by day I cry out; at night I clamor in your presence.
Ps 119:169	3	Let my prayer come before you; incline your ear to my call for help.
Jb 10:15	4	For my soul is surfeited with troubles
Jb 17:1		and my life draws near to the nether world.
Pss 69:16; 143:7	5	I am numbered with those who go down into the pit; I am a man without strength.

	6	My couch is among the dead,
		    like the slain who lie in the grave,
		Whom you remember no longer
		    and who are cut off from your care.

7   You have plunged me into the bottom of the pit,
        into the dark abyss.

Ps 69:3, 16   8   Upon me your wrath lies heavy,

Pss 42:8; 88:8   and with all your billows you overwhelm me.

Jb 19:13   9   You have taken my friends away from me;
                        you have made me an abomination to them;

Ps 142:8; Lam   I am imprisoned, and I cannot escape.
3:7
                    II

10 My eyes have grown dim through affliction;
        daily I call upon you, O Lord;
        to you I stretch out my hands.

Pss 6:6; 30:   11 Will you work wonders for the dead?
10; 115:17
Ba 2:17   Will the shades arise to give you thanks?

Is 38:18   12 Do they declare your kindness in the grave,
                        your faithfulness among those who have perished?

13 Are your wonders made known in the darkness,

Jb 26:6; Ap 9:   or your justice in the land of oblivion?
11
                    III

14 But I, O Lord, cry out to you;
        with my morning prayer I wait upon you.

15 Why, O Lord, do you reject me;

Pss 69:18;   why hide from me your face?
102:3
Jb 13:26; Ps   16 I am afflicted and in agony from my youth;
25:16
Ps 39:3   I am dazed with the burdens of your dread.

Jb 6:4   17 Your furies have swept over me;

Ps 39:11   your terrors have cut me off.

18 They encompass me like water all the day;
        on all sides they close in upon me.

19 Companion and neighbor you have taken away from me;

Jb 17:13f; Ps   my only friend is darkness.
107:10

This is a clear example of a sick man's lament. He is about to sink into the pit, into the dark abyss (2-7; on the relation between "abyss" and "sheol," see §14d). The wrath of God (cf. §11h) is upon him, he thinks (vv 8, 15, 17); seeing this, his friends have abandoned him (vv 9, 19; cf. Ps 38:12). This suppliant, like the one of Ps 6, recalls in his prayer that no thanksgiving to God, no praise of his will ever come from sheol, the world of the dead (vv 10-13). No firm hope or anticipation of joy is expressed by this sad man who wrote, "I am afflicted and in agony from my youth" (v 16). His analysis of suffering, like that of Job, does not reach the level where redemptive values are considered, as in the notion of Christian sacrifice.

The term "your terrors" in verse 17 "refers to the *demons of illness* serving as Yahweh's instruments of punishment." This statement of Mowinckel (II, p. 9) is related to his controversial idea that worshippers in the psalms often complain of evil enemies who cause illness by "their damaging words" (Pss 38:13; 41:6-9), their fatal witchcraft, that is, and their evil wishes (cf. §12g + 14d *c. fi.*).

Whereas in *JB* the difficult *bammētîm hopšî* (v 6) is rendered "alone, down among the dead," it appears in *CV* as "my couch is among the dead," like in the new Latin Psalter. Other commentators are divided by the following debate: is a *leprosarium* a "house of liberation," because at the end of his life, the leprous, considered as "dead," was liberated from Death, as a slave from his master (Jb 3: 19)? Or is the *leprosarium* a "house of reclusion," as suggested in 2 Kgs 15:5: from the day he became a leper, king Azaria was confined to a *bēt haḥopšît* (could not the expression be a euphemism)? Then why not read with Grelot in Ps 88:6: "My confinement (is) among the dead"?

PSALM 102 (101)

Prayer in Time of Distress

1 *The prayer of an afflicted one when he is faint and pours out his anguish before the Lord.*

I

2 O Lord, hear my prayer,

Ps 119:169
    and let my cry come to you.

Pss 88:15;
143:7
3 Hide not your face from me
    in the day of my distress.

Incline your ear to me;
    in the day when I call, answer me speedily.

4 For my days vanish like smoke,
    and my bones burn like fire.

5 Withered and dried up like grass is my heart;

I forget to eat my bread.

6 Because of my insistent sighing

Ps 109:24
    I am reduced to skin and bone.

7 I am like a desert owl;
    I have become like an owl among the ruins.

Ps 77:4
8 I am sleepless, and I moan;
    I am like a sparrow alone on the housetop.

9 All the day my enemies revile me;

Is 65:15
    in their rage against me they make a curse of me.

10 For I eat ashes like bread

Ps 42:4
    and mingle my drink with tears.

Ps 88:17
11 Because of your fury and your wrath;
    for you lifted me up only to cast me down.

Wis 2:5
12 My days are like a lengthening shadow,

Jb 8:9; 14:2;
Ps 109:23
    and I wither like grass.

II

13 But you, O Lord, abide forever,

Lam 5:19
    and your name through all generations.

Is 60:1ff
14 You will arise and have mercy on Sion,
    for it is time to pity her,
    for the appointed time has come.

15 For her stones are dear to your servants
    and her dust moves them to pity.

Is 59:19; 60:3;
66:18
16 And the nations shall revere your name, O Lord
    and all the kings of the earth your glory.

17 When the Lord has rebuilt Zion
    and appeared in his glory;

18 When he has regarded the prayer of the destitute,
    and not despised their prayer.

Pss 22:31; 90:
16
19 Let this be written for the generation to come,
    and let his future creatures praise the Lord:

20 "The Lord looked down from his holy height,

Ps 11:4
    from heaven he beheld the earth.

21 To hear the groaning of the prisoners,
    to release those doomed to die" —

22 That the name of the Lord may be declared in Zion;
    and his praise in Jerusalem.

Is 60:3f
23 When the peoples gather together,

Zech 8:22; Ps 96:3ff		and the kingdoms, to serve the Lord.
Ps 105:1		III
	24	He has broken down my strength in the way; he has cut short my days.
	25	I say: O my God,
Is 38:10; Jer 17:11		Take me not hence in the midst of my days; through all generations your years endure.
Lam 5:19; Ps 55:24	26	Of old you established the earth, and the heavens are the work of your hands.
Jb 14:12; Heb 1:11f	27	They shall perish, but you remain though all of them grow old like a garment.
Is 51:6		
Is 65:17		Like clothing you change them, and they are changed,
	28	but you are the same, and your years have no end.
	29	The children of your servants shall abide,
Is 51:8		and their posterity shall continue in your presence.

Interpreters readily admit that in this penitential psalm (see on
*Ps 6) two supplications have been united, one individual, the other
collective. In the first (vv 2-13; 23-28), Canon Osty writes (p. 272),
a sick man, burning with fever and insulted by his enemies, implores
Eternal God to let him enjoy in peace the last few years of his life;
in the second supplication (vv 14-23, 29) the community prays to
God for the restoration of Zion and its establishment as the religious
center of the world (cf. §14c, c. fi.). Verse 29 is a conclusion to both
sections of the psalm.

For other commentators the structure of the psalm illustrates perfectly how an individual lament can become collective when adopted
by the community for liturgical purposes. Kraus believes that hymnic
elements have been normally added to the original individual supplication. Weiser maintains easily the unity of the psalm in the framework
of a cultic ceremony. Ps 102, writes Mowinckel, is a fine example of
such a forward-looking congregational lament, in which an individual
is speaking on behalf of the community, as the person whose heart
is especially loaded with the sufferings and the pressure of his time"
(I, p. 221). The psalm could in fact be classified with the collective
laments and the first part of the poem (vv 2-12) read as a figurative
description of Israel in exile. In many verses (cf. 16, 23, 27) the tone
is eschatological.

PSALM 109 (108)

Prayer against a Slanderous Enemy

1 *For the leader. A psalm of David.*

I

Ps 35:22

O God, whom I praise, be not silent,

2   for they have opened wicked and treacherous
                                    mouths against me.

Pss 64:4; 120: 3f

They have spoken to me with lying tongues,

3 and with words of hatred they have encompassed me
    and attacked me without cause.

4 In return for my love they slandered me,
    but I prayed.

Prv 17:13; Ps 35:12
Jer 18:20; Ps 69:11f

5 They repaid me evil for good
    and hatred for my love.

II

6 Raise up a wicked man against him,

Zech 3:1

    and let the accuser stand at his right hand.

7 When he is judged, let him go forth condemned,
    and may his plea be in vain.

8 May his days be few;

Acts 1:20

    may another take his office.

Ex 22:22

9 May his children be fatherless,
    and his wife a widow.

Jer 18:21; Is 65:13
Jb 5:4f

10 May his children be roaming vagrants and beggars;
    may they be cast out of the ruins of their homes.

11 May the usurer ensnare all his belongings,

Jb 20:18

    and strangers plunder the fruit of his labors.

12 May there be no one to do him a kindness,
    nor anyone to pity his orphans.

Is 14:21; Ps 137:9
Jb 18:19; Ps 21:11

13 May his posterity meet with destruction;
    in the next generation may their name be blotted out.

14 May the guilt of his fathers be remembered by the Lord;

Jer 18:23; Ex 20:5

    let not his mother's sin be blotted out;

15 May they be continually before the Lord,

Ps 34:17

    till he banish the memory of these parents from the earth.

16 Because he remembered not to show kindness,

but persecuted the wretched and poor

Jb 20:19   and the brokenhearted, to do them to death.

17 He loved cursing; may it come upon him;
he took no delight in blessing; may it be far from him.

18 And may he be clothed with cursing as with a robe;

Nm 5:24   may it penetrate into his entrails like water
and like oil into his bones;

19 May it be for him like a garment which covers him,
like a girdle which is always about him.

III

20 May this be the recompense from the Lord upon my accusers
and upon those who speak evil against me.

Pss 34:9; 145:9   21 But do you, O God, my Lord, deal kindly with me
for your name's sake;
in your generous kindness rescue me;

22 For I am wretched and poor,
and my heart is pierced within me.

Ps 102:12; Jb 30:22
Ex 10:19; Jl 2:20   23 Like a lengthening shadow I pass away;
I am swept away like the locust.

24 My knees totter from my fasting,

Ps 102:6   and my flesh is wasted of its substance.

Pss 69:12; 70:4; 123:4
Ps 22:8   25 And I am become a mockery to them;
when they see me, they shake their heads.

26 Help me, O Lord, my God;
save me, in your kindness,

27 And let them know that this is your hand;
that you, O Lord, have done this.

2 Sm 16:12;
Nm 22:6
Pss 83:17f;
119:78   28 Let them curse, but do you bless;
may my adversaries be put to shame,
but let your servant rejoice.

29 Let my accusers be clothed with disgrace

Jer 20:11   and let them wear their shame like a mantle.

30 I will speak my thanks earnestly to the Lord,

Ps 22:23   and in the midst of the throng I will praise him,

31 For he stood at the right hand of the poor man,
to save him from those who would condemn him.

This peculiar psalm could reflect in part a trial by ordeal (cf.

Nm 5:22), called after the author of this lament had been accused of sorcery and held responsible for the death of a poor man (v 16), presumably caused by magically effective curses (v 17f). If this hypothesis, proposed also by Weiser, is correct, the awful imprecations (vv 6-19; cf. §14d) listed in the psalm could have been pronounced by the enemies during the trial. This would also explain the use of the singular in these verses. But in verse 20 the terrible words are applied to the adversaries: "May this be the recompense from the Lord upon my accusers." Is it a wish that what they said should happen to them, that they might fall in the pit they have dug (cf. *Pss 35:8; 57:7; §12e), or, more precisely, that God bring them down "by their own tongue" (Ps 64:9)? Or else is it a way of avoiding the effect of the curses (cf. §14d) by returning them upon the adversaries? If they are genuine imprecations of the psalmist, they reflect a religious standard yet unaware of the evangelical level of forgiveness. Gunkel did call Ps 109 the only "pure" imprecation psalm. What exasperates this and other psalmists (cf. 35:12; 38:21) is the fact that ungrateful accusers repay evil for good and hatred for love (v 5). After the litany of imprecations, the prayer for help is renewed in moving terms: "I am wretched and poor, and my heart is pierced within me" (v 22). "Let them know, says the psalmist to God, that this is your hand; that you, O Lord, have done *this*" (v 27). Could "this" refer to the death of the poor man (v 16) the psalmist is accused of killing? Of course "divine action" can mean also an accident or a natural calamity.

PSALM 120 (119)

A Complaint against Treacherous Tongues

1 A *song of ascents.*

I

In my distress I called to the Lord,
 and he answered me.

Ps 12:3ff

2 O Lord, deliver me from lying lip,
 from treacherous tongue.

Pss 63:12;
139:20

II

1 Sm 3:17;
14:44

3 What will he inflict on you, with more besides,

Ps 109:2   O treacherous tongue?

                        4 Sharp arrows of a warrior
Prv 16:27; Ps   with fiery coals of brushwood.
11:6
Ps 140:11   III

Gn 10:2   5 Woe is me that I sojourn in Meshech,

Gn 25:13   that I dwell amid the tents of Cedar!

                        6 All too long have I dwelt
                           with those who hate peace.

                        7 When I speak of peace,
Ps 140:3   they are ready for war.

This psalm figures among the "Pilgrim Songs" (cf. §3c) possibly because its author is away from Jerusalem, among barbarians, represented by Meshech (cf. Gn 10:2) "an ancient people of Northeastern Asia Minor," or Cedar (cf. Gn 25:13), "a tribe of the North Arabian desert" (CV). These names, referring to places far apart, are probably metaphorical, so that little is known of the real setting in life of the psalm. According to JB, Meshech is "the country of the Moschoi, a Caucasian people, Gn 10:2; Ez 27:13, where Gog is later to be king, Ez 38:2. The Arabs of Kedar lived in the Syrian desert. The psalmist makes 'Meshech' and 'Kedar' synonymous with barbarian."

"In my distress I called to the Lord, and he answered me" (v 1), writes the psalmist. What follows, "O Lord, deliver me from lying lip . . ." could be a hidden quotation recalling his prayer (cf. Ps 41: 5) and the whole psalm would be a "testimony" (Weiser), recited during a cultic ceremony. Other authors read the first verse in the present: "When I am in trouble, I call to Yahweh, and he answers me" (JB). For Weiser, however, "it is unnecessary and hardly legitimate, though fashionable nowadays, to translate the perfect tenses by the present tense, thus marking the whole psalm as a prayer of lament" (p. 742; see on *Ps 63). Whatever it is, a lament or a "recapitulated supplication," the poem seems to allude again to a trial by ordeal (cf. Ps 109) because of the mention of an oath in verse 3. By being untruthful the adversary works his own destruction. He will be hit by the arrow (cf. 7:13; 11:2; 57:4; 64:3) of his own "treacherous tongue" (cf. Ps 64:9) and burned with the charcoal (cf. *Ps 11:6) intended for others (cf. Prv 25:22; Rm 12:20).

PSALM 130 (129)

Prayer for Pardon and Mercy

1 *A song of ascents.*

I

Pss 18:5; 95:
4; 139:15
Jon 2:3; Lam
3:55
2 Chr 6:40; 7:
15
Neh 1:6f

Out of the depths I cry to you, O Lord;
    Lord, hear my voice!
2 Let your ears be attentive
    to my voice in supplication:

II

3 If you, O Lord, mark iniquities,

Jb 9:2

    Lord, who can stand?

Ex 34:7; Ps
103:3
Rm 2:4

4 But with you is forgiveness,
    that you may be revered.

III

5 I trust in the Lord;

Ps 119:42

    my soul trusts in his word.

Pss 25:1; 42:2

6 My soul waits for the Lord

Pss 5:4; 90:
14; 143:8

    more than sentinels wait for the dawn.

IV

More than sentinels wait for the dawn,

Is 21:11; 26:9

7   let Israel wait for the Lord,
For with the Lord is kindness

Ps 19:15; Lk
2:38
Pss 19:15; 25:
22

    and with him is plenteous redemption.
8 And he will redeem Israel
    from all their iniquities.

The *De profundis* is both a "Song of ascents" (cf. §3c) and a penitential psalm (cf. *Ps 6). Martin Luther, reports Weiser, "has classed the psalm with the 'Pauline' psalms (Pss 32, 51, 130, 143) as the best psalms of the Psalter," also the best, presumably, in relation to his doctrines. Deeply affected by sin because of a God-given perception of its seriousness, the psalmist displays true repentance and hopes for forgiveness. The last two verses could be a later liturgical addition. If not, they express, as in other psalms the psalmist's religious sensitiveness toward fellowship in cult, belief and redemption (v 7).

The psalm is mostly associated, in the Church, to the liturgy of

the dead, because the mention of "depths" has suggested very soon
the abyss in which popular representation places the abode of the souls
in purgatory. Rather, perhaps the association arose from the idea of
judgment: "If you, O Lord, mark iniquities, Lord, who can stand?"
(v 3) In fact no one can live that hour without anguish unless he relies
on God's mercy (v 4). Quoting verse 3 (cf. Ps 143:2), Mowinckel
observes: "The psalmists agree with the author of the poem of Job
that, face to face with God, all creatures are unclean and sinful" (II,
p. 13). Š. Porubčan suggests that Ps 130 is a "pilgrim song" rather
than a penitential psalm. Are not the souls of the dead pilgrims?

PSALM 140 (139)

Prayer for Deliverance from the Snare of the Wicked

<table>
<tr><td></td><td>1</td><td colspan="2">For the leader. A psalm of David.</td></tr>
<tr><td></td><td></td><td>I</td><td></td></tr>
<tr><td></td><td>2</td><td colspan="2">Deliver me, O Lord, from evil men;</td></tr>
<tr><td>Ps 27:12</td><td></td><td></td><td>preserve me from violent men,</td></tr>
<tr><td></td><td>3</td><td colspan="2">From those who devise evil in their hearts,</td></tr>
<tr><td>Ps 120:7</td><td></td><td></td><td>and stir up wars every day.</td></tr>
<tr><td>Pss 52:4; 55:
22; 58:5
Sir 12:16; Rm
3:13</td><td>4</td><td colspan="2">They make their tongues sharp as those of serpents;
the venom of asps is under their lips.</td></tr>
<tr><td></td><td></td><td>II</td><td></td></tr>
<tr><td></td><td>5</td><td colspan="2">Save me, O Lord, from the hands of the wicked;
preserve me from violent men</td></tr>
<tr><td>Ps 57:7</td><td></td><td colspan="2">Who plan to trip up my feet —</td></tr>
<tr><td>Jer 18:22</td><td>6</td><td colspan="2">the proud who have hidden a trap for me;
They have spread cords for a net;</td></tr>
<tr><td>Pss 119:110;
142:4
Ps 31:15</td><td></td><td></td><td>by the wayside they have laid snares for me.</td></tr>
<tr><td></td><td>7</td><td colspan="2">I say to the Lord, you are my God;
hearken, O Lord, to my voice in supplication.</td></tr>
<tr><td></td><td>8</td><td colspan="2">O God, my Lord, my strength and my salvation;
you are my helmet in the day of battle!</td></tr>
<tr><td></td><td></td><td>III</td><td></td></tr>
<tr><td></td><td>9</td><td colspan="2">Grant not, O Lord, the desires of the wicked;
further not their plans.</td></tr>
<tr><td></td><td>10</td><td colspan="2">Those who surround me lift up their heads;</td></tr>
</table>

Pss 5:11; 141:
10

        may the mischief which they threaten overwhelm them.

Gn 19:24; Rm
12:20
Nm 16:31f

11 May he rain burning coals upon them;

        may he cast them into the depths, never to rise.

Pss 11:6; 55:
24

    IV

12 A man of wicked tongue shall not abide in the land;

        evil shall abruptly entrap the violent man.

13 I know that the Lord renders

        justice to the afflicted, judgment to the poor.

14 Surely the just shall give thanks to your name;

Pss 11:7; 16:
11; 17:15

        the upright shall dwell in your presence.

This psalm has affinities with Psalm 64 in which also the "enemies" (cf. §12g) are slanderers armed with sharp tongues (v 4 in both psalms). As in Ps 120, so also in Ps 140 the accused prays that his enemies be destroyed by their own curses, the "burning coals" intended for their victim (vv 9-11; cf. *Ps 11:6). His hope is well founded: "I know that the Lord renders justice to the afflicted, judgment to the poor" (v 13).

PSALM 141 (140)

Prayer of a Just Man To Be Saved from Wickedness

1 *A psalm of David.*

    I

    O Lord, to you I call; hasten to me;

        hearken to my voice when I call upon you.

Pss 50:14;
116:17
Rev 5:8; Ex
30:8
Pss 28:2; 50:
14; 63:5

2 Let my prayer come like incense before you;

        the lifting up of my hands, like the evening sacrifice.

    II

3 O Lord, set a watch before my mouth,

        a guard at the door of my lips.

Ps 119:36

4 Let not my heart incline to the evil

        of engaging in deeds of wickedness

Ps 94:16

    With men who are evildoers;

Prv 5:3; 27:6

        and let me not partake of their dainties.

Eccl 7:5

5 Let the just man strike me; that is kindness;

Prv 9:8; 25:
12
1 Sm 15:13

        let him reprove me; it is oil for the head,

    Which my head shall not refuse,

Ps 33:1   but I will still pray under these afflictions.

Is 3:15; 8:14   6   Their judges were cast down over the crag,
                      and they heard how pleasant were my words
                 7   As when a plowman breaks furrows in the field,
                      so their bones are strewn by the edge of the nether world.

                      III

Pss 25:15;   For toward you, O God, my Lord, my eyes are turned;
145:15   in you I take refuge; strip me not of life.
                 9   Keep me from the trap they have set for me,
                      and from the snares of evildoers.

Pss 5:11; 69:   10   Let all the wicked fall, each into his own net,
23   while I escape.

Little is known of the particular circumstance of this psalm, partly because verses 6 and 7 are corrupt and obscure. Yet it seems that the psalmist is plagued with temptation (vv 3, 4, 9) arising from the conduct of "evildoers" (vv 4, 9; cf. Ps 73:8-10). Prayer is remarkably compared to incense and the lifting of hands, that is, supplication (cf. Pss 28:2; 63:5; 77:3; 88:10; 119:48; 134:2; 143:6) to "evening sacrifice" (v 3). Some authors see in this "a spiritualization and a deepening of the idea of God and of man's intercourse with him which puts the psalm in the same class with Pss 40, 50, 51, 69 and 71" (Weiser). There will be more to say about that in connection with *"sacrificium laudis"* of Ps 50:14.

The difficult verses 6-7 Weiser leaves untranslated (cf. *Ps 53:7). Tournay's latest attempt at their interpretation is well documented. Some of the biblical parallels he used are included in the list supplied here next to the *CV* text. His translation would appear in English as follows:

5. Let the just strike me kindly to amend me,
   but never let the oil of the wicked anoint my head,
   for my ornament is the prayer I oppose to their malice.
6. They are delivered to the grip of the Rock, their judge:
   he will hear my words, for they are delectable.
7. As a millstone grinds against the soil
   so their bones are strewn about the rim of sheol.

The general meaning of Ps 141 is clear, writes Tournay. The prayer of the faithful will be answered; it will hasten the punishment of the wicked, to whom *lex talionis* will be applied (cf. §12e, 14d). All evil-doers will perish but the just man will escape unscathed from the temptations. The psalmist's only liking is for prayer, which he offers up, in fragrant fumes, like an evening sacrifice (cf. Pss 50:14; 51:19; 69:31f). The incense of his prayer wraps the worshipper up like a splendid ornament. The psalm, it is claimed, comes from a "didactic" milieu as the references to wisdom literature indicates. It shows special affinities with Prv 15:26-32 and the date of its origin can be set in the third century B.C.

Verse 5 can be compared with one of the sayings of Ahiqar, from Egyptian wisdom circles. The Ahiqar sayings have been found on eleven fifth century B.C. sheets of palimpsest papyrus recovered half a century ago in Elephantine (Aswan). Ahiqar is mentioned in the Book of Tobit (1:22; 14:10 etc.); his presence and writings are associated with Assyrian kings Sennacherib (704-681) and Esarhaddon (680-669). Ahiqar used to say: "My son, let the wise man strike thee with many blows, and let not the fool salve thee with sweet salve" (II: 73 Syriac; in Charles, II, p. 738; cp. Eccl 7:5).

PSALM 142 (141)

Prayer of a Prisoner in Dire Straits

1 Sm 22:1; 24:1f Ps 57:1	1	*A maśkîl of David. A prayer when he was in the cave.*
		I
	2	With a loud voice I cry out to the Lord;
		with a loud voice I beseech the Lord.
	3	My complaint I pour out before him;
		before him I lay bare my distress.
Jb 17:1; Ps 143:4 Ps 139:24	4	When my spirit is faint within me,
		you know my path.
		II
		In the way along which I walk
Pss 140:6; 141:9		they have hid a trap for me.
	5	I look to the right and see,
		but there is no one who pays me heed.
Lam 3:7		I have lost all means of escape;
		there is no one who cares for my life.

III

6 I cry out to you, O Lord;

Pss 73:28; 91: 2, 9

Pss 15:5; 116:9

    I say, "You are my refuge,

      my portion in the land of the living."

7 Attend to my cry,

Ps 79:8

    for I am brought low indeed.

Rescue me from my persecutors,

    for they are too strong for me.

Ps 88:9

8 Lead me forth from prison,

    that I may give thanks to your name.

The just shall gather around me

    when you have been good to me.

This persecuted psalmist (v 7) is cut away from his friends, isolated and perhaps kept in prison (vv 5, 8) by his enemies. Having lost all means of escape (v 5), his only hope lies with the Lord, who knows his path (v 4), that is, his past and destiny. The Lord is also the psalmist's "portion in the land of the living," a statement possibly related to a liturgical action. Among the *Heilgeschichte* events experienced in the cult, those which belong to God's entire redemptive work in history (cf. *Ps 66), A. Weiser lists also the *redistribution of the land* (cf. Pss 16:5f; 25:13; 37:9, 11; 60:6ff; 61:5). According to Dt 31:9ff, he writes, "it was carried out every seven years in the autumn within the framework of the Covenant Festival and presumably followed the tradition of the conquest and distribution of the land" (*The Psalms*, p. 44; cf. §13b). In fact, for the Israelite believer the Covenant was life's domain and his "portion" was the Lord (cf. Pss 16:5, 11; 27:13; 73:26; 119:57; Lam 3:24). After his release by God's might the psalmist will rejoice in the fellowship of worshippers (vv 7-8; on the idea "God is my portion," see *Ps 73:26).

PSALM 143 (142)

Prayer of a Penitent in Distress

1 *A psalm of David.*

I

O Lord, hear my prayer;

    hearken to my pleading in your faithfulness;

    in your justice answer me.

2 And enter not into judgment with your servant,

Jb 9:2; 14:3f
Eccl 7:20; Rm 3:20

    for before you no living man is just.

II

3 For the enemy pursues me;

Ps 7:6

    he has crushed my life to the ground;

Lam 3:6

    he has left me dwelling in the dark, like those long dead.

Ps 142:4

4 And my spirit is faint within me,

Ps 77:4

    my heart within me is appalled.

Ps 77:6, 12f

5 I remember the days of old;

Ps 1:2

    I meditate on all your doings,

    the works of your hands I ponder.

6 I stretch out my hands to you;

Ez 19:13; Ps 63:2

    my soul thirsts for you like parched land.

III

7 Hasten to answer me, O Lord,

    for my spirit fails me.

Pss 10:1; 69:18; 102:3
Pss 28:1; 88:5

Hide not your face from me

    lest I become like those who go down into the pit.

Pss 5:4; 17:15

8 At dawn let me hear of your kindness,

    for in you I trust.

Jb 21:14; Pss 25:4; 86:11
Pss 25:1; 86:4

Show me the way in which I should walk,

    for to you I lift up my soul.

9 Rescue me from my enemies, O Lord,

    for in you I hope.

IV

Pss 5:9; 51:3

10 Teach me to do your will,

Pss 26:12; 94:18

    for you are my God.

Is 63:11; Wis 1:5

May your good spirit guide me

Pss 94:18; 121:3

    on level ground.

11 For your name's sake, O Lord, preserve me;

Pss 31:2; 71:2; 119:142

    in your justice free me from distress,

12 And in your kindness destroy my enemies;

Pss 54:7; 116:16

    bring to nought all my foes,

    for I am your servant.

The suppliant of this "penitential" psalm (see *Ps 6) is persecuted, perhaps on the verge of being brought to court by his powerful enemies (vv 3, 9, 12). He hopes to be heard in the morning (v 8), for sunrise symbolizes joy and hope (cf. Pss 90:14; 101:8; see on *Ps 5:4). His spirit is faint, failing (vv 4, 7), his heart appalled (v 4), presumably from fear. Having from the beginning noted the natural sinfulness of man and his impurity before God (v 2), he proceeds to ask for God's guidance to walk in the right path (vv 8, 10), firmly convinced that his moral deviations have brought him to this fearful state. Yet he boasts to be a "servant of God" and feels to be on good ground to ask for the destruction of his enemies and the annihilation of his foes (v 12).

It is noteworthy that in verse one God's justice is mentioned in parallel with his faithfulness. This explains why the psalmist can say: "In your justice answer me." The saving aspect of God's justice is implied in these statements. What problems this involved is discussed elsewhere (§11e). It is not difficult to see why the "absolution," a solemn prayer for the dead chanted after a mass of requiem, begins with the following words: "Enter not into judgment with thy servant, O Lord; for, save thou grant him forgiveness of all his sins, no man shall be justified in thy sight (Ps 143:2). Wherefore suffer not, we beseech thee, the sentence thou pronouncest in judgment upon one whom the faithful prayer of thy Christian people commends to thee, to be a doom which shall crush him utterly" (cf. Rm 3:20; Gal 2:16). Besides, not a few descriptive elements of Ps 143 are metaphors connected with darkness, death and pit (vv 3, 47), easily adapted to burials. In the Church's Latin Office, Ps 143 is recited at Lauds on Fridays, the antiphon being verse 9: "Rescue me from my enemies, O Lord, for in you I hope." With few corrections, mainly in verse 12, the psalm can can be applied to the suffering Christ. In the Missal, the Gradual of Passion Sunday and the Offertory of Monday in the Holy Week are drawn from verses 9 and 10.

M. Dahood finds in verses 10b-11 of Ps 143 confirmation of one of his less acceptable suggestions: that ṣedāqâh, in some contexts, "means approximately *meadow*" (on Ps 5:9). This follows the main line of thought discussed in connection with *Ps 36:10, namely that in poetic passages of the Bible is featured the motif of the Elysian Fields, the abode of the blessed after death. The "meadow" motif would appear in Ps 5:9: "Lead me into your meadow (*bᵉsidqātekā; CV* "in your justice") because of my rivals, your way make level before me." It is also represented, Dahood thinks, in Ps 69:28f, in an eschatological context: "Add to them punishment upon punishment and let them not enter your meadow. Let them be blotted out of the book of the living, and let them not be enrolled among the just." Lastly comes Ps 143:10b-11: "With your good spirit lead me into the level land; for your name's sake, O Yahweh, grant me life in your meadow."

§21. PSALMS OF CONFIDENCE OF THE INDIVIDUAL

(a) *General character*

The "psalms of confidence" are in reality the "motives of confidence" from the corpus of the lamentation developed into independent psalms (A. Bentzen, *Introduction to the Old Testament,* I, p. 156). We read, for example, in a well known lament:

> In you our fathers trusted;
>> they trusted, and you delivered them.
> To you they cried, and they escaped;
>> in you they trusted, and they were not put to shame (Ps 22:5f).

Most of the elements constituting in fact the lament are found in the psalms of confidence, but here the confidence motif predominates. The idea of security (cf. 4:9; 16:8f; 27:1-5) and of peace, even during sleep (cf. 3:6; 4:5, 9; 16:7), is frequently mentioned. The joy which this quietude provides (cf. 4:8; 16:6, 9, 11; 23:6) is often associated with the temple, where God is likely to reveal himself (cf. 11:7; 16:11) and grant the prayers of his faithful (cf. 3:5; 11:4; 23:6; 27:4). In these psalms the personal tone is more apparent than in the thanksgivings. In her instructive study of the confidence motif in the psalms J. Thévenet has carefully examined also the vocabulary of "confidence" (cf. Ps 43-56) and even presented her findings in a four-column conspectus of words found in the Massoretic Text, with their equivalents in the Septuagint, the Vulgate and the new Latin Psalter (p. 116f). Some forty years previously J. Begrich had investigated the expressions of confidence of the Israelite (individual) laments and their Babylonian counterpart (see bibliog.).

(b) *These are the psalms of confidence of the individual*: Pss 3, 4, 11, 16, 23, (27), (62), (121), 131.

PSALM 3

Trust in God in Time of Danger

2 Sm 15:13ff   1 A psalm of David, when he fled from his son Absalom.

I

2 O Lord, how many are my adversaries!

3   Many rise up against me!
       Many are saying of me,
       "There is no salvation for him in God."

Dt 33:29; Prv   4 But you, O Lord, are my shield;
2:7
Sir 11:13; Pss   my glory, you lift up my head!
5:13; 18:3
Pss 27:6; 110:   II
7
Ps 5:3   5 When I call out to the Lord,
                    he answers me from his holy mountain.

Prv 3:24   6 When I lie down to sleep,

Pss 5:4; 18:36;   I wake again, for the Lord sustains me.
27:9
                 7 I fear not the myriads of people
                    arrayed against me on every side.

III

Jer 2:27   8 Rise up, O Lord!
                    Save me, my God!
                    For you strike all my enemies on the cheek;

Ps 58:7; Jb   the teeth of the wicked you break.
29:17
Jer 3:23; Jon   9 Salvation is the Lord's!
2:9
Pss 7:11; 115:   Upon your people be your blessing!
12; 134:3

According to the ascription this psalm was composed by David when he fled from his son Absalom. There is no way of proving or disproving the value of this precision, but the psalmist could well have been a royal worshipper, imperiled as he is by so many adversaries (v 2), by "myriads of people" (v 7). Presumably, Weiser suggests, the psalm belongs to the royal ritual, in which the idea of Yahweh's warfare against enemies formed the *Heilgeschichte* framework. It is true that the psalmist's absolute confidence in prayer rests on the saving deeds of the Lord experienced in the past.

Dahood finds in verse 4 the divine title "Suzerain," by reading *māgān* instead of *māgēn*, "shield" (*CV*). His argument proceeds from

Ps 84:12 which, he says, "virtually defines a suzerain": "For Sovereign (*šemeš*) and Suzerain (*māgān*) is Yahweh; God bestows favors and honors." *Shemesh* (= *Ugar. špš*) was the title of the Pharaoh or of the Hittite overlord, explains Dahood. As for "Suzerain" the root concept is *māgan*, "to give, bestow, hand over," frequent in Ugaritic and found also in Phoenician. In Pss 84:10 and 89:19, *māgān*, "Suzerain," would balance respectively the titles of "anointed" and "king." If one accepts to read *māgān* in Gn 15:1, then the title is associated with its root meaning, "to give": "Fear not, Abraham, I am your Suzerain who will reward you very greatly." The conceptual relationship between "suzerain" and "benefactor" comes out in Lk 22:25: "The kings of the heathen lord it over their subjects, and those in authority are called Benefactors." "In the historical prologues of suzerainty or vassal treaties, Dahood also notes, emphasis was laid upon the past benevolent acts of the great king, and the advantages that would accrue to the vassal who accepted the treaty were set forth. In other words, the great king represented himself as a benefactor, so that the transition from *māgān*, "benefactor," to "suzerain," may have occurred within this terminological framework" (cf. §13c). These various associations are found in Ps 84:12: "For Sovereign and Suzerain is Yahweh; God bestows favors and honors."

Other suggestions proposed by Dahood in connection with Ps 3 can be usefully mentioned here. Read in verse 7: "I fear not the *shafts* of people, deployed against me on every side." The root *rbb* is understood as signifying "to shoot arrows" and not "myriads" (cf. Ps 18:44; Jb 16:13). Verse 8 yields better meaning if *kî* is taken as an "emphatic particle with the precative or optative perfect": "O that you yourself [O Yahweh] would smite all my foes on the jaw!" (cf. Pss 9:5; 39:10 etc.) Smitten on the jaw the adversaries will no longer be able to calumniate the psalmist with their slanderous "shafts"!

PSALM 4

Joyful Confidence in God

1 *For the leader; with stringed instruments. A psalm of David.*

I

2 When I call, answer me, O my just God,
     you who relieve me when I am in distress;
     Have pity on me, and hear my prayer!

Pss 6:3; 9:14

II

3 Men of rank, how long will you be dull of heart?
  Why do you love what is vain and seek after falsehood?

Ps 31:22
4 Know that the Lord does wonders for his faithful one;
  the Lord will hear me when I call upon him.

Eph 4:25
5 Tremble, and sin not;

Ps 149:5
  reflect, upon your beds, in silence.

Dt 33:19; Ps
20:4
Pss 27:6; 51:
21
6 Offer just sacrifices,
  and trust in the Lord.

III

Pss 31:17; 67:
2; Nm 6:25
Dn 9:17; Prv
16:15
7 Many say, "Oh, that we might see better times!"
  O Lord, let the light of your countenance shine upon us!

8 You put gladness into my heart,

Prv 3:10; Dt
33:28f
  more than when grain and wine abound.

9 As soon as I lie down, I fall peacefully asleep,
  for you alone, O Lord,
  bring security to my dwelling.

If Ps 3 is a "morning hymn" because of verse 6, Ps 4 can be called an "evening hymn" on account of verses 5 and 9. Verse 2, which does not fit too well in the context, may have been altered somehow when the psalm became a liturgical prayer of supplication. The central stanza of the psalm (vv 3-6) would reflect a priestly exhortation to a group of influential people ("men of rank"), inviting them to avoid sin and trust in the Lord. The supplication "lift upon us the light of thy face" (v 7:litt.) refers probably to an ancient liturgical benediction (cf. §3c and Nm 6:25). The "beds" of verse 5 (cf. Ps 149:5) could allude to the place of prayerful prostration: Ps 95:6 and Sir 50:17 (cf. BJ).

Much could be said in favor or against Dahood's interpretation of the psalm as "a prayer for rain" (cf. JBL 1966, p. 485f). "Drought is in the land; the psalmist (a ḥāsîd; cf. §12c) is much distressed, while the pusillanimous leaders of the people criticize Yahweh and seek rain from the nature deities. The psalmist reminds those of little faith that Yahweh will hear their prayer if they but examine their consciences, weep for their sins, and offer legitimate sacrifices. The correct exegesis of some of the phrases flows from the comparison with similar phrases and contexts in the other psalms that are prayers for rain, such as 60:10-14, 67, 85." It can be readily admitted that verse 3b translated, "how long will you worship inanities or consult idols?", refers to various practices of idolatry. The "prayer for rain" interpretation depends basically on the meaning of *ṭob* in verse 7. The claim is that the word means "rain" in this and other biblical texts:

> Ps   4:7 : Many keep saying, "Who will show us rain?"
> Ps 85:13: With a loud voice Yahweh gives his rain,
>   and our land gives its produce.
> Dt 28:12: Yahweh will open for you his treasury of rain (*'ôṣārô*
>   *haṭṭôb*),
>   the heavens, to give your land its rain in due season.
> Jer   5:25: And your sins have withheld the rain from you.

That *haṭṭôb* can be translated "the rain" in this last example is shown by comparing the statement with Jer 3:3, "So that the showers (*rᵉbîbîm*) were withheld" and Am 4:7: "I withheld from you the rain (*geshem*)." In translating Ps 4:7b, "the light of your face has fled (*nāsâh*) from us (*'ālēnû*), O Yahweh," Dahood explains that *nāsâh*, from *nūs*, "represents an archaic third-person masculine singular of the Canaanite *qatala* type as in Ugaritic," and that in "Northwest Semitic" (*'al*) with verbs of fleeing can denote "from," as more than one study has shown. As consequence, he adds, *Ps 67 should also be classified as "a prayer for rain," because of verse 2: "May he make his face shine upon us." According to L. Dürr, the setting in life and the vocabulary of Ps 4 points to its being contemporary with the Book of Malachi (5th cent.).

PSALM 11 (10)

Unshaken Confidence in God

1 *For the leader. Of David.*

I

In the Lord I take refuge; how can you say to me,
   "Flee to the mountain like a bird!

2 For, see, the wicked bend the bow;
      they place the arrow on the string
      to shoot in the dark at the upright of heart.

3 When the pillars are overthrown,
      what can the just man do?"

Pss 121:1;
124:7
Gn 19:17; Ez
7:16
Mt 24:16; Pss
18:34; 55:7
Pss 7:13; 37:
14
Ps 57:5

Ps 64:4

Pss 24:2; 82:5

II

Dt 26:15; 1 Kgs 8:30 Hb 2:20; Is 66:1; Mt 5:34	4 The Lord is in his holy temple; the Lord's throne is in heaven. His eyes behold,
Pss 66:7; 102: 20 Ps 7:10	his searching glance is on mankind. 5 The Lord searches the just and the wicked;
Ps 5:7	the lover of violence he hates.
Gn 19:24; Ez 38:22 Rev 14:10; 16: 19; 20:9 Ps 103:6; Jb 33:26 Ps 17:15; Is 38:11; 1 Cor 13:12	6 He rains upon the wicked fiery coals and brimstone; a burning blast is their allotted cup. 7 For the Lord is just, he loves just deeds; the upright shall see his face.

Advised by friends or disciples (vv 1-3) to flee from a great peril, the psalmist prefers to take refuge in the temple (v 4), for the Lord controls the destinies of the just and of the wicked (5-7), as the mention of the biblical figure of the cup suggests (cf. Pss 16:5; 23: 5; 75:9; Is 51:17; Jer 25:15; Ez 23:32; Hb 2:16). "Fiery coal and brimstone" probably refers to the Genesis stories about Sodom and Gomorrah (Gn 19:24; Ex 38:22; Jb 18:15). The phrase "see the face of God," Weiser explains, "is derived from the language of the cultus and refers to the theophany as the climax of the rites performed in the cult when the worshipper experiences the presence of his God with joy and trembling" (cf. Pss 24:6; 42:3). With reference to Ps 68:5 he asserts that in the cult theophany there is no clear distinction between the epiphany of God in the heavens and his appearance in the sanctuary. Thus Ps 11 declares: "The Lord is in his holy temple; the Lord's throne is in heaven" (v 4). This can be compared with Jesus' saying: "But I say to you, Do not swear at all, either by heaven, for it is the throne of God, or by the earth, for it is his footstool, or by Jerusalem, for it is the city of the great King" (Mt 5:34-35).

Are "the pillars" of verse 3 the foundations of "public order" (*CV*) or those of ethics and religion, entrusted to the rulers (*BJ*, referring to Is 19:10; Ps 82:5)? According to *The Interpreter's Bible,* "the supporters of the psalmist point out that his cause is tumbling to pieces, and he is about to be buried in the ruins." In Dahood's opinion, no "just man" is involved in the verse, but "the Just One," God himself: "When foundations are being torn down, what is the Just One doing?" The answer is given in the next verse. *Saddîq* is a divine appellative which recurs in Pss 31:19 and 75:11 (cf. §11e + 12b). "The complaint of the poet, Dahood writes, is not unlike the reasoning of the practical atheist in Ps 10:4-5, who was convinced that God in his heavens was too far removed to intervene in behalf of justice" (cf. §10a).

Quite striking also is Dahood's version of the last verse: "For the Just One is Yahweh, who loves just actions; Our face shall gaze upon the Upright one." He finds in it "the breakup of the stereotyped phrase (as in v 4) found in Dt 22:4 . . .": "A God of faithfulness and without iniquity, the Just and Upright one is he." Dahood then comments: "The vision of God mentioned here is doubtless that of Pss 16:11; 17:15; 41:13; 49:16; 73:26, which suggests a belief in an afterlife in the presence of Yahweh. If perfect justice is not attained in this life, it will be in the next; this seems to be the ultimate motive for the psalmist's confidence." The difficulty of the Hebrew text (singular subject with plural verb) is attributed by *BJ* to an emendation introduced to avoid saying that God can be seen in this life (v 7). But, *BJ* suggests, the "theological scruple" (cf. Gn 32:30) was unfounded since the text merely states that the upright will stand in the presence of God like servants before a benevolent and generous master, to receive his favors: cf. Pss 15:1; 16:11; 17:15; 24:6; 27:8; 105:4; Is 38:11; Gn 33:10; Jb 33:26.

PSALM 16 (15)

God the Supreme Good

1 *A miktam of David.*

I

Keep me, O God for in you I take refuge;

2   I say to the Lord, "My Lord are you.

1 Sm 2:2; 4:8   Apart from you I have no good."

3 How wonderfully has he made me cherish

Ps 34:10   the holy ones who are in his land!

4 They multiply their sorrows

1 Sm 26:19   who court other gods.

Blood libations to them I will not pour out,

Os 2:19   nor will I take their names upon my lips.

Pss 11:6; 23:5   5 O Lord, my allotted portion and my cup,

Jb 22:25   you it is who hold fast my lot.

Mi 2:4; Sir   6 For me the measuring lines have fallen on pleasant sites;
45:20
Nm 18:20; Dt   fair to me indeed is my inheritance.
10:9; Lam 3:
24; Wis 3:14;   II
Pss 37:18;
105:11

                    7 I bless the Lord who counsels me;

Pss 4:5; 17:3;   even in the night my heart exhorts me.
Jer 12:2
Acts 2:25ff   8 I set the Lord ever before me;

Pss 21:8; 30:   with him at my right hand I shall not be disturbed.
7; 121:5
                   9 Therefore my heart is glad and my soul rejoices,

Pss 6:6; 49:   my body, too, abides in confidence;
16; Nm 16:33
Acts 2:27f; 13:   10 Because you will not abandon my soul to the nether world,
35f
Dn 12:2; 2   nor will you suffer your faithful one to undergo
Mc 7:9; 12:43
                                                              corruption.

Prv 5:6; Ps 1:   11 You will show me the path to life,
6
Ps 140:14   fullness of joys in your presence,

                    the delights at your right hand forever.

The various historical interpretations of this psalm belong to three types. Some place the setting in life of the psalm soon after the return from the Babylonian captivity, mainly because of similarities with passages of Deutero-Isaiah (cf. §14c) regarding sacrifices to the gods, distributions of lots (vv 4-5; cf. Is 57:5ff; 65:3-7), atmosphere of joy (vv 9-11; cf. Is 62:4f). The psalmist's zealous opposition to idolatry would indicate, it is also thought, that he was one of the hasidim or "saints" (v 3; cf. §12c) of the inter-testamental period. The psalm would reflect the conflict opposing Old Testament religion and new sects or cults of the Hellenistic age. A third interpretation is mainly represented by Weiser who discovered in this psalm also indications (cf. the renunciation of foreign gods) that its origin traces back to a pre-exilic cult of the covenant festival (cf. §13c). The poem would be the personal confession of a worshipper in which he sets forth what the encounter with God in the sanctuary means to him.

This psalmist, it seems, received less than his share of suffering. He is satisfied with his lot and he thankfully blesses the Lord (vv 5-7). With the Lord at his right hand he lives confidently soul and body, for, he adds, "thou will not abandon my soul to the nether world, nor will you let your saint (hasîd) see the pit" (8-10). The word šahat, "pit," may mean also "corruption," "decay" (cf. Jb 17:14), so that the

Septuagint's text is not necessarily pioneering in the translation which the New Testament has applied to Christ's resurrection (Acts 2:27): "For thou wilt not abandon my soul to Hades, nor let thy Holy One see corruption" (cf. 13:35). This can be compared with *JB*'s rendering of Ps 16:10: "For you will not abandon my soul to Sheol, nor allow the one you love to see the Pit." An afflicted man, reflecting on the problem of retribution, also tried in Ps 73:24 to express his conviction that the last word is not to death: "With your counsel you guide me, and in, the end you will receive me in glory." Other similarities link the two psalms (comp. Ps 16:7-8 and Ps 73:23-24). It is not excluded that what the psalmist hopes for is the privilege granted Enoch and Elijah (cf. Ps 49:16 and §14d).

Building on the premise that "the language and style of the psalm are peculiarly Phoenician," Dahood says of the psalm: "This profession of faith was composed by a Canaanite convert to Yahwism." The *professio fidei* (v 2) is followed by the abjuration of the false Canaanite gods ("the holy ones") once served (vv 3-4) and by the enumeration of the joys and blessings of the psalmist's new life (5-11). The belief in immortality (vv 10-11) was "well known among the Canaanites." In the very beginning the poet addresses himself to *"El,"* "the ancient Canaanite and patriarchal designation of the chief deity." C. Schedl also admits that the *qᵉdôšîm* (cf. §12d) and *'addîrê* of verse 3 are Canaanite deities. It would appear that Dahood's interpretation, served by his own translation, does fit in the context (but cf. §12b). Verses 1 to 4 are rendered as follows:

> Preserve me, O El,
>   for I have sought refuge in you.
> I said, "O Yahweh, you are my Lord,
>   there is none above you."
> As for the holy ones who were in the land,
>   and the mighty ones in whom was all my delight:
> May their travail-pains be multiplied,
>   prolong their lust.
> I surely will not pour libations to them from my hands,
>   nor will I raise their names to my lips.

According to R. P. Bierberg the last two verses of Ps 16 refer to Christ literally and exclusively, while the subject of the rest of the psalm is David literally (and Christ only typically). Other authors would prefer to say that the whole psalm in its literal sense refers both to David and to Christ, to David in a vaguer and less perfect way, and to Christ more clearly and perfectly (a case of *sensus plenior*). For A. Vaccari the words of verse 10 apply to both David and Christ in their proper sense, yet in a fuller sense to Christ who rose from the dead, while David's body knew corruption but will not be subject to *eternal* corruption. The psalmist's insight of the afterlife for the blessed is probably well rendered in Dahood's version of verse 11: "You will make me know the path of life eternal, filling me with happiness before you, with pleasures at your right hand forever."

PSALM 23 (22)

The Lord, Shepherd and Host

1 A *psalm of David.*

I

The Lord is my shepherd; I shall not want.

Jer 23:3; Jn 10:11ff
Ez 34:14; Pss 80:2: 95:7
Is 49:10: Gn 48:15

2   In verdant pastures he gives me repose;

Beside restful waters he leads me;

Jer 31:25; Ps 100:3
Is 40:11; Ez 34:16
Is 48:9: Prv 4: 11; Ps 25:4

3   he refreshes my soul.

He guides me in right paths

for his name's sake.

Is 50:10; Jb 10:21
Pss 84:7; 138: 7
Mi 7:14; 1 Sm 17:43

4 Even though I walk in the dark valley

I fear no evil; for you are at my side

With your rod and your staff

that give me courage.

II

Pss 22:27; 78: 19
Is 65:13; Ps 27:11
Lk 7:46; Ps 92:11
Pss 11:6; 16:5; 116:13

5 You spread the table before me

in the sight of my foes;

You anoint my head with oil;

my cup overflows.

6 Only goodness and kindness follow me

all the days of my life;

And I shall dwell in the house of the Lord

for years to come.

Childlike confidence in God, in peace and serenity, is the predominant note of this psalm, rightly considered to be one of the finest in the Psalter. Apparently the psalm expresses clearly a few simple ideas. Yet it is diversely interpreted, especially since it is not easy to determine the *Sitz im Leben* of the composition. W. E. Gössman remarks that the various translations of the poem reflect men's different ways of understanding God. According to Weiser the author experienced during a divine service what a blessing is communion with God. Recalling his past life he saw it as spent under the vigilant care of the Lord, amidst all kinds of perils. The divine service which inspired him could have been a hymn praising Yahweh, the "shepherd of Israel" (Ps 80:1), who has led the covenant people throughout salvation history (Is 40:11; 63:14; Ez 34:10ff; Pss 95:7; 100:3).

"It is a significant fact, notes Mowinckel (II, p. 127), that this psalm actually breaks all the patterns of 'form history.' Being a pure psalm of confidence, it cannot immediately be classified under any of the 'categories' or 'types' of style history. A real poet using the traditional cultic forms of style has here created a poem which has its own type. It is an expression of the religious traditions of the people of the covenant. It is also an expression of the conception of God with which they were entrusted, and of the personal experiences of God in their own lives and the attitude to life created by these." Along the cultic line also, J. Eaton suggests that "new force is gained by relating to the king's symbolic cultic role the journey into the valley of the shadow of death, the restoration of life or soul, the manifestation of righteousness and the greater glory of God . . ." (cf. §8d). For A. L. Merrill the psalm would describe a royal coronation ritual involving a procession which proceeds from the temple to the spring and perhaps includes a "circumambulation of the holy city" (cf. Ps 48:13ff).

In a special study of the psalm, E. Vogt advances the opinion that Ps 23 is to be linked with a thanksgiving sacrifice offered by a pilgrim, presumably for a favor experienced very recently, perhaps as he passed through a dark valley (v 4). Elsewhere in the psalms thanksgiving is often followed or accompanied by the offering of a sacrifice (cf. 66:13ff; 116:17ff) or of a sacrificial meal (Pss 22:26f; 63:6). The temple itself is called "the house of rest" (1 Chr 28:2) and "the place of rest" of the Lord's ark (Ps 132:8, 14). "The waters of rest" in verse 2 of the psalm and other indications could suggest that God the Shepherd is host to the psalmist in his temple. Having guided him through difficult and perilous paths he now "restoreth his soul," he feeds him (*rōʻi*) and his guests at the sacrificial meal. If the "dark valley" of verse 4 is understood metaphorically, the calamity alluded to could be a false accusation in court. Then the expression "paths of righteousness" (v 3b *ad. litt.*) could be another confession of innocence (Pss 5:8; 28:11f; 143:8-10; cf. *Ps 101). The psalmist's slanderers, his "adversaries," happened to wander in the temple while he was celebrating and thus he could say: "You spread the table before me in the sight of my foes" (v 5). In the fourteenth century B.C. an official of the city of Irqata (= 'Arqah, N.E. of Tripoli, Lebanon) wrote to the pharaoh of El-Amarna (cf. §9d): "Let the king, our lord, listen to the words of his faithful servant and give a present to his servant, while our enemies see and eat dust" (Letter 100: S. A. B. Mercer, vol. I, p. 341). No precise date can be determined for the psalm's composition. Since however it seems to feature some of Deutero-Isaiah's description of the repatriation (cf. Is 40:11; 49:9f) and the (second) temple is (re) built, the date could very well be the fifth-fourth century.

It has. been suggested or restated by E. Power, and accepted by others (e.g., Morgenstern, Koehler), that the *šebeṭ* and *miš'enet* of verse 4 are the two rods which are carried regularly by the Palestinian shepherd, the former as a weapon, the second as a guiding staff or as a weapon. E. Power believed that *šlḥn* ("table") owes its origin to a dittography of the initial letter of the following word *ngd*. So he read *šelaḥ,* a word "used collectively for weapons in Joel 2:8." Thus he translated verses 4b-5:

> The club and thy staff,
>   they comfort me.
> Thou preparest arms for my defense
>   against my enemies.
> Thou anointed my head with oil;
>   my cup is full.

For Dahood "the psalmist is quietly confident that Yahweh is his shepherd, who will guide him through the vicissitudes of this life to the eternal bliss of Paradise" (cf. the theme of the "Elysian fields," on *Pss 1, 36, 143). Corresponding to this interpretation, the verbs of verses 2-3 are rendered as future rather than as present. Also "the house of the Lord" (v 6) is understood as "the heavenly dwelling of Yahweh" (cf. Pss 27:4; 31:3; 36:9; Is 6:4).

In his study of the psalm G. Rinaldi mainly stressed how the psalm reflects the biblical theme of "rest." *Mᵉnûhâ,* "riposo," he shows, was one of the great gifts of God to the covenant-people. A large number of biblical texts, in the two Testaments, treat the theme of the divine Shepherd: they are studied in my *The Names and Titles of Jesus,* pp. 65-71. Among the "admonitions of Ipu-wer," written in Egypt, probably before the time of Abraham, we read the following description of the ideal king: Men shall say, "He is the herdsman of all men, evil is not in his heart. Though his herds may be small, he has spent the day caring for them" (*ANET,* p. 443). "Just as Yahweh chose David to be 'the shepherd of his people,' writes Mowinckel (I, p. 56), so 'shepherd' is a standing attribute of the king of Mesopotamia. It is his calling to 'tend the black-headed' (i.e., men). Hammurabi is 'the beneficent shepherd' (*re'u mušallimu*), and so likewise in Egypt."

PSALM 27 (26)

Trust in God

1 *Of David.*

A

I

The Lord is my light and my salvation;
  whom should I fear?
The Lord is my life's refuge;
  of whom should I be afraid?

2 When evildoers come at me
  to devour my flesh,
My foes and my enemies
  themselves stumble and fall.

3 Though an enemy encamp against me,
  my heart will not fear;
Though war be waged upon me,
  even then will I trust.

II

4 One thing I ask of the Lord;
  this I seek:
To dwell in the house of the Lord
  all the days of my life,
That I may gaze on the loveliness of the Lord

Margin references:

Pss 25:5; 35:3; 36:10
Is 10:17; 60:19f; Mi 7:8
Ps 31:2

Jb 19:22; Pss 14:4; 57:5

Mi 7:8

Ps 23:6

Ps 90:17; Prv 3:17

and contemplate his temple.

Ps 76:3   5 For he will hide me in his abode
in the day of trouble;

2 Sm 7:2; Ps
15:1   He will conceal me in the shelter of his tent,
Ps 40:3; Is
30:29   he will set me high upon a rock.
Pss 3:4; 110:7   6 Even now my head is held high
above my enemies on every side.

And I will offer in his tent

Pss 54:8; 66:
15   sacrifices with shouts of gladness;
Pss 7:18; 28:
7; 57:8   I will sing and chant praise to the Lord.

                                   B

                     I

          7 Hear, O Lord, the sound of my call;
Pss 25:16; 30:
11   have pity on me, and answer me.
Ps 24:6; 2 Sm   8 Of you my heart speaks; you my glance seeks;
21:1
Hos 5:15; Am   your presence, O Lord, I seek.
5:4
Pss 13:2; 44:   9 Hide not your face from me;
25
Pss 19:12; 34:   do not in anger repel your servant.
23
Pss 3:6; 18:36   You are my helper: cast me not off;
forsake me not, O God my savior.

Is 49:15; Jer   10 Though my father and mother forsake me,
31:20   yet will the Lord receive me.

                     II

          11 Show me, O Lord, your way,
Pss 5:9; 25:5;   and lead me on a level path,
27:11
Ps 23:5   because of my adversaries.

          12 Give me not up to the wishes of my foes;
Ps 35:11   for false witnesses have risen up against me,
Ps 140:2   and such as breathe out violence.

          13 I believe that I shall see the bounty of the Lord
Is 38:11; Ps   in the land of the living.
142:6
          14 Wait for the Lord with courage;
be stouthearted, and wait for the Lord.

One proposed analysis of this psalm safeguards its unity: a man
unjustly accused is away from the temple when he expresses his trust
in God (vv 1-6); having reached the temple he formulates his supplication (vv 7-13) and obtains an answer: "wait for the Lord!" (v 14)
The same desire of God's proximity is expressed in both parts (vv

4-5 and 8-9). Although he admits that the whole psalm is uniform in metrical measure, Podechard believes it really consists of two poems: a triumphant thanksgiving (1-6) and an anxious supplication (7-14). In the view of H. Schmidt the psalm reflects a judgment liturgy (*Gerichtsliturgie*).

E. Vogt has noted points of comparison between Pss 23 and Ps 27:1-6. "Ps 23, he writes, had its origin in the ceremony after thanksgiving: it is not itself a *Danklied,* but a general statement and expression of confidence phrased in the present tense. Ps 27:1-6 grew out of exactly the same situation; it is animated by the same sense of thankfulness and confidence, which is the result of a bitter experience" (p. 210). The only difference in the situation, adds Vogt, lies in the fact that the recital of Ps 23 followed the sacrifice, before or during the sacrificial banquet, while Ps 27 preceded the liturgy: "I will offer in his tent sacrifices with shouts of gladness; I will sing and chant praise to the Lord" (v 6). Ps 27:1-6, like Ps 23, uses present tenses and both speak of God in the third person. Different images express similar ideas in much the same phrase pattern:

Ps 23:1, "The Lord is my shepherd . . ."
   27:1, "The Lord is my light . . ."
   23:4, "Even though I walk in the dark valley I fear no evil . . ."
   27:3, "Though an army encamp against me, my heart will not fear . . ."
   23:2f, "In verdant pastures he gives me repose; beside restful waters he leads me; he refreshes my soul . . ."
   27:5, "For he will hide me in his abode in the day of trouble; He will conceal me in the shelter of his tent . . ."
   23:5, "You spread the table before me in the sight of my foes . . ."
   27:6, "Even now my head is held high above my enemies on every side."
   23:6, "And I shall dwell in the house of the Lord for years to come."
   27:4, "One thing I ask of the Lord; this I seek: to dwell in the house of the Lord all the days of my life."

In the second part of Ps 27 we read: "Show me, O Lord, your way, and lead me on a level path" (v 11), while Ps 23:3 has: "He guides me in right paths" — but the Hebrew words are different. In Ps 27: 7-14 also the "adversaries" use "false witnesses" (v 12) to attain their ends. H.-J. Kraus considers verse 14 to be a priestly oracle (cf. §8e) linked to the psalm only later.

In verse 4 Mowinckel (I, p. 6) thinks, the rare verb *biqqēr* would allude to an "augural sacrifice" (cf. Ps 5:4). For him also, the worshipper in Ps 27:1-6 "is no doubt a king in the typically bad situation of vassal king" (I, p. 238; cf. §13c). To "behold the beauty of the god" (v 4: *nō'am,* "pleasantness"), Mowinckel writes (I, p. 238), is an old cultic expression also found in Egypt (cf. *Ps 30), which originally meant the corporeal vision of the unveiled statue of the god at the festivals, as the highest religious experience. In Yahwism it has become a metaphor for the more spiritual experience of the grace and benevolence of Yahweh manifested especially at the festival of his personal "epiphany" in the Temple. The verse obviously alludes to the position of the king as the sacral leader of the festal cult; his highest desire is to hold this position with its personal relation to Yahweh also in the future.

Verse 13 is translated by Dahood: "In the Victor do I trust, to behold the beauty of Yahweh in the land of life eternal." We already know the origin of the divine appellative "the Victor" (see *Pss 7 and 22). As for the "beauty" (*tûb* = "bounty" in *CV*) of Yahweh it is spoken of also in Ex 33:19 and *tûb* equally designates "beauty" in Hos 10:11 and Zech 9:17. The concept of "life eternal" (see *Ps 21:5), notes Dahood, was known to the Late Bronze Age author who wrote: "Ask for life eternal and I will give it to you, immortality and I will bestow it upon you" (2 Aqht:IV:27f).

PSALM 62 (61)

Trust in God alone

Ps 39:1; 1 Chr 16:41	1 *For the leader; 'al Idithun. A psalm of David.*
	I
	2 Only in God is my soul at rest;
Pss 51:16; 65: 6	from him comes my salvation.
	3 He only is my rock and my salvation,
Ps 94:22	my stronghold; I shall not be disturbed at all.
Pss 6:4; 74:10	4 How long will you set upon a man and all together

beat him down

Pss 56:3; 57:4
as though he were a sagging fence, a battered wall?

Pss 40:3; 61:
3; 91:14
5 Truly from my place on high they plan to dislodge me;

Ps 55:22f
they delight in lies;

They bless with their mouths,

Ps 63:12
but inwardly they curse.

II

6 Only in God be at rest, my soul,

Mi 7:7
for from him comes my hope.

Jer 3:23; Ps
25:5
7 He only is my rock and my salvation,

Ps 18:2, 7
my stronghold; I shall not be disturbed.

8 With God is my safety and my glory,

he is the rock of my strength; my refuge is in God.

Is 26:4
9 Trust in him at all times, O my people!

Pour out your hearts before him;

God is our refuge!

III

Pss 38:6f; 49:
13
10 Only a breath are mortal men;

Eccl 1:2; Ps
49:3
an illusion are men of rank;

Pss 78:39; 89:
48; Is 40·15
In a balance they prove lighter,

Jb 31:6; Prv
16:12
all together, than a breath.

Ez 22:29
11 Trust not in extortion; in plunder take no empty pride;

Jb 31:24f; Ps
52:9
though wealth abound, set not your heart upon it.

Jb 40:5
12 One thing God said; these two things which I heard:

13 that power belongs to God, and yours, O Lord, is kindness;

Jb 34:11; Jer
17:10
and that you render to everyone according to his deeds.

Rm 2:6

Repeatedly this psalmist calls God "my rock, and my salvation, my stronghold" (vv 3, 7). Again: "With God is my safety and my glory, he is the rock of my strength; my refuge is in God" (v 8). This language would come from a man who is in much the same situation as that of Ps 63. Persecuted by enemies he has found refuge in the temple where an oracle has reassured him (vv 12-13). In fact that sort of revealed assurance through an oracle (cf. §8e) is especially attested, writes Mowinckel (I, p. 219), in Pss 6, 28, 31, 62. The theme of trust and confidence, particularly of trust *in God alone,* dominates the whole psalm. Yet it is more explicit in the first part (vv 1-9), while the second part (10-12) recalls sapiential truths: the vanity of man and of wealth, the equity of God who renders to every one according to his deeds. This, Weiser thinks, illustrates the connection between cultic experience and hortatory "wisdom": "It is in the union of power and grace that the essential nature of the Old Testament belief in God is truly expressed; for power without grace does not admit of any trust, and grace without power is deprived of its ultimate seriousness." Before God, man is small but in his grace he can trust. All this is expressed in the form of the so-called "numerical proverb" (vv 12-13), frequent in wisdom literature (cf. Prv 6: 16; Jb 5:19; Sir 23:16).

PSALM 121 (120)

The Lord Our Guardian

1 *A song of ascents.*

I

Is 38:14; Hos 13:9 Pss 11:1; 25: 15:; 87:1 Jer 3:23	I lift up my eyes toward the mountains; whence shall help come to me?
Pss 115:5; 124:8	2 My help is from the Lord, who made heaven and earth.

II

1 Sm 2:9; Ps 66:9
Prv 3:24ff
	3 May he not suffer your foot to slip;
	    may he slumber not who guards you:
	4 Indeed he neither slumbers nor sleeps,
	    the guardian of Israel.

III

	5 The Lord is your guardian; the Lord is your shade;
Is 4:6; Pss 16: 8; 73:23 Is 25:4; 49:10	he is beside you at your right hand.
2 Kgs 4:18ff; Gn 31:40	6 The sun shall not harm you by day, nor the moon by night.

IV

Ps 97:10	7 The Lord will guard you from all evil; he will guard your life.
Dt 28:6; 32: 10 2 Sm 3:25; Ps 131:3	8 The Lord will guard your coming and your going, both now and forever.

Although Jerusalem is not expressly mentioned, it is perhaps alluded to under the word "mountains" (v 1). The whole poem is easily understood as a religious valediction. It is not surprising then that the psalm is one of the "pilgrim songs" (cf. §3c). In his farewell words the traveller asks: "I lift up my eyes toward the mountains; whence shall help come to me?" A priest, a friend, or a relative answers ("my" was probably added by mistake): "(my) Help is from the Lord . . ." (vv 2-8). Day and night God is the guardian of every man in their goings and comings (cf. §11bc), just as he has been in *Heilsgeschichte* the "guardian of Israel" (v 4). It is true that the ancients feared the action of the moon (cf. Mt 17:15, a "lunatic") as well as of the sun (Is 49:10; Jdt 8:3). But the mention of the "moon" in Ps 121:6 could have been required by parallelism (cf. Jos 10:12). For Mowinckel Ps 121 is a complex liturgy including a blessing addressed to an individual representing the congregation (II, pp. 50 and 76).

PSALM 131 (130)

Humble Trust in God

	1 A *song of ascents. Of David.*
Pss 115:9ff; 146:5 Mi 6:8	O Lord, my heart is not proud, nor are my eyes haughty;
	I busy not myself with great things,
Ps 139:6	nor with things too sublime for me.
Is 30:15	2 Nay rather, I have stilled and quieted
Mt 18:3	my soul like a weaned child.
Is 66:12f	Like a weaned child on its mother's lap, [so is my soul within me]
	3 O Israel, hope in the Lord,
Ps 121:8	both now and forever.

After perhaps many disillusions encountered in realizing ambitious projects, this psalmist has quieted his soul and obtained a more balanced state of mind with a good dose of humility. The implied statement that God is like a mother for the faithful is featured in the Deutero-Isaian hymn to Mother Zion (Is 66:7-13): "As a mother comforts her son, so will I comfort you" (v 13). In the same context God says: "Can a mother forget her infant, be without tenderness for the child of her womb? Even should she forget, I will never forget you" (Is 49:15). Humble trust in God, illustrated in this short poem, was obviously a major element in the inner life of the *'anāwîm* and the *saddîqîm,* the "poor" and the "righteous," who presumably were natural candidates for psalm writing (cf. §12ab).

§22. THANKSGIVINGS OF THE INDIVIDUAL

The thanksgiving comes as the final act in the drama of a human situation. The prayer and trust of the suppliant have not been in vain. His request has been granted or at least help is assured. This assurance may have been delivered to him through a kind of prophetic revelation received in the cult (cf. §8e). If the deliverance is not yet a reality the suppliant's confidence rests on his faith in the word of God. This is the case, it seems, in these laments, like Pss 22 and 28, which end with a thanksgiving.

H. Gunkel expressed as follows what he thought distinguished the hymn from the thanksgiving: "The difference is that the songs of thanks shout for joy over the specific deed which God has just done for the one giving thanks, while the hymns sing the great deeds and the majestic attributes of God in general" (*Einleitung . . .* p. 276). C. Westermann has the following comment on this quotation: "Does not this observation say quite clearly that there exists between hymn and song of thanksgiving really *no* difference of type, or category, and the song of thanks, of the individual and of the people, is really another type of hymn? The result is then, that in the Psalter there are two dominant categories, the hymn (including the Psalm of thanks) and the lament" (*The Praise . . . ,* p. 18; cf. §7b). As H. Ringgren remarks, "thanksgiving is not primarily an expression of gratitude to God, but rather the admission or acknowledgment that it is God who has acted and that the psalmist is entirely dependent on him. Thanksgiving is a confession [cf. the *"confitebor"* of the old Latin Psalter] and a proclamation of God as the one from whom all good gifts come. Thus thanksgiving is no less theocentric than the praise of God's greatness" (*The Faith . . . ,* p. 77). Thanksgiving, he adds, is the proper response to God's actions, but it expresses itself in praise: "Thanksgiving is simply one way of praising God, and it is characteristic that the Greek translation of the Old Testament usually renders *todah* [= thanksgiving] as *ainesis,* i.e., praise" (p. 78). The difference between the "hymns" and the "songs of thanks," concludes C. Westermann, "lies in the fact that the so-called hymn praises God for his actions and his being as a whole (*descriptive praise*), while the so-called song of thanks praises God for a specific deed, which the one who has been delivered recounts or reports in his song (*declarative praise;* it could also be called confessional praise)" (p. 31; cf. §7b). Two thanksgiving psalms can be read outside the Psalter, those of Hezekiah (Is 38:10-20) and of Jonah (2:3-10). "It is characteristic of true piety that it not only turns to God in time of distress, but also remembers to thank him in times of success and prosperity" (H. Ringgren, p. 77). It is possible that copies of the supplications of individuals were kept in the temple archives for further use, H. Schmidt thinks (p. VII). Thus would the thanksgiving have been joined sometimes to the lament, when at the thanksgiving ceremony the two texts were handled together (cf. Pss 6, 7, 13, 30, 31, 40, 56, 57, 109).

(a) The *structure* of these thanksgivings consists normally of the following elements:

1) *Introduction*: in which the psalmist expresses his intention to thank God (cf. 9:2; 138:2) or simply states: "It is good to give thanks to the Lord." It is often noted where the thanksgiving takes place. "In the vast assembly" (40:10; cf. 22:23, 26; 26:12), "in the assembly of the people ... in the council of the elders" (107:32), "in the gates of the daughter of Sion" (9:15), "in the presence of the angels" (138: 1; cf. 89:6), "at your holy temple" (138:2). The vast audience is typical of the thanksgiving setting: "Sing praise to the Lord enthroned in Zion; proclaim among the nations his deeds" (9:12); "I will give thanks to you among the peoples, O Lord, I will chant your praise among the nations" (57:10; cf. 67:3; 96:3; 105:1). The *introduction* is sometimes omitted or replaced by wisdom sayings (cf. 32:1; 34:12-15; 40:9), which like to infer doctrine from concrete examples (cf. 10:19; 30:6; 34:6-9). Descriptions contrasting the wicked and the just are not unusual (cf. Pss 10 and 92:7-15). Hymnic themes (cf. Pss 9:3-12; 30:5) sometimes occur at the very beginning (cf. Ps 92: 2f).

2) The *main section* consists essentially in describing the peril from

which the psalmist has been wonderfully delivered (cf. Ps 30:12). The abrupt change of the situation must be proclaimed (Ps 40:6-11). "There are some differences in the description of the distress according to its character. If the danger has been caused by the *sins* of the subject of the psalm this is of course mentioned. This is called *'positive confession,'* and the *grace of God* in forgiving the sin and saving the people or the individual speaking in the poem from the sufferings, regarded as punishment for the transgressions, is emphasized. On the other hand, if the misfortune has been caused, not by the sins of the psalmist, but by the wickedness of enemies, we find the so-called 'negative confession': The prayer protests *innocence* and exalts the *justice of Yahweh* manifested in the liberation of the innocent from their distress. These two variations correspond to the two main forms of *psalms of lamentation,* viz., the *penitential* psalms and the psalms of *innocence"* (A. Bentzen, *Introduction . . .* I, p. 153). Every favor granted to the Israelite constitutes a testimony of God's faithfulness to the covenant-people. Hence the community is invited to take part in the thanksgiving song (cf. Pss 32:11; 107:1). In fact, as G. von Rad notes, it is as if the deliverance was granted to the individual mainly for the benefit of the community. The proper place for the proclamation of God's saving deeds is the community (I, p. 359). Sometimes the narration of the peril recalls the very words pronounced during the crisis: "I said, 'I confess my faults to the Lord,' and you took away the guilt of my sin" (32:5). If the transition is not indicated a lament seems to be involved (cf. 30:9). *'Amartî,* "I said," could be translated in some cases by "I thought" (30:7; 31:23; 117:11; cf. C. J. Labuschagne). The recollection of the peril serves an additional purpose: to experience once again the effects of God's saving deed. Finally, the thanksgiving was the normal occasion to fulfill the vows made during the distress (cf. Pss 22:26; 116:14, 17). More will be said about the votive thanksgiving sacrifice in connection with the community thanksgiving (§25).

3) Only a few psalms of this category seem to have a distinctive *conclusion* or ending: invitation to praise (cf. 32:11), resolution (30:13), praise (138:8).

(b) The thanksgiving psalms of an individual are the following: (9/10), 30, 32, 34, 40 (vv 2-12), 41, (92), (107), 116. 138.

PSALM 9 (9A)

Thanksgiving for the Overthrow of Hostile Nations

1   *For the leader; according to Muth labben. A psalm of David.*

I

2   I will give thanks to you, O Lord, with all my heart;
     I will declare all your wondrous deeds.

3   I will be glad and exult in you;

Pss 7:18; 18:50; 86:12   I will sing praise to your name, Most High,

4   Because my enemies are turned back,
     overthrown and destroyed before you.

II

5   For you upheld my right and my cause,

Ps 7:9, 12   seated on your throne, judging justly.

Ps 59:6   6   You rebuked the nations and destroyed the wicked;

Jb 18:17   their name you blotted out forever and ever.

Jer 49:13   7   The enemies are ruined completely forever;

Gn 19:29   the remembrance of the cities you uprooted has perished.

III

Pss 29:10; 48:15   8   But the Lord sits enthroned forever;
Ps 89:15   he has set up his throne for judgment.

Jer 11:20; Ps 75:3   9   He judges the world with justice
Pss 96:10. 13; 98:9   he governs the peoples with equity.

Is 25:4; Ps 31:3   10   The Lord is a stronghold for the oppressed,
     a stronghold in times of distress.

Ps 36:11   11   They trust in you who cherish your name,
     for you forsake not those who seek you, O Lord.

IV

12   Sing praise to the Lord enthroned in Sion;
     proclaim among the nations his deeds;

Pss 19:15; 49:16   13   For the avenger of blood has remembered;
Jb 16:18   he has not forgotten the cry of the afflicted.

V

Pss 6:3; 25:16   14   Have pity on me, O Lord; see how I am afflicted by my foes,
Wis 16:13   you have raised me up from the gates of death,

15   That I may declare all your praises

Ps 48:3   and, in the gates of the daughter of Zion, rejoice
                            in your salvation.

VI

16 The nations are sunk in the pit they have made;

Sir 27:26; Ps 7:16
      in the snare they set, their foot is caught;

Ps 58:12
17 In passing sentence, the Lord is manifest;

Ps 5:11
      the wicked are trapped by the work of their own hands.

VII

Ps 55:16
18 To the nether world the wicked shall turn back,

Ps 50:22
      all the nations that forget God.

19 For the needy shall not always be forgotten,

Prv 23:18
      nor shall the hope of the afflicted forever perish.

20 Rise, O Lord, let not man prevail;

      let the nations be judged in your presence.

1 Mc 4:32
21 Strike them with terror, O Lord;

      let the nations know that they are but men.

PSALM 10 (9B)

Prayer for Help against Oppressors

I

Pss 44:10f; 74:1
1 Why, O Lord, do you stand aloof?

      Why hide in times of distress?

2 Proudly the wicked harass the afflicted,

Ps 9:16
      who are caught in the devices the wicked have contrived.

II

Pss 37:35; 94: 3
Jb 1:5
3 For the wicked man glories in his greed,

      and the covetous blasphemies, sets the Lord at nought.

Is 29:15; Jb 22:13
Zeph 1:12; Pss 14:1; 36:2
4 The wicked man boasts, "He will not avenge it";

      "There is no God," sums up his thoughts.

5 His ways are secure at all times;

      your judgments are far from his mind;

Ps 73:8
      all his foes he scorns.

6 He says in his heart, "I shall not be disturbed;

      from age to age I shall be without misfortune."

Rm 3:14
7 His mouth is full of cursing, guile and deceit;

Ps 140:4
      under his tongue are mischief and iniquity.

8 He lurks in ambush near the villages;

Is 32:7; Hb 3: 14
Prv 1:11
      in hiding he murders the innocent,

      his eyes spy upon the unfortunate.

Hos 6:9; Ps 17:12
Jer 5:26; Jb 38:40
Jb 24:14

9 He waits in secret like a lion in his lair;
  he lies in wait to catch the afflicted;
  he catches the afflicted and drags them off in his net.

10 He stoops and lies prone
  till by his violence fall the unfortunate.

Ez 9:9; Jb 22:13
Pss 13:2; 73:11; 94:7

11 He says in his heart, "God has forgotten;
  he hides his face, he never sees."

    III

Mi 5:8; Is 11:15; 33:10
Pss 20:7; 138:7

12 Rise, O Lord! O God lift up your hand!
  Forget not the afflicted!

Zeph 1:12

13 Why should the wicked man despise God,
  saying in his heart, "He will not avenge it"?

14 You do see, for you behold misery and sorrow,
  taking them in your hands.
  On you the unfortunate man depends;

Ex 22:21f;
Hos 14:4

  of the fatherless you are the helper.

15 Break the strength of the wicked and of the evildoer;
  punish their wickedness; let them not survive.

    IV

Jer 10:10; Ps 93:1

16 The Lord is king forever and ever;
  the nations have perished out of his land.

17 The desire of the afflicted you hear, O Lord;
  strengthening their hearts, you pay heed

Dt 10:18

18 To the defense of the fatherless and the oppressed,
  that man, who is of earth, may terrify no more.

There is no need of repeating here why the Septuagint and the Vulgate are probably right in transmitting as one original psalm the double Hebrew composition. In favor of the original unity of this psalm is its acrostic character (cf. §6d), now partially lost in the poorly preserved text (*CV*). J. Enciso suggests that the division of the psalm, as transmitted in the *MT* could have taken place after the Maccabean victory. This would explain that LXX preserved the unity of the psalm. A. Weiser considers as evident that the celebration of the feast of Yahweh's covenant (cf. §13c) was the occasion when "the psalm" was recited. The reference to God as to the King enthroned (9:5; 10:16) in Zion (9:12f) to pass judgment on the nations (9:5, 8f, 17f, 20f) could verily point to a cult festival. Besides, he thinks that an accurate consideration of the tenses used suggests that the "two psalms" represent a "prayer of supplication." Mowinckel (I, p. 219) classifies them as one of the "national (congregational) psalms" (cf. §23).

Yet it is better to read the composition as a thanksgiving, thus analyzed by E. Podechard: "The object of the psalm is the lot of the humble and of the faithful, oppressed by evildoers. The psalmist starts with a particular case, his own. After having expressed his joy and thanked God who has delivered him from his enemies, he offers higher and more general considerations on the misdeeds of the wicked. According to his petition, God's intervention will repress the evildoers and liberate their victims from persecution" (p. 49). Still more precisely, Podechard believes (p. 53), the so-called "nations" (the *gôyîm*: 9:6, 16, 18, 20f; 10:16; not the *'ummîm* of 9:9 or the *'ammîm* of 9:12) are the proud and arrogant, identified with the wicked, already by parallels (9:6, 16-18; 10:15f), explicitly in 10:2: "Proudly the wicked (*rāšā'*) harass the afflicted . . ." The enemies are the same throughout both psalms; only the victims change. The psalmist considers himself first, victim already released (Ps 9), then the mass of the humble still persecuted (Ps 10; on evildoers see §12g).

Various names used in the psalms (9-10) refer to the same category; they are: the poor, the humble or the afflicted (*'ānî*: 10:2, 9; *'aniwwîm*: 9:19; *'anāwîm*: 10:17; *'aniyyîm;* 9:13; 10:12), the needy (*'ebyôn*: 9:19), the oppressed (*dāk*: 9:10; 10:18), the unfortunate (*ḥlk*: 10:8, 10), the innocent (*nāqî*: 10:8), the orphan (*yātôm*: 10: 14, 18), and all those who seek God and cherish His name (9:11). One may ask, with Van der Berghe, if the *'ānî* is the weak, the humble (or humbled), the oppressed, the persecuted, the sick man or the poor. Does the term refer to individuals, to social categories or to the nations? We have attempted to find an answer to some of these questions (cf. §12abc) and also to determine in what sense God is the "avenger of blood" (9:13; cf. §11d). Another question raised by Ps 10 is that of the practical atheist (vv 4f, 11ff; see §10a).

According to R. Gordis the psalmist identified his own enemies with those of his group and, seeing his group of the "humble" and the "poor" as the authentic Israel, he identified the foes with the enemies of the nation. H. Junker believes that Ps 9/10 centers on the theme of the reign of God. In a first part (vv 2-13) the psalmist anticipated in a hymn the triumph of the justice and glory of God's eternal reign. Then he prayed for the advent of the reign (vv 14-21) and finally he complained about the delay of the reign of God (Ps 10). Parsing with M. Buttenwieser the verbs of Ps 9:5-7 as "precative perfects" (= optative perfects: cf. *Psalms* I, p. 39 and *Pss 4:8; 67:7), Dahood sees Ps 9/10 "as a lament throughout":

> Oh that you would defend my right and my cause,
> sit upon the throne, O righteous Judge!
> Rebuke the nations, destroy the wicked,
> blot out their name forever and ever.
> The foes — may they be destroyed,
> a heap of ruins forever;
> Root out their gods,
> may their memory perish (Ps 9:5-7).

The translation of *'ārîm* by "gods" in this context (v 7) is not at all required, it seems, even though that meaning can be maintained in Mi 5:13: "And I will root out your *asherim* and will destroy your gods (*'ārēkā*)." In this case *'ārîm* is related to a root *gyr,* meaning "to protect" in Ugaritic. Understanding *'ōlām* (*CV:* "forever") as referring to "primeval time" (cf. Pss 77:6; 92:9; 93:12; Is 51:9), and *le* as meaning "from," Dahood translates Ps 9:8: "Behold (*hmh* of v 7; cf. *CBQ* 1954, p. 16) Yahweh has reigned from eternity, has established his throne for judgment" (cf. Ps 29:10). Verse 13 he plausibly translates: "For he cares for those who mourn, their lament he remembers; He does not forget the cry of the afflicted." Parallelism is thus improved and the difficult "avenger of blood" is avoided. On the basis of Ugaritic *dmn,* parallel to *bky,* "to cry," *dammîm* (for MT *dāmîm,* "blood") is interpreted as "those who mourn." A similar use of the root *dmm* founds Dahood's version of Ps 4:5: "Be disquieted, but do not sin, examine your conscience, upon your beds *weep.*" The translation Dahood proposes of Ps 10:3-5 cannot be discussed here, but it shows how differently a Hebrew text can be understood:

> For the wicked boasts of his desire,
> and the despoiler worships his appetite.
> The wicked condemns Yahweh:

"Since the Lofty One will not avenge his anger,
God will not upset his plans,
And his wealth will last for all time."
O Exalted One, your decrees are far from him,
with all his being he sniffs at them.

The proposed translation of verse 4, it is noted, "tries to make clear
that the wicked man does not deny the existence of God but only his
intervention in human affairs" (cf. §10a). Psalm 10 ends by this praise
to God:

The desire of the afflicted you hear, O Lord;
strengthening their hearts, you pay heed
To the defense of the fatherless and the oppressed,
that man, who is of earth, may terrify no more (vv 17f).

One of the special titles of God is in fact to be the Defender of the
lowly, of the orphan and of the widow, the Guardian of the little ones
(cf. §11c).

PSALM 30 (29)

Thanksgiving for Deliverance from Death

Ezr 6:16f; 1
Mc 4:36f

1 *A psalm. A song for the dedication of the temple. Of David.*
2 I will extol you, O Lord, for you drew me clear

Pss 35:19; 38:
17
    and did not let my enemies rejoice over me.

A

3 O Lord, my God,

Pss 41:5; 103:
3
    I cried out to you and you healed me.

Jon 2:7

4 O Lord, you brought me up from the nether world;

Pss 30:4; 69:
16
    you preserved me from among those going down into the
           pit.

Ps 31:24

5 Sing praise to the Lord, you his faithful ones,

Pss 33:21; 97:
12
    and give thanks to his holy name.

Is 54:7; Jb 14:
13

6 For his anger lasts but a moment;
    a lifetime, his good will.
At nightfall, weeping enters in,

Pss 5:4; 17:
15; 46:6
    but with the dawn, rejoicing.

B

I

7 Once, in my security, I said,

Ps 16:8   "I shall never be disturbed."

Pss 26:3; 73: 8 O Lord, in your good will you had endowed me with
1   majesty and strength;
          but when you hid your face I was terrified.

II

9 To you, O Lord, I cried out;
   with the Lord I pleaded:

10 "What gain would there be from my lifeblood,
    from my going down into the grave?

Is 38:18   Would dust give you thanks

Pss 6:6; 88:   or proclaim your faithfulness?
11f
Ba 3:2f; Ps 11 Hear, O Lord, and have pity on me;
27:7
Pss 18:36; 33:   O Lord, be my helper."
20
III

Jer 31:13; Est 12 You changed my mourning into dancing;
9:22
Is 61:3   you took off my sackcloth and clothed me with gladness,

Ps 7:6   13 That my soul might sing praise to you without ceasing;
          O Lord, my God, forever will I give you thanks.

This psalmist recovered from an illness which had almost taken him to the grave (vv 3-4). At the hour of danger he realized that he had falsely founded his security on human capabilities (v 8). The medicinal or educational character of the "wrath" of God is recalled (v 6; cf. §11h). According to the heading, the psalm was used for the Jewish feast of Dedication (cf. Jn 10:22). The *Hanukkâh* commemorated first the restoration of worship (1 Mc 4:59), interrupted when Antiochus Epiphanes desecrated the temple in 167, and then also the miraculous deliverance from Syrian domination. To celebrate this event, notes Mowinckel (II, p. 199), "no new festival psalm was composed ... but the most suitable psalm from the Psalter was chosen and given a new meaning, namely Ps 30. The Maccabees felt restricted to the canonical psalm collection."

In verse 2 Dahood reads *'ōyᵉbay,* "my Foe," as *plurale excellentiae,* referring to Death, "the archfoe of the stricken poet" (cf. on *Ps 13: 3, 5). The same author concedes various meanings to the words derived from the root *rg'*. In *Ps 35:20 it was used to designate the "oppressed"; in Ps 30:6 it denotes "death": "For death is in his anger, life eternal in his favor; In the evening one falls asleep crying, but at dawn there are shouts of joy." *Rega'* could also mean "Perdition," i.e., "the place of death," or Sheol, as in Ps 6:11 and Nm 16:21. Besides, "to fall asleep" is "symbolic language" for "to die." Then one may conclude that "dawn is a symbol of resurrection and immortality . . . . The psalmist is convinced that eternal life will follow" (on the meaning of "morning" see on *Ps 5:4).

Neb-Re, an artisan of ancient Egypt's nineteenth Dynasty (the Exodus period), composed a memorial prayer to Amon-Re after the god had cured his son. His thanksgiving goes to "Amon-Re . . . the august god, he who hears the prayer, who comes at the voice of the poor and distressed (cf. Ps 10:18), who gives breath (to) him who is weak . . . May he grant to me that my eyes look at this beauty (cf. *Ps 27) . . . Thou art Amon-Re, Lord of Thebes, who rescued him who is in the underworld (cf. Ps 30:4) . . . He says: though it may be that the servant is normal in doing wrong, still the Lord is normal in being merciful. The Lord of Thebes does not spend an entire day angry. As for his anger — in the completion of a moment there is no remnant (cf. Ps 30:6), and the wind is turned about in mercy for us . . . (*ANET*, p. 380). In this Egyptian thanksgiving also, recovery from serious illness is described as a deliverance from Sheol. References to similarities particularly striking have been added to the text. As a whole the Egyptian composition is notably inferior in inspiration as compared with the biblical psalm.

PSALM 32 (31)

Remission of Sin

1 *Of David. A maśkîl.*

I

Hos 14:13; Rm 4:7f
Is 1:18

    Happy is he whose fault is taken away,
      whose sin is covered.

2 Happy the man to whom the Lord imputes no guilt,
    in whose spirit there is no guile.

II

3 As long as I would not speak, my bones wasted away

Ps 38:9	with my groaning all the day,
Ps 38:5	4 For day and night your hand was heavy upon me;
	my strength was dried up as by the heat of summer.
Ps 38:19	5 Then I acknowledged my sin to you,
2 Sm 12:13; Jb 31:33 Prv 28:13; Jas 5:16 1 Jn 19	my guilt I covered not. I said, "I confess my faults to the Lord," and you took away the guilt of my sin.
Pss 30:5; 37: 28	6 For this shall every faithful man pray to you in time of stress.
Ps 18:5	Though deep waters overflow, they shall not reach him.
	7 You are my shelter; from distress you will preserve me; with glad cries of freedom you will ring me round.

III

Pss 31:4; 48: 15	8 I will instruct you and show you the way you should walk;
Pss 31:23; 33: 13f	I will counsel you, keeping my eye on you.
Jer 4:22; Ps 14:1 Ps 49:13	9 Be not senseless like horses or mules; with bit and bridle their temper must be curbed, else they will not come near you.

IV

Ps 34:22	10 Many are the sorrows of the wicked,
Pss 16:11; 34: 8, 21	but kindness surrounds him who trusts in the Lord.
	11 Be glad in the Lord and rejoice, you just;
Ps 33:1	exult, all you upright of heart.

In its literary structure this psalm is a true thanksgiving. It is also a penitential psalm (cf. *Ps 6), dealing mainly with the remission of sin. It reflects a past experience of sin, not a present one, as Ps 51. The psalmist had tried to cover up his guilt, but suffering having sharpened his moral sensitiveness (cf. Ps 119:67, 71) he confessed his sin (v 5). Thus he was "saved": he was forgiven, his "fault" taken away (vv 1-2; cf. Ps 25:18; Lv 10:17; Jn 1:29). This "beatitude" of the forgiven is quoted by Rm 4:6-8 as recited by David and is used by Paul to illustrate justice credited without works. This psalm carries also sapiential teaching and confirms a principle laid down by Proverbs: "He who conceals his sins prospers not, but he who confesses and forsakes them obtains mercy" (28:13). The doctrine is supplemented by the First Epistle of John: "If we say that we have no sin, we deceive ourselves, and the truth is not in us. If we acknowledge our sins, he is faithful and just to forgive us our sins and to cleanse us from all iniquity. If we say that we have not sinned, we make him a liar, and his word is not in us" (1:8-9; cf. §12e).

Psalm 32 is recited by the Church on All Saints day and in the Office for the deceased. Verse 11 is quoted in the liturgical texts in honor of the martyrs: "Be glad in the Lord and rejoice, you just; exult, all you upright of heart." In the Greek ritual the priest, after administering baptism, says three times with the faithful: "Happy is he whose fault is taken away, whose sin is covered" (v 1). The expression "covered" is a correct literal translation of the Hebrew *kᵉsûy*. The meaning is suggested by the parallel phrase "whose fault is taken away" (*nᵉśûy*). The verse is part of a "benedictory word" (vv 1-2) which serves as a means of instruction and exhortation. In the second part of the psalm (vv 8ff), addressed to "you" in the style of wisdom literature, the author warns against obstinacy of heart and calls upon the "upright of heart" to rejoice in the Lord. "Psalm 32, writes Mowinckel (II, p. 142), voices strong and completely personal views about the happiness in recognizing and confessing one's sin; the traditional basic type is fairly well hidden behind the personal and didactic."

PSALM 34 (33)

Praise of God, the Protector of the Just

1 Sm 21:13ff	1	*Of David, when he feigned madness before Abimelech, who forced him to depart.*
		I
Pss 66:20; 145:2	2	I will bless the Lord at all times; his praise shall be ever in my mouth.
Ps 103:1f	3	Let my soul glory in the Lord; the lowly will hear me and be glad.
Pss 29:2; 35:27	4	Glorify the Lord with me, let us together extol his name.
		II
	5	I sought the Lord, and he answered me and delivered me from all my fears.

6 Look to him that you may be radiant with joy,

Pss 31:2; 69:7

and your faces may not blush with shame.

7 When the afflicted man called out, the Lord heard,
and from all his distress he saved him.

8 The angel of the Lord encamps

Pss 32:10; 37:
18, 25
Pss 100:5;
106:1
Pss 2:12; 40:5

around those who fear him, and delivers them.

9 Taste and see how good the Lord is;

happy the man who takes refuge in him.

Pss 16:3; 31:
20; 33:18

10 Fear the Lord, you his holy ones
for nought is lacking to those who fear him.

Lk 1:53

11 The great grow poor and hungry;
but those who seek the Lord want for no good thing.

III

Prv 4:1; 8:32

12 Come, children, hear me;
I will teach you the fear of the Lord.

1 Pt 3:10ff

13 Which of you desires life,
and takes delight in prosperous days?

14 Keep your tongue from evil
and your lips from speaking guile;

Am 5:14; Prv
3:7

15 Turn from evil, and do good;
seek peace, and follow after it.

Sir 15:19

16 The Lord has eyes for the just,
and ears for their cry.

Pss 5:6; 21:9;
Rev 21:7
Lam 4:16; Pss
37:28, 38

17 The Lord confronts the evildoers,
to destroy remembrance of them from the earth.

18 When the just cry out, the Lord hears them,

Ps 145:19

and from all their distress he rescues them.

Mt 11:28

19 The Lord is close to the brokenhearted;
and those who are crushed in spirit he saves.

Jb 36:15; Ps
38:3

20 Many are the troubles of the just man,
but out of them all the Lord delivers him;

Ps 37:18, 25

21 He watches over all his bones;

Jn 19:36; Ex
12:46
Pss 32:10; 37:
2, 20

not one of them shall be broken.

22 Vice slays the wicked,
and the enemies of the just pay for their guilt.

Pss 27:9; 31:
6; 44:27

23 But the Lord redeems the lives of his servants;
no one incurs guilt who takes refuge in him.

In this as in other alphabetic psalms (cf. §6d) the logical sequence of thoughts is not always observed. If verse 23 began, as it seems, with the (missing) letter *waw* (*wᵉ*), its place would be after verse 6. Most alphabetic psalms are believed by some to have originated in the sixth century B.C., like the Book of Lamentations. The hymnic introduction (vv 1-4) is followed by the psalmist's testimony in which he draws generalizing conclusions from his personal experience (vv 5-11). The sapiential pattern of presentation is even more apparent in the second part of the psalm (12-23), with its instructions and exhortations. The category of the "poor of Yahweh" encountered in Ps 9/10 is also represented in Ps 34. They are called the "poor" (*'anā-wîm*: vv 3, 7), the "holy ones" (*qᵉdôšîm*: v 10), the "just" (*ṣaddîqîm*: 20, 22), the "servants" (*'abādîm*) of the Lord (v 23). They are the humble clients of God, those who seek Him (v 11), who fear Him (8, 10), who take refuge in Him (v 9), when they are "crushed in spirit" (v 19; litt. "broken of heart"). The Psalter was the favorite prayer book of this *corpus piorum,* who would speak to God as "the generation of thy sons" (Ps 73:15; see §12a-d). The psalmist tries to communicate what experimental knowledge he has of retribution: security, prosperity and joy belong to the virtuous protected or delivered by God, Savior and Redeemer (cf. §11d). At El-Amarna, in the tomb of pharaoh Ai (14th cent.), was found an inscription transmitting a text which corresponds word for word to Ps 34:13: "Which of you desires life, and takes delight in prosperous days?" (cf. M. Sandman, *Texts from the time of Akhenaten: Bibl. Aeg.* VIII, 1938, p. 99). It is not known how the Egyptian phrase found its way to the Psalter (cf. *RB* 1950, pp. 174-179 and §9c).

The psalm heading alludes to an episode of David with Achish, the king of Gath (1 Sm 21:11-16). Perhaps the original heading read *'ākîš melek gat* (Akish, king of Gath) which, through scribal error, could easily have been shortened to *'ākîš melek,* then to *'abîmelek* (in the biblical story of 1 Sm 21, it was at the court of the Philistine king Achish that David feigned insanity after he had departed from the priest Ahimelek). By linking *ta'amû,* "taste" (v 9) and *tithallēl,* "let . . . glory" (v 3) of Ps 34 with *ta'mô,* "his good taste" and (*wᵉ*)*yithôlēl,* "he feigned himself mad" of 1 Sm 21:14, a scribe, with a typically rabbinical touch, gave the psalm a davidic reference.

PSALM 40 (39)

Gratitude and Prayer for Help

1 *For the leader. A psalm of David.*

A

I

Lam 3:25

2 I have waited, waited for the Lord,
and he stooped toward me and heard my cry.

Ps 28:1

3 He drew me out of the pit of destruction,
out of the mud of the swamp;
He set my feet upon a crag;

Pss 61:3; 94:18

he made firm my steps.

Pss 33:3; 96:1

4 And he put a new song into my mouth,

Is 42:10

a hymn to our God.

Is 41:14

Many shall look on in awe
and trust in the Lord.

II

Jer 17:7; Prv 16:20
Pss 34:9; 94:12

5 Happy the man who makes the Lord his trust;
who turns not to idolatry
or to those who stray after falsehood.

6 How numerous have you made,

Jb 5:9; Pss 26: 7; 65:6

O Lord, my God, your wondrous deeds!
And in your plans for us

Dt 4:34

there is none to equal you;
Should I wish to declare or to tell them,
they would be too many to recount.

III

Am 5:21f; Ps 50:8ff
Ps 51:18; Is 50:4
Jer 7:23; 1 Sm 15:22
Is 1:10-20; Mi 6:6ff
Heb 10:5ff

7 Sacrifice or oblation you wished not,
but ears open to obedience you gave me.
Holocausts or sin-offerings you sought not;

8 then said I, "Behold I come;
in the written scroll it is prescribed for me,

9 To do your will, O my God, is my delight,

Dt 6:6; Jer 31:33

and your law is within my heart!"

Pss 36:7; 85:14

10 I announced your justice in the vast assembly;

Pss 107:22; 111:1

I did not restrain my lips, as you, O Lord, know.

11 Your justice I kept not hid within my heart;

your faithfulness and your salvation I have spoken of;

Pss 25:10; 89:15

I have made no secret of your kindness and your truth

in the vast assembly.

B

I

12 Withhold not, O Lord, your compassion from me;
     may your kindness and your truth ever preserve me.

13 For all about me are evils beyond reckoning;
     my sins so overcome me that I cannot see;
     They are more numerous than the hairs of my head,
     and my heart fails me.

II

Ps 70:2-6

14 Deign, O Lord, to rescue me;

Ps 38:23

     O Lord, make haste to help me.

Pss 25:3; 35:26; 53:6
Pss 38:13; 54:5

15 Let all be put to shame and confusion
     who seek to snatch away my life.
     Let them be turned back in disgrace
     who desire my ruin.

16 Let them be dismayed in their shame

Pss 35:16; 42:11

     who say to me, "Aha, aha!"

17 But may all who seek you

Pss 35:9; 48:11

     exult and be glad in you,
     And may those who love your salvation

Pss 35:27; 48:11

     say ever, "The Lord be glorified."

Pss 25:16; 35:10

18 Though I am afflicted and poor,
     yet the Lord thinks of me.

Pss 18:36; 33:20

     You are my help and my deliverer;
     O my God, hold not back!

The first section of this psalm (vv 2-11) is the thanksgiving of a man who has been rescued from the danger of death, while the second section (vv 14-18 = Ps 70) is a typical supplication of one afflicted and persecuted. In between there are two transition verses. For Weiser the whole psalm can be regarded as one unity, if one admits the presence, here as elsewhere, of a "tension between the possessing of the assurance of faith and the striving for it." In the first section the worshipper would tell of past experiences (vv 2-11) which comfort and reassure him in face of a new calamity (12-18).

Several phrases and thoughts of verses 14-18 recur in Ps 35:4, 21, 26f).

The psalmist's statement that obedience is better than sacrifice (vv 7-9) follows a trend of thought expressed by Samuel (1 Sm 15: 22) and other prophets (cf. Is 1:10-20; Mi 6:6-8). The problem is discussed in connection with *Ps 50:14 and 51:18. In the Epistle to the Hebrews, Ps 40:7-9 is quoted from the Septuagint and applied to Christ's sacrifice of perfect obedience: "Bulls' blood and goats' blood are useless for taking away sins, and this is what he said, on coming into the world:

> You who wanted no sacrifice or oblation,
> prepared a body for me.
> You took no pleasure in holocausts or sacrifices for sin;
> then I said,
> just as I was commanded in the scroll of the book,
> "God, here I am! I am coming to obey your will" (10:5-7: *JB*).

The exact meaning of Ps 40:7-9 in the *MT* is still a matter of dispute. It is linked in part with a broader problem, that of the original structure of the psalm. This has been carefully studied by E. Vogt. It is beyond our scope to discuss in detail his proposals, which are radical enough. The text, he believes, suffers from a misplaced verse and additions. Verse 13 should be read after verse 2. The following lines were added later to verses 7-9:

> In volumine libri scriptum est id quo teneor,
>   aures fodisti mihi.
> Facere voluntatem tuam, Deus meus, volo,
>   et lex tua est in medio viscerum meorum.

In this marginal note to the psalmist's rather liberal views on sacrifice the "pious reader" had scribbled his wish to abide entirely by the law. N. H. Ridderbos maintains the unity of the psalm and considers verses 2-12 as an introduction to the rest of the poem. Following Eerdmans ("Essays . . . , p. 268ff), he translates verse 8: "Then have I said: Lo, I come with the written scroll with me." The psalmist, supposedly the king, declares: "On the day of my coronation I presented myself before you with a copy of the law with me, symbolizing my intention of living according to thy will. I carry thy law in my heart."

A few of Dahood's sundry suggestions can be mentioned here. In verse 2, "Constantly I called Yahweh" makes better sense than "I have waited, waited for the Lord." *Qāwâh* (meaning II) does seem to mean "to call" (or "to proclaim") in other biblical texts, such as in Ps 52:11: "And before your devoted ones I shall proclaim how sweet is your name" (cf. Jb 17:13). Knowing that "with the verbs of refusing, withholding, etc.," the preposition *l* denotes "from," as in Ugaritic, a more precise translation of verse 11b can be obtained: "I did not hide your kindness, nor your fidelity from the great congregation." "Kindness and fidelity" may be personified here (vv 11f) also (cf. Pss 23:6; *25:21), as "two attendants who protect the psalmist against sundry dangers — in the present context, against the danger of wild animals" (cf. v 13 and §11e). The meaning of verse 3 becomes clearer if read in the light of the interpretation of Sheol proposed above (§14d).

PSALM 41 (40)

Thanksgiving after Sickness

1 *For the leader. A psalm of David.*

I

Sir 4:10

Prv 14:21; Tb 4:7f

2 Happy is he who has regard for the lowly and the poor;
    in the day of misfortune the Lord will deliver him.
3 The Lord will keep and preserve him;
    he will make him happy on the earth,
    and not give him over to the will of his enemies.
4 The Lord will help him on his sickbed,

Pss 37:18, 25; 55:23

    he will take away all his ailment when he is ill.

II

5 Once I said, "O Lord, have pity on me;

Pss 39:10f; 103:3

    heal me, though I have sinned against you.
6 My enemies say the worst of me:
    'When will he die and his name perish?'
7 When one comes to see me, he speaks without sincerity;

his heart stores up malice;

when he leaves he gives voice to it outside.

8   All my foes whisper together against me;

against me they imagine the worst:

9   'A malignant disease fills his frame';

and 'Now that he lies ill, he will not rise again.'

Jer 20:10; Jb 19:13f
Ps 55:14f; Jn 13:18

10   Even my friend who had my trust

and partook of my bread, has raised his heel against me.

III

Pss 25:16; 51:3

11   But you, O Lord, have pity on me, and raise me up,

that I may repay them."

12   That you love me I know by this,

that my enemy does not triumph over me,

13   But because of my integrity you sustain me

and let me stand before you forever.

* * *

Ps 59:6

14   Blessed be the Lord, the God of Israel,

Neh 9:5; Dn 2:20

from all eternity and forever. Amen. Amen.

Didactic and hortative generalities (vv 2-4) introduce this thanksgiving psalm, which from verse 5 recalls the supplication expressed during a grave illness (vv 4, 9). The disease is described as "malignant" (v 9: "a thing of Belial"; cf. Dt 13:14; Pss 18:5; 101:3). Anciently sickness was generally considered as punishment for personal sins (cf. Pss 32:4; 38:3ff; 107:17 and Job, *passim*). Stressing the cultic setting of the psalm's origin, A. Weiser believes that the "lowly" (*dal*) of verse 2 is the psalmist himself, and that the "beatitude" is destined to those of the community who by "paying attention" to his praise will partake of the grace of the Lord.

Though he admits having been a sinner (v 5), the psalmist speaks of his "integrity" (v 13). His confession of innocence could refer only to the false accusations or insinuations of his adversaries (vv 8-9). To Mowinckel (II, pp. 6, 37), Ps 41 is good proof of his theory that the "enemies" of sick psalmists were generally those who by magically effective curses or evil words and wishes (cf. vv 6, 9; see §14d) increased illness and danger of death (but see §12g). Not being yet disciplined in the love for one's enemies (cf. Lk 6:27f), the psalmist all too humanly begs the Lord: "Raise me up, that I may repay them" (v 11). The translation of verses 12-13 is crucial for the interpretation of the whole psalm. *CV* has understood that the man has been cured, and after recalling his supplication he now praises God (cf. also Weiser, Kraus, *RSV et al.*). L. R. Fisher's thesis is "that Ps 41 is an old Thanksgiving Psalm. It is probably related to a time when the king was ill and his enemies tried to overthrow him. Since he was healed and his enemies were not successful, the king's scribes changed the wording a little, and they used the psalm to teach loyalty to the king, to insure the dynastic line against the rebels." There would be a Ugaritic parallel for the thought pattern (*UT* 127:43-57; C. H. Gordon, p. 194).

Another opinion can be defended: the psalm is a supplication (cf. *JB*). Eerdmans ("Essays . . . ," p. 274ff) translates verses 11-12: "But thou, O Jahu [= Yahweh], have mercy upon me and raise me up, that I may requite them. By this I will know that thou delightest in me if mine enemy will not exult over me and thou hast held me up in mine integrity and hast set me before thy face for ever." Eerdmans also suggests a setting in life which would explain the strange sapiential introduction of the psalm. "The psalm appears to be a prayer of a sick man lying down on his bed. Therefore it cannot have been said in the temple as is generally assumed. He was not alone. A visitor was with him. This man opened the prayer by reciting a dogmatic utterance, speaking of Jahu in the third person, as of the protector of those who consider the poor. From this we infer that he was a singer, who came to attend the patient, whom he knew as notorious for helping the poor. After this he turned to the patient and continued, addressing Jahu in the second person "Thou hast overturned him by his sickness."

Other remarks of Eerdmans are worth noticing. "In the subsequent prayer (vv 5-13) the sick man himself proceeds to ask Jahu for mercy, without describing the nature of the ailment. He is merely complaining of the fact that his visitors do not have any hope of his recovery. Therefore he called them names, enemies and haters they were to him. The only accusation brought against them was that they presumed his ailment to be incurable, saying 'when shall he die?' There is no proof of any malicious joy about his misfortune."

In this "prayer for healing," the psalmist, according to Dahood, tells the Lord: "Instead of putting me into Sheol after death, directly take me to yourself that I might encounter you face to face for all eternity" (cf. vv 3, 13). This is more easily understood if in verse 3 we read: "Do not put him into the maw (*nefesh*) of his Foe" (cf. Ps 16:10), a prayer for "the grace of assumption". (cf. *Ps 17:15). What Job hoped for in his distress was to have his innocence proved before God by a "mediator" who would stand as a witness:

I know my vindicator lives,
A guarantor upon the dust will stand;
Even after my skin is flayed,
Without my flesh I shall see God.
I will see him on my side,
My own eyes will see him unestranged,
My heart faints within me (tr. *The Anchor Bible*).

PSALM 92 (91)

Praise of God's Just Government of Mankind

1 *A psalm; a song for the Sabbath day.*

I

2 It is good to give thanks to the Lord,
Pss 9:3; 97:9   to sing praise to your name, Most High,

3 To proclaim your kindness at dawn
Pss 57:4; 98:3   and your faithfulness throughout the night.

Pss 71:22; 98:   4 With ten-stringed instrument and lyre,
5f   with melody upon the harp.

Pss 89:17; 97:   5 For you made me glad, O Lord, by your deeds;
12   at the works of your hands I rejoice.

II

Pss 86:10; 96:   6 How great are your works, O Lord!
3   how very deep are your thoughts!
Wis 17:1

7 A senseless man knows not,
Ps 76:6   nor does a fool understand this.

8 Though the wicked flourish like grass
and all evildoers thrive,

Pss 37:28; 73:   9 They are destined for eternal destruction;
17   while you, O Lord, are the Most High forever.
Pss 9:8; 125:1

III

10 For behold, your enemies, O Lord,

for behold, your enemies shall perish;

Pss 64:3; 94: 16
Ps 18:3; Dt 33:17
Ps 23:5

all evildoers shall be scattered.

11 You have exalted my horn like the wild bull's;

you have anointed me with rich oil.

12 And my eye has looked down upon my foes,

and my ears have heard of the fall of my wicked

adversaries.

IV

Ps 1:3

13 The just man shall flourish like the palm tree,

like a cedar of Lebanon shall he grow.

14 They that are planted in the house of the Lord

Pss 52:10; 128:3

shall flourish in the courts of our God.

15 They shall bear fruit even in old age;

vigorous and sturdy shall they be,

16 Declaring how just is the Lord,

Dt 32:4; Ps. 89:27

my Rock, in whom there is no wrong.

Various literary elements meet in this psalm, although the thanksgiving theme, which opens the poem, seems to be primarily intended. According to Mowinckel (II, 28, 29, 37), Ps 92 can be classified as a royal national (collective) thanksgiving psalm, like Pss 18 and 138. The "king-ego" style (cf. §23a) is presumably discernible here also and in verse 11 the psalmist says to the Lord: "You have exalted my horn like the wild bull's; you have anointed me with rich oil." The metaphor of the horn symbolizes power (Pss 75:5; 89:18; 112:9), that of the king especially: "The Lord will judge the ends of the earth; he will give strength to his king, and exalt the horn of his anointed" (1 Sm 2:10). The horn is also a symbol of Davidic descent (Ps 132:17; Lk 1:69). In given contexts, anointing with oil would, in itself, primarily refer to the king: "There Zadok the priest took the horn of oil from the tent, and anointed Solomon" (1 Kgs 1:39). Not so much anointing in general (cf. Ps 132; Am 6:6; Eccl 9:8) as anointing in public worship (cf. Ps 23:5) can also be read in Ps 92:11. The mention of musical instruments (v 4) also points to a liturgical setting for the psalm. Perhaps the psalmist spent one or more days in the temple (v 3; cf. Pss 55:17; 134:2).

In the second temple the Levitical choir chanted each day of the week a psalm to accompany the libation of wine (cf. Sir 50:15ff) that

followed the *tamid* (perpetual) offering (cf. *Mishnah, "Tamid,"* 7:3-4).
Of these "Levitical Psalms" (24, 48, 81, 82, 92, 94) only Ps 92
has in Hebrew a superscription to indicate its liturgical use. This
would suggest, N. M. Sarna thinks, that it was the first of the group
to be selected, the others having been chosen after the close of the
Hebrew Psalter. In the Septuagint five superscriptions reflect the liturgical use: Pss 24 (23), 48 (47), 92 (91), 93 (92), 94 (93). Ps 92,
Sarna claims, was selected for the Sabbath reading (cf. §8c) because
its contents were felt to correspond to the two dominant themes of
the biblical Sabbath, "the cosmogonic and the socio-moral." The
presence of the first motif is indicated by a Ugaritic parallel:

> Now thine enemy, O Baal,
> Now thine enemy wilt thou smite,
> Now wilt thou cut off thine adversary (68:8f; Gordon, p. 180).

> For, behold, thine enemies, O Lord,
> For, behold, thine enemies shall perish;
> All workers of iniquity shall be scattered (Ps 92:10).

H. L. Ginsberg has pointed out (*Orientalia,* 1936, p. 180) that in
the first two lines of each of these passages practically the same rhythm
is present as in Ps 29:1, 5, 7, 8 (with some emendations). The parallel
is more convincing, notes Sarna, if examined in the light of a known
oriental and biblical device: express the evil deeds and punishment
of the historical wicked in terms of the mythical conflict of God with
the rebellious forces of primeval chaos (cf. §9b + 11a). The overthrow of the wicked is in fact stressed in this psalm (vv 8-12). The
cosmogonic theme is also represented by the creation motif alluded
to in verse 6: "How great are your works!" (cf. Ps 104:1, 24) But
the institution of Sabbath (cf. v 1) is connected with creation (Gn 2:3;
Ex 20:11). Besides, creation means order, passage from chaos *to*
cosmos, also an effect of divine righteousness (cf. Pss 89:10, 15; 96:
10), while the injustice of evildoers shakes the foundations of the
earth (Ps 82:2-5). In this sense the "socio-moral theme" of Ps 92,
the problem of the wicked and the righteous, can be related to the
cosmogonic motif.

Some reflections of Ps 92 supposedly belong to a theme called
Gerichtsdoxologie, in which the psalmists declare just the judgments

of God, his intervention in favor of the just, against the wicked (cf. Pss 7:10ff; 11:6-9; 51:6; 119:75; 145:7, 13, 17). In Ps 101 that sense of justice is attributed to the pious prince, while Ps 139 praises divine knowledge, required to pronounce infallible judgments. The best example of such "doxology of judgment" is Achan's act of praise before his execution (Jos 7:19ff). "Through the doxology of judgment, writes G. von Rad, the guilty person not only acknowledged the justice of his punishment; his confession also had a very concrete significance in sacral law, for the actions against him were thereby brought to an end (1 Kgs 8:33; cf. Ezr 10:7ff; Is 12:1f: *OT Theol.,* v. 1, p. 358).

PSALM 107 (106)

God the Savior of Men in Distress

Pss 100:5; 106:1 1 Chr 16:34; Dn 3:89 Jer 33:11; Is 62:12	1	"Give thanks to the Lord, for he is good, for his kindness endures forever!"
	2	Thus let the redeemed of the Lord say,
Pss 19:15; 49: 16; 136:24		those whom he has redeemed from the hand of the foe
Is 43:5f; 49: 12	3	And gathered from the lands,
Zech 8:7f		from the east and the west, from the north and the south.

A

I

Mt 8:15; 32: 10	4	They went astray in the desert wilderness; the way to an inhabited city they did not find.
Is 49:10	5	Hungry and thirsty, their life was wasting away within them.
	6	They cried to the Lord in their distress; from their straits he rescued them;
Jer 31:9; Is 40:3; 43:19 Dt 6:10	7	And he led them by a direct way to reach an inhabited city.
	8	Let them give thanks to the Lord for his kindness
Pss 106:2; 136:4		and his wondrous deeds to the children of men,
Is 40:10; 55:1	9	Because he satisfied the longing soul
Ps 22:27; Lk 1:53		and filled the hungry soul with good things.

II

Is 42:7, 22; Ps 88:19 Is 49:9; Jb 36:8f	10	They dwelt in darkness and gloom, bondsmen in want and in chains,
Is 63:10	11	Because they had rebelled against the words of God

Ps 7:18		and scorned the counsel of the Most High.
Ps 106:42	12	And he humbled their hearts with trouble;
		when they stumbled, there was no one to help them.
	13	They cried to the Lord in their distress;
		from their straits he rescued them.
Is 42:7, 16; 49:9 Is 52:2; Ps 69:34	14	And he led them forth from darkness and gloom
		and broke their bonds asunder.
	15	Let them give thanks to the Lord for his kindness
		and his wondrous deeds to the children of men,
	16	Because he shattered the gates of brass
Is 45:2; 61:1		and burst the bars of iron.

III

17 Stricken because of their wicked ways
    and afflicted because of their sins,

Jb 6:7

18 They loathed all manner of food,
    so that they were near the gates of death.

19 They cried to the Lord in their distress;
    from their straits he rescued them.

Is 55:11; Wis 16:12

20 He sent forth his word to heal them
    and to snatch them from destruction.

21 Let them give thanks to the Lord for his kindness
    and his wondrous deeds to the children of men.

2 Chr 29:31; Ps 69:32

22 Let them make thank offerings
    and declare his works with shouts of joy.

IV

23 They who sailed the sea in ships,
    trading on the deep waters,

24 These saw the works of the Lord
    and his wonders in the abyss.

25 His command raised up a storm wind

Jon 1:4f; Ps 89:10
Jon 2:4

    which tossed its waves on high.

26 They mounted up to heaven; they sank to the depths;
    their hearts melted away in their plight.

Is 29:9

27 They reeled and staggered like drunken men,
    and all their skill was swallowed up.

Jon 1:14

28 They cried to the Lord in their distress;
    from their straits he rescued them.

29 He hushed the storm to a gentle breeze,

Mk 4:39		and the billows of the sea were stilled;
	30	They rejoiced that they were calmed,
		and he brought them to their desired haven.
	31	Let them give thanks to the Lord for his kindness
		and his wondrous deeds to the children of men.
	32	Let them extol him in the assembly of the people
		and praise him in the council of the elders.

B

Is 50:2	33	He changed rivers into desert,
Is 35:7; 41: 18; 42:15 Sir 39:23		water springs into thirsty ground,
	34	Fruitful land into salt marsh,
Gn 19:23ff		because of the wickedness of its inhabitants.
Is 41:18	35	He changed the desert into pools of water,
Ps 114:8		waterless land into water springs.
	36	And there he settled the hungry,
Ez 36:35f		and they built a city to dwell in.
Is 65:21; Jer 31:5	37	They sowed fields and planted vineyards,
		and they obtained a fruitful yield.
Dt 7:13	38	He blessed them, and they became very many;
		nor did he suffer their cattle to decrease.
	39	And they dwindled and were brought low
		through oppression, affliction and sorrow.
Jb 12:18	40	But he who pours out contempt upon princes,
Jb 12:24f		and sends them astray through a trackless waste,
	41	Lifted up the needy out of misery
Ps 113:7f		and made the families numerous like flocks.
Jb 22:19; Ps 97:12 Jb 5:16	42	The upright see this and rejoice,
		and all wickedness closes its mouth.
	43	Who is wise enough to observe these things
Os 14:10; Is 63:7		and to understand the favors of the Lord?

Although this psalm does reflect a community thanksgiving (v 32), recited before the offering of the sacrifice (v 22), it should be listed with the psalms of the individual because in it groups come in turn to thank God for personal favors. Some commentators find in the opening verses indications that a rather ancient private thanksgiving has been reread and applied to Israel. This application could follow the deeper theological insight which tends to set the particular

favors in the general *Heilsgeschichte* pattern, since, as we have seen
(§22a, 2), every grace bestowed to the individual confirms God's
faithfulness toward the covenant-people.

Perhaps the psalm belonged to a *Dankfestliturgie* (a thanksgiving
festival) inaugurating the thanksgiving season. The opening cry of
praise, "Give thanks to the Lord, for he is good, for his kindness
endures forever!" frequently mentioned in the Bible (already: Jer
33:11; cf. §11f), belongs to the temple liturgy. Together with verses
2 and 3 it constitutes an introduction to the whole psalm. Yet it
seems more true to say that verses 1-9 belong together and recapitulate,
under one image, the innumerable instances of salvation: as the
chosen people has been brought from the wilderness to the land
of promise, thus from scattered places pilgrims have come to the
Holy City to mingle in a common thanksgiving their various experiences.
In the remaining stanzas three particular groups express their thanks
for having been delivered from their respective afflictions: captivity
or prison (10-16) grave illness (17-22), peril at sea (23-32). The
presence of the refrain in verse 8 would favor the interpreters who
read in verses 4-9 also a particular thanksgiving, in which God is
praised as the rescuer of wanderers lost in the wilderness. The second
part (vv 33-43) expresses in hymnic form the tribute of the community to the divine *Heilsgeschichte* deeds, now actuated in the cult.
Verses 4-9 could allude to the exodus from Egypt and verses 10-16 to
the return from the Babylonian captivity, the second exodus (compare
Is 42:10ff; 49:10f; 51:10f). Verse 16 is almost identical with Is
45:2 (cf. Is 61:1).

PSALM 116 (114-115)

Thanksgiving to God for Help in Need

A

1 Alleluia

I

I love the Lord because he has heard
    my voice in supplication,

2 Because he has inclined his ear to me
    the day I called.

Ps 18:5f   3 The cords of death encompassed me;
    the snares of the nether world seized upon me;

I fell into distress and sorrow,

Jon 2:8 4 And I called upon the name of the Lord,

"O Lord, save my life!"

II

Ex 34:6 5 Gracious is the Lord and just;

yes, our God is merciful.

Pss 72:12;
116:6 6 The Lord keeps the little ones;

I was brought low, and he saved me.

7 Return, O my soul, to your tranquillity,

for the Lord has been good to you.

Ex 56:14 8 For he has freed my soul from death,

Is 25:8; Ap
21:4 my eyes from tears, my feet from stumbling.

9 I shall walk before the Lord

Pss 27:13;
142:6 in the lands of the living.

B

2 Cor 4:13 10 I believed, even when I said,

"I am greatly afflicted";

11 I said in my alarm,

Rm 3:4; Pss
12:3; 62:10 "No man is dependable."

12 How shall I make a return to the Lord

for all the good he has done for me?

Ex 25:29; Ps
23:5 13 The cup of salvation I will take up,

and I will call upon the name of the Lord;

14 My vows to the Lord I will pay

in the presence of all his people.

Is 43:4 15 Precious in the eyes of the Lord

Wis 3:5f; Ps
97:10 is the death of his faithful ones.

Ps 82:2, 16 16 O Lord, I am your servant;

I am your servant, the son of your handmaid;

you have loosed my bonds.

Lv 7:11; Ps
107:22 17 To you will I offer sacrifice of thanksgiving,

and I will call upon the name of the Lord.

18 My vows to the Lord I will pay

Is 31:8 in the presence of all his people,

19 In the courts of the house of the Lord,

in your midst, O Jerusalem.

This one Hebrew psalm appears in the Septuagint and Vulgate
as Pss 114 and 115. Before offering the sacrifice he had promised

(v 14) when his life was threatened (vv 3, 8, 15), the psalmist appears in front of the community (v 14) to give his thanksgiving testimony, which includes generalizing conclusions (vv 5, 6, 15), as well as personal recollections. If the psalm is rather recent, the "cup of salvation" (v 13) could refer to the Jewish wine libation (cf. *Ps 92). It may also refer to a judgment ordeal similar to the one mentioned in Nm 5:19-28. More probably the "cup of destiny" is meant (cf. *Ps 11:6) and perhaps, as in Ps 16:5, does it allude to what Weiser (p. 175) calls "the festival cup of Yahweh," which, it is presumed, was passed around at cultic meals to signify the sharing of divine grace.

The personal or private thanksgiving psalm, writes Mowinckel (II:31), belonged to the ritual of the thank-offering feast. Some elements of the ceremony are preserved in Ps 116. "The psalm is sung where the sacrificial act is taking place, that is at the sanctuary, in the temple (Ps 116:19), before the assembled congregation, the 'godfearing,' 'the righteous,' 'the worshippers of Yahweh' and so on. Probably before the sacrificial act itself (Ps 116:17ff; Jonah 2:10), while it was being prepared, the offerer would appear with the 'cup of salvation' in his hand and empty the wine as a drink-offering upon the altar, while calling on the name of Yahweh (Ps 116:13); then the song of thanksgiving would follow, whether sung by himself or by one of the temple servants — most probably, no doubt, the latter." Elsewhere Mowinckel notes that it is in the thanksgiving psalms that "we perhaps meet with most deviations from the common style." Ps 116 in particular "is distinguished by the irregular, back and forth treatment of the traditional elements and by its Hebrew, which is anything but classical" (II, p. 142).

PSALM 138 (137)

Hymn of a Grateful Heart

1 *Of David.*

I

Ps 9:2

    I will give thanks to you, O Lord, with all my heart,

    [for you have heard the words of my mouth;]

Pss 8:6; 35:5; 91:11

      in the presence of the angels I will sing your praise;

Ps 5:8

2 I will worship at your holy temple

and give thanks to your name,

Pss 25:10; 57:
4; 117:2

Because of your kindness and your truth;
for you have made great above all things
your name and your promise.

3 When I called, you answered me;

Is 40:29

you built up strength within me.

II

Ps 68:33

4 All the kings of the earth shall give thanks to you, O Lord,
when they hear the words of your mouth;

5 And they shall sing of the ways of the Lord:
"Great is the glory of the Lord."

Is 57:15

6 The Lord is exalted, yet the lowly he sees,
and the proud he knows from afar.

III

Ps 23:4

7 Though I walk amid distress, you preserve me;

Ps 10:12

against the anger of my enemies you raise your hand;
your right hand saves me.

8 The Lord will complete what he has done for me;

Pss 118:29;
136:1

your kindness, O Lord, endures forever;
forsake not the work of your hands.

This liturgical prayer draws a lot on other psalms. The psalmist will sing his praise in the presence of *'elōhîm* (v 1). Is God meant by this word, or are these "divine" beings (cf. §10g) demythologized *elōhîm* of the celestial phoenician court? (cf. Pss 58:2; 82:1, 6) The Greek and Latin Psalters read "angels" (cf. *Ps 8:6). *Neged 'elōhîm* can be translated also "in the face of the gods," with the meaning: despite the false gods (cf. Ps 96:5). The psalmist speaks, as it seems, from the forecourt of the temple; he looks toward the sanctuary where he will prostrate and worship (cf. Ps 5:8). Already perhaps he has experienced in the cult theophany this "kindness and fidelity," once proclaimed by God himself at Sinai (Ex 34:6) and so often recalled in the Pss: 40:12; 57:4; 61:8; 85:11; 89:15, 25; 115:1; 138:2; cf. §11f).

Possibly, writes Mowinckel (II, p. 29), some apparently quite individual thanksgiving psalms, like Pss 92 and 138, must be interpreted in the same way as Ps 18, a pure royal psalm of thanksgiving. In some cases, he adds (II, 36f), "the terms used in the psalm seem to suggest that the worshipper is to be thought of as a person in high position, perhaps the king or the governor, and that the distress had a more or less *political* character, as in Pss 18 and 138 . . . . In the account of the distress *enemies* sometimes play a part. In the royal psalms, such as Pss 18 and 138, the case is clear: we have the political enemies of the king, and those probably foreigners, as a rule, as in the royal laments."

CHAPTER SIX

LAMENTS

Psalms of Confidence, and Thanksgivings: of the Community

The literary structures in this family of psalms are similar to those of the corresponding categories related to the individual. Yet the situation is different: the distress to be removed, the favor obtained requesting a thanksgiving are now the concern of the community. The normal setting of collective prayer being the cult, these psalms of the community are likely to have originated in a liturgical milieu of feasts and rites celebrated in the sanctuaries.

§23. LAMENTS OF THE COMMUNITY

(a) *General character*

Quite obviously these psalms are to be associated with days of humiliation, fast or prayer proclaimed for special occasions arising from national distress. Penitential rites of various kinds would accompany the national prayer for deliverance: cf. Jos 7:5-9; Jgs 20: 23, 26; 1 Sm 7:6; 1 Kgs 8:33ff; Jer 14:2. These calls to repentance and prayer (cf. Jl 1:13f) were specifically intended to temper God's wrath aroused by grievous sins, to atone for them, to remove impurity from the midst of Israel or to move God to intervene for his people.

It is not impossible, thinks A. Bentzen, that "an element of penitence has also been involved in the great *annual festivals,* already in pre-exilic days" (I, p. 155).

As "unquestionably communal or national laments" Mowinckel lists: Pss 12, 14, 44, 58, 60, 74, 79, 80, 83, 89, 144 and Lam 5 (I, p. 194). These are national laments *in the we-form,* for which there does not seem to be any evidence in Babylonia, where the king spoke for the community in the I-form, even in public distress. Apart from the "national (congregational) psalms" proper which describe a disaster that has already taken place, Mowinckel identifies another series of psalms, in which Yahweh's protection is sought against a threatening danger. These are the *protective psalms,* which include: Pss 3, 5, 7, 11, 20, 26, 27, 28, 36, 52, 54, 57, 61, 62, 63, 64, 71, 77, 83, 86, 139, 140, 144 (cf. I, p. 219f + *Ps 71).

Among the biblical "psalms of lamentation proper" there are some, Mowinckel believes (I, p. 219), which apparently are quite personal and yet are in reality national (congregational) psalms. Such national laments *in the I-form* would include: Pss 9-10, 13, 31, 35, 42-43, 55, 56, 59, 69, 94, 102, 109, 142 (cf. I, pp. 225-246). More probably, however, only one of them (Ps 94) is a national lament, the others being individual (private) laments or thanksgivings (Ps 9-10). In fact the debate on the *"ich"* of the psalms is an old one, but it has never been proved convincingly that in so many cases the psalmist speaking in the I-form is in reality the king or a leader of the people representing the community and expressing its collective interests (see on *Ps 59; cf. Pss 44, 77, 108). Already in 1888 R. Smend had strongly advocated the collective sense of the "I" in a large number of psalms. More recently A. Bentzen has expressed the opinion "that the line of demarcation between 'national' and 'individual' psalms must not be drawn too mechanically. For there is a possibility that the original connection of the psalms with the royal ritual must involve the conclusion that 'individual' psalms, originally to be used by the king, on account of the position of the king as 'incarnation' not only of God, but also of the nation, in reality are 'national' psalms" (I, p. 155).

The views of Smend and his followers are strongly opposed by Hermann Gunkel and by E. Balla, the latter arguing that of alleged "collective" *Ichpsalmen* of the Psalter, Ps 129 is the only example in which the people are poetically personified (p. 114). In his final conclusion Balla also warns against accepting an allegorizing interpretation of the psalms to the detriment of the obvious meaning expressed by the words (p. 150).

A few literary elements belong more clearly to the national laments then to the private supplications. The enemies referred to are non-Israelites, considered also as God's own enemies. A salvation-oracle (*Heilsorakel*) is usually expected, as often featured in the penitential services (cf. 2 Chr 20:14-19; Pss 60:8ff; 85:9). The negative oracle of Jer 14-15 could illustrate the background of many national laments. Gradually the Israelites learned to interpret even divine punishment as medicinal and the *Heilsorakel* was entirely replaced by the confession of sins and a begging for forgiveness (cf. Ezr 9:5ff; Dn 9:5f). National laments often appeal to the *magnalia Dei* of the *Heilsgeshichte* (cf. §10f) to motivate the request for God's intervention (cf. Pss 44 and 80). Our classification ascribes to this category a greater number of psalms than is usual (considering only the psalms in the "We"-form). The uncertain are indicated by the brackets and discussed in the respective introductions.

(b) The laments of the community are the following: Pss (12), 44, (58), 60, 74, (77), 79, 80, (82), (83), 85, 90, (94), (106), (108), 123, (126), 137.

PSALM 12 (11)

Prayer against Evil Tongues

	1 *For the leader; "upon the eighth." A psalm of David.*
	I
Is 57:1	2 Help, O Lord! for no one now is dutiful;
Mi 7:2; Is 59:15	faithfulness has vanished from among men.
Pss 31:19; 54:22	3 Everyone speaks falsehood to his neighbor;
Jr 9:7; Is 59:3f; Ps 55:22	with smooth lips they speak, and double heart.
	II
Jb 5:21; Ps 31:19	4 May the Lord destroy all smooth lips,
	every boastful tongue,
Ps 17:10	5 Those who say, "We are heroes with our tongues;
	our lips are our own; who is lord over us?"
	III
Pss 25:15; 35:10	6 "Because they rob the afflicted, and the needy sigh,

Is 33:10; Ps
10:12

now will I arise," says the Lord;
"I will grant safety to him who longs for it."
IV

Ps 19:8

7 The promises of the Lord are sure,

Prv 30:5; Pss
18:31; 19:11

like tried silver, freed from dross, sevenfold refined.

8 You, O Lord, will keep us
and preserve us always from this generation,

9 While about us the wicked strut
and in high place are the basest of men.

Psalm 12 is identified by Mowinckel as a "national complaint" (I, pp. 200, 207), and described as "a promise about the rescue of Israel from the pressure of alien rule" (II, p. 216). The foreign nation is alluded to only in very general terms (I, p. 220f). Yet the main elements of the lament appear in the psalms: initial cry (Help, O Lord!), lament (vv 2-3), supplication (4-5), oracle (6), expression of confidence (7-8), lament again (9). It is the supplication of an individual (cf. v 6) who identifies his cause with that of the just, as opposed to the wicked. The prophetic tone is noticeable, especially in verse 2 (cf. Mi 7:2; Is 57:1; 59:15). Other commentators define our psalm as "a liturgy of some sort," which, like Is 33, "is to be accounted for by its origin in the festival cult" (Weiser). These two interpretations are not incompatible if we admit Mowinckel's view that "the psalms of lamentation are in fact also cultic liturgies containing both the lament and the supplication itself, then Yahweh's promise of help through the temple prophet, and finally the thanksgiving or the confidence of being heard with a reference to the promise" (II, p. 76). Such a definition would apply especially to Pss 12, 60, and 108.

It is alleged that Ps 12 lends support to the opinion that the magic power of curses is attested in the psalms (cf. §14d). The masters of falsehood say: "We are heroes with our tongues; our lips are our own; who is Lord over us?" (v 5; cf. Jb 32:22; Jer 2:31; Ps 31:19) More convincingly it can be held that the psalm provides a good example of an *"oracle d'exaucement"* (cf. §8e), of an oracular assurance that the prayer has been heard: "Because they rob the afflicted, and the needy sigh, *now I will arise* (cf. §13d), says the Lord; "I will grant safety to him who longs for it" (v 6). Previously the psalmist had noted sadly (v 2) that a generation was disappearing, that of the saints (*ḥasîdîm*) and the faithful (*'emûnîm*).

PSALM 44 (43)

Israel's Past Glory and Present Need

1 *For the leader. A maśkil of the sons of Core.*

I

2 O God, our ears have heard,
> our fathers have declared to us,
The deeds you did in their days,
> in days of old:

3 How with your own hand you rooted out the nations
> and planted them;
you smashed the peoples, but for them you made room.

4 For not with their own sword did they conquer the land,
> nor did their own arm make them victorious,
But it was your arm and your right hand
> and the light of your countenance, in your love for them.

5 You are my king and my God,
> who bestowed victories on Jacob.

6 Our foes through you were struck down;
> through your name we trampled down our adversaries.

7 For not in my bow did I trust,
> nor did my sword save me;

8 But you saved us from our foes,
> and those who hated us you put to shame.

9 In God we gloried day by day;
> your name we praised always.

II

10 Yet now you have cast us off and put us in disgrace,
> and you go not forth with our armies.

11 You have let us be driven back by our foes;
> those who hated us plundered us at will,

12 You marked us out as sheep to be slaughtered;
> among the nations you scattered us.

13 You sold your people for no great price;
> you made no profit from the sale of them.

14 You made us the reproach of our neighbors,
> the mockery and the scorn of those around us.

15 You made us a byword among the nations,

Marginal references:

2 Sm 7:23; Is 63:7f
Ps 78:3

Pss 33:16; 80:9

Dt 8:17f

Jos 24:12

Pss 17:36; 20:7
Pss 31:17; 67:2
Pss 5:3; 145:1

Ps 20:2

Hos 1:7

Lv 26:7

Ps 64:11

Pss 10:1; 60:3-7
Ex 15:3; Jgs 5:4
Pss 35:1-3; 60:12
Dt 28:25

Lv 26:33; Dt 4:27; 28:64
Is 52:3; Jgs 2:14; 3:8
Dt 32:30

Dn 9:16

Pss 38:12; 55:14f

Pss 31:12; 42:
11; 69:13   a laughingstock among the peoples.

16 All the day my disgrace is before me,
   and shame covers my face

17 At the voice of him who mocks and blasphemes,
   and in the presence of the enemy and the avenger.

III

18 All this has come upon us, though we have not forgotten you,
   nor have we been disloyal to your covenant;

19 Our hearts have not shrunk back,
   nor our steps turned aside from your path,

Jer 9:10   20 Though you thrust us down into a place of misery
   and covered us over with darkness.

21 If we had forgotten the name of our God

Is 1:15   and stretched out our hands to a strange god,

22 Would not God have discovered this?

Jer 11:20   For he knows the secrets of the heart.

Ba 3:33   23 Yet for your sake we are being slain all the day;

Rm 8:36   we are looked upon as sheep to be slaughtered.

IV

24 Awake! Why are you asleep, O Lord?
   Arise! Cast us not off forever!

Jb 13:24; Ps
13:2   25 Why do you hide your face,
Ps 69:18   forgetting our woe and our oppression?

Pss 7:6; 119:
25   26 For our souls are bowed down to the dust,
   our bodies are pressed to the earth.

27 Arise, help us!

Pss 19:15; 25:
22   Redeem us for your kindness' sake.

In this community lament God is reminded of his past favors to Israel (vv 2-9), as contrasting with the present situation (10-23), which requires the help of the Lord (24-27). Various afflictions constitute the national calamity: defeat in battle (v 11), deportation (v 12), loss of prestige (15-16), destruction of cities (v 20), divine indifference (vv 5, 10). Not a few elements of the description are traditional *clichés* (cf. Am 1:6, 9; Jer 9:11; 10:22; 49:33; Is 13:22; 34:13; 63:7f) which may apply to any of the troubled periods of Israel's history: the Assyrian invasion (2 Kgs 18-19), the Babylonian invasion (2 Kgs 23:29 to 25:26; cf. Pss 74, 79, 80), "the national degradation of the Persian period." Religious persecution is not clearly alluded to even in verses 18-23, and there is no special ground for assigning the psalm to the Maccabean period. "The place of jackals" (*meqôm tannîm*) in verse 20 can mean devastation (cf. Is 34:13; Jer 9:10) or the desert where the Jews took refuge during the persecution of Antiochus Epiphanes (cf. 1 Mc 2:29; 9:33).

In verses 5-9 is proclaimed the saving intervention of God *acting alone*, the basic creed of the "holy war" (cf. §13d, 14b and Ps 35:1f). On the expression "my God" in verse 5 as relating to the God of Israel, see O. Eissfeldt (*ZAW*, 61, 1945-48, pp. 10-16). Not pharisaic theology in its initial stage but an excessive reliance on the covenant-bond seems to be reflected in verses 18-23. Some prophets, like Jeremiah, have to explain that Israel's infidelity can and must bring a break in the covenant, followed by disasters, even the exile.

Heilsgeschichte seen in the light of faith consists mainly in saving deeds wrought by the God of history (vv 2-9; cf. Ps 78:3; Dt 8:17f; Jos 24:12; 2 Sm 7:22f; Hos 1:7). For the same reason a national disaster is naturally ascribed to divine abandonment (vv 18-23). The opening verse, "O God, our ears have heard, our fathers have declared to us . . ." can refer to national tradition or to *Heilsgeschichte* recitals in the cult. The first person singular in verses 5, 7, 16 speaks for a leader who represents the nation (cf. §23a). Other national calamity psalms (74, 79, 80) deal with some of the themes exposed in Ps 44. For Mowinckel (I, 219) there are only three "national psalms of lamentation" proper: Pss 44, 74, 89. In them is found "a rather general description of the distress or disaster which the enemy has already brought upon land and people and king . . . . They were no doubt occasioned by a day of prayer and fasting after one or more lost battles, or perhaps the sack of the town."

The psalmist's question in verse 24: "Awake! Why are you asleep, O Lord?" is similar to Elijah's taunt addressed to the prophets of Baal in 1 Kgs 18:27, "Perhaps he is asleep and needs to be awakened." Widengren in *Myth, Ritual, and Kingship,* p. 191, argues from this formula of Ps 44 to a dying and rising Yahweh (see §8d) but, as Dahood correctly notes, "a merely formal parallel does not permit one to infer a parallel meaning (cf. W. L. Moran in *Biblica* 1959, p. 1027). Mythical formulas must be interpreted in light of the dominating Hebrew concept of history, and vivid poetic images can scarcely be made the basis for serious theological discussion. The sleep of God, who really does not and cannot sleep (Ps 121:4), simply means that by remaining inattentive to the prayer of his people he gives the impression of being asleep."

PSALM 58 (57)

Against Unjust Judges

1 *For the leader. (Do not destroy!) A miktam of David.*

I

Pss 29:1; 82:6; 84:8

2 Do you indeed like gods pronounce justice
    and judge fairly, you men of rank?

Mi 2:1

Dt 16:19

3 Nay, you willingly commit crimes;
    on earth you look to the fruits of extortion.

4 From the womb the wicked are perverted;

Ps 51:7

    astray from birth have the liars gone.

Dt 32:33

5 Theirs is poison like a serpent's,
    like that of a stubborn snake that stops its ears,

6 That it may not hear the voice of enchanters

Jer 8:17; Eccl 10:11

    casting cunning spells.

II

Jb 29:17; Ps 3:8

7 O God, smash their teeth in their mouths;
    the jaw-teeth of the lions, break, O Lord!

Jb 11:16; Wis 16:29
Ps 64:4

8 Let them vanish like water flowing off;
    when they draw the bow, let their arrows be headless
                shafts.

9 Let them dissolve like a melting snail,

Jb 3:11, 16; Eccl 6:4f

    like an untimely birth that never sees the sun.

Na 1:10; 2 Sm 23:6
Jb 21:18; Ps 35:5

10 Unexpectedly, like a thorn-bush,
    or like thistles, let the whirlwind carry them away.

Ps 94:1ff; Na 1:2

11 The just man shall be glad when he sees vengeance;

Ps 68:24; Is 63:1-6

    he shall bathe his feet in the blood of the wicked.

12 And men shall say, "Truly there is a reward for the just;

Jb 19:29; Mal 3:18

    truly there is a God who is judge on earth!"

To understand this psalm and Ps 82 one must have in mind the "process whereby Yahwism came to terms with the local shrine-gods by means of the idea of divine judgment" (Weiser) on the wicked, delivered mostly in the cult. The gods of the Canaanite shrines were reduced to a lower rank and finally dispossessed completely of their power (cf. §10g). The court "gods" could be, here (v 2) and in

Ps 82:1, degraded divinities still in a way responsible for certain spheres of human life. According to ancient belief divine behavior is reflected in the "affairs of men." In spite of the wholesale conversion to Yahwism something survived of the tension between Yahweh and the other gods. Mowinckel who notes this (I, 148) sees the evildoers of Ps 58 mostly as "the national enemies of Israel, or the heathen oppressors and their helpers within Israel" (I, p. 208).

The invocation is missing from this psalm, which starts with a lament in the form of an accusation directed against the gods of the oppressors (vv 2-3; cf. Mowinckel, I, p. 196). It is not sure, not even in this psalm, that curse (vv 5-10) is used as an operative power against the enemy. Imprecations were also part of the ritual for eliminating sinners (cf. Dt 27:11-26 and §14d). As perverted from the womb and astray from birth (v 3), the wicked lie outside the covenant fellowship. The wish for vengeance, expressed in verse 11, is better understood, if not justified, when read in that context.

R. Pautrel has proposed the following Latin translation of three difficult verses of the psalm (7-9):

> Dissipentur sicut aqua quae recedit,
>   calcabunt arenam et sitient.
> Pereant sicut partus exiens in tabem,
>   abortus mulieris qui non vidit solem.
> Antequam oriantur spinae languescat rhamnus
>   vivum tamquam siccum evellant eum.

A paraphrase in English can be attempted: "Let them disappear like a mirage, sand and thirst will be their lot; let them perish like a foetus in decay, like an untimely birth that saw no light; before the thorns grow, let the thorn-bush decay; uproot it green as if it had withered." All these metaphors illustrate one theme: the abortive destiny of the wicked.

PSALM 60 (59)

Prayer after Defeat in Battle

Ps 45:1   1 *For the leader; according to "The Lily of..." A Miktam*
            2 *of David (for teaching) when he fought against Aram Naha-*
2 Sm 8:2f   *raim and Aram Soba; and Joab, coming back, killed twelve*

thousand Edomites in the "valley of salt."

I

Pss 44:10-17;
74:1

3 O God, you have rejected us and broken our defenses;
you have been angry; rally us!

Is 24:19

4 You have rocked the country and split it open;

Pss 46:4; 68:9

repair the cracks in it, for it is tottering.

5 You have made your people feel hardships;

Is 51:17; Jer
25:15

you have given us stupefying wine.

Is 49:22; Ex
17:15

6 You have raised for those who fear you a banner
to which they may flee out of bowshot

Ps 108:7-14

7 That your loved ones may escape;
help us by your right hand, and answer us!

II

Ps 108:8ff

8 God promised in his sanctuary:

Sir 50:26

"Exultantly I will apportion Sichem,

Gn 33:17

and measure off the valley of Socchoth.

Ob 19

9 Mine is Galaad, and mine Manasse;

Gn 49:10; 2
Sm 2:4

Ephraim is the helmet for my head; Juda, my scepter;

Is 11:14; 25:
10f

10 Moab shall serve as my washbowl;

Ob 18-21; Ps
110:1

upon Edom I will set my shoe;

Ob 19; Is 11:
14

I will triumph over Philistia."

III

Pss 31:22;
108:11
Is 34:6; 63:1;
Am 1:11

11 Who will bring me into the fortified city?
Who will lead me into Edom?

12 Have not you, O God, rejected us,

Is 42:13; Ps
44:10

so that you go not forth, O God, with our armies?

Pss 76:4-7;
135:10
Hos 1:7

13 Give us aid against the foe,
for worthless is the help of men.

14 Under God we shall do valiantly;

Hb 3:12; Ps
44:6

it is he who will tread down our foes.

It is not sure that all the sections of this psalm date from the same period and reflect the same historical situation. The divine utterance of verses 8-10 has a wider scope than the lament (vv 3-7) and not the same object. It probably reflects conditions of the Davidic era (comp. v 8 and Nm 24:17). Yet later it was incorporated in the psalm, probably in pre-exilic times, when God would still be said to lead the people in battle (vv 12, 14; cf. Pss 44:10; 60:12; 68:8; Ex 15:3) as he did in the desert (Nm 4:14). Was the particular circumstance, as Weiser puts it, a military assembly rallied round the banner (v 6) of Yahweh (cf. Ps 20:6; Ex 17:15f), perhaps during a campaign against the territory of Edom: "O Lord, when you went out of Seir, when you marched from the land of Edom, the earth quaked and the heavens were shaken, while the clouds sent down showers" (Jgs 5:4; cf. Ob vv 1-21).

The oracle (vv 8-10) takes the form of a divine utterance borrowed from the sacred tradition of the distribution of the land (see on *Ps 142), in which is proclaimed once again Yahweh's ownership of the land of Canaan (Weiser). Yahweh's battle cry, "I will exult" (v 8), is sounded against Israel's frontier enemies. Victory is assured (*BJ*). Verses 7-14 are read again in Ps 108:7-14. From this Mowinckel concludes (II, p. 59) that "the same promise might reappear in different psalms, at different times . . . that oracles might be used over again . . . that they made up a permanent feature of the liturgy itself, and that the wording would usually be rather stereotyped and according to pattern." Yet in Ps 60 the oracular promise, he adds, was formulated with reference to a definite historical situation: a war against Edom and other neighboring peoples. Yet the wording was re-used for a new situation (Ps 108).

PSALM 74 (73)

Prayer in Time of National Calamity

1 *A maśkîl of Asaph.*

I

Pss 10:1; 60:3-7
Ps 38:2

Why, O God, have you cast us off forever?
Why does your anger smolder against the sheep
of your pasture?

Pss 49:16; 69:37; 78:71
Dt 7:6; Is 63:17
Ex 15:17; Hos 48:12

2 Remember your flock which you built up of old,
the tribe you redeemed as your inheritance,
Mount Sion, where you took up your abode.

3 Turn your steps toward the utter ruins;
toward all the damage the enemy has done in the sanctuary.

4 Your foes roar triumphantly in your shrine;
they have set up their tokens of victory.

5 They are like men coming up with axes to a clump of trees;

6 and now with chisel and hammer they hack at all
its paneling.

Is 64:10; 2
Kgs 25:8f
Ps 79:1

7   They set your sanctuary on fire;

  the place where your name abides they have razed

      and profaned.

8   They said in their hearts, "Let us destroy them;

  burn all the shrines of God in the land."

Ez 7:26; Lam
2:9
Ps 6:4

9   Deeds on our behalf we do not see; there is no prophet now,

  and no one of us knows how long ....

Ps 62:4; 77:8

10 How long, O God, shall the foe blaspheme?

  shall the enemy revile your name forever?

11 Why draw back your hand

Is 52:10

  and keep your right hand idle beneath your cloak?

II

Pss 55:20; 89:
10-15

12 Yet, O God, my king from of old,

  you doer of saving deeds on earth,

13 you stirred up the sea by your might;

Ez 29:3; 32:2;
Gn 1:21
Ex 14:30; Is
27:1
Jb 3:8

  you smashed the heads of the dragons in the waters.

14 You crushed the heads of Leviathan,

  and made food of him for the dolphins.

Hb 3:10; Gn
1:9
Pss 77:17f;
104:10
Gn 1:16

15 You released the springs and torrents;

  you brought dry land out of the primeval waters.

16 Yours is the day, and yours the night;

Pss 33:6, 9;
95:5
Jb 38:8-11

  you fashioned the moon and the sun.

17 You fixed all the limits of the land;

  summer and winter you made.

18 Remember how the enemy has blasphemed you, O Lord,

  and how a stupid people has reviled your name.

Ps 68:14

19 Give not to the vulture the life of your dove;

  be not forever unmindful of the lives of your afflicted

      ones.

Ps 78:37

20 Look to your covenant,

  for the hiding places in the land and the plains

      are full of violence.

Pss 9:10; 113:
7; 115:6

21 May the humble not retire in confusion;

  may the afflicted and the poor praise your name.

Is 33:10; Ps
73:20

22 Arise, O God; defend your cause;

  remember how the fool blasphemes you day after day.

23 Be not mindful of the voice of your foes;

  the uproar of those who rebel against you is unceasing.

This psalm is concerned with a national calamity involving the temple. Its destruction by the Babylonians in 587 could be meant (cf. 2 Kgs 25:9; Is 64:10): utter destruction, burning down and profanation included (vv 3-8). All this does not apply fully to the deeds of Antiochus Epiphanes who burned the doors of the temple(1 Mc 4:38; 2 Mc 1:8), then desecrated the sanctuary (1 Mc 1:23, 39; 2 Mc 6:5). In this period though the silence of the prophetic word (v 9) is more explicitly noted (1 Mc 4:46; 9:27; 14:41). Besides, ancient sources say Epiphanes was Epimanes, "the fool." Yet verse 22 may not allude to any one sinner: "Remember how the fool blasphemes you day after day." The phrase, "there is no prophet now" (v 9), could also refer to the absence of Ezekiel and Jeremiah or reflect a reality expressed in the Lamentations on Jerusalem: "Her prophets have not received any vision from the Lord" (2:9). Reference to the Babylonian invasion is also favored by the apparent indefinite duration of the temple calamity, whereas in the Maccabean events, the sanctuary was rededicated after only three years (1 Mc 1:54; 4:52).

Having described the calamity, the psalmist recalls from the *Heilsgeschichte* tradition a series of divine saving deeds (vv 12-17): the crossing of the Sea of reeds (Ex 14:30), the defeat of the Egyptians (cf. Ez 29:3; 32:4), the exodus miracles (cf. Ex 17:6; Nm 20:11), the miraculous crossing of the Jordan river (cf. Jos 3:15). In all this God's creative power was also active, especially against the watery chaos (cf. Ps 89:10f). With the mention of the water dragons and of Leviathan (vv 13f; cf. Ps 104:26; Is 27:1; Jb 3:8; 7:12), Canaanite mythical imagery is used for extolling God's supreme mastery of nature (cf. §9b, 11a and J. L. McKenzie). Such divine grandeur, the psalmist concludes (vv 18-23), cannot tolerate the perpetuation of blasphemy.

The lament's aim is to move Yahweh to act in favor of the suppliant(s). The motivation often refers to his past deeds (cf. Ps 74: 12-17) and especially to his honor, by showing that Yahweh's cause is at stake. This will obviously be the case, if, for example (as in Ps 74), the temple itself has been laid waste. In this context it seems less indicated to seek for the lament's motivation a precise historical setting. On the other hand, a purely cultic and dramatic setting cannot be admitted, although such an interpretation does contain elements of truth. The following views of F. Willesen illustrate well, it would seem, both the method and the excesses of a certain "myth and ritual" school of exegesis (cf. §8d).

"In the following pages," Willesen writes, "I hope to indicate that the psalms (= 74 and 79) have no relation whatsoever to any historic occurrences, but are completely cultic. If this be true, the determination of their type as 'national psalms of lamentation' must fall, and it will come out that originally they were ritual laments with a fixed position in the cult drama of the New Year festival..." (p. 289). Then he attempts to prove that in the Semitic world the (cultic) profanation of the temple and the (ritual) death of the god are bound up inseparably. So the cultic weeping and lamentation accompanying the god to Sheol have been integrating parts of the act of temple profanation too. Texts would indicate "that the temple had to undergo a purification prior to the procession and the inthronization of the deity, and this postulates a preceding profanation ceremony. Would it be too audacious to interpret the purification of the postexilic Jewish Temple on the day of Atonement as a reminiscence of the ritual expulsion of the Chaos power from the house it had seized with the result of menacing misfortune to all creatures?" (p. 298) There is little doubt about the answer, but let us read the application to Ps 74.

"If this interpretation be consistent the verses are a decisive evidence partly of the presence of the cultic drama in Israel, and partly of the connection of Ps 74 with this cult. The course of the drama may then be this: After the introduction follow the rites representing the conquest of the sanctuary by the Chaos powers, viz., the roaring, the bringing in of signs followed by burning and complete ritual destruction. One of the sites, the disposition of the hostile signs, is explained by verses 5-6: the performing persons take the axes, Ba'al's insignia, into the sacred house after having removed Jahweh's signs, and this act is described further by an allusion to a — no doubt well known — mythic idea: it has to look like the behavior of Ba'al when felling Jahweh's forest, i.e., that the actors are cutting, hewing, and hammering with their tools on the wooden furniture destined for this purpose. After this casual flash on the sacred acts generally forgotten long ago the cultic text proceeds with the next picture, the burning of the ruined building" (p. 305).

With less imagination it can be found that some aspects of Israelite cosmogony are reflected in verse 15: "You released the springs and torrents; you brought dry land out of the primeval waters." In connection with the description of Sheol (§14d) the views of J. A. Emerton have been mentioned. Applying these to Ps 74:15 he concludes that the whole verse "describes the removal of the primeval waters from the earth. God cleft open springs, so that the water might descend through them" and thus allow dry land to appear.

PSALM 77 (76)

Lament and Comfort in Time of Distress

Ps 62:1	1	*For the leader; 'al Idithun. A psalm of Asaph.*
		I
	2	Aloud to God I cry;
		aloud to God, to hear me;
	3	on the day of my distress I seek the Lord.
		By night my hands are stretched out without flagging;
Ps 119:28		my soul refuses comfort.
	4	When I remember God, I moan;
Lam 3:20; Jon 2:8		when I ponder, my spirit grows faint.
	5	You keep my eyes watchful;
		I am troubled and cannot speak.
Dt 32:7; Ps 143:5	6	I consider the days of old;
Ps 119:52	7	the years long past I remember.
Pss 63:7; 119:148		In the night I meditate in my heart;
		I ponder, and my spirit broods:
Pss 13:2; 74: 10; 79:5	8	"Will the Lord reject forever
Is 49:14f		and nevermore be favorable?
	9	Will his kindness utterly cease,
Lam 3:22		his promise fail for all generations?
	10	Has God forgotten pity?
		Does he in anger withhold his compassion?"
	11	And I say, "This is my sorrow,
		that the right hand of the Most High is changed."
	12	I remember the deeds of the Lord;
		yes, I remember your wonders of old.
Ps 1:2	13	And I meditate on your works;
		your exploits I ponder.

II

Dt 32:4

Pss 71:19; 86:8

Ex 15:11

Neh 1:10; Ps 19:15
Gn 46:26f

Na 1:4

Pss 71:20; 86:13

Hb 3:10; Ps 18:12

Pss 97:4; 135:7; 144:6
Ex 19:18; Hb 3:10f

Pss 66:6; 78:13

Hb 3:15; Is 43:16; 51:10
Wis 14:3

Ex 12:51; Ps 78:52f

Hos 12:13; Is 63:11f

14 O God, your way is holy;
  what great god is there like our God?
15 You are the God who works wonders;
  among the peoples you have made known your power.
16 With your strong arm you redeemed your people,
  the sons of Jacob and Joseph.
17 The waters saw you, O God;
  the waters saw you and shuddered;
  the very depths were troubled.
18 The clouds poured down water;
  the skies gave forth their voice;
  your arrows also sped abroad.
19 Your thunder resounded in the whirlwind;
  your lightning illumined the world;
  the earth quivered and quaked.
20 Through the sea was your way,
  and your path through the deep waters,
  though your footsteps were not seen.
21 You led your people like a flock
  under the care of Moses and Aaron.

It is not so much a past calamity as the precarious situation of the nation which constitutes the object of this lament. Mowinckel would classify it with the "protective psalms" (cf. §23a and *Ps 71), in which God's protection is sought against a threatening danger (I, p. 219f). Yet, as Mowinckel himself admits, it is possible that "the whole people has been struck by disaster" (p. 227). The speaker is the representative of the people. He lived in a difficult period, after the exile (*BJ*). Although the psalm has unity, it consists of two parts: a lament (vv 2-10) and a hymn (12-21). Verse 11 links both parts and expresses the main concern of the psalmist, the "intriguing" ways of God: "This is my sorrow, that the right hand of the Most High is changed." For sleepless nights he has brooded on that problem. Yet in the stylized form of the theophany tradition (cf. Ex 19:18) he testifies to God's saving deeds (vv 14-23), in terms often similar to probably older writings, as Habakkuk 3:10-11:

Into streams you split the earth;
at sight of you the mountains tremble.
A torrent of rain descends;
the ocean gives forth its roar.

H. G. May believes that the "many waters" of Ps 77:20 are the waters of the Red Sea (cf. Hb 3:15), as in Ps 74:13f. John L. McKenzie, however, concludes his study of Ps 74:13ff with the following remark: "The weight of probabilities suggests that the phenomenon described in Ps 74:13-15 are creative works, and not the historical events of Exodus; and that the imagery employed is derived from Semitic — principally Canaanite — mythology" (p. 282). The English translation refers twice to the "meditation" of the psalmist. In Hebrew two different words are used: *śîaḥ* (v 7) and *hāgâh*. There exact meaning has been explained (§12f).

PSALM 79 (78)

The Destruction of Jerusalem and Its Temple

1 *A psalm of Asaph.*

I

2 Kgs 25:9ff;
Ps 94:5
Lam 1:10

O God, the nations have come into your inheritance;
they have defiled your holy temple,

Ez 25:3

they have laid Jerusalem in ruins.

Jr 7:33; Ps
68:37
1 Mc 7:17

2 They have given the corpses of your servants
as food to the birds of heaven,

Pss 52:11; 85:
9
Zeph 1:17

the flesh of your faithful ones to the beasts of the earth.

3 They have poured out their blood like water
round about Jerusalem,

Jer 8:1ff; 14:
16; 34:20
Zeph 2:8

and there is no one to bury them.

4 We have become the reproach of our neighbors,

Pss 44:14; 69:
9; 89:42

the scorn and derision of those around us.

II

Pss 77:8; 80:5

5 O Lord, how long? Will you be angry forever?
Will your jealousy burn like fire?

Ex 20:5; Dt
4:24
Sir 36:2; Ps
78:49ff

6 Pour out your wrath upon the nations that acknowledge
you not,

upon the kingdoms that call not upon your name;

Jer 50:7; Ps 14:4
Jer 10:25

7 For they have devoured Jacob
  and laid waste his dwelling.

Jer 11:10

8 Remember not against us the iniquities of the past;

Is 64:8

  may your compassion quickly come to us,

Ps 142:7

  for we are brought very low.

III

Pss 65:6; 85:5

9 Help us, O God our savior,

Ez 20:44; 36:22

  because of the glory of your name;

Pss 65:4; 85:3

  Deliver us and pardon our sins
  for your name's sake.

Ex 32:12; Mal 2:17
Jl 2:17; Pss 42:4; 115:2

10 Why should the nations say,
  "Where is their God?"
  Let it be known among the nations in our sight

Dt 32:43; Jl 4:21

  that you avenge the shedding of your servants' blood.

IV

11 Let the prisoners' sighing come before you;
  with your great power free those doomed to death.

Gn 4:24; Lv 26:21
Ps 137:7

12 And repay our neighbors sevenfold into their bosoms
  the disgrace they have inflicted on you, O Lord.

Jer 23:1ff; Ez 34:1ff

13 Then we, your people and the sheep of your pasture,
  will give thanks to you forever;

Is 43:21; Pss 78:6; 89:2

  through all generations we will declare your praise.

The destruction of Jerusalem and of the temple, with the massacre involved, forms the historical background of this national lament. Yet in spite of the details provided, it is as little possible here as in Pss 44 and 74 to ascertain that the calamity described is the catastrophe of 587. At any rate the mention of "our neighbors" in verse 12 (cf. Pss 44:14; 80:7; 89:42) seems to indicate that verses 10-13 are directed against Moab, Ammon, Edom, who before (2 Kgs 24:2) or after the fall of Jerusalem roamed in Judea to plunder (cf. Ez 35:10; 36:5). The text of verses 6-7 occurs in Jer 10:25, and verse 5 is typically in the style of national laments: "O Lord, how long? Will you be angry forever? Will your jealousy burn like fire?" (*Pss 13:2; 44:24; 74:1; 80:5; 89:47) The avenging (*neqāmâh*) of innocent blood (v 10) is a theme well attested in the psalms (cf. Pss 18:48;

58:11; 94:1; 149:7) and is related to God's deeds as *gô'ēl* ("re-deemer"; cf. §11d) of his people (cf. Pss 19:15; 78:35), a notion initially expressed in the ancient Exodus hymn (Ex 15:13) and fully used in Deutero-Isaiah (cf. Is 43:1, 7; 15). Although God is prayed to avenge "his servants' blood" (v 10), the "innocence motivation" is not proposed and allusion is made to the "iniquities of the past" (v 8). Finally, the image of the sheep and shepherd (v 13) serves to illustrate the relation of God with his people both at the end of this psalm and in the beginning of the next one (cf. *Ps 23).

PSALM 80 (79)

Prayer for the Restoration of the Lord's Vineyard

Ps 45:1	1	*For the leader; according to "Lilies." Eduth. A psalm of Asaph.*
		I
Ez 34:11; Ps 23:1	2	O shepherd of Israel, hearken,
		O guide of the flock of Joseph!
Ex 25:22; 1 Sm 4:4 Nm 2:18-23; 2 Sm 6:2 Ps 18:11	3	From your throne upon the cherubim, shine forth before Ephraim, Benjamin and Manasse.
		Rouse your power,
Pss 78:5f; 82: 8		and come to save us.
Jer 31:18; Ps 35:1-3 Pss 67:2; 89: 16	4	O Lord of hosts, restore us; if your face shine upon us, then we shall be safe.
		II
Is 64:8; Pss 6:4; 79:5	5	O Lord of hosts, how long will you burn with anger while your people pray?
	6	You have fed them with the bread of tears and given them tears to drink in ample measure.
	7	You have left us to be fought over by our neighbors,
Ps 44:14		and our enemies mock us.
	8	O Lord of hosts, restore us; if your face shine upon us, then we shall be safe.
		III
Is 5:1-7; 27: 2f Hos 10:1; Jer 2:21	9	A vine from Egypt you transplanted; you drove away the nations and planted it.

Ps 44:3
10 You cleared the ground for it,
  and it took root and filled the land.
11 The mountains were hidden in its shadow;
Nm 24:6; Ez 19:11
  by its branches, the cedars of God.
12 It put forth its foliage to the Sea,
Zech 9:10; Ps 72:8
  its shoots as far as the River.

IV

13 Why have you broken down its walls,
  so that every passer-by plucks its fruit,
Jer 12:10
14 The boar from the forest lays it waste,
Pss 79:10; 85: 6
  and the beasts of the field feed upon it?
15 Once again, O Lord of hosts,
  look down from heaven, and see;
Take care of this vine,
16 and protect what your right hand has planted
  [the son of man whom you yourself made strong].

V

17 Let those who would burn it with fire or cut it down
  perish before you at your rebuke.
18 May your help be with the man of your right hand,
  with the son of man whom you yourself made strong.
19 Then we will no more withdraw from you;
  give us new life, and we will call upon your name.
20 O Lord of hosts, restore us;
  if your face shine upon us, then we shall be safe.

The historical situation of this lament could have been similar to that supposed in Pss 44 and 60: whereas in the past the Israelites were led by God from victory to victory, now they are mocked by their enemies, threatened by their neighbors (cp. *Ps 79:12) and fed with the bread of tears (vv 5-8). The vine, which is Israel, has become a great tree (vv 9-12) and yet now it is abandoned to looting and destruction (13-14). It is high time for the Lord to arise with power (v 3) and hearken to the prayer of the refrain: "O Lord of hosts, restore us; if your face shine upon us, then we shall be safe" (vv 4, 8, 20). In this refrain the meaning of the whole psalm is condensed, as well as the main object of supplication in all the national laments: a return to normal relations between Yahweh and the covenant people. It will be brought about by God's initiative in restoring and reconverting the faithful (*hašîbēnû!*), in saving them by a new theophany encounter. In the allegory of the vine (vv 8-14) the pattern of *Heilsgeschichte* appears in a traditional form (cf. Gn 49:22f; Is 5:1-7). There is an historical connection between the title "Lord of hosts" of the refrain and his "throne upon the cherubim" (see §11b).

For years the date of the psalm's composition has been the subject of debate among scholars. It is generally agreed that the *terminus a quo* is the period following king Solomon's death, since the mention of "Israel," of "Joseph," of "Ephraim, Benjamin and Manasse" (vv 2, 3) seems to suppose the divided kingdom. From the tenth to the second century almost every possible date has been proposed. O. Eissfeldt would settle for one between 732 and 722. H. Heinemann has stated his proposal clearly. "Our contention is that the evidence points unmistakably in one direction: that the Psalm belongs to a much earlier period, preceding the division of the kingdom and, even more precisely, before the rise of Judah to predominance. Only thus can we understand why there is no mention of Judah, why 'Joseph' is used as a synonym for Israel and why special place is accorded to Benjamin. The Psalm must have been composed in the time of Saul. Thus it becomes obvious why the author should think that the salvation of Israel depends on Benjamin, or rather on the *'iš yemini* — a phrase actually applied to Saul in 1 Sm 9:1 and 21:7. The situation of a country 'wholly overrun by enemies' (Kirkpatrick) is entirely in accord with conditions at the time of Saul, prior to his victory over the Philistines. Israel, at the moment reflected in the Psalm, is indeed going to war, and calls upon its God to lead it to victory, as He had done so often before. The memory of the Ark and its miraculous powers was still fresh."

More probably, Mowinckel believes (II, p. 152), Ps 80 originated from "some North-Israelite sanctuary, such as Bethel . . . and belongs in all probability to the last days of the Northern Kingdom." Having translated verse 18: "May your hand protect the man at your right, the son of man who has been authorized by you," *JB* comments: "Probable allusion to Zerubbabel (Hag 1:1; Esd 3:2) rather than to Benjamin ('Son of the right hand'), Amaziah ('Yahweh is trusty'; cf. 2 Chr 25:15), or Israel (cf. Ex 4:22)" (cf. Ps 132:10). Zerubbabel, high-commissioner in Jerusalem, began rebuilding the temple in 520 B.C. (cf. Esd 5:2).

PSALM 82 (81)

Judgment against Wicked Judges

1 A *psalm of Asaph.*

Ps 89:7

God arises in the divine assembly;

Is 3:13f

he judges in the midst of the gods.

I

2 "How long will you judge unjustly

Zech 7:9; Jer 22:3

and favor the cause of the wicked?

Dt 1:17; Is 1: 17

3 Defend the lowly and the fatherless;

2 Chr 19:7; Jer 5:28

render justice to the afflicted and the destitute.

Ex 23:6; Ez 22:29

4 Rescue the lowly and the poor;

Pss 12:6; 68:6

from the hand of the wicked deliver them.

II

5 "They know not, neither do they understand;

they go about in darkness;

Prv 8:27; Pss 11:3; 104:3

all the foundations of the earth are shaken.

Jn 10:34; Pss 29:1; 58:1

6 I said: You are gods,

all of you sons of the Most High;

7 Yet like men you shall die,

Is 14:12; Ez 28:17

and fall like any prince."

Pss 58:12; 76: 10; 94:2

8 Rise, O God; judge the earth,

Zech 2:17

for yours are all the nations.

Why is this world full of injustice? Because the judges themselves are wicked and easily bribed. This prophetic teaching (cf. Is 1:17f; 3: 14f; Mi 3:1-11), eschatological in tone (cf. Is 24:21f), is presented in the psalm with a *mise en scène* (v 1) inspired by Canaanite mythology. The ancient literary themes involving assemblies of the gods, in judicial court, are used also elsewhere in the psalms (cf. Ps 58). For the greater part of the psalm, the divine judge speaks in the course of a cult theophany (vv 2-7; cf. §13d); the gods of the nations are doomed because they have failed to procure justice and have been imitated on earth by their human counterparts. A prayer follows the divine revelation: "Rise, O God; judge the earth, for yours are all the nations" (v 8; on divine care for the lowly, vv 3f, see §11c).

Psalm 82 raises the problem of Israel's and the psalmists' monotheism. What status had the gods of the nations? The answer to that question has been attempted elsewhere (§10g). In Ps 82 also any existence or function independent of Yahweh is denied them. They are even sentenced to death like ordinary mortals (v 7). In *The Old Testament against its environment,* G. Ernest Wright favors a literal interpretation of the psalm: the scene is a heavenly council, composed of the "gods of the nations" with Yahweh as the head of the assembly. Mowinckel (I, p. 150) adds that the idea of an assembly of gods belongs to the festival of new year and enthronement, when the coming year's destiny was determined. It was in such an assembly of "sons of gods" and "saints," i.e., divine beings, that Yahweh once portioned out the nations amongst the "sons of gods" whom he made governors over them (cf. Dt 32:8f; 33:2f). The *'elohim* can hardly be the human, Israelite judges, Wright thinks, in spite of Jn 10:34, nor Hasmonean kings (Duhm), nor the deified kings of the Hellenistic age (Buttenwieser). In his comprehensive and instructive study of the psalm, J. Morgenstern proposed that the *'elohim* were "fallen angels" and that the clue to the original indictment of the psalm was to be looked for in the well-known story of Gn 6:1-4. "There is no doubt, Wright declares, that his reconstruction makes excellent sense, but in reality it is tearing a short composition to pieces on tenuous evidence in order to rebuild it according to one's own notions" (p. 32, n. 39).

R. T. O'Callaghan has related to Ps 82 extracts of a Ugaritic poem. In it, when King Keret is sick, his son, *Ilhu,* queries of him: "Wilt thou die, then, Father, like mortals?" Then, when Keret has recovered, his son *Yṣb* is prompted to say to him (t. 127, 27-34; Gordon, p. 194): "Thou hast let thy hands fall into mischief, Thou dost not judge the cause of the widow nor adjudicate the case of the brokenhearted." Keret apparently neglects the welfare of his realm as a *result* of his mortal sickness, but in Ps 82 such neglect of justice is the *cause* of the sentence of mortality. O'Callaghan believes that in spite of the Ugaritic parallels it can still be maintained that the psalmist meant human judges in verses 2 and 6. A. González also rejects the determining character of the Ugaritic parallels and would set the date of the psalm's composition about Deutero-Isaiah's time.

PSALM 83 (82)

Prayer against a Hostile Alliance

1   A *song; a psalm of Asaph.*

    I

2   O God, do not remain unmoved;

Is 62:6; Ps
109:1
        be not silent, O God, and be not still!

3   For behold, your enemies raise a tumult,
        and they who hate you lift up their heads.

4   Against your people they plot craftily;

Jer 11:9; Ps
71:10
        they conspire against those whom you protect

5   They say, "Come, let us destroy their nation;
        let the name of Israel be remembered no more!"

Ps 2:2

6   Yes, they consult together with one mind,
        and against you they are allied:

7   The tents of Edom and the Ismaelites,

1 Chr 5:10;
19f
Ex 17:8
        Moab and the Agarenes,

8   Gebal and Ammon and Amalec,
        Philistia with the inhabitants of Tyre;

2 Sm 2:9

9   The Assyrians, too, are leagued with them;
        they are the forces of the sons of Lot.

    II

Jgs 7:12-25;
Is 9:3
Jgs 4-5

10 Deal with them as with Madian;
        as with Sisara and Jabin at the torrent Cison,

11 Who perished at Endor;

Jer 8:2; 25:
33
        they became dung on the ground.

12 Make their nobles like Oreb and Zeb;
        all their chiefs like Zebee and Salmana,

13 Who said, "Let us take for ourselves
        the dwelling place of God."

Is 17:13

14 O my God, make them like leaves in a whirlwind,

Is 29:5; Pss
35:5; 58:10
Ez 21:3
        like chaff before the wind.

15 As a fire raging in a forest,

Is 5:24; 10:17
        as a flame setting the mountains ablaze,

Pss 50:3;
135:7
Jer 25:32; Jb
27:21
Pss 71:13;
109:28

16 So pursue them with your tempest
        and rout them with your storm.

17 Darken their faces with disgrace,

that men may seek your name, O Lord.

18 Let them be shamed and put to rout forever;
    let them be confounded and perish,

Dt 4:39; Is 19 Knowing that you alone are the Lord,
42:8
Dn 4:22; Pss   the Most High over all the earth.
7:18; 87:5

Rather than a precise historical situation this psalmist has probably
in mind the general state of tension which naturally opposes Godfearing Israel and the surrounding Gentile nations, supported by
Assyria. From the silence on Babylon though, it may be assumed that
the psalm was composed between the ninth and the seventh centuries
(Weiser). Others believe, however, that the period of Nehemiah can
be alluded to (cf. Hen 2:19; 4:1f; 6:1). In fact Israel has rarely been
without hostile neighbors (cf. 1 Mc 5:3ff). In the first series of imprecations (vv 10-13) it is wished that the divine judgment in the cult
will bring upon the present enemies of Israel the fate which fell upon
her former enemies, during the period of the Judges (ch 4). The God
of history is also the theophany God (§13d) whose power can mobilize
nature's forces against the enemies of His Name (vv 14-19). An
ultimate result of the judgment will be, it is hoped, that men will
seek God's name and acknowledge supreme divine dominion (vv 17,
19).

In some psalms, Mowinckel suggests (II, p. 51f), the original
cursing word has been replaced by the prayer asking Yahweh to crush
the enemy (cf. §14d). "But a prayer like the one in Ps 83:10ff, with
its elaborate description of the disaster imprecated on the enemies of
the people, is evidently connected with the ancient cursing formulas,
such as seers and other 'divine men' ('îš 'elōhîm) and possessors of
the effectual word would use against the enemy before the battle; with
such words Balak expected Balaam to slay the Israelites for him" (Nm
23-24).

PSALM 85 (84)
Prayer for Complete Restoration

1 For the leader. A psalm of the sons of Core.
   I
2 You have favored, O Lord, your land;

Ps 14:7   you have restored the well-being of Jacob.

Is 40:2   3 You have forgiven the guilt of your people;

Pss 32:179:9;   you have covered all their sins.
103:3

4   You have withdrawn all your wrath;
    you have revoked your burning anger.

II

Pss 79:9; 106: 21

5   Restore us, O God our savior,
    and abandon your displeasure against us.

6   Will you be ever angry with us,

Pss 80:13f; 89:39-52

    prolonging your anger to all generations?

7   Will you not instead give us life;
    and shall not your people rejoice in you?

Is 54:7; Pss 26:3; 73:1
Is 51:5

8   Show us, O Lord, your kindness,
    and grant us your salvation.

III

9   I will hear what God proclaims;

Pss 55:19; 122:6ff
Pss 79:2; 97: 10

    the Lord — for he proclaims peace
    To his people, and to his faithful ones,
    and to those who put in him their hope.

Is 56:1

10 Near indeed is his salvation to those who fear him,

Hag 2:7; Ez 11:23
Pss 25:10; 89: 15; 115:1
Hag 2:9; Zech 9:10

    glory dwelling in our land.

11 Kindness and truth shall meet;
    justice and peace shall kiss.

12 Truth shall spring out of the earth,

Mal 3:20

    and justice shall look down from heaven.

13 The Lord himself will give his benefits;

Zech 8:12

    our land shall yield its increase.

Is 45:8; Ps 40: 10f

14 Justice shall walk before him,
    and salvation, along the way of his steps.

Some interpreters read in v 2 an explicit mention of the return from the Babylonian exile: "Thy favor, O Lord, is for thy land, you bring back *the captives* of Jacob" (*BJ*). Awkwardly following the Vulgate, the Douay version translates: "Lord, thou hast blessed thy land; *thou hast turned away the captivity of Jacob.*" In better style, Msgr. Knox writes: "What blessings, Lord, thou hast granted to this land of thine, *restoring Jacob from captivity,* pardoning thy people his guilt . . . ." The majority of present interpreters, however, understand the expression *šabtā š^ebît ya'aqōb* as referring more generally to a restoration of "the fortunes of Jacob" (*RSV,* Weiser), of "the destiny of Jacob" (Osty), or of "the well-being of Jacob" (*CV*). Msgr. Kissane translates, "Thou hast shown favour to thy land, thou hast changed the fortunes of Jacob," then explains: "This psalm is a message of hope to the returned exiles who during the early years after the return from exile were discouraged because their condition fell far short of the glorious and happy state which had been foretold by the prophets." Deutero-Isaiah, especially, had depicted the restoration almost as a return to paradise (cf. 51:3). The content of the psalm is perhaps more accurately summed up by *BJ*: after a slow and difficult start, the repatriated will enjoy a happier period (cf. Pss 14:7; 80:4; 126:1-6), the one foreseen in Deutero-Isaiah, 45:8; 51:5; 56:1; 58:8) and in Zechariah (8:12; 9:10). The first stanza of the psalm (vv 2-4) does reflect the atmosphere of the beginning of the "book of consolation" (Deutero-Isaiah):

Comfort, give comfort to my people,
   says your God.
Speak tenderly to Jerusalem, and proclaim to her
   that her service is at an end,
   her guilt is expiated;
Indeed, she has received from the hand of the Lord
   double for her sins (Is 40:1-2).

The second stanza, the complaint, is more dependent on the reflections of the prophets who lived the experiment of the Restoration (cf. §14c): "You expected much, but it came to little" (Hag 1:9). The reason given is that they were not concerned with rebuilding the temple. In the same vein Zechariah writes: "O Lord of hosts, how long will you be without mercy for Jerusalem and the cities of Juda that have felt your anger these seventy years?" (1:12)

Some authors prefer to understand the psalm in the light of the tradition of the festival cult celebrated at the autumn feast, alluded to in verse 13b: "Our land shall yield its increase." With that interpretation the psalm could be pre-exilic. Weiser reads also in the psalm an illustration of his favorite theme: the necessary tension in genuine faith between what is possessed (*habender Glaube*) and what is expected (*harrender Glaube*). After the complaint a prophet from among the community "hears what God proclaims" and interprets it (vv 9-14): salvation is near, glory will dwell (again: cf. Ez 11:23; Hag 2:9) in the land, truth will spring out of the earth, and justice shall look down from heaven. In verses 11-14 the divine attributes and social virtues are poetically personified (comp. Pss 89:15; 97:2).

Psalms 85 and 126, writes Mowinckel (I, p. 223), "can most naturally be interpreted as prayers for peace and a happy year, and most probably they belonged to the festival of harvest and new year; at any rate they have the idea of a 'turning of the destiny' in common with this festival; for this term originally indicates the 'turning' which every new year means and is expected to involve. Especially in Ps 126 it is most natural to take the mention of sowing and reaping as referring to real life, and not merely as a metaphor for 'salvation' in general, the hoped-for restoration . . . . Both psalms mentioned justify the prayer for a 'turning' by referring to a particular occasion known to everybody, on which God had turned the destinies of the people; this probably is a reference to the restoration after the Exile."

PSALM 90 (89)

God's Eternity and Man's Frailty

Dt 33:1; Jos 14:6	1	*A prayer of Moses, the man of God.*
		I
		O Lord, you have been our refuge
		through all generations.
Prv 8:25; Jb 38:8	2	Before the mountains were begotten
		and the earth and the world were brought forth,
Hb 1:12; Ps 93:2		from everlasting to everlasting you are God.
Gn 2:7; 3:19; Jb 34:15	3	You turn man back to dust,
		saying, "Return, O children of man."
	4	For a thousand years in your sight
2 Pt 3:8		are as yesterday, now that it is past,
Jgs 7:19		or as a watch of the night.
	5	You make an end of them in their sleep;
Is 40:6ff; Ps 103:15f		the next morning they are like the changing grass,
	6	Which at dawn springs up anew,
Jb 14:2		but by evening wilts and fades.
		II
Zeph 1:18; Ps 78:59	7	Truly we are consumed by your anger,
Dt 32:22; Ps 95:11		and by your wrath we are put to rout.
	8	You have kept our iniquities before you,

Os 7:2; Ps 69:
6
Dt 32:26

Eccl 6:12

Is 65:20

Sir 18:8; Ps
89:48
Jb 20:8; 103:
15f

Dt 32:29

Pss 6:4; 13:2ff

Pss 5:4; 59:
17; 130:6

Pss 89:2; 102:
19

    our hidden sins in the light of your scrutiny.

9 All our days have passed away in your indignation;
    we have spent our years like a sigh.

10 Seventy is the sum of our years,
    or eighty, if we are strong,
    And most of them are fruitless toil,
    for they pass quickly and we drift away.

11 Who knows the fury of your anger
    or your indignation toward those who should fear you?

III

12 Teach us to number our days aright,
    that we may gain wisdom of heart.

13 Return, O Lord, How long?
    have pity on your servants!

14 Fill us at daybreak with your kindness,
    that we may shout for joy and gladness all our days.

15 Make us glad, for the days when you afflicted us,
    for the years when we saw evil.

16 Let your work be seen by your servants
    and your glory by their children;

17 And may the gracious care of the Lord our God be ours;
    prosper the work of our hands for us!
    [Prosper the work of our hands!]

The psalm is ascribed to Moses by the heading, presumably because it contains material alluding to stories of Gn 1-3 and to Dt 32-33. Besides, the ascription is a precious witness of the high esteem in which tradition held the psalm. Although by its content the poem owes much to wisdom, its structure and main thoughts suggest that it is a community lament (cf. vv 12-17), not associated with any precise situation. Human life is reconsidered against the background of the eternal being of God. While God is from everlasting (v 2; cf. Ps 93:2; Hb 1:12; Prv 8:25), man has to return to dust (v 3; cf. Gn 3:19; Pss 89:48; 103:14; 104:29). Human beings disappear as grass in the Orient vanishes under the scorching sun (vv 5-6; cf. Pss 103:15f; 128:6; Is 40:6f). The brevity of human life is rightly explained by the judgment of God on sin (vv 7-11; cf. Gn 6:3, 13). In this reflection centered on the notion of time the psalmist has remarkably adapted sapiential maxims to the requisites of prayer.

Sometimes, Mowinckel notes (I, p. 91), a meditation takes a hymnal form: the introductory part of Ps 90 (vv 2-4) has become a song of praise to God's everlastingness as a background to a prayer of mercy towards short-lived man (see on *Ps 139). In fact it can be said that the description of the brevity of human life corresponds to the complaint of the lament. Yet the main point of Ps 90, Mowinckel writes, is not the hymn but "the prayer for the Eternal God not to overlook the short life of a man and let it pass away in misfortune, but to have mercy upon his congregation which consists of such short-lived people" (II, p. 75).

The insistence on the individual's personal claims precludes an early date for the psalm. Mowinckel (I, p. 221) attempts to characterize more precisely the original setting of Ps 90. "Later on, Judaism had a series of annual days of public penance and fasting in remembrance of the great disasters associated with the fall of the kingdom and the destruction of city and temple (Zech 7:5; 8:19). On these occasions they would complain of the permanent distress, of the degradation of Israel and the oppression and dishonor of gentile supremacy and ask for deliverance, revenge and re-establishment. To this category probably belong for instance Pss 90 and 137." These psalms, he adds, (I, p. 222), including also, it seems, Pss 58, 82, 106, 123, 125, are closely connected — like the later ones of new year and enthronement — with the Jewish hope of future re-establishment: "The eyes of the poet and congregation are turned towards the future, praying for the fulfillment of Israel's hope, the turning of the fate" (see on *Ps 85). The Jewish penitential prayer of the fast days had a nocturnal character. This is perhaps reflected in Ps 90:5f and elsewhere (cf. Is 26:9; Ps 77:3), when God's answer is expected in the morning (see on *Ps 5:4).

PSALM 94 (93)

A Warning to Israel's Oppressors

A

I

Na 1:2; Dt 32:35	1 God of vengeance, Lord,
Ps 80:2	God of vengeance, show yourself.
Ps 82:8	2 Rise up, judge the earth;
Lam 3:64	render their deserts to the proud.

Mal 2:17; Ps
13:2ff
Pss 6:4; 89:47

3 How long, O Lord, shall the wicked,
   how long shall the wicked glory,

1 Sm 2:3; Jer
12:1
Ps 10:3

4 Mouthing insolent speeches,
   boasting, all the evildoers?

II

5 Your people, O Lord, they trample down,

Ps 79:1

   your inheritance they afflict.

Ez 22:7

6 Widow and stranger they slay,

Is 1:17; 10:2

   the fatherless they murder,

Ez 9:9; Pss
10:11; 73:11
Jb 22:13; Pss
84:9; 132:2

7 And they say, "The Lord sees not;
   the God of Jacob perceives not."

III

8 Understand, you senseless ones among the people;

Prv 1:22; 8:5

   and you fools, when will you be wise?

Ex 4:11

9 Shall he who shaped the ear not hear?

Prv 20:12; Ps
33:13f

   or he who formed the eye not see?

10 Shall he who instructs nations not chastise,
    he who teaches men knowledge?

11 The Lord knows the thoughts of men,

1 Cor 3:20

    and that they are vain.

B

I

Pss 40:5; 128:
1
Jb 5:17; Ps
119:71

12 Happy the man whom you instruct, O Lord,
    whom by your law you teach,

13 Giving him rest from evil days,
    till the pit be dug for the wicked.

1 Sm 12:22

14 For the Lord will not cast off his people,

Sir 47:22

    nor abandon his inheritance;

15 But judgment shall again be with justice,
    and all the upright of heart shall follow it.

II

16 Who will rise up for me against the wicked?

Pss 92:10;
119:78

    Who will stand by me against the evildoers?

17 Were not the Lord my help,

Ps 115:17

    I would soon dwell in the silent grave.

Pss 27:11; 66:
9; 121:3

18 When I say, "My foot is slipping,"
    your kindness, O Lord, sustains me;

19 When cares abound within me,
    your comfort gladdens my soul.

III

20 How could the tribunal of wickedness be leagued with you,
    which creates burdens in the guise of law?
21 Though they attack the life of the just

Gn 9:4; Is 59:
7; Mt 12:7
Pss 48:4; 144:
2
1 Sm 2:2; Dt
32:31
Ps 95:1
    and condemn innocent blood,
22 Yet the Lord is my stronghold,
    and my God the Rock of my refuge.
23 And he will requite them for their evildoing,
    and for their wickedness he will destroy them;

Ps 101:8
    the Lord, our God, will destroy them.

There is a mixture of various literary elements in this psalm. The first part (1-11) is a prayer imploring the "God of vengeance" (*'el neqāmôt*) to pronounce judgment on the evildoers, and not to let the faith of the just be strained beyond limits. The second part (16-23) is a hymn of praise and thanksgiving, joined to the first part by a transition stanza (vv 12-15). Wisdom thought and expression is especially noticeable in the middle part of the poem (vv 8-15). Yet by content and style (cf. vv 5, 14) the psalm is mainly a national lament. With reference to *Ps 44 we have seen that Mowinckel (I, p. 219) links up Ps 94 in the series of I-psalms which also belong to the national psalms of lamentation. The psalmist, most likely the king, represents the congregation on the day of penance.

Verse 20 is notoriously difficult. A. Allgeier published in 1950 on the verse an article which is a history of its exegesis. It is in fact instructive to note how differently the verse could be rendered by scholars. Moreover there seems to be a deep theological thought involved, to be elucidated. In the following shorter review of mainly modern authors the Douay and *CV* versions represent respectively the Vulgate and the New Latin Psalter: (1) Douay, (2) *CV*, (3) *RSV*, (4) Briggs, (5) R. A. Knox, (6) Kissane, (7) Weiser, (8) Kirkpatrick, (9) Crampon, new edit., (10) *JB*, (11) *Bible de la Pléiade*, (12) Osty, (13) H.-J. Kraus.

(1) Doth the seat of iniquity stick to thee,
     who framest labour in commandment?
(2) How could the tribunal of wickedness be leagued with you,
     which creates burdens in the guise of law?

(3) Can wicked rulers be allied with thee,
Who frame mischief by statute?

(4) Can the throne of engulfing ruin be allied to thee,
Which frameth trouble by statute?

(5) What part have these unjust judges with thee?
Thy punishments are for the breakers of thy law.

(6) Will He ally with thee, O throne of iniquity,
That devisest trouble by statute?

(7) Can the throne of destruction be allied with thee,
Which frames mischief on the basis of statutes?

(8) Shall the throne of iniquity have fellowship with thee,
Which frameth mischief by a law?

(9) Est-il donc ton allié, le tribunal d'iniquité,
qui crée l'affliction sous couvert de la loi?

(10) You never consent to that corrupt tribunal
that imposes disorder as law . . .

(11) Aurais-tu pour allié un tribunal criminel,
inventeur de peines contraires aux lois?

(12) Te ferais-tu l'allié d'un tribunal inique,
pratiquant la violence à l'abri de la loi?

(13) Hat der Thronsitz des Verderbens Gemeinschaft mit dir,
der Unheil schafft gegen die Satzung?

All these translations, except the first and (?) last, refer to the wicked tribunal or throne, the verb *yōsēr,* "creates," "frames" (Latin: "fingere"). A typical comment is given by Kissane: "This verse takes up the thought of 16. Is God to make Himself accomplice of the wicked by condoning his crimes?" Much in the same line of thought, Kirkpatrick had written: "Though He may tolerate them for a time, it is inconceivable that Jehovah should let these rapacious judges shelter themselves under his authority." On the contrary, Allgeier would, with the Vulgate, consider "God" as governing the participle *yōsēr* and translate verse 20b: "der du bildest Leid auf Grund eines Gesetzes." The verse, he comments (p. 28), touches a basic problem of theodicy (also discussed in Job): suffering is not contrary to faith in God. The fundamental motivation, however, of divine ordinations is ultimately beyond man's understanding. The expression *ḥōq yhwh* can mean a *Grundgesetz* which sets a divine pattern of conduct. Thus in Ps 2:7:

"I will point out to you a *ḥōq yhwh.*" So perhaps could the following translation of Ps 94:20 express the psalmist's idea:

> Can the tribunal of iniquity be leagued with you,
> who establishes suffering on the basis of a law?

PSALM 106 (105)

Israel's Confession of Sin

1 Alleluia

A

Give thanks to the Lord for he is good,
> for his kindness endures forever.

2 Who can tell the mighty deeds of the Lord,
> or proclaim all his praises?

3 Happy are they who observe what is right,
> who do always what is just.

4 Remember me, O Lord, as you favor your people;
> visit me with your saving help,

5 That I may see the prosperity of your chosen ones,
> rejoice in the joy of your people,
> and glory with your inheritance.

B

I

6 We have sinned, we and our fathers;
> we have committed crimes; we have done wrong.

7 Our fathers in Egypt
> considered not your wonders;
> They remembered not your abundant kindness,
> but rebelled against the Most High at the Red Sea.

8 Yet he saved them for his name's sake,
> to make known his power.

9 He rebuked the Red Sea, and it was dried up,
> and he led them through the deep as through a desert.

10 He saved them from hostile hands
> and freed them from the hands of the enemy.

11 The waters covered their foes;

Marginal references:
Jer 33:11; Ps 107:1
Pss 98:1; 107:8
Ps 1:2
Is 56:2
Neh 5:19, 31
Is 65:9; Ps 105:11
Ps 95:8ff
Lv 26:40; 1 Kgs 8:47
Dn 9:5
Ex 14:11ff; Nm 14:11
Ez 20:14; 36:21f
Pss 78:13; 114:3
Na 1:4; Ex 14:21-31
Is 50:2; 63:13
Pss 55:19; 107:2

not one of them was left.

12 Then they believed his words

Ex 15.1ff   and sang his praises.

II

13 But soon they forgot his works;

Nm 11:4ff,
31ff   they waited not for his counsel.

14 They gave way to craving in the desert

Ex 15:24; Ps
95:9   and tempted God in the wilderness.

Pss 105:39f;
107:4ff
Nm 11:33 15 He gave them what they asked

but sent a wasting disease against them.

III

16 They envied Moses in the camp,

Nm 16:1-35   and Aaron, the holy one of the Lord.

17 The earth opened and swallowed up Dathan,

Dt 11:6   and covered the faction of Abiram.

18 Fire broke out against their faction;

Is 26:11   a flame consumed the wicked.

Ex 32:1-29;
Dt 9:8-29
Acts 7:41 19 They made a calf in Horeb

and adored a molten image;

Jer 2:11 20 They exchanged their glory

for the image of a grass-eating bullock.

Jer 2:32; Ps
88:2 21 They forgot the God who had saved them,

who had done great deeds in Egypt,

Ps 72:18 22 Wondrous deeds in the land of Ham,

terrible things at the Red Sea.

23 Then he spoke of exterminating them,

but Moses, his chosen one,

Withstood him in the breach

Ez 22:30; Dt
9:25   to turn back his destructive wrath.

V

Nm 14:1-19;
Jer 3:19
Ez 20:6 24 Yet they despised the desirable land;

they believed not his word.

Dt 1:27 25 They murmured in their tents,

Ps 89:31f   and obeyed not the voice of the Lord.

26 Then with raised hand he swore against them

Nm 14.32; 1
Cor 10:5
Lv 26:33   to let them perish in the desert,

27 To scatter their descendants among the nations,

Ez 20:23; 36:
19   and to disperse them over the lands.

VI

Nm 25:1-15   28 And they submitted to the rites of Beelphegor
Dt 26:14; Is 8:19   and ate the sacrifices of dead gods.
Nm 14:11   29 They provoked him by their deeds,
                   and a plague attacked them.
Sir 45:23   30 Then Phinees stood forth in judgment
                   and the plague was checked;
              31 And it was imputed to him for merit
                   through all generations forever.

VII

Ps 89:47   32 They angered him at the waters of Meriba,
Nm 20:12; Dt 1:37; 4:21   and Moses fared ill on their account,
              33 For they embittered his spirit,
                   and the rash utterance passed his lips.

VIII

Jgs 1:21, 27-35   34 They did not exterminate the peoples,
Dt 7:2   as the Lord had commanded them,
Lv 18:3   35 But mingled with the nations
                   and learned their works.
Jgs 2:12-19; Ez 20:8   36 They served their idols,
                   which became a snare for them.
2 Kgs 16:3   37 They sacrificed their sons
Dt 32:17; Bar 4:7   and their daughters to demons,
1 Cor 10:20   38 And they shed innocent blood,
Ez 16:20   the blood of their sons and their daughters,
Lv 17:7; Pss 97:7; 115:4ff   Whom they sacrificed to the idols of Chanaan,
Nm 35:33; Jer 7:31; 19:4f   desecrating the land with bloodshed;
              39 They became defiled by their works,
Ex 34:16; Jer 3:6f   and wanton in their crimes.

C

              40 And the Lord grew angry with his people,
                   and abhorred his inheritance;
Jgs 2:14-23   41 He gave them over into the hands of the nations,
                   and their foes ruled over them.
              42 Their enemies oppressed them,
                   and they were humbled under their power.
Is 63:9   43 Many times did he rescue them,
                   but they embittered him with their counsels

and were brought low by their guilt.

2 Kgs 14:26;
Is 63:9
Acts 7:34

44 Yet he had regard for their affliction
when he heard their cry;

Lv 26:42; Ps
105:8
Ps 111:5

45 And for their sake he was mindful of his covenant
and relented, in his abundant kindness,

46 And he won for them compassion

Ezr 9:9

from all who held them captive.

47 Save us, O Lord, our God,
and gather us from among the nations,
That we may give thanks to your holy name

1 Chr 16:35f

and glory in praising you.

* * *

48 Blessed be the Lord, the God of Israel, through all eternity!

Pss 41:14; 89:
53

Let all the people say, Amen! Alleluia.

Although this psalm has much in common with the history Pss 78 and 105, "its basic mood is to be compared rather with a national penitential lament." Weiser notes also that according to the *Community Rule* the renewal of the Covenant at Qumran included the following ceremonies:

1. The praise of God in a hymn sung by the priest and Levites and the congregation's response, "Amen. Amen."
2. The recital by the priests of the divine saving deeds ($\d{s}id^eq\hat{o}t$ '$\bar{e}l$).
3. The recital by the Levites of the "sins of the Israelites."
4. The confession of sins of those who "enter into the Covenant," made in recognition of God's righteousness and mercy (cf. M. Burrows, *The Dead Sea Scrolls* II, pl. I, 18-II, 1).

In that context Ps 105 could be compared to the *Heilsgeschichte* recital, while Ps 106 would represent the Levitical recital of the sins. *BJ* sees in the first three couplets (vv 1-5) and the last (v 48) a liturgical frame. The enclosed "historical psalm," it adds, belongs to the literary category of national confessions: cf. 1 Kgs 8:33f; Is 63:7 to 64:11; Neh 9:5-37; Dn 9; Bar 1:15 to 3:8. Mowinckel, on the other hand (II, p. 111f), describes Ps 106 as an "historical penitential psalm" and lists it as one of the non-cultic poems (cf. §8a). Ps 106 and Ps 1 deal with a favorite subject of "learned psalmography": Instruction about the destinies of good and evil people. D. G. Castellino, who holds that Pss 58, 77, 82 are community laments, classifies Ps 106 in the category he calls *liturgia della fedeltà jahvistica: Pss* 78, 81, 95, 105, 106.

To compare the historical account of Ps 106 with the extant biblical narratives makes interesting study in the longer commentaries. Independent treatment of the same matter usually responds to a theological intent. Thus, as Weiser remarks, the tradition of the Exodus (vv 6-23) "is considered from the point of view of the unbelief of the people who negligently pass by the wonderful works of God and rebel against his will." Verse 47a reads: "Save us, O Lord, our God, and gather us from among the nations." "This statement," notes Kirkpatrick (introduction to Ps 105), "which at first sight might seem to imply that no return had yet taken place, must be understood as a prayer for the completion of the restoration by the return of the Israelites from all the countries in which they were scattered" (see on *Ps 105). Verse 48 is a doxology seemingly added later to end the Fourth Book of the Psalter. It recurs in 1 Chr 16:36 (see also on *Ps 96).

PSALM 108 (107)

Prayer for Victory

1 *A song; a psalm of David.*

I

Ps 57:8-12

2 My heart is steadfast, O God; my heart is steadfast;
  I will sing and chant praise.

3 Awake, O my soul; awake, lyre and harp;
  I will wake the dawn.

4 I will give thanks to you among the peoples, O Lord;
  I will chant your praise among the nations,

Pss 36:6; 103:11

5 For your kindness towers to the heavens,
  and your faithfulness to the skies.

6 Be exalted above the heavens, O God;

Pss 96:3; 113:4
Ps 60:7-14

  over all the earth be your glory!

7 That your loved ones may escape,
  help us by your right hand, and answer us.

II

Ps 60:8ff

8 God promised in his sanctuary:

"Exultantly I will apportion Sichem,
and measure off the valley of Succhoth;
9 Mine is Galaad, and mine Manasse,
Ephraim is the helmet for my head; Juda, my scepter;
10 Moab shall serve as my washbowl;

Dt 25:9; Ru 4: 7f

upon Edom I will set my shoe;
I will triumph over Philistia."

Ob 14; Ps 60: 11
Ps 125:1

11 Who will bring me into the fortified city?
Who will lead me into Edom?
12 Have not you, O God, rejected us,

Nm 14:14; Pss 44:10; 68:8

So that you go not forth, O God, with our armies?
13 Give us aid against the foe,
for worthless is the help of men.
14 Under God we shall do valiantly

Ps 44:6

it is he who will tread down our foes.

At a period which is not anterior to the formation of the Elohistic collection (cf. §3b) an "editor" has combined for liturgical purposes Ps 57:8-12 and Ps 60:7-14 into one psalm, our Ps 108. The first part (vv 2-7) is a thanksgiving, hymnic in form, which in *Ps 57 indicated that this lament had been written after the granting of the petition. The second part (vv 9-14) is an oracle of consolation introduced in the national lament (*Ps 60) explained above. Pss 12, 60 and 108 contain various elements typical of cultic liturgies (see *Ps 12).

PSALM 123 (122)

Israel's Prayer in Persecution

1 *A song of ascents.*

I

To you I lift up my eyes
who are enthroned in heaven.
2 Behold, as the eyes of servants

Pss 25:15; 69: 4

are on the hands of their masters,
As the eyes of a maid
are on the hands of her mistress,

So are our eyes on the Lord, our God,
    till he have pity on us.

II

3 Have pity on us, O Lord, have pity on us,
    for we are more than sated with contempt;
4 Our souls are more than sated
    with the mockery of the arrogant,
    with the contempt of the proud.

Neh 3:36

Pss 44:14f;
109:25
Jb 12:5

This short unpretentious yet moving poem, one of the "songs of ascents" (§3c), was recited by a genuinely pious and sincere man, in the name of the community. In it he stresses how dependent of God, enthroned in heaven, is the company of the just, constantly in need, and satiated with humiliation. His interpretation of the right attitude of man towards God correctly combines reverential awe, which prevents undue familiarity, and trusting love, which is proper to sons and not to slaves. As expression of a humble feeling of dependence, Ps 123 can be compared to Ps 131. According to *JB* the psalm was "probably composed shortly after the return from exile or in the time of Nehemiah; the restored community was exposed to the contempt and hostility of surrounding pagans (cf. Neh 2:19; 3:36)."

PSALM 126 (125)

The People's Prayer for Full Restoration

1 *A song of ascents.*

I

When the Lord brought back the captives of Zion,
    we were like men dreaming.
2 Then our mouth was filled with laughter,
    and our tongue with rejoicing.
Then they said among the nations,
    "The Lord has done great things for them."
3 The Lord has done great things for us;
    we are glad indeed.

II

4 Restore our fortunes, O Lord,

Pss 14:7; 85:2

Jb 8:21; Ps
107:42

Lk 1:49

Is 25:8f; Ez
36:35f

Ps 85:5

like the torrents in the southern desert.

5 Those that sow in tears

Jn 16:20   shall reap rejoicing.

Jer 31:9   6 Although they go forth weeping,

carrying the seed to be sown,

They shall come back rejoicing,

Bar 4:23; Rev   carrying their sheaves.
21:4

This "pilgrim song" seems to reflect a situation similar to the one proposed for *Ps 85: the material and social conditions the poet witnesses fulfill very incompletely the splendid restoration promised by the prophets (cf. Ps 59:9-11). With the *šibat* of verse 1 recurs the translator's problems: should we read "When the Lord brought back the captives of Sion . . ." (*CV,* Kissane, *BJ,* Osty, New Latin Psalter) or with Briggs, "When Yahweh restores the prosperity of Zion, we are like dreamers"? (also A. Weiser) According to Kraus also, we should read "Als Yahwe wandte Zions Geschick" ("When the Lord changed the fate of Sion") because, he says, *šibat* is obviously a scribal error. Ps 85:5 and Ps 126:4, he thinks, recommend reading either *šebut* (Ketib) or *šebit* (*Qere*). Yet *šibat* may well be retained, as it is attested in an eighth century B.C. Aramaic suzerainty treaty from Syria (cf. *CBQ* 1958, pp. 449ff: verse 24 of the Beirut *Sfire* inscription; cf. J. A. Fitzmyer, p. 119f). Why not translate: "When the Lord brought about the return to Zion we were like dreamers." And in verse 4 the meaning is quite certainly: Let the return of the "returnees" be like rushing streams in the Negeb. J. Morgenstern reads: "Restore our fortune, O God, even as the water-courses in the Negeb!" J. Strugnell, making explicit what is implicit in Hebrew, translates verse 1b: "Then were we as men who had been (were) healed" and refers to Jb 39:4; Is 38: 16; Hos 6:11 to 7:1.

"Those that sow in tears shall reap rejoicing" (v 5) was probably a proverbial saying, which Jesus, according to the fourth Gospel, expressed otherwise: "Unless the grain of wheat fall into the ground and die, it remains alone. But, if it die, it brings forth much fruit" (12:24). In Ps 126:5, writes Mowinckel (I, p. 147), "we have a reference to the crops of the coming year, which are to be safeguarded by the harvest feast. But the thought goes further. The turning of destiny involves all conceivable happiness, in a moral as well as a material sense." The idea that rejoicing follows weeping (vv 5-6) finds expression also in the Fourth Gospel: "You shall weep and lament, but the world shall rejoice; and you shall be sorrowful; but your sorrows shall be turned into joy" (16:20).

PSALM 137 (136)

The Exile's Remembrance of Sion

I

Ez 3:15

1 By the streams of Babylon
   we sat and wept
   when we remembered Sion.

2 On the aspens of that land

Is 24:8
   we hung up our harps,

3 Though there our captors asked of us
   the lyrics of our songs,
   And our despoilers urged us to be joyous:
   "Sing for us the songs of Sion!"

II

4 How could we sing a song of the Lord
   in a foreign land?

Jer 51:50

5 If I forget you, Jerusalem,
   may my right hand be forgotten!

6 May my tongue cleave to my palate
   if I remember you not,
   If I place not Jerusalem

Ps 122:1
   ahead of my joy.

III

Is 34:5-15; Ob
2ff
Ez 25:12ff;
Lam 4:21f
Ps 79:12

7 Remember, O Lord, against the children of Edom,
   the day of Jerusalem,
   When they said, "Raze it, raze it
   down to its foundations!"

Is 47:1ff; Jer
50-51

8 O daughter of Babylon, you destroyer,
   happy the man who shall repay you
   the evil you have done us!

Is 14:21; Hos
14:1
2 Kgs 8:12;
Lk 19:44

9 Happy the man who shall seize and smash
   your little ones against the rock!

The psalmist, a repatriated exile, recalls some features of the sad experiences of the Israelite captives in Babylonia. Ezechiel also had been with "the exiles who lived at Tel Abib by the river Chobar" and for seven days, he writes, "I sat among them distraught" (3:15). Their harps were idle, hung on the aspens. How could they sing in a foreign land the praises of God, who seemingly had abandoned them; how could they desecrate the holy hymns and their own souls by entertaining a pagan and mocking audience? A. Guillaume even feels quite certain that by *tôlelîm* (*CV*, "captors") in verse 3 "harsh, pitiless slave-drivers" are meant. The hated Edomites (cf. Is 34:5-15; Jr 49:7-22; Ez 25:12ff) were allied with the Babylonians to bring about the "day of Jerusalem" (v 7), the catastrophe of 587-6 (cf. Lam 4:21f; Am 1:11f; Ob 2-9). They even seized that opportunity for settling in southern Judah.

The poet feels Babylon did not get the right treatment when spared by Cyrus. He lets himself be dominated by "his mounting rage" and "plunges into the abyss of human passion" (Weiser). Isaiah also, prophesying against Babylon proclaimed: "The bows of the young men shall be smashed, their infants dashed to pieces before their eyes" (3:15f; cf. Jer 14:1). The prayer, Mowinckel observes (II, p. 52), passes into a direct curse in a particularly refined form (in v 9), namely as a word of blessing on the person who shall inflict the most cruel revenge against the hated enemy. Yet "the little ones" of verse 9 could also mean the adults (cf. Lam 1:5); all the Babylonians being the "children" of the personified "daughter of Babylon" (cf. Ps 87:4f; Lk 19:44). The imprecation is directed against the future generation of enemies of God and of Israel. Among the calamities mentioned in the "admonitions of Ipu-wer" (see on *Ps 23) the following is mentioned: "Why really, the children of nobles are dashed against the walls. The (once) prayed-for children are (now) laid out on the high ground . . ." (*ANET*, p. 442). So the fate of the little ones seems to have been used elsewhere also as one among conventional lament motifs. In Jeremiah's letter to the exiles God urged them to settle normally in Babylon and "promote the welfare of the city (LXX: 'country') to which I have exiled you; pray for it to the Lord, for upon its welfare depends your own" (Jer 29:7). Yet in another context the same Jeremiah described the coming "vengeance of the Lord" against Babylon (51:1-64). But this was a prophecy, not a wish!

According to J. Enciso, the psalms without heading were incorporated later in the Psalter, when the use of "titles" had ceased.
For five of these, Pss 1, 2, 104, 119, 137, the subject-matter pointed
to their choice as introductory compositions to the respective collections they prelude to. In the third collection of David (137-145)
the main theme would be prayers for help against the enemies, among
whom Edom and Babylon occupied the first rank. Mowinckel (II, p.
130) also believes that "the psalm is considerably later than the
'return.'" The poet, he writes, was not among those carried away.
This composer of psalms in Zion sees himself as a wandering harp-
player. "Through his conventionalized, not realistic image, the poet
has given an incomparably touching expression to the elegiac sentiment
which grips him when he pictures to himself the emotions and situation
of those who were forcibly evacuated to the land of the enemy." In this
psalm as in many others traditionalism and personality merge success-
fully.

§24. PSALMS OF CONFIDENCE OF THE COMMUNITY

(a) *General character*

Even in the private psalms the confidence motif has generally
a collective bearing since the suppliant prays as a member of the covenant and the favor expected is for the benefit of the community (cf.
§22a, 2). Biblical confidence relies on God alone (Is 30:15), any
other support being excluded (cf. Is 31:1; Ps 40:5). This firm trust
in the Lord is expressed both in urgent need and in the normal situa-
tions of human life. The three collective psalms of confidence follow
much the same pattern as the corresponding private poems. Psalm 46
is added by some to this category while Ps 115 is listed by others with
the hymns. There are good reasons to maintain our classification. The
key ideas of the three psalms include: the invitation to set fully one's
trust in God (115:9ff; 125:1), rock of security (125:1f), source of
blessing (115:15; 129:8) and peace (125:5).

(b) The psalms of confidence of the community are: (115), 125,
    (129).

PSALM 115 (113B)

The Greatness and Goodness of the True God

I

1 Not to us, O Lord, not to us

Ez 36:22f; Ps 113:4

Pss 23:3; 25:10
     but to your name give glory
     because of your kindness, because of your truth.

2 Why should the pagans say,

Mal 2:17; Jl 2:17

Pss 53:2; 79:10
     "Where is their God?"

Ps 135:6
3 Our God is in heaven;
     whatever he wills, he does.

II

Jer 10:3; Ps 135:15ff
4 Their idols are silver and gold,
     the handiwork of men.

Bar 6:7ff
5 They have mouths but speak not;
     they have eyes but see not;

6 They have ears but hear not;
     they have noses but smell not;

7 They have hands but feel not;
     they have feet but walk not;
     they utter no sound from their throat.

Is 44:9f
8 Their makers shall be like them,
     everyone that trusts in them.

III

Pss 55:24; 131:1ff

Pss 33:20; 40:18
9 The house of Israel trusts in the Lord;
     he is their help and their shield.

Ps 118:2ff
10 The house of Aaron trusts in the Lord;
     he is their help and their shield.

Mal 3:16; Acts 10:2

Eccl 8:12; Ps 15:4
11 Those who fear the Lord trust in the Lord;
     he is their help and their shield.

Pss 3:9; 67:2; 128:5
12 The Lord remembers us and will bless us:
     he will bless the house of Israel;
     he will bless the house of Aaron;

13 He will bless those who fear the Lord,
     both the small and the great.

14 May the Lord bless you more and more

Dt 1:11   both you and your children.
                 15 May you be blessed by the Lord,
Pss 104:2;   who made heaven and earth.
121:2
                 16 Heaven is the heaven of the Lord,
                        but the earth he has given to the children of men.
Pss 6:6; 88:   17 It is not the dead who praise the Lord,
11f
Is 38:18; Sir   nor those who go down into silence;
17:23
Pss 94:17;   18 But we bless the Lord,
113:2
Ps 134:1   both now and forever.

The central idea of this psalm is found in vv 9-11, where the three classes of Israel, the laity of Israelite birth, the priests and "those who fear the Lord" express their confidence in God. This sort of litany, the benediction which follows (vv 12-15) and the hymn (16-18) featured, it seems, in a liturgy glorifying the name of God (vv 1-3). While the true "God is in heaven" (v 3), distinct from and infinitely above mankind, the idols are earthly and dependent on their human makers. Traditional formulas describe the powerlessness of the images of the gods (vv 4-8; cf. Ps 95:5; Dt 4:28; 1 Sm 12:21; Hb 2:18ff; Jer 10:3ff; 16: 19f; Is 40:19f; 44:9f). Such descriptions presumably drew their stylized forms from their use in covenant liturgies which included the renunciation of the foreign gods (cf. Gn 35:2; Jos 24:14-25). Decisive against the gods is the fact that they are not alive. On earth human activity's highest living expression is the praise of God. Where this is impossible, as in Sheol, life is at its minimum (cf. §14d).

Mowinckel describes Ps 115 as a "liturgy for a day of penance" (II, p. 50) and believes it is also "marked by the spirit of *early Judaism* and its whole conception of God after the full victory of monotheistic thought" (I, p. 98). In these "younger psalms" (also Pss 135:15-18; 96:6; 97:7), he adds, it is not the struggle against Canaanite influences which we face; it is the spirit of self-conscious "Judaism," feeling its superiority over the stupid polytheism of the surrounding "idolaters." Yet there is no compelling reason to classify the psalm as recent. "Judaism" began with Ezra and even in pre-exilic times there were "proselytes" (cf. Ex 18:9-12; 1 Kgs 8:41ff; 2 Kgs 5:17). Furthermore it is not certain that "those who fear the Lord" (v 11; cf. Pss 118:4; 135:20) are proselytes. The expression can designate the whole community of the just (cf. Pss 61:6; 103:17), although in New Testament times it did refer to those who sympathized with Judaism without accepting circumcision (cf. Acts 10:2; 22, 35; 13: 16, 26). In the Greek and Latin versions Ps 115 is joined to Ps 114 to form one psalm (113), but originally they were probably distinct (see on *Ps 114).

PSALM 125 (124)

The Lord the Protector of Israel

1 *A song of ascents.*

I

Is 24:23; 25:7   They who trust in the Lord are like Mount Zion,

Is 28:16; Ps 108:11   which is immovable; which forever stands.

Ps 112:6   2 Mountains are round about Jerusalem;

Pss 92:9; 135:13   so the Lord is round about his people,

Dt 32:10; Mt 28:20   both now and forever.

II

3 For the scepter of the wicked shall not remain

Is 57:13; 60:21; 65:9   upon the territory of the just,

     Lest the just put forth

Ps 119:134   to wickedness their hands.

III

4 Do good, O Lord, to the good

Ps 18:26   and to the upright of heart.

5 But such as turn aside to crooked ways

     may the Lord lead away with the evildoers!

Ps 122:6ff; Gal 6:16   Peace be upon Israel!

Those who put their trust in God are immovable like Mount Zion, which was believed to be deeply rooted in the center of the earth (see on *Ps 46 and *Ps 48). The faith of the just is exposed to great temptations if "the sceptre of the wicked," foreign domination probably, remains too long upon the territory of the just (v 3; cf. §12b), Yahweh's holy inheritance (cf. *Ps 142:6). So a prayer for faith preservation is formulated (v 4). The call on the judgment of God to isolate the just from the wicked (vv 3, 5) and the allusions to the danger of apostasy seem to reflect an eschatological thought pattern already preluding to apocalyptic developments.

PSALM 129 (128)

Prayer for the Overthrow of Israel's Foes

1 *A song of ascents.*

I

Much have they oppressed me from my youth,
    let Israel say,

Ps 124:2f

2 Much have they oppressed me from my youth;
    yet they have not prevailed against me.

Is 51:28

3 Upon my back the plowers plowed;
    long did they make their furrows.

4 But the just Lord severed
    the cords of the wicked.

II

5 May all be put to shame and fall back
    that hate Zion.

Is 37:27

6 May they be like grass on the housetops,

Is 40:6ff; Ps
129:5f

    which withers before it is plucked;

7 With which the reaper fills not his hand,
    nor the gatherer of sheaves his arms;

8 And those that pass by say not,

Ru 2:4; Ps
118:26

    "The blessing of the Lord be upon you!

Pss 67:8;
134:3

    We bless you in the name of the Lord!"

This psalm also includes elements of a community lament (cf. vv 5-7), but the expression of confidence predominates: as in the past, Israel will survive (vv 1-3) and its enemies will be confounded (vv 5-8), under the just judgment of God (v 4). Weiser describes the psalm as a liturgical formulary of the Israelite covenant community (cf. §13c). Those "that hate sin" (v 5) could be, he thinks, Israelites of the Northern Kingdom, opposed to the Jerusalem cult. Cultic imprecations, recalled in verses 5-8, were employed against them. According to Mowinckel (I, p. 45), on the other hand, Ps 129 illustrates well that use of the I-psalms in which the singer represents the "corporate, greater I" of the congregation. The usage would be "normal, ancient, Israelite cultic style." Yet, according to E. Balla (p. 114), Ps 129 is, of all the *Ichpsalmen* of the Psalter, the only example in which the people are poetically personified (cf. §23a).

§25. THANKSGIVINGS OF THE COMMUNITY

(a) *General character*

These psalms praise God and thank him for his general favors. They celebrate his saving intervention on behalf of Israel or of the just, mainly the poor and the weak. Hymnic elements do appear in some of these psalms (see §23a). According to G. Pidoux the hymns celebrate Yahweh's interventions in Israel's early history, while the collective thanksgivings are concerned rather with recent deeds of deliverance (*Du Portique à l'Autel,* p. 65). Postexilic eschatological prophecy will also express itself in a type of national thanksgiving (cf. Is 26:7-19; Zech 9:9-17).

It is likely that thanksgiving festivals constituted the original setting of the private and national thanksgiving psalms. Features of these liturgical ceremonies have been preserved, mainly in the thanksgiving psalms of the community. He who wishes to express his gratitude comes to the temple with a victim (66:13ff). Having been greeted by the worshippers present (32:1f), he announces his intention to praise God, "to declare all his wondrous deeds" (9:2), since his personal experience testifies to the merciful ways of divine Providence (30:6; 34:17-23).

The votive offering of a sacrifice (cf. Pss 65:2; 116:18) often accompanies the prayer of the thanksgiving: "I will bring holocausts to your house; to you I fulfill the vow which my lips uttered and my words promised in my distress" (66:13f; cf. 22:26; 76:12). Possibly some psalms were composed precisely to accompany the *tôdâh,* the thanksgiving sacrifice (cf. the heading of Ps 100), mentioned in various texts: Am 4:5; Jer 17:26; 33:11; Jon 2:10; Lv 7:12; 22:29. The same word *tôdâh* means in other texts "praise" (Jer 30:19; Is 51:3; Ps 26:7) of gratitude (Jos 7:19; Ezr 10:11; cf. *Ps 27:6). In Ps 50:14 instead of "Offer to God praise as your sacrifice" it is suggested to read "Offer to God a thanksgiving sacrifice" (cf. Pss 50:23; 107:22; 116:17). God does not condemn the offering of sacrifices (Ps 50:8-13), but the qualified value of animal sacrifice (see on *Ps 51:18) is sometimes recalled. As Aben Esra puts it: "The sacrifices are not useful to God, but to man" (see R. Pautrel, "Immola Deo . . .", p. 239; E. Podechard, *Le Psautier,* I, p. 226f; H.-J. Kraus, *Psalmen,* p. 309f; S. Mowinckel, II, p. 90f).

Other elements of sacrificial rites are attested in the psalms (cf. §8b). In a lament the suppliant declares: "I wash my hands in innocence, and I go around your altar, O Lord, giving voice to my thanks, and recounting all your wondrous deeds" (26:6f). Processions around the altar could be an ancient rite of semitic religions. The "prophets of Baal," in Elijah's time, "limped about the altar which they had made" (1 Kgs 18:26). The association of "innocence" with the altar reminds one of the purifying oath (*Reinigungseid*) described in 1 Kgs 8:31f. In the second part of Ps 22 the thanksgiver says: "So by your gift will I utter praise in the vast assembly; I will fulfill my vows before those who fear him. The lowly shall eat their fill" (v 26f). It is probable that this thanksgiving (vv 23-32) was uttered during a ritual meal offered to the "poor" (cf. §12a), among whom the psalmist willingly counted himself (v 25). Some authors read in Ps 22:27 an allusion to the messianic banquet (Is 25:6; 55:1; 65:13; Prv 9:1f; Ps 23:5) rather than to a ritual meal associated with the communion sacrifice (Lv 7: 15; Dt 14:29; 16:13). Ps 118 contains instructive indications concerning the thanksgiving liturgy: entry into the temple (vv 19f), exclamation of the worshippers (vv 22-26), procession (v 27), thanksgiving proper, (5-18), and a responsory of a choir or of the congregation (vv 1-4 and 29). The main section includes a description of the distress (5-7; 10-13), particular (14-18) and general (8-9) deductions and finally the repetition of the psalmist's intention (28). As for the structure of these collective psalms it follows the same pattern as the similar psalms of the individual.

(b) These are the thanksgivings of the community: Pss (65), (66), 67, (68), (118), 124.

PSALM 65 (64)

Thankgsivings for God's Blessings

1   *For the leader. A psalm of David. A song.*

I

2   To you we owe our hymn of praise,
O God, in Sion;

Pss 61:6, 9;
66:13f

To you must vows be fulfilled,
you who hear prayers.

Is 66:20f	3	To you all flesh must come
	4	because of wicked deeds.
		We are overcome by our sins;
Pss 51:3ff; 79:9		it is you who pardon them.
	5	Happy the man you choose, and bring
		to dwell in your courts.
Pss 22:27; 63:6; 78:19		May we be filled with the good things of your house,
		the holy things of your temple!

II

Pss 40:6; 66:3f	6	With awe-inspiring deeds of justice you answer us,
Pss 62:2; 79:9		O God our savior,
Is 66:19		The hope of all the ends of the earth
		and of the distant seas.
Jb 38:7	7	You set the mountains in place by your power,
		you who are girt with might;
Pss 32:7; 93:3f; Mt 8:26 Is 17:12; Ps 2:1	8	You still the roaring of the seas,
		the roaring of their waves and the tumult of the peoples.
Is 66:18f	9	And the dwellers at the earth's ends are in fear at your marvels;
Pss 19:5; 63:4		the farthest east and west you make resound with joy.

III

Ps 104:10-30	10	You have visited the land and watered it;
		greatly have you enriched it.
Is 30:25; Jb 38:25		God's watercourses are filled;
		you have prepared the grain.
	11	Thus have you prepared the land: drenching its furrows,
Am 9:13		breaking up its clods,
		Softening it with showers,
		blessing its yield.
	12	You have crowned the year with your bounty,
Jl 4:13		and your paths overflow with a rich harvest;
	13	The untilled meadows overflow with it,
		and rejoicing clothes the hills.
	14	The fields are garmented with flocks
		and the valleys blanketed with grain.
Is 44:23; Jl 2:22f		They shout and sing for joy.

The statement in verse 2, "To you must vows be fulfilled, you who hear prayers," seems to imply that this community thanksgiving takes place after God had answered prayers for rain in a time of drought. The psalm could also have been sung at the harvest festival which, it is said, coincided with the New Year festival celebrated in the spring since the reign of Josiah. This "thanksgiving psalm of the harvest feast," writes Mowinckel (I, p. 162f), is also one of the enthronement psalms (cf. §13a). Verses 6-9 celebrate the victory of God over the primordial ocean. "The dwellers at the earth's ends" are not remote nations but the "demonic powers of the *tᵉhōm* around the earth," "the helpers of Rahab" (Jb 9:3), conquered at the moment of creation (cf. §9b, 11a). The regular return of the rainy season (vv 10-14) was an annual blessing resulting from the establishment of the "right order" in the beginning.

In Ps 65 the congregation thanks God for benefits of a general character: graces of the sanctuary (vv 2-5), mastery over natural elements (6-8), blessing of fertility (10-14). Notions typical of the thanksgiving are featured: vows have to be fulfilled (v 2), God hears prayers (v 2), God answers in his justice (v 6). Temporal blessings of the community constitute the immediate object of the thanksgiving. This serves the psalmist as a starting-point for reviewing man's relationship with God. He reaffirms especially that only with God's grace can man overcome his sin and approach to God (vv 3-5). In this psalm, as throughout the Psalter, the divine purpose is seen achieving itself in history by divine rule which dominates the whole world from its very beginning (vv 6-9). To the retreatant wishing to acquire a greater love of God St. Ignatius Loyola suggests that he meditate on the way God is at work for us in the gifts of nature, including plant and animal life. A similar insight seems to have been in the psalmist's mind when he describes God himself as active in the fertility of the land (vv 10-14; cf. *Ps 104).

PSALM 66 (65)

Praise of God, Israel's Deliverer

1 *For the leader. A psalm; a song.*
  Shout joyfully to God, all you on earth,

Pss 65:9; 69:31   2   sing praise to the glory of his name;
  proclaim his glorious praise.

Pss 65:6; 71:
16ff
Pss 18:45; 81:
16
Ps 7:18

Pss 57:9f; 86:
12

Is 44:27; 50:2

Ps 77:20f

Ps 11:4

Pss 45:18; 68:
30ff

Pss 69:3; 73:
18; 121:3

Is 48:10

Ps 38:3

Is 51:23

Pss 65:2; 76:
12

Pss 54:8; 96:8

3 Say to God, "How tremendous are your deeds!
    for your great strength your enemies fawn upon you.

4 Let all the earth worship and sing praise to you,
    sing praise to your name!"

I

5 Come and see the works of God,
    his tremendous deeds among men.

6 He has changed the sea into dry land;
    through the river they passed on foot;
    therefore let us rejoice in him.

7 He rules by his might forever;
    his eyes watch the nations;
    rebels may not exalt themselves.

8 Bless our God, you peoples,
    loudly sound his praise;

9 He has given life to our souls,
    and has not let our feet slip.

10 For you have tested us, O God!
    You have tried us as silver is tried by fire;

11 You have brought us into a snare;
    you laid a heavy burden on our backs.

12 You let men ride over our heads;
    we went through fire and water,
    but you have led us out to refreshment.

II

13 I will bring holocausts to your house;
    to you I will fulfill the vows

14 Which my lips uttered
    and my words promised in my distress.

15 Holocausts of fatlings I will offer you,
    with burnt offerings of rams;
    I will sacrifice oxen and goats.

16 Hear now, all you who fear God, while I declare
    what he has done for me.

17 When I appealed to him in words,
    praise was on the tip of my tongue.

18 Were I to cherish wickedness in my heart,
    the Lord would not hear;

19   But God has heard;
         he has hearkened to the sound of my prayer.

Pss 34:1; 68:   20   Blessed be God who refused me not
20, 36   my prayer or his kindness!

The unity of the psalm can be maintained if we suppose, with Weiser, that the community thanksgiving festivals supplied the framework within which the worshippers' vows could be fulfilled (cf. 1 Sm 1:21; 2:1-10) and personal thanksgivings recited. For H. Schmidt Pss 66 and 106 are liturgies for the offering of votive thanksgiving sacrifices (cf. Ps 66:13).

The occasion for the festival in which Ps 66 featured was the deliverance from a great national danger, as it appears in verses 8-12, where the community thanksgiving recalls aspects of the calamity. This section of the poem is preceded by an hymnal introduction in praise of the *Heilsgeschichte* God (vv 1-7): "Come and see the works of God, his tremendous deeds among men" (v 5), sacred history actualized in the cult. "The psalm presents itself as the response of the cult community to the recital of the *Heilsgeschichte* tradition which has taken place in a previous cultic act; this act was understood as a present action of God directed towards the members of the cult community themselves and causing all historical differences of space and time to disappear in face of the reality of God, so that participants in the cult, in facing God, faced the same situation in which the people of God had once found themselves at the time of the Exodus and their entry into the Promised Land" (Weiser).

Mowinckel believes that the real thanksgiving occurs in the second part (vv 13-20) where, in "king-ego" style, a leading representative speaks in the name of the people. E. Podechard (p. 282) says that the leader of the nation illustrated with his personal *Heilsgeschichte* experience what protection God provides to Israel. The influence of Deutero-Isaiah on the psalm could suggest a postexilic date.

Psalm 66 is a good example of the way dimensions of time and space are reduced to a present (cf. vv 3, 5) in the cult, and broadened to include all peoples (vv 4, 8): the whole cosmos centers in the temple, where the singers are the stage-managers who orchestrate the worshipping praise of all nations (cf. §8b). Enlightened Christians believe that universal *Heilsgeschichte* is re-experienced in their paschal liturgy. In the resurrection of Christ, the Head of renewed humanity, divine salvation concentrates. To this central event can apply Ps 66: 12, especially in the German translation: "Du hast uns herausgeführt in die Freiheit" (Kraus, Lohfink): "You have led us out to freedom." Paschal themes related to the Exodus do in fact feature in Ps 66 (cf. v 6). In the Roman Missal verses 2, 3 constitute the Introit of the Third Sunday after Easter. In the LXX and Vulgate the title "psalm of the resurrection" is applied to Ps 66, presumably because of verse 9: "He has given life to our souls, and has not let our feet slip."

PSALM 67 (66)

Harvest Prayer That All Men May Worship God

1 *For the leader; with stringed instruments. A psalm; a song.*

I

Nm 6:22ff; Ps 45:3
Pss 4:7; 31: 17; 44:4

2 May God have pity on us and bless us;
    may he let his face shine upon us.
3 So may your way be known upon earth;

Gn 12:2f; Jer 33:9
Is 43:9; 49:6; 61:11

    among all nations, your salvation.
4 May the peoples praise you, O God;
    may all the peoples praise you!

II

Pss 48:12; 75: 10; 118:24

5 May the nations be glad and exult
    because you rule the peoples in equity;

Is 49:6; 52:10

    the nations on the earth you guide.
6 May the peoples praise you, O God;
    may all the peoples praise you!

III

Ex 23:16; Lv 26:4
Ez 34:27; Ps 3:9

7 The earth has yielded its fruits;
    God, our God, has blessed us.
8 May God bless us,

Ps 129:8

    and may all the ends of the earth fear him!

This psalm featured as part of the harvest-thanksgiving festival celebrated in autumn: "The earth has yielded its fruits; God, our God, has blessed us" (v 7). It is, like the majority of the psalms, very theocentric in thought structure. Its main concern is that God's salvation be revealed to the nations and be praised by all peoples. The Giver, not the gift is central; not the blessing of the harvest (as in the fertility-rites) but the divine deed is celebrated in the Israelite cult. The tone of the psalm is firmly expressed in the refrain (vv 4, 6) and already felt in the opening prayer (v 2), similar to the "Aaronite blessing": "The Lord bless you and keep you! The Lord let his face shine upon you, and be gracious to you! The Lord look upon you kindly and give you peace!" (Nm 6:24ff) God's providential rule appears to concentrate on Israel's destinies. But divine intervention in this particular case discloses what pattern of salvation awaits the whole world.

Commenting upon some ideas involved in the "enthronement psalms," Mowinckel (I, p. 185) writes: "We shall not be able fully to realize the emotions of poet and congregation when, in Ps 93, creation is mentioned as the basis of kingship, unless we have also realized the actual re-experience of the saving work of creation through the growth and the crops of the blessed year, which is expressed by the authors of harvest festival thanksgiving psalms like 65 or 67." Parsing *nat^{e}nâh* as a "precative perfect" (see on Ps 4:8; cf. *Ps 3), Dahood translates Ps 67:7: "May the earth give her produce, may God, our God, bless us," and comments: "The psalm is thus a prayer for rain rather than a hymn of thanksgiving for blessings bestowed; the presence of the jussive *y^{e}bār^{e}kēnu* points to the same conclusion." Helen G. Jefferson notes that Ps 67 is one of four psalms (also 29, 93, 100) having 71% of its vocabulary paralleled by Ugaritic roots. In itself this statistic only shows that Ugaritic and Hebrew are related languages. But she concludes: "The cultic coloring of Ps 67, its vocabulary and style, all point to Canaanite influence. This supports the theory that Ps 67 is pre-exilic in origin." It can be doubted, however, that Canaanite influence does necessarily indicate such an early date (cf. §9d).

PSALM 68 (67)

God's Triumphal Procession

1   *For the leader. A psalm of David; a song.*

I

Nm 10:35; Pss 7:7; 73:20 Is 33:3	2 God arises; his enemies are scattered, and those who hate him flee before him.
Wis 5:14	3 As smoke is driven away, so are they driven;
Ps 97:5	as wax melts before the fire,
Dt 33:2; Nm 16:35	so the wicked perish before God.

4 But the just rejoice and exult before God;
   they are glad and rejoice.

II

Pss 7:18; 18:
10f
Is 19:1; Dt
33:26
Ps 68:34

5 Sing to God, chant praise to his name,
   extol him who rides upon the clouds,
   Whose name is the Lord;
   exult before him.

Dt 10:18; Bar
6:37
Pss 69:34; 72:
12

6 The father of orphans and the defender of widows
   is God in his holy dwelling.

7 God gives a home to the forsaken;

Ps 146:7

   he leads forth prisoners to prosperity;
   only rebels remain in the parched land.

III

8 O God, when you went forth at the head of your people,

Ex 13:21; Ps
78:14ff
Hb 3:6; Jgs 5:
4

   when you marched through the wilderness,

9 The earth quaked; it rained from heaven at the presence
                                               of God,

Pss 60:4; 77:
19

   at the presence of God, the God of Israel.
   [This is Sinai.]

Ps 65:11

10 A bountiful rain you showered down, O God,
                        upon your inheritance;
    you restored the land when it languished;

11 Your flock settled in it;

Ex 16:4f; Ps
78:24f

    in your goodness, O God, you provided it for the needy.

IV

12 The Lord gives the word;
    women bear the glad tidings, a vast army:

Jgs 5:22

13 "Kings and their hosts are fleeing, fleeing,
    and the household shall divide the spoils.

Jgs 5:16; Gn
49:14
Ps 74:19

14 Though you rested among the sheepfolds,
    the wings of the dove shone with silver,

Jgs 8:25f

    and her pinions with a golden hue.

Ps 91:1

15 While the Almighty dispersed the kings there,

Jgs 9:48f

    snow fell on Salmon."

V

16 High the mountains of Basan;
    rugged the mountains of Basan.

17 Why look you jealously, you rugged mountains,

Pss 15:1; 48:
3

    at the mountain God has chosen for his throne,

Ez 43:7	where the Lord himself will dwell forever?
2 Kgs 6:17; Is 66:15	18 The chariots of God are myriad, thousand on thousands; the Lord advances from Sinai to the sanctuary.
2 Sm 5:6f; Jer 31:12 Ps 7:8; Eph 4:8	19 You have ascended on high, taken captives, received men as gifts — even rebels; the Lord God enters his dwelling.

VI

Pss 66:20; 72: 17ff Is 46:3; 63:9	20 Blessed day by day be the Lord, who bears our burdens; God, who is our salvation.
	21 God is a saving God for us; the Lord, my Lord, controls the passageways of death.
Ps 110:6	22 Surely God crushes the heads of his enemies, the hairy crowns of those who stalk about in their guilt.
	23 The Lord said: "I will fetch them back from Basan; I will fetch them back from the depths of the sea,
Pss 63:10; 69: 3, 15 Dt 32:42; Ps 58:11 Ps 59:16; 1 Kgs 21:19f	24 So that you will bathe your feet in blood; the tongues of your dogs will have their share of your enemies.

VII

	25 They view your progress, O God,
2 Sm 6:5; Ps 132:8	the progress of my God, my King, into the sanctuary;
	26 The singers lead, the minstrels follow, in their midst the maidens play on timbrels.
Pss 40:10; 89: 6 Jer 2:13; 17: 13	27 In your choirs bless God; bless the Lord, you of Israel's wellspring!
	28 There is Benjamin, the youngest, leading them; the princes of Juda in a body,
Is 8:23; 2 Par 30:1f	the princes of Zabulon, the princes of Nephthali.

VIII

	29 Show forth, O God, your power, the power, O God, with which you took our part;
	30 For your temple in Jerusalem
Pss 67:4ff; 72: 10; 76:11 Ez 29:2f	let the kings bring you gifts.
	31 Rebuke the wild beast of the reeds,
Jer 46:20; Pss 22:22; 75:11	the herd of strong bulls and the bullocks, the nations. Let them prostrate themselves with bars of silver; scatter the peoples who delight in war.
	32 Let nobles come from Egypt;
Is 45:14	let Ethiopia extend its hands to God.

IX

Ps 67:4   33 You kingdoms of the earth, sing to God,
                         chant praise to the Lord
Ps 68:5; Hb   34   who rides on the heights of the ancient heavens.
3:8
                         Behold, his voice resounds, the voice of power:
                 35   "Confess the power of God!"
                         Over Israel is his majesty;
                         his power is in the skies.
Pss 59:6; 71:   36 Awesome in his sanctuary is God, the God of Israel;
22
Pss 28:8; 29:   he gives power and strength to his people.
11
Ps 34:1   Blessed be God!

The fact that the text is poorly preserved in some sections (cf.
vv 12-15) renders even more difficult the interpretation of this psalm
already obscured by brief allusions to too many scattered events. Yet
the general real life setting of the psalm may well have been the autumn
covenant festival (§13c). Two verses are especially significant in that
respect:

Rain in abundance, O God, thou didst shed abroad;
thou didst restore thy heritage as it languished — (v 9 = 10:
RSV).
Thy solemn processions are seen, O God,
the processions of my God, my King, into the sanctuary — (24 =
25: RSV).

At the heart of that festival, Weiser explains, is the revelation of God,
who according to ancient thought, comes to his sanctuary from Mount
Sinai and by his presence "actualizes" his redemptive work. This sacral
act of salvation "is executed in a stylized pattern of sacred phrases and
rites cast in a fixed form by tradition; and the psalm refers to this,
though mostly only in brief hints." The main phases of Heilsgeschichte
(salvation history) are celebrated in this triumphal hymn, which is
introduced by the departure words of Moses addressed to the theophany
God (§13d) on the sacred Ark: "Arise, O Lord, that your enemies
may be scattered, and those who hate you may flee from you" (Nm
10:35; cf. Is 33:3). It could be the signal for the procession to leave.

 BJ lists as follows the sequence of events evoked by the psalm: the
exodus from Egypt, the wandering in the desert, marked by various

incidents (rebellion, theophany, manna and quail), the victories at the time of the Judges (Deborah, Gedeon) and the settlement in Zion (David, Solomon), the stories about Elijah and Elisha, the tragic fate of the Achab family, the solemn pasch of Hezekiah. It seems that the unpleasant allusions to Egypt in verse 31 are more recent than the original psalm. The Deutero-Isaiah universalist views reflected in verses 29-33 could also point to a post-exilic re-edition of the psalm. The basic antiquity of the psalm seems to be indicated by its use of formulas like "rider of the clouds" (vv 5, 34). Other archaic expressions, *qōdeš,* "sanctuary" (vv 18, 25), *miqdāšîm,* "sanctuaries" (36) and "the voice of power" (34) suggest to Eerdmans that the psalm was composed during the reign of David. W. F. Albright has stated (p. 3) that "fully half of the unique words which strew Ps 68 may be elucidated by Ugaritic." He also believes that this psalm consists of a string of about thirty *incipits* (beginnings of poems) written not much later than the Solomonic period. A more likely interpretation would be that of H. Schmidt, for whom Ps 68 is a collection of short autonomous poems, sung on the same occasion: procession in honor of Yahweh (vv 25f) and of his enthronement at the New Year Festival (cf. §13a).

Mowinckel writes that Ps 68 is an old originally North Israelite psalm later adapted for the epiphany festival in Jerusalem (II, p. 152). Ps 68, he also believes, is a procession psalm for the "festival of light" (cf. Ps 118:27). It celebrated Yahweh's triumphal entry as king at the feast of tabernacles (I, p. 170, 182). In fact, he says, Pss 24, 68, 118, 132 were written for festal processions (I, p. 5). Other authors suggest that Ps 68 reflects the cultic traditions associated with an ancient Israelite sanctuary at Mount Thabor. This would explain the attention given to the Deborah victory over Sisara (vv 13-17 and Jgs 4:12ff). As reported by Weiser, "Gaster (*Thespis* . . . p. 415ff) takes Ps 68 to be the libretto of the pantomine performed at the Canaanite New Year Festival, which in his opinion was worked over for liturgical use in the Yahweh cult; he believes that *bāšān* (vv 16, 23) alludes to the chaos dragon and corresponds to the Ugaritic *btn,* a designation that would fit in very well with the phrase *the depths of the sea* in verse 23." Weiser is probably right though in his opinion that the interpretation from Israelite tradition is the more natural one in view of the whole tenor of the psalm. (*Btn,* in Ugaritic means "serpent, dragon"; on the destruction of *Bashan's* kingdom, cf. Nm 21:33ff).

Because of the special character of this psalm it seems advisable to mention sundry suggestions made to help understand the more difficult passages (the numbers indicate the verses).

(5) "Extol him who rides upon the clouds." *JB* reads: "Build a road for the Rider of the Clouds," while the revised Latin Psalter has, "Lay a road for him who rides through the desert." "One and the same epithet is applied to *Ba'l* as *rkb 'rpt* (1 Aqht: 43:44) and to God as *rōkēb bā'arābôt* (Ps 68:5)" (C. H. Gordon, p. 292). "The expression *The Rider of the Clouds* as a divine epithet is very ancient, since it occurs in Chanaanite literature even before the time of Moses, and it is not uncommon in the Old Testament. Cf. Dt 33:26; Ps 18: 10ff; 68:34; Is 19:1; Hb 3:8" (*CV*). Parsing *l* of *lē'lōhīm* as vocative *lamedh* (see v 33), M. Dahood translates: "Sing, O gods, chant, O his heavens, pave the highway for the Rider of the Clouds!"

(7) W. F. Albright proposed in *HUCA* the following improved translation of verse 7: "It is Yhwh who causeth the single to set up house, who setteth free prisoners with music, but who causeth rebels to tent in the wasteland" (cf. *Ps 113:9).

(9) Emending verse 9 with the help of Jgs 5:4f and the Targum, E. Vogt finds the following meaning: "The earth quaked, the heavens swayed, the mountains shook before the Lord, before the Lord, the God of Israel." Instead of "[This is Sinai]" Dahood reads "The One of Sinai," and explains: "Because he created Sinai as his sanctuary (v 18), and because he appeared there to Moses at the momentous point in Israelite history, Yahweh received the epithet *zeh sīnay,* "The One of Sinai" (also in Jg 5:5)."

(10) Whether we have a scribe's inspired mispelling or a rare Hebrew root, D. W. Goodwin believes, we need not alter the consonantal text in order to obtain a satisfactory translation of verse 10: "An abundance or rain will thou give freely, O God, a stream, subsided and exhausted, thou wilt restore it."

(12) Reading *'imrâh mebaśśeret,* R. Tournay translates verse 12: "The Lord gives an order, it serves notice of a vast army." With this would fall the allusion to female heralds.

(13) Having read in verse 13, "May the kings of the *hosts* bow themselves, bow themselves, the country's pasture land share the boon,"

Dahood explains that the "brighter stars" empty their contents upon Palestine.

(14) Various attempts have been made to elucidate verse 14. Even though the Rubenites had not cooperated, their Israelite brothers scored a great victory and collected a large booty of gold and silver (R. Tournay). The dove is Israel (cf. Hos 7:11; 11:11; Ps 74:19) or perhaps an object of art found in the booty: an image of the Phoenician goddess Astarte (cf. 1 Kgs 11:5, 33), represented with a dove, symbolizing love (cf. E. Podechard, "Psaume LXVIII," p. 516).

(15) R. Tournay proposes that the snow which fell on Salmon was a rain of "salt" (cf. Jgs 9:45). Hoar-frost is compared to salt in Sir 43:18f. But S. Iwry sees in the text no allusion to any miraculous event; Read: "When Shaddai scattered the kings, as snow dries up (*khtš šlg*) in Zalmon."

(18) According to Albright (*Fs. Mowinckel*), the original text of verse 18 could have been "The chariots of Yahweh were two (?) thousand, two myriads the bowmen of my Lord, when they brought the Holy Ark?) from Sinai." Reading also *šin'ān* as "archer," and *yābam,* as "creator," Dahood has the following rendering: "God's chariots were twice ten thousand, thousands the archers of the Lord, who created Sinai as his sanctuary." Cf. Ex 15:17; Ps 78:54.

(19) Instead of the rather queer idea that God "received men as gifts," one should probably read, with Dahood, in verse 19: "You received gifts from (*ba*) their hands (*'d*)" (see on *Ps 17:4).

(23) Completing suggestions advanced since 1959 at least, P. D. Miller amends the *MT* of verse 23 to read *'ešbam bāšān* and translates: "Said the Lord: I muzzled the Serpent, I muzzled the Deep Sea." The elucidation of the text is based on a Ugaritic parallel: "I muzzled *tannin,* I muzzled him. I smote the twisting serpent" (*'nt*: III:37f; cf. *JBL* 1961, p. 270f). F. C. Fensham relies also on Ugaritic to read in the same verse: *miḥōr bāšān 'āšib* and translates: God said: "From the hole of the snake I will bring back, I will bring back from the depths of the sea" (cf. Is 11:8). Other suggestions and discussions in Dahood's *Psalms* II, p. 145f.

(33) Dahood's translation: "O kings of the earth, sing! O gods, sing praises to the Lord!" This supposes the use of vocative *lamedh* (cf.

on *Ps 33 and *VD* 45, 1967, pp. 32-46) and the meaning "kings" given to *mamlekoth* ("kingdoms"), as in Phoenician and in biblical passages: 1 Sm 10:18; 1 Kgs 10:20; 2 Chr 9:19; 12:8; Is 47:5; Jer 1: 15; 25:26; Pss 79:6; 102:23; 135:11. But "kingdoms" fits also well in the context.

PSALM 118 (117)

Hymn of Thanksgiving to the Savior of Israel

1 Alleluia

A

Pss 100:5;
136:1ff
Jer 33:11; 2
Chr 5:13
Pss 115:9ff;
135:19ff

Give thanks to the Lord, for he is good,
    for his mercy endures forever.

2 Let the house of Israel say,
    "His mercy endures forever."

3 Let the house of Aaron say,
    "His mercy endures forever."

4 Let those who fear the Lord say,
    "His mercy endures forever."

B

I

5 In my straits I called upon the Lord;
    the Lord answered me and set me free.

Pss 27:1; 56:
12
Heb 13:6; Ps
56:5

6 The Lord is with me; I fear not;
    what can man do against me?

7 The Lord is with me to help me,

Ps 54:9

    and I shall look down upon my foes.

8 It is better to take refuge in the Lord

Ps 146:3

    than to trust in man.

9 It is better to take refuge in the Lord
    than to trust in princes.

II

10 All the nations encompassed me;
    in the name of the Lord I crushed them.

11 They encompassed me on every side;
    in the name of the Lord I crushed them.

12 They encompassed me like bees,
    they flared up like fire among thorns;

in the name of the Lord I crushed them.

13 I was hard pressed and was falling,

Pss 3:6; 146:
9; 147:6
but the Lord helped me.

Pss 59:17; 94:
22
Ex 15:2; Is
12:2
14 My strength and my courage is the Lord,

and he has been my savior.

III

Neh 12:27, 43
15 The joyful shout of victory

in the tents of the just:

Ex 15:6; Is
62:8
"The right hand of the Lord struck with power:

16   the right hand of the Lord is exalted;

the right hand of the Lord has struck with power."

17 I shall not die, but live,

Is 38:19
and declare the works of the Lord.

18 Though the Lord has indeed chastised me,

yet he has not delivered me to death.

C

I

Ps 24:7f; Is
26:2
19 Open to me the gates of justice;

I will enter them and give thanks to the Lord.

20 This gate is the Lord's

the just shall enter it.

21 I will give thanks to you, for you have answered me

and have been my savior.

Acts 4:11; Lk
20:17
Zech 3:9; 4:7;
1 Pt 2:7
Eph 2:20
22 The stone which the builders rejected

has become the cornerstone.

Mt 21:42
23 By the Lord has this been done;

it is wonderful in our eyes.

24 This is the day the Lord has made;

Ps 67:5
let us be glad and rejoice in it.

25 O Lord, grant salvation!

O Lord, grant prosperity!

II

Mt 2:19; 23:
39
Ps 128:5
26 Blessed is he who comes in the name of the Lord;

we bless you from the house of the Lord.

27 The Lord is God, and he has given us light.

Lv 23:40; 2
Mc 10:7
Ex 27:2; 38:
2; Neh 8:15
Join in procession with leafy boughs

up to the horns of the altar.

28 You are my God, and I give thanks to you;

O my God, I extol you.

29 Give thanks to the Lord, for he is good;
Pss 106:1;
138:8
      for his kindness endures forever.

Psalm 118 is very illuminating for the study of the ancient thanksgiving liturgy (cf. §25a). Mowinckel (I, p. 180f) attributes special importance to Ps 118, as illustrating what took place at the so-called "enthronement festival" (cf. §13a). Some of his remarks deserve attention. The psalm, like the procession, starts outside the "Gate of Righteousness," very likely the innermost temple gate, through which only "the righteous" — the congregation in a state worthy of the cult — are allowed to enter. In Babylonia also temple gates were named according to various blessings supposedly received when entering (cf. H. Zimmern, in Z. d. Deutschen Morg. Ges., 76, 1922, p. 49). The request to open the Gate of Righteousness (v 19-20; see on *Ps 24) is preceded by a thanksgiving (vv 1-18) in which the king or the leader of the congregation testifies in the name of the community that God has been the savior of Israel throughout the ages. One "concentrated picture" recalls how, when Israel was encompassed about by the nations, the king destroyed them in the name of Yahweh. Here, Mowinckel believes, the "saga has been conventionalized on the model of the myth about *the fight of nations*" (p. 180).

Then follow a short thanksgiving (vv 21-25) and a prayer for prosperity (v 26), to which the priests answer with a blessing from the house of the Lord on those who are now coming (in procession) in his holy Name (v 26). What the priests say then, "The Lord is God, and he has given us light" (v 27), could reflect the Aaronite benediction (Nm 6:25) and allude to the "festival of light" of the feast of Tabernacles. The invitation to join in a cultic "dance" around the altar, "with leafy boughs," could be in relation to an aspect of the Feast of Booths: "On the first day you shall gather foliage from majestic trees, branches of palms and boughs of myrtles and of valley poplars, and there for a week you shall make merry before the Lord, your God" (Lv 23:40; cf. Neh 8:15; 2 Mc 10:7; Mk 11:8). A third hymn concludes the psalm (vv 28-29). It includes the thanksgiving of the king (v 28) and of the choir (v 29), probably sung during the "festal dance."

When the representative of the people has ended his thanksgiving (vv 5-21), the congregation, speaking in the third person, opens its hymn with the following words: "The stone which the builders rejected has become the cornerstone" (v 22). It alludes to various texts (cf. Zech 3:9; 4:7; Is 8:14; 28:16) which have been interpreted in a messianic sense and applied to Christ (Mt 21:42; Acts 4:11; Rm 9:33; 1 Cor 3:11; Eph 2:20; 1 Pt 2:4f). The simile of the corner-stone could point to the restoration of Israel when the temple was rebuilt after the exile (cf. Agg 1:9; Zech 1:16). In the psalm itself "the parable illustrates the change that has taken place in the fortunes of the saved man: he was rejected, despised and persecuted by men, but was saved and honored by God and was entrusted by him with a parti-cularly important task. The interpretation of this saying in late Judaism as referring to David and to the Messiah ... is presumably based on the correct recollection that the king appeared in the cult in the rôle of David (cf. Ps 18) and that the royal cult entailed that at any given time the tradition of his ancestor was revived in the person of the actual representative of the Davidic dynasty" (Weiser).

According to *JB,* Ps 118 may have been used for the feast described in Neh 8:13-18 (cf. Ezr 3:4; Zech 14:16; Ex 23:14). Ps 119 could then have been connected with the reading from "the book of the law of God." B. D. Eerdmans ("Foreign elements ..., p. 130) thinks Ps 118 is pre-exilic. Among the indications he finds for that early date is the admission of the laymen into the inner-court of the temple, where the great altar stood. They are told (v 27) to bind their festal-sacrifices with cords to the horns of the altar. In the post-exilic period the laymen had to make their prosternations in the outer-court and attend to the offering of their sacrifices, standing on the threshold of one of the gates, leading into the innercourt, where priests and levites officiated. Eerdmans believes that the psalmist was a zealous missionary and that verses 10-12 allude to the circumcision of his proselytes. So he translates:

All the gojim [non-Israelites] compassed me about
    when I had them circumcised (*'amîlām*) in the name of Jahu.
They surrounded me, encircling me,
    when I had them circumcised in the name of Jahu.
They surrounded me like bees,
    they were quenched like the fire of thorns,
    when I had them circumcised in the name of Jahu.

Thus were the gojim appeased by their circumcision and incorporated "in the congregation of Jahu."

PSALM 124 (123)

The Lord the Rescuer of His People

1 *A song of ascents. Of David.*

I

Had not the Lord been with us,

Ps 118:2   let Israel say,

2   had not the Lord been with us —

When men rose up against us,

Prv 1:12; Ps 129;1f   3   then would they have swallowed us alive.

When their fury was inflamed against us,

Pss 18:5; 69: 2f   4   then would the waters have overwhelmed us;

The torrent would have swept over us;

5   over us then would have swept

the raging waters.

II

6 Blessed be the Lord, who did not leave us

a prey to their teeth.

Prv 6:5; Ps 11:1   7   We were rescued like a bird

Ps 91:3   from the fowler's snare;

Broken was the snare,

and we were freed.

8 Our help is in the name of the Lord,

Pss 121:2; 134:3   who made heaven and earth.

The dangers and trials from which Israel has been preserved or liberated by the grace of God are evoked in such conventional and stylized metaphors that it is hardly possible even to suggest any specific historical circumstance as the background for this psalm. The adversaries have almost swallowed up Israel (v 3) as the dragon Babylon has swallowed Jerusalem (Jer 51:34). The metaphor of the raging waters (vv 4, 5; cf. Pss 18:5; 42:8; 69:2) can easily be linked with the mythical power of the primeval abyss (cf. §9b, 11a). Israel has also been saved from the teeth of the beasts of prey and from the fowler's snare (vv 6, 7). Salvation, revelation of the divine Name and creation (cf. v 8) are frequently associated in the cult. This and the initial notice, "let Israel say" (v 1), could indicate a liturgical use of the psalm.

Verse 7 borrows from the imagery of bird hunting. This seems also implied in our Lord's saying: "Take heed to yourselves . . . lest that day come upon you suddenly as a snare" (Lk 21:34f). Although biblical references for this comparison are available (cf. Hb 1:15; Is 24:17; Hos 7:12; Ez 32:3), its origin can be traced to ancient Oriental representations. On the "stela of the vultures" can be seen a large human figure (the god Ningirsu or Eannatum, the king of Lagash) smiting with a mace human figures, with shaved faces and heads, contained in a net. The limestone stela, from Tello in ancient Sumer, is now at the Louvre Museum (cf. *ANEP*, fig. 298, and A. Parrot, *Terre du Christ*, Neuchâtel, 1965, p. 102).

CHAPTER SEVEN

RØYAL PSALMS

§26. THEIR GENERAL CHARACTER

It has been said and repeated that the basic reality in human life was for the Israelite not the individual but the community. Within the nation the king was the representative of the whole. Mowinckel can even assert: "The covenant between Yahweh and Israel and between Yahweh and David is one and the same thing." Such being the importance of the king, it is no wonder that psalms have been composed in his honor. In truth, the unity of this category of "royal psalms" rests basically on one fact: they all concern the king. They have no special literary structure although some of the themes are predominant: divine adoption, the throne's stability, the prophecy of Nathan, prayers for the king, oracles promising him happiness and prosperity.

The traditional view which held that David wrote most of the psalms was inclined to increase considerably the number of "royal psalms." When the Davidic authorship was reappraised (cf. §4g) the opposite tendency came to the fore. Mowinckel tells us what happened next: "But in its earlier phase modern scientific study of the psalms tended to deny the presence of any royal figure in the psalms, and it was maintained that they had been largely composed in Jewish times, after the Exile, out of the private experiences of ordinary people in the joys and sorrows of daily life, and through impulses from certain individual prophets . . . . Where we do meet a royal figure, as in the so-called 'messianic' psalms, this figure was interpreted as a personification of the people of Israel. Gunkel was the first to re-conceive of the royal psalms as real king psalms, and place this interpretation on a sure scientific foundation" (I, p. 46f). Conclusions should not be drawn too easily from the presence of themes of royalty, since motifs of royal psalms were sometimes taken over by private, unknown suppliants (cf. H. J. Kraus, *Psalmen*, I, p. 412). Mowinckel devotes in fact a whole chapter to the *"I" and "We" in the Psalms — the Royal Psalms* (I, pp. 42-80). The problem of the *Ichpsalmen* has been examined above (§23a). It can be recalled here that unless the king is mentioned explicitly or implicitly it is usually difficult to prove that the "I"-speaker is a royal figure, when the context points to the interests of a private individual.

The cultic role of the king has been overemphasized by the so-called "Myth and Ritual School" (see §8d and G. E. Wright, p. 66f). J. L. McKenzie's statement of about ten years ago remains valid: "The arguments raised against this theory by many scholars I accept as decisive, and hence I interpret the messianic character of the Israelite king without any reference to his place in the cult" (*CBQ* 1957, p. 26). "Hebrew kingship and its ideology, he adds, cannot be explained as a derivation or a borrowing from foreign ideologies because of its connection with the kingship of Yahweh, which is a distinctive Hebrew belief." The king has a "unique position" in the religion of Israel. "He is a charismatic officer, the successor of the judges . . . . To the king is attributed superhuman strength and wisdom and the possession of the spirit of Yahweh . . . . He is the incorporation of his people, and in him are recapitulated the covenant of Israel and the promises and obligations which flow from the covenant" (p. 36f; cf. J. De Fraine, *L'aspect . . . ,* p. 371ff). Israelite kingship, observes Wright, "never achieved the sanctity of the absolutism which is encountered elsewhere . . . . The conception of Yahweh as the covenant-Lord of Israel, the Chosen People, prevented the Israelite monarchy from presuming too much and left independent religious leaders free to pronounce judgment on the kings for doing evil in the sight of Yahweh. It also permitted a people of Yahweh to survive destruction and exile, and attempt to rebuild a holy community without a king in the light of the wilderness period" (p. 67f). In his extensive study of ancient oriental king ideology, K.-H. Bernhardt rejects the "ritual pattern" theory (cf. §8d) and advocates an explanation of royal ideology based on the historical rejection of the kingship and on the traditions of the nomadic period (see especially his 3rd chapter: pp. 51-66). As for K. R. Crim, he agrees generally with H.-J. Kraus' explanation centered on the assumption of an annual festival in Jerusalem commemorating the election of David (see §13b).

The temporal monarch is in fact the delegate of Yahweh, the Eternal King of Israel: Ex 15:18; Nm 23:21; Jgs 8:23; 1 Sm 8:7; 12:12; 1 Kgs 22:19; Is 6:5. For this reason the king's throne in Jerusalem is called "throne of the Lord" (1 Chr 29:23) or "the throne of the kingdom of the Lord over Israel" (1 Chr 28:5). The permanency attributed to the dynasty in the language of court etiquette was freely wished to the king himself: "He asked life of you: you gave him length of days forever and ever" (Ps 21:5). "Eternal duration" was a quality associated with kingship by the ancient conventional court-style. In the economy of divine revelation such hyperbolic language heralded the advent of messianism. It must be noted again that the line of division between individual and eschatological kingship is somewhat difficult to draw. "The historical king appears with traits which are sometimes superhuman, or very near it. He is, at least in the widest sense, a messianic figure. The accession of a successor of David was a new sign that the national hope of a historical or an eschatological future persevered, that the blessing of Yahweh still rested upon the figure of Israel through the king" (McKenzie, p. 27; on "royal messianism," see §15c). W. H. Brownlee has recently suggested that sacral kingship has been introduced in Israel and Judaism as belonging to an "angelic" category (cf. RB 1966, pp. 171-175). Four times David is compared to an angel of God: 1 Sm 14:17, 20, 27; 29:9. According to Zech 12:8, in messianic times the "house of David shall be godlike, like an angel of the Lord . . ." (12:8). To king Ahasuerus Esther said: "My Lord, you looked to me like an angel of God, and my heart was moved with fear of your majesty" (Est 5:2; cf. Prv 16:14f).

§27. THE HISTORICAL SETTING

In Gunkel's classification, the royal psalms (2, 18, 20, 21, 45, 72, 101, 110, 132) form one of the five main categories (cf. §7a). The psalms deal with native Israelite kings of the pre-exilic period (Ps 45 which mentions a princess of Tyre, in verse 13, is presumably dedicated to a king of the northern kingdom). Various occasions of the official life of these Davidic monarchs constitute the historical setting of the royal psalms: enthronement (Pss 2, 72, 101, 110), royal wedding (Ps 45), songs related to the king's warring exploits (18, 20, 21, 144A), lament (Ps 89:47ff), and the anniversary of the founding of the Davidic dynasty and its royal sanctuary on Mount Zion (132; cf. Gunkel-Begrich, *Einleitung* . . . , p. 145f). This historical situation of the royal psalms will be more precisely investigated in the respective introductions. On the royal psalms can be consulted the studies of K. H. Bernhardt, K. R. Crim, J. De Fraine, G. B. Gray, A. R. Johnson, J. L. McKenzie, R. Nogosek, G. von Rad, K. H. Rengstorf, G. Widengren.

§28. TEXT AND INTRODUCTION

The royal psalms are: Pss 2, (18), 20, 21, 45, 72, 89, 101, 110, 132, (144).

PSALM 2

The Universal Reign of the Messiah

I

Acts 4:25; Rev 11:18	1	Why do the nations rage
		and the peoples utter folly?
Wis 6:1-21	2	The kings of the earth rise up,
Pss 48:5; 83:6		and the princes conspire together
Ps 20:7		against the Lord and against his anointed:
Ps 149:8; Na 1:13	3	"Let us break their fetters
		and cast their bonds from us!"

II

Pss 59:9; 150:1	4	He who is throned in heaven laughs;
Is 40:15f		the Lord derides them.
	5	Then in anger he speaks to them;

he terrifies them in his wrath:

6 "I myself have set up my king
    on Sion my holy mountain."

III

7 I will proclaim the decree of the Lord:
    The Lord said to me, "You are my son;
    this day I have begotten you.

8 Ask of me and I will give you
    the nations for an inheritance
    and the ends of the earth for your possession.

9 You shall rule them with an iron rod;
    you shall shatter them like an earthen dish."

IV

10 And now, O kings, give heed;
    take warning, you rulers of the earth.

11 Serve the Lord with fear, and rejoice before him;

12 with trembling pay homage to him,
    Lest he be angry and you perish from the way,
    when his anger blazes suddenly.
    Happy are all who take refuge in him!

Marginal references:
- 2 Sm 7:14; 1 Chr 17:13
- Is 49:1; Acts 13:33
- Pss 89:27; 110:3
- Heb 1:5; 5:5
- Is 49:6; 53:2
- Dn 7:14
- Ps 110:6
- Rev 2:27; 12:5; 19:15
- Jgs 5:3; Wis 6:1f
- Is 49:23; Ps 72:9
- Ps 21:10
- Pss 34:9; 55:24; Prv 16:20

Pss 1 and 2 have no title. Both together would constitute, according to *BJ,* a sort of preface to the whole Psalter, by evoking some of its main moral and messianic teachings. Ps 1 begins and Ps 2 ends with a "beatitude." By its subject-matter, thinks J. Enciso (see on *Ps 137), Ps 2 is well adapted to fill its role as prologue to various collections: the first and second collection of David, the collections of Asaph, of the sons of Core and of the reign of God. These groups of psalms, it is thought, would have one theme in common: God's universal reign. Jewish and Christian traditions alike consider Ps 2 as messianic, like Ps 110, on which it likely depends. It is attributed to David by Acts 4:25 (see §16a for detailed references to the New Testament). Prominent literary and conceptual developments proper to the royal psalms find expression in Ps 2: the king as son of God, the stability of the Davidic dynasty, the divine oracles at the coronation ceremony, royal messianism.

A king of Judah recites this psalm at his own enthronement. The change of ruler should not be a signal for vassals to revolt (vv 1-3). God guarantees the perpetuation of the dynasty (4-6). After the divine proclamation instituting the new king (7-9), a warning is addressed to the rulers of the earth (10-12). Since Israel has ever been a modest kingdom, with no vassals worthy to be called kings, the world-wide setting of the psalm (see on *Ps 66) is partly literary and imitates the royal ceremonial pattern of the great oriental empires (see also below: the consequence of divine adoption). As a matter of fact, the divine installation of a kinglet is for the psalmist an occasion to dissert on God's universal dominion. While strife and ambition agitate the kings of the earth and the nations (cf. Is 17:12), the great Monarch smiles down serenely on this agitation from his heavenly throne (cf. Is 18:4) or terrifies the whole world with his thundering voice (cf. Is 17:13).

The divine proclamation (vv 7-9; cf. *Ps 19:4) is better understood against the background of ancient *royal protocol (cf. von Rad, "Das judäische Königsritual," *TLZ* 72, 1947, pp. 211-216). Yet here a new dimension is added, the eschatological one (cf. §14a), for this particular Davidic kingship is a prototype of the expected messianic kingship at the end of times, when the reign of God will be established in the whole world. In the last stanza (10-12) the Israelite king is out of the picture and the real intent of the psalm is again manifest: that all the rulers of the earth acknowledge with awe and serve with fear God as the universal Lord of the earthly kingdoms. The New Testament has applied to the messiahship and the divine sonship of Jesus the statements of Ps 2: cf. Acts 4:25ff; 13:33; Heb 1:5; 5:5. The same typology is verified whenever it is stated that Jesus is king, the son of David (cf. §15c).

Having recalled that the Israelite king had a role to play as mediator of the Covenant (cf. 2 Kgs 23:3), G. H. Jones has the following to say about Ps 2:7: In proclaiming the "decree of Yahweh," "the king on his enthronement was accepting the Covenant of Yahweh, which had as its visible sign the decree which he was declaring." If it was not a written document, the "decree" certainly was fixed in content and form. At his enthronement the king would say: "I will repeat concerning the decree of Yahweh . . . ." According to the Egyptian ritual of enthronement the reference was to a written document expressing the divine legitimacy of the king, his calling and enthronement by the deity, and the further destiny and "name" that will thereby be his. The "decree" or "edict" of Ps 2:7, adds Mowinckel (I, 62), is thus a confirmation of the covenant with David (2 Sm 7).

In verses 7-8, comments K. H. Rengstorf, an unidentified king of the pre-exilic period mentions at his accession the Royal Protocol or Oracle (*ḥōq*), which promises him dominion over the whole world. The phrase, "ask of me and I will give you," would be a peculiar feature of the Enthronement ritual of Jerusalem and Judea. J. Dupont has explained how the New Testament authors have given to the triumph of Jesus an enthronement setting: only after his Passion is Jesus declared Son of God, Lord and King. As man he had to "be born" to the glory he possessed eternally as the Son. In this sense it is said of Him in a paschal context: "Thou art my son, I this day have begotten thee" (Heb 1:5; Ps 2:7; cf. Rm 1:4).

Divine adoption is in fact one of the features of ancient coronation rites: "You are my son; this day I have begotten you" (Ps 2:7; cf. 89:27f). Nathan's prophecy also declared: "I will be a father to him and he a son to me" (2 Sm 7:14; cf. 1 Chr 22:10; 28:6). Following the revised Latin Psalter (and the Septuagint), *CV* translates Ps 110:3: "Yours is princely power in the day of your birth, in holy splendor; before the daystar, like the dew, I have begotten you." But the Israelite king was in no way divinized. The title *Elohim* bestowed upon him by an obscure text (Ps 45:7) is also attributed to less important officials (cf. Ps 58:2). In Egypt and in Assyro-Babylonia the king was considered son of a god. But in Israel divine adoption coincides with the coronation. The Israelite king is not divine by natural generation (cf. M. Noth, "Gott, König, Volk im Alten Testament" [1950], in *Gesammelte Studien zum Alten Testament,* pp. 188-229). "*I beget you* is an audacious poetical hyperbole which prepared the way for expressing supra-dynastic messianism. As a result of divine adoption the king in Zion is entitled to a universal dominion. The whole earth belongs to Yahweh, who makes his adopted son his heir and his delegate" (J. Steinmann, p. 28). The role of the Israelite king then reflects in a way the universal dominion of the Lord over the nations (Pss 47:3, 9; 89:12; Is 45:1; 52:10).

The "genuinely archaic flavor" of the psalm's language suggests to Dahood "a very early date (probably the tenth century)." So this author at least is not impressed by A. Robert's contention that "all the verses of the Ps, 6 and 12 excepted, include terms characteristic of the post-exilic language." "Nothing decisive can be said against a pre-exilic dating" of the psalm, states Mowinckel (I, p. 65, n.). B. Lindars finds some evidence for assuming that "the men of Qumran . . .

understood the psalm to be concerned with Davidic kingship. Everything points to the conclusion that they were right, once it is agreed
that the acrostic is too insecure to be accepted as the decisive factor"
(p. 67). Already in 1885 an acrostic beginning had been perceived
in Ps 2 by G. Bickell (cf. *VT* 1967, p. 62). Developing a suggestion
of R. H. Pfeiffer, M. Treves now finds plenty of evidence to support
his claim that the king of Ps 2 is one of the Hasmoneans. Then he
adds: any remaining doubt is dispelled by the acrostic: the phrase in
Hebrew formed with the first letter of each verse can be translated:
"Sing ye to Jannaeus the First and his wife." That, Treves contends,
was written at the accession of Jannaeus, in the year 103 B.C. Such
a late date for the psalm is, however, very unlikely.

Other studies that merit consideration attempt to elucidate obscure or difficult passages. The meaning "to forgather," applied to
rāgāš (*CV,* "rage") by Briggs ("consent together") is accepted by
Dahood, who notes that in Pss 55:15 and 64:3, the word is associated
with that meaning to *sōd,* "council," represented by *nôsᵉdû* in Ps
2:2. The meaning of *yehᵉgû* (*CV,* "utter") in verse 1 is clarified by
that of "to number," attested for *hāgâh* in a military context of a Ugaritic text (*Krt*:90-91). If *rîq* (*CV,* "folly") can mean "troops" (cf. Gn
14:14), then sufficient evidence is produced to support the translation
of verses 1-2 proposed by Dahood:

> Why do the nations forgather,
>   and the peoples number their troops?
> Why do kings of the earth take their stand,
>   and the princes make common cause
> Against Yahweh and against his anointed?

The following added comment seems equally relevant: "There is no
point in trying to identify the kings historically. By the time of the
composition of this psalm (probably tenth century) they had become
stock literary figures who belong to the genre of royal psalms. They
should be classed with the kings of Ps 48:5. If an historical background must be sought, the El Amarna correspondence (cf. §9d)
offers graphic descriptions of the plottings and intrigues of the petty
kings of Syria-Palestine against the Egyptian suzerain and against
one another."

Some years ago A. Kleber applied to verse 9 known elements of the rite of the smashing of earthen vessels: at certain state functions of the Ancient East, vessels inscribed with the names of the hostile rulers or rebellious subjects, or of harmful things were ceremoniously dashed to the ground and broken with a stick or pounder, in order to give symbolic expression to the intention of destroying the objects of fear or hatred. In Revelation the "Son of God" says "to the rest in Thyatira: To him who overcomes and who keeps my works unto the end, I will give authority over the nations. And he shall rule them with a rod of iron, and like the potter's vessel they shall be dashed to pieces, as I also have received from my Father; and I will give him the morning star" (2:26ff).

Reading $n^e\check{s}\bar{e}$ *qāber*, "men of the grave," instead of MT *naššeqû bar* (litt., "kiss the son"), Dahood translates v 11: "Serve Yahweh with reverence, and live in trembling, O mortal men!" This is followed by the remark: "The Yahwist king is portrayed as railing against the Canaanite concepts of divine kingship." But does not the "Yahwist king" also claim for himself a "divine kingship"? Besides, there is a kind of consensus among other scholars (Rowley, Closen, Weiser, Kraus, *BJ, Osty*) for accepting the textual emendation proposed by A. Bertholet a long time ago (*ZAW*, 1908, p. 58f; cf. *Bib* 1940, pp. 288-309; 426ff): unite differently the words of verses 11f and read *ûbir'ādâh naššeqû beraglāw*: "with trembling kiss his feet." To this emendation accepted by him in 1925 A. Vaccari substituted in 1949: "Pay homage to him with trembling" (cf. *Liber Psalmorum* and *CV*). "Foot-kissing (Ps 2: 12; cf. Is 49:23) as a sign of subjection and homage was a general oriental custom, known both from Egypt, and Babylonia-Assyria" (Mowinckel, I, p. 55, with references).

PSALM 18 (17)

Thanksgiving for Help and Victory

1 *For the leader. Of David, the servant of the Lord, who sang to the Lord the words of this song when the Lord had rescued him from the grasp of all his enemies and from the hand of Saul.*

A

I

2 Sm 22; Ps 43:2   2 I love you, O Lord, my strength,

Gn 49:24; Dt 32:4   3   O Lord, my rock, my fortress, my deliverer.

Pss 28:1; 31:
2ff
Pss 3:4; 25:5;
33:17
Lk 1:69

My God, my rock of refuge,
> my shield, the horn of my salvation, my stronghold!
4 Praised be the Lord, I exclaim,
> and I am safe from my enemies.

II

Jon 2:3-6; Jb
22:11
Pss 32:6; 42:
8; 69:3

5 The breakers of death surged round about me,
> the destroying floods overwhelmed me;
6 The cords of the nether world enmeshed me,
> the snares of death overtook me.
7 In my distress I called upon the Lord
> and cried out to my God;
> From his temple he heard my voice,
> and my cry to him reached his ears.

III

Jgs 5:4f; Hb
3:10
Ex 19:18; Sir
16:17
Pss 46:4; 97:4

8 The earth swayed and quaked;
> the foundations of the mountains trembled
> and shook when his wrath flared up.

Ex 15:8; Jb
36:33
Ps 97:3

9 Smoke rose from his nostrils,
> and a devouring fire from his mouth
> that kindled coals into flame.

Ps 144:5

10 And he inclined the heavens and came down,
> with dark clouds under his feet.

Ex 37:7ff; 1
Sm 4:4
Pss 80:2; 99:
1; 104:3
1 Kgs 8:12; Ps
77:18
Pss 97:2; 135:
7
Hb 3:4

11 He mounted a cherub and flew,
> borne on the wings of the wind.
12 And he made darkness the cloak about him;
> dark, misty rain-clouds his wrap.

Dt 4:11; Ps
120:4
Ex 19:19; Jb
36:33
Jb 37:2; Ps
29:4f
Zech 9:14

13 From the brightness of his presence
> coals were kindled to flame.
14 And the Lord thundered from heaven,
> the Most High gave forth his voice;

Wis 5:21; Ps
144:6

15 He sent forth his arrows to put them to flight,
> with frequent lightnings he routed them.
16 Then the bed of the sea appeared,
> and the foundations of the world were laid bare,
> At the rebuke of the Lord,
> at the blast of the wind of his wrath.

Ps 144:7

17 He reached out from on high and grasped me;
> he drew me out of the deep waters.

Pss 42:8; 69:2f

18 He rescued me from my mighty enemy

and from my foes, who were too powerful for me.
19 They attacked me in the day of my calamity,
but the Lord came to my support.
20 He set me free in the open,
and rescued me, because he loves me.

IV

1 Sm 26:23   21 The Lord rewarded me according to my justice;
according to the cleanness of my hands he requited me;
22 For I kept the ways of the Lord
and was not disloyal to my God;
23 For his ordinances were all present to me,
and his statutes I put not from me,
Dt 18:13   24 But I was wholehearted toward him,
and I was on my guard against guilt.
25 And the Lord requited me according to my justice,
according to the cleanness of my hands in his sight.
1 Sm 2:30   26 Toward the faithful you are faithful,
Ps 125:4   toward the wholehearted you are wholehearted,
27 Toward the sincere you are sincere,
but toward the crooked you are astute;
Prv 3:34   28 For lowly people you save
Jb 22:29   but haughty eyes you bring low;
1 Kgs 11:36;   29 You indeed, O Lord, give light to my lamp;
Jb 29:3
2 Sm 22:29;   O my God, you brighten the darkness about me;
Ps 139:12
30 For with your aid I run against an armed band,
and by the help of my God I leap over a wall.
Dt 32:4   31 God's way is unerring,
Ps 12:7   the promise of the Lord is fire-tired;
Prv 30:5   he is a shield to all who take refuge in him.

B

I

Is 45:21   32 For who is God except the Lord?
Dt 32:4; Is   Who is a rock, save our God?
44:8
33 The God who girded me with strength
and kept my way unerring;
Hb 3:19; Pss   34 Who made my feet swift as those of hinds
11:1; 61:3
Dt 32:13; Is   and set me on the heights;
58:14
Jb 29:20; Ps   35 Who trained my hands for war
144:1
Jb 20:24; Ps   and my arms to bend a bow of brass.
7:14

II

36   You have given me your saving shield;

Pss 3:6; 20:7;
40:18
          your right hand has upheld me,
          and you have stooped to make me great.

Jb 18:7; Pss
17:5; 21:8
37   You made room for my steps;
          unwavering was my stride.

Ps 21:9
38   I pursued my enemies and overtook them,
          nor did I turn again till I made an end of them.

39   I smote them and they could not rise;
          they fell beneath my feet.

III

40   And you girded me with strength for war;

2 Sm 8:11f
          you subdued my adversaries beneath me.

41   My enemies you put to flight before me,

Ps 25:19
          and those who hated me you destroyed.

42   They cried for help — but no one saved them;

Hb 1:2
          to the Lord — but he answered them not.

43   I ground them fine as the dust before the wind;
          like the mud in the streets I trampled them down.

IV

44   You rescued me from the strife of the people;

Rev 2:26f
          you made me head over nations;
          A people I had not known became my slaves;

45   as soon as they heard me they obeyed.

Ps 144:7
     The foreigners fawned and cringed before me;

Mi 7:17
46   they staggered forth from their fortresses.

C

47   The Lord live! And blessed be my Rock!

Pss 18:3; 62:7
          Extolled be God my savior.

48   O God, who granted me vengeance,
          who made peoples subject to me

49   and preserved me from my enemies,
          Truly above my adversaries you exalt me
          and from the violent man you have rescued me.

Rm 15:9
50   Therefore will I proclaim you, O Lord, among the nations,

Pss 7:18; 21:
14
          and I will sing praise to your name,

1 Sm 2:10; Ps
20:7
51   You who gave great victories to your king
          and showed kindness to your anointed,

1 Kgs 2:33; Ps
78:70
          to David and his posterity forever.

This royal psalm of thanks describes how, when the king was already in the jaws of death, overwhelmed by the floods of Destruction, he called in his distress upon the Lord (vv 1-7), and the theophany God, revealing himself in his awful majesty, rescued his anointed (vv 8-20) on account of his loyalty and innocence (21-31). The account of the theophany follows the cultic pattern described elsewhere (§13d). By associating the king's deliverance with Israel's at the Red Sea (cf. v 16) the rescuing of God's anointed (v 51) is linked with the very foundation of the *Heilsgeschichte* tradition. The "protestation of innocence" (21-25) does not here derive from pharisaic self-righteousness but it is "an affirmation of faith in the covenantal faithfulness of God, which may be experienced by those who in obedience to God's ordinances keep their faith in him" (A. Weiser; cf. §12e). In the second part of the psalm God is praised and thanked for the "grace of kingship" (Weiser) renewed in Israel, and especially for having prepared the king for war (vv 32-35), given him victory over his enemies (36-43) and confirmed his ascendancy over the nations (44-46). Although the style remains somewhat grandiose in this second part, the cosmic background of the first part is replaced by a more plausible account of events dealing with war and political prisoners. Two hymnic stanzas of praise begin (2-4) and end (47-51) the psalm.

The ascription of the psalm to David by the heading (v 1) is confirmed in 2 Sm 22, where the text of the poem is thus introduced: "And David spoke to the Lord the words of this song on the day when the Lord delivered him from the hand of all his enemies, and from the hand of Saul." There exists no compelling reason to exclude the possibility that David did compose the psalm. The parallels indicated from subsequent biblical texts may be dependent on the psalm or other common traditions. The so-called "Deuteronomic style in verses 21ff," writes Weiser, "is confined to phrases which are by no means characteristic only of the Deuteronomic literature." He indicates other features which seem to assign the psalm to an early date, as, for example, the king's archaic method of fighting on foot (vv 30, 34, 37). The expression *bᵉnê nēkār,* "the foreigners," is, however, found only in Ez 44:7, in the last chapters of Isaiah (cf. 60:10), in Neh 9:2 and in Ps 144:7, 11, dependent on Ps 18 (cf. *BJ*). This does not favor a pre-exilic date of the psalm. Besides, the passage from Micah, parallel to verses 45b-46, is post-exilic: "They shall come quaking from their fastnesses, trembling in fear of you [the Lord]" (Mi 7:17b).

Not so much a single victory over the enemies as probably a series of providential saving deeds lie behind this enthusiastic praise, especially in the second part. The text may have suffered alterations during its long history. The cosmic dimension attributed to an event affecting a small kingdom indicates here again that the *prima intentio* of the psalm, in the first part especially, is the celebrating of the majesty of God which transcends the limits of time and place, while it manifests itself in some historical event (see on *Ps 66).

Dahood's annotations on Ps 18 begin with the psalm's heading where he reads "from the hand of Sheol" instead of "from the hand of Saul." The poet's delivery from Sheol forms the subject-matter of verses 4-7. Not only that, Dahood observes, but "rescue from the grasp of all his enemies and from the hand of Sheol fairly summarizes the contents of the entire poem." An unpublished psalm in Akkadian, found at Ras Shamra, begins with the words, "Since the day you delivered me from the mouth of Death." The psalmist's interest in Sheol will of course appear even greater, if in verses 4, 18, 49 the "adversaries" are identified with "the Foe," Death personified (see on *Pss 30:2 and 13:3, 5), and if "the destroying floods (v 5)" are "the torrents of Belial," with the explanation that the word *Belial* derives from the root *bl'*, "to swallow" (hence "throat"). Add to this Dahood's reading of verse 20a: "He brought me out of the broad domain" (= Sheol; cf. Ps 31:9). Read also an allusion to Sheol in verse 8: "The nether world (*'ereṣ*) reeled and rocked, the foundations of the mountains shuddered." Other texts which place the foundations of the mountains in the underworld would include Dt 32:22; Is 24:18; Jer 31:37; Mi 6:2; Jon 2:7. Already in his *Schöpfung und Chaos in Urzeit und Endzeit* (Göttingen, 1895), p. 18, n. 1, Gunkel had observed that in Ex 15:12, Is 14:12 and Eccl 3:21, *'ereṣ* denoted "nether world." In some biblical passages *'ereṣ* (usually = "land," "earth") does seem to mean "nether world." In Dahood's list the following references to psalms are given: 7:6; 18:8; 22:30; 41:3; *61:3, 10; 71:20; 95:4; 106:17; 141:7; 143:3; 147:6; 148:7 (on Sheol see §14d).

Should the poetic "wings of the wind" disappear from verse 11? Dahood proposes to read: "He mounted the Cherub and flew, and soared on wings outstretched" (*kanepē rewaḥ*: "the wings of broadness"; cf. Ps 104:3). In verse 43 also, Dahood notes, the Masoretes have erroneously read *'al p^{e}nē rū^{a}ḥ,* "on the face of the wind," instead of *'al p^{e}nē rewaḥ,* "upon the square": "I pulverized them like dust in the square, like the mud in the streets I trampled them." To this Dahood adds: "The image of God flying upon the Cherub of extended wings" is related to the widely mistranslated and misinterpreted phrase of Ez 28:14, *k^{e}rūb mimšaḥ hassōkēk,* "the overshadowing Cherub of wings outstretched" (cf. Vulg.: "Cherub extentus"). The use of *mšḥ* with the meaning "to measure, extend" is attested in Ugaritic (t. 76, 11:22-23; Gordon, p. 182): "Your powerful wings will Baal stretch out, Baal will stretch them out for flight." The more common meaning, "to anoint," attached to *mšḥ,* is not to be retained in Ez 28:14: "With an *anointed* guardian cherub I placed you" (*RSV*).

If the "enemies" do not in fact appear before verse 18, then Dahood's translation of verse 15 gives a better meaning: "He forged his arrows and scattered them, he multiplied his shafts and dispersed them." The pronouns "them" refer to the arrows and the shafts. The latter are "bolts of lightning." The biblical poet, explains Dahood, ascribed to Yahweh the attributes of the Canaanite artisan-god Kothar. The point of the Aqhat (Ugaritic) legend is that the mortal Aqhat came into possession of a miraculous bow designed by Kothar for the hunt-goddess Anath (Dahood, p. 115). The theme of the artisan-God forging the weapons of the psalmist recurs in verse 35: "Who trained my hands for battle, lowered the miraculous bow into my arms," and also in Ps 7:14: "O that he would create the weapons of death, make his arrows into flaming shafts." The effect of lightning is more apparent in Dahood's translation of verse 16:

> The fountain heads of the sea were exposed,
>   and the world's foundations were laid bare,
> At your roar, O Yahweh,
>   at the blast from your nostrils.

Referring to a more traditional translation of verse 35 (cf. *CV*), S. Mowinckel (I, p. 54) points to other parallel sources: "When the king in Ps 18:34 says about Yahweh that 'he teacheth my hands to war, so that I can bend a bow of bronze,' this may be illustrated by an Egyptian picture of the God Seth teaching Pharaoh Thutmose to use a bow." "Of all the psalms, he adds (I, p. 72), Ps 18 is the one which has the most Egyptian style, and reminds one most directly of hymns to the 'god' Pharaoh, with their highflown descriptions of his majesty's overwhelming victories over all the wretched and wicked 'foreign' nations — poetical descriptions which are not always in accordance with the historical results of the 'victories.' One suspects the composer of Ps 18 of having studied the poetical art of Egypt, and that he too lays more stress on grandiose description and ebullient enthusiasm than on actual facts."

Arguing that the dative (double-duty) suffix, "to me," required with *tā'îr*, "*to* (cause to) shine," is to be supplied from *nērī*, "my lamp," Dahood reads in verse 29: "You shine for me; my lamp is Yahweh, my God illumines my darkness." In 2 Sm 22:29 we read in fact (*RSV*): "Yea, thou art my lamp, O Lord; and my God lightens my darkness." Compare with Ps 139:12 (Dahood): "Darkness is not too dark for you and the night shines for you like the day; as the darkness, so the light." — A better parallelism certainly results from translating verse 42 with *mošia'* understood as "Savior" (cf. §11d): "They implored, but the Savior was not there, the Most High Yahweh, but he did not answer them" (Dahood). This is how *The Anchor Bible* reads verses 44-46 (as compared with *CV*):

> You delivered me from the shafts of people,
>   protected me from the venom of nations.
> An alien people must serve me,
>   as soon as they hear, they obey me;
> Foreigners cringe before me.
> Foreigners shrivel up,
>   and their hearts are seized with anguish.
> May Yahweh live!
> Praised be my Mountain!
> And exalted the God of my triumph!

F. M. Cross and D. N. Freedman have published (*JBL* 1953, pp. 15-34) a detailed study of 2 Samuel 22 = Ps 18: "Both texts, they note, have been revised and modernized considerably in the course of transmission, but 2 Sam 22 preserves a number of archaic readings, which point to a minimal date in the ninth-eighth centuries B.C. for the written composition of the poem." Among the "archaic linguistic phenomena" can be mentioned here the use of the preposition *b* to mean 'from' and the presence of enclitic *mem* [cf. *Ps 31:18], both of which have been subject to editorial revision. Important also is the conclusion "that the imperfect form of the verb was the common, generally used verb form in old Israelite poetry, as in old Canaanite poetry, and that its time aspect was determined by the context, not the presence or absence of the conjunction" (i.e., *"waw consecutive"*). "It seems clear, these scholars add, that the author of the psalm drew on a number of older sources. The theophany in verses 8-16 with its Canaanite associations is of a piece with the ancient poetry of Israel, belonging to the period of the Judges and early monarchy. Similarly in verses 26-27, an old gnomic couplet with sing-song rhythm and anthropopathic conceptions, apparently is quoted by the psalmist.... It remains a question as to whether the psalm is an amalgamation of two or more independent odes, or a single poem sharply divided into separate parts." The Davidic authorship of the psalm is not excluded since "a tenth century date for the poem is not at all improbable" (p. 20f).

PSALM 20 (19)

Prayer for the King in Time of War

1 *For the leader. A psalm of David.*

I

1 Sm 7:8   2 The Lord answer you in time of distress;

Prv 18:10; Ps 44:6   the name of the God of Jacob defend you!

1 Kgs 8:30-44   3 May he send you help from the sanctuary,

Pss 14:7; 128:5   from Sion may he sustain you.

Ps 4:6   4 May he remember all your offerings

1 Sm 7:9; Pss 51:21; 61:6   and graciously accept your holocausts.

Ps 21:3   5 May he grant you what is in your heart

    and fulfill your every plan.

2 Chr 20:19; Ps 21:6   6 May we shout for joy at your victory

    and raise the standards in the name of our God.

Prv 10:24; Ps 37:4   The Lord grant all your requests!

II

Pss 2:2; 18:51   7 Now I know that the Lord has given victory to his anointed,

Pss 56:10; 132:10   that he has answered him from his holy heaven

Dt 26:15; Ps 20:7   with the strength of his victorious right hand.

Hos 1:7; Mi 5:9   8 Some are strong in chariots; some, in horses;

Is 31:1; 36:9;
2 Chr 14:11
1 Sm 17:45;
Ps 33:16f
Is 40:31; Ps
18:37

> but we are strong in the name of the Lord, our God.
> 9 Though they bow down and fall,
> 　　yet we stand erect and firm.
> 10 O Lord, grant victory to the king,
> 　　and answer us when we call upon you.

It has been suggested, on good grounds, that various speakers intervene in this psalm: a priest (vv 2-4), the congregation (v 6), a priest or a cult prophet (v 7), the congregation again (vv 8-10). Perhaps the psalm was part of a sacrificial liturgy performed before the king departed for the battlefield (cf. 1 Sm 7:9; 13:9; 1 Kgs 8:44; 2 Chr 20:18f). In that sense Ps 20 could be listed among the so-called "protective psalms" (cf. *Ps 71). Other commentators would associate the psalm with a fixed liturgy, namely that of New Year's day, when Yahweh was glorified as King. Accordingly Weiser translates verse 10: "O Lord, do help us, O King, who answers us in the day we call."

The aim of the cultic ceremony in which Ps 20 featured was to obtain that the "grace of kingship" be sent from Mount Zion (v 3), the usual site of God's epiphany (cf. Am 1:2). The assurance that the prayer has been heard (v 7) is variously explained: oracle, sacrificial evidence, prophetic pronouncement, cultic theophany, or, more simply, news from the battlefront. Yet the assurance is not too surprising to any one who takes seriously the promise that divine help is guaranteed to God's anointed (cf. Ps 18:5; comp. Pss 56:10; 60: 8; 140:13). A different, perhaps better, translation of verse 7 is proposed in *The Anchor Bible*: "Now I know that Yahweh has given his anointed victory, has granted him triumph from his sacred heaven, and from his fortress has given victory with his right hand" (see on *Pss 8:2f and 78:26).

The prophets have consistently preached that it is not the will of God that Israel should compete with the other nations in resting confidence on the best weapons of war, like horse-drawn chariots (vv 8-9; cf. Dt 17:16; Hos 1:7; 14:4; Mi 5:9; Is 31:1; Zech 8:9; Pss 33: 16f; 147:10f). "Ps 20, as well as Ps 21, writes Mowinckel (I, p. 224), is partly addressed to the king himself, and in these psalms, as well as in Ps 72, the intercession is distinguished by piling up words of blessing; an evidence of the religious and style-historical connection between the prayer and the word of blessing, which is the cultic origin of the intercession" (For the dating of Pss 20 and 21, cf. §5e).

PSALM 21 (20)

Thanksgiving and Prayers for the King

1 *For the leader. A psalm of David.*

I

2 O Lord, in your strength the king is glad;
    in your victory how greatly he rejoices!

Ps 20:5   3 You have granted him his heart's desire;
    you refused not the wish of his lips.

4 For you welcomed him with goodly blessings,
    you placed on his head a crown of pure gold.

Dt 5:30; 6:24   5 He asked life of you: you gave him
Is 38:4ff; 2   length of days forever and ever.
Kgs 20:6
1 Kgs 1:31;   6 Great is his glory in your victory;
Neh 2:3
Pss 20:6; 61:   majesty and splendor you conferred upon him.
7; 72:17
2 Sm 1:29; 1   7 For you made him a blessing forever;
Chr 17:27
Gn 12:2; 48:   you gladdened him with the joy of your presence.
20
Pss 7:18; 46:   8 For the king trusts in the Lord,
5; 50:14
Pss 16:8; 18:   and through the kindness of the Most High he
37; 112:6   stands unshaken.

II

Pss 18:38; 34:   9 May your hand reach all your enemies,
17   may your right hand reach your foes!

Hos 7:7; Is   10 Make them burn as though in a fiery furnace,
30:33
Mal 3:19   when you appear.

2 Sm 2:37   May the Lord consume them in his anger;
    let fire devour them.

Lam 2:20; Jb   11 Destroy their fruit from the earth
18:19
Pss 34:17;   and their posterity from among men.
109:13
    12 Though they intend evil against you,

Prv 24:21   devising plots, they cannot succeed,

13 For you shall put them to flight;

Ps 45:6   you shall aim your shafts against them.

14 Be extolled, O Lord, in your strength!

Pss 7:18; 89:   We will sing, chant the praise of your might.
14

In this psalm again, *blessings* (*bir^ekôt*, v 4) and "saving help" (*y^ešû'âh*: vv 2, 6), proper to the "grace of kingship" are celebrated. They include, according to Weiser, such realities as convey terms like "glory," "splendor," "majesty," "sovereignty," "life," "length of days," "joy," "salvation," "victory." Perhaps the psalm was part of a coronation ritual (cf. v 4). Both the "cultic representation of the blessings" (vv 2-7) and the prayer (vv 9-13) may have been recited by a priest in the presence of the king, while verses 8 and 14 would be the congregation's antiphon (like Ps 20:6c). F. C. Fensham suggests that "Ps 21 may be an enthronement psalm which is closely connected to the renewal of the covenant . . . . A possible time of origin is during the reign of Hezekiah" (716-687). E. Beaucamp would deny that Ps 21 is a royal *Te Deum*. Should we not, he asks, consider verses 9-14 as addressed to Yahweh? The psalm is a "coronation liturgy" as could be also Pss 5, 16, 23, 27, 42-43, 61, 63, 84, 91, 101 etc. One of the blessings, "length of days forever and ever," has been interpreted in a messianic sense by late Judaism and by some commentators as referring to the everlasting reign of the Davidic dynasty. More simply, these hyperbolical expressions are quite common in ancient court etiquette, reflected also in the Bible (cf. 1 Kgs 1:31; Neh 2:3; Is 53:10; Dn 2:4). Being God's anointed, his "vicegerent" (cf. *Ps 2), the king shares in a way divine fulness of life, as he does divine majesty and divine authority. The king was considered as the dispenser to the nations of the blessings he received: "for you made him a blessing forever" (v 7). Hence the great importance attributed to the "grace of kingship."

Alterations in the text may account for the fact that verses 9-13 refer partly to the king and partly to God (see below). In the ancient "song of Moses" already, God is called a "man of war" (Ex 15:3; cf. §14b), while the mention of "fire" evokes the "jealousy" of God (Ex 20:5), the Sinai theophany (cf. Dt 4:12; 5:5, 22-25; Ps 18:14f) and the eschatological day of judgment (Am 1:4-14; 2:2-5; Mal 3:2; 4:1). The psalm ends with a call which is also an element of the theophany in the cult: "Arise, O Lord!" (cf. §13d)

Dahood would entitle Ps 21: "A psalm of thanksgiving for the royal victory prayed for in the preceding psalm." Verses 9-13 describe the victorious battle: the subject is Yahweh and the imperfect forms are used to describe past narrative action (as in "archaic Hebrew poetry"; see on *Ps 18): "Your left hand overtook all your foes, your right hand overtook those who hate you . . ." etc. The favor asked for and granted, as mentioned in verses 5-7, would be "eternal life" (see on *Ps 27:13; cf. Prv 12:28). Accordingly Dahood reads in verses 5a and 7b: "Life eternal he asked of you . . . you will make him gaze with happiness upon your face" (cf. *Pss 16:11; 17:15). The king, it is explained, was thought to receive the gift of immortality on the day of his coronation (cf. Ps 2:7). Another royal attribute is described as "splendor and majesty" (v 6). This corresponds to the Akkadian concept of *melammu,* denoting "a characteristic atttribute of the gods consisting of a dazzling aureole or nimbus which surrounds the divinity. The king as representative and likeness of the gods also has such an aura, which constitutes the divine legitimation of his royalty. This *melammu* is bestowed upon him when he becomes king" (Dahood). Mowinckel, for his part, notes (I, p. 56) that the king's prayer for "life" and "length of days forever and ever" (v 5) often recurs both in Egyptian and Mesopotamian royal inscriptions. The "promising notes" of Pss 21 and 72, he believes, are probably not to be looked upon as direct oracles, "but as the words of an inspired psalmist, as echoes of such oracles inserted into the intercessions and blessing wishes which the poet-singer puts into the mouth of the congregation. Once more they bring out the close relationship between temple prophet and psalmist, or rather, show that in fact the two would in many cases be one and the same person."

PSALM 45 (44)

Nuptial Ode for the Messianic King

Pss 60:1; 80:1   1 For the leader; according to "Lilies." A maśkil of the sons
                     of Core. A love song.
                     I
                  2 My heart overflows with a goodly theme;
                        as I sing my ode to the king,
                        my tongue is nimble as the pen of a skillful scribe.
                     II
                  3 Fairer in beauty are you than the sons of men;
                        grace is poured out upon your lips;
Pss 3:9; 21:7;   thus God has blessed you forever.
67:2, 7
                  4 Gird your sword upon your thigh, O mighty one!
Ps 21:6   in your splendor and your majesty ride on triumphant.

<table>
<tr><td>Is 9:6; 11:4</td><td>5</td><td>In the cause of truth and for the sake of justice;
and may your right hand show you wondrous deeds.</td></tr>
<tr><td>Ps 21:13</td><td>6</td><td>Your arrows are sharp; people are subject to you;
the king's enemies lose heart.</td></tr>
<tr><td>2 Sm 7:16; Is 9:1
Heb 1:8f; Pss 33:14; 55:20
Is 11:4</td><td>7</td><td>Your throne, O God, stands forever and ever;
a tempered rod is your royal scepter.</td></tr>
<tr><td></td><td>8</td><td>You love justice and hate wickedness;
therefore God, your God, has anointed you
with the oil of gladness above your fellow kings.</td></tr>
<tr><td></td><td>9</td><td>With myrrh and aloes and cassia your robes are fragrant;</td></tr>
<tr><td>1 Kgs 22:39;
Am 3:15; 6:4</td><td></td><td>from ivory palaces string music brings you joy.</td></tr>
<tr><td></td><td>10</td><td>The daughters of kings come to meet you;</td></tr>
<tr><td>1 Kgs 9:28;
Jb 22:24</td><td></td><td>the queen takes her place at your right hand
 in gold of Ophir. </td></tr>
</table>

III

<table>
<tr><td>Jos 24:2</td><td>11</td><td>Hear, O daughter, and see; turn your ear,</td></tr>
<tr><td>Gn 12:1; Ez 16:3</td><td></td><td>forget your people, and your father's house.</td></tr>
<tr><td></td><td>12</td><td>So shall the king desire your beauty;
for he is your lord, and you must worship him.</td></tr>
<tr><td>Is 60:5f</td><td>13</td><td>And the city of Tyre is here with gifts;
the rich among the people seek your favor.</td></tr>
<tr><td></td><td>14</td><td>All glorious is the king's daughter as she enters;</td></tr>
<tr><td>Ex 28:12, 39;
Is 61:6</td><td></td><td>her raiment is threaded with spun gold.</td></tr>
<tr><td></td><td>15</td><td>In embroidered apparel she is borne in to the king;
behind her the virgins of her train are brought to you.</td></tr>
<tr><td></td><td>16</td><td>They are borne in with gladness and joy;
they enter the palace of the king.</td></tr>
</table>

IV

<table>
<tr><td></td><td>17</td><td>The place of your fathers your sons shall have;
you shall make them princes through all the land.</td></tr>
<tr><td>Gn 17:7; 35:11
Is 60:15; Ps 66:3, 8</td><td>18</td><td>I will make your name memorable through all generations;
therefore shall nations praise you forever and ever.</td></tr>
</table>

This poem, Mowinckel thinks, is "the only example in the whole of Israelite psalm poetry of a true hymn to the king" (I, p. 74). It is not in fact a purely royal hymn, for the divine grace of kingship gets the real attention of the poet. Quite surprisingly Weiser offers no cultic interpretation of the psalm, which he calls "the only example of a profane lyric in the Psalter." It is, he adds, "a song of praise in honor of a young king and his consort, a princess of Tyre (v 13), which was composed and recited by a court-poet on the occasion of the ruler's wedding." The admonition served to the bride, "forget your people and your father's house," may be meant to avert the danger of other royal wives who would import idolatry and foreign customs into the kingdom of other Solomons or Achabs. In fact the mention of a "princess of Tyre" (v 13) seems a reference to royalty of the northern kingdom of Israel, as would indicate also the allusion to "ivory palaces" (v 9; cf. 1 Kgs 22:39; Am 3:15; 6:4). Such was the value of the hymn that it was soon interpreted as referring to the Messiah and as such was incorporated in the Psalter. To illustrate the superiority of Christ over the angels, the *Epistle to the Hebrews* states that in Ps 45:8-9 (*LXX*) it is written of the Son:

Thy throne, O God, is forever and ever,
and a sceptre of equity is the sceptre
    of thy kingdom.
Thou hast loved justice and hated iniquity;
therefore God, thy God, has anointed thee
with the oil of gladness above thy fellows (1:8-9).

The *ho theos* is correctly understood by R. E. Brown (*TS* 1965, p. 562) as a vocative and *Hebrews* here unequivocally applies the title "God" to Jesus. The psalm may be read also in the typical sense as referring to Christ and his bride the Church (cf. Mt 9:15; 25:1-13; Jn 3:29; 2 Cor 11:2; Eph 5:21-32; Rev 19:7; 21:9). Other Christian interpreters consider Ps 45 as directly messianic, that is, written by the inspired writer himself as celebrating the sacred nuptials of the messianic King with Israel (cf. Ez 16:13; Is 62:5; Ct 3:7, 11; 4:11) or with the Church. Since every Davidic king was a prospective Messiah (cf. §15c), it could well be that the very words of this lyric poem, written for an Israelite wedding, can now be read, in the fuller sense, as speaking of the "marriage of the Lamb" (Rev 19:7). From his thorough study of Ps 45, Philip J. King concludes (p. 129) that the poem is messianic in the typical sense: we promptly perceive in the person of the historical king (Solomon probably) of the royal psalm a prefiguring of the ideal sovereign of future times, the King-Messiah.

The king is handsome, notes Dahood, because God has favored him "from eternity" (v 3; see on *Ps 9:8), like other predestined individuals (cf. Ps 139:16; Is 49:1, 5; Jer 1:5; Gal 1:15). Considering the difficulty of telling the king, "Your throne, O God, stands forever and ever" (v 7), Dahood reads *kissē'ᵃkā* ("a denominative *piel* from *kissē'*, "throne") and translates: "The eternal and everlasting God has enthroned you!" This translation deprives of their main argument the proponents of an allegorical interpretation of the psalm. The poem does not any more apply to an earthly monarch an attribute strictly divine. Besides, one must always reckon with the figurative hyperbolic language of *Hofstil*, "style de cour" (cf. Ph. J. King, pp. 103-115 and R. Pautrel, "Le style . . ."). The divine vocative is maintained in *BJ* and qualified "titre protocolaire." In 2 Sm 14:17 the wise woman sent by Joab tells king David: "My lord is like the angel of God to discern good and evil." But this formula (cf. §26) is similar to God's reflection after the Fall: "Behold, the man has become like one of us, knowing good and evil" (Gn 3:22, *RSV*). Noting that Ps 45 is a *maśkîl* psalm (v 1), a poem, he says, involving a symbolic meaning, C. Schedl would place the nuptial ode beside Isaiah's prophetic songs on the Messiah's birthday (Is 7:14) and enthronement (Is 9:1). To the same messianic cycle, he adds, belong Pss 2, 72 and 110. Finally *bᵉtûlôt*, "virgins," in verse 15, should be read in the singular, thinks Dahood, like Phoenician *btlwt*, "maiden" (cf. *ḥokmôt*, Prv 9:1) and verse 15 can be translated: "Let the maiden be led to the king, let her companions be brought to her."

PSALM 72 (71)

The Kingdom of the Messiah

1 *Of Solomon.*

I

O God, with your judgment endow the king,

Is 9:6
    and with your justice, the king's son;

2 Sm 23:3
Is 9:5f; 11:3;
Jer 23:5
2 He shall govern your people with justice

    and your afflicted ones with judgment.

Zech 9:10
3 The mountains shall yield peace for the people,

Is 45:8; 52:7
    and the hills justice.

4 He shall defend the afflicted among the people,
    save the children of the poor,
    and crush the oppressor.

II

2 Sm 7:16; Ps 45:7
Ps 61:7

5 May he endure as long as the sun,
    and like the moon through all generations.

6 He shall be like rain coming down on the meadow,

Hos 6:3; Is 32:2; 45:8

    like showers watering the earth.

7 Justice shall flower in his days,

Ps 89:38

    and profound peace, till the moon be no more.

III

Pss 2:8; 98:3

8 May he rule from sea to sea,

Dt 11:24; Zech 9:10

    and from the River to the ends of the earth.

Sir 44:21; Ps 2:11
Mi 7:17; Is 49:23; 60:9
Pss 45:13; 48: 8; 68:30
Mt 2:11; Is 45:14; 60:6
Gn 49:10; 1 Kgs 10:1
Is 42:4,10

9 His foes shall bow before him,
    and his enemies shall lick the dust.

10 The kings of Tharsis and the Isles shall offer gifts;
    the kings of Arabia and Saba shall bring tribute.

11 All kings shall pay him homage,
    all nations shall serve him.

IV

Pss 35:10; 74: 21
Prv 31:8f

12 For he shall rescue the poor man when he cries out,
    and the afflicted when he has no one to help him.

13 He shall have pity for the lowly and the poor;

Jb 29:12

    the lives of the poor he shall save.

Pss 19:15; 49: 16
Ps 116:15

14 From fraud and violence he shall redeem them,
    and precious shall their blood be in his sight.

V

15 May he live to be given the gold of Arabia,
    and to be prayed for continually;
    day by day shall they bless him.

Is 27:6

16 May there be an abundance of grain upon the earth;

Hos 14:6f; Am 9:13

    on the tops of the mountains the crops shall rustle
                    like Lebanon.

Is 49:20; 54:1

    the city dwellers shall flourish like the verdure
                   of the fields.

Ps 21:7

17 May his name be blessed forever;
    as long as the sun his name shall remain.

Gn 12:3; 48: 20; Zech 8:13

    In him shall all the tribes of the earth be blessed;

Sir 44:21   all the nations shall proclaim his happiness.

* * *

Pss 68:20; 71:   18   Blessed be the Lord, the God of Israel,
22; 89:53
Pss 71:16ff;   who alone does wondrous deeds.
75:2
                   19   And blessed forever be his glorious name;
Nm 14:21   may the whole earth be filled with his glory.
                        Amen. Amen.
                   20   The prayers of David the son of Jesse are ended.

Christian commentators entitle this psalm "The promised king" (*JB*) or "The Kingdom of the Messiah" (*CV* and the revised Latin Psalter). The Targum also has interpreted it as referring to the Messiah. Although the psalm is not quoted by the New Testament, it features in the Church's official prayers for Christmas, the Epiphany (com. vv 10, 15 and Mt 2:11), Holy Thursday, Christ the King and Holy Trinity. Almost half of the psalm consists of wishes that simply cannot be fulfilled in the world's present or foreseeable conditions. Even ancient Oriental court style (*Hofstil,* cf. *Ps 2) cannot account for all the hyperbolic expressions. Some commentators read in the psalm Israel's hope for the coming of *the ideal king* as the prophets have depicted him (cf. Is 9:5; 11:3; Zech 9:9f). In verse 15 it is written: "May he live ... to be prayed for continually," and the whole psalm can be interpreted as an intercession for the king (cf. A. Barucq, *L'expression ...,* p. 438). This has worried past literal messianists, since we do not pray for the divine Messiah, although we do for his coming. Yet we say to God: "Thy kingdom come!" (Mt. 6:10) Besides, messianic texts do not describe all the aspects of the future reality. Finally, "to pray for" can be equivalent to expressing a "wish," a "blessing" or a "prediction." Ps 72, Mowinckel writes (I, p. 69), "becomes [in the latter part] a formula of blessing which reminds one strongly of the promises of the prophets as it oscillates between blessing and prediction. The officiating priest who recites the psalm ... speaks on behalf of the congregation and in the form of a petition. But he is also the representative of Yahweh and pronounces strong and effective words with a ring of certainty."

According to the "titles" mentioned in the Septuagint and some Hebrew manuscripts, Solomon would be the subject of the psalm, presumably because of verses 1, 2 and 10 (cf. 1 Kgs 3:12ff, 28; 10:

1-13). Perhaps Ps 72 featured, like other royal psalms (cf. 20 and 21), in the liturgy of the king's enthronement. Since the Israelite king was considered as God's representative, it is not too unexpected that attributes of the kingship of God be drawn upon to express the hoped for prosperity and justice of the new reign. Again, since Nathan's prophecy (2 Sm 7:1-17), all Davidic princes were candidates for the Messianic promotion (cf. §15c), and thus could the celebration of their accession be illumined with the reality of the eschatological kingdom. It is generally thought that verses 18-19 represent a doxology concluding the second book of the Psalter. If this is not the case, if they belong to Ps 72, then the verses could shed light on the psalm's meaning: "The king's reign and its blessing are the reflection of the sovereign rule of God and of his salvation, and his fame is overshadowed by the 'glory' (*kābôd*) of God who alone does wondrous things" (Weiser). P. W. Skehan has shown that Ps 72 is a unity. It has five stanzas (the doxology excluded), each with four full lines of Hebrew verse (1-4; 5-8; 9-11; 12-15; 16:17).

Ps 72 is pre-exilic if it describes the reign of an Israelite king. The apparent allusions to post-exilic biblical passages can be explained of course as later editorial or messianic adaptations. Yet it could be, observes R. Pautrel, that the psalm is post-exilic and sings the glory of a non-Israelite king or kingdom. Does not Yahweh call Cyrus "my shepherd" and "his anointed"? (Is 44:28; 45:1) "It is worth noting, writes Mowinckel (I, p. 55), that when the Israelite psalmist wishes to express the king's universal sovereignty, he does so in images which are formed from the Babylonian point of view, and which originated there," as when he writes: "May he rule from sea to sea, and from the River to the ends of the earth" (72:8; cf. 89:26; cf. §9b). R. Tournay reads in verse 16 an allusion to a myth, current in ancient Lebanon: the awakening of Melqart, the great Baal of Tyre, the god of vegetation, marked the appearance of spring (cf. 1 Kgs 18: 27). The allusion, he adds, would rather point to the post-exilic period. In verse 9 the difficult *ṣiyyîm* is retained by *JB* with the explanation: "The word, meaning the animals or demons of the desert (Is 13:21; 34:14; Jer 50:39; Ez 34:28), here refers to subjugated heathen states (cf. Is 27:1; Dn 7:3, etc.; Rev 13:1, etc.)." The first part of the verse is translated: "The Beast will cower before him and his enemies grovel in the dust."

PSALM 89 (88)

Prayer for the Fulfillment of God's Promises to David

Ps 88:1

1 A *maśkíl* of Ethan the Ezrahite.

I

Is 63:7

2 The favors of the Lord I will sing forever;

Pss 79:13; 90:16

through all generations my mouth shall proclaim
your faithfulness.

Is 54:10

3 For you have said, "My kindness is established forever";

Pss 57:4; 92:3

in heaven you have confirmed your faithfulness:

Is 55:3

4 "I have made a covenant with my chosen one,

Pss 18:51; 132:10f

I have sworn to David my servant:

5 Forever will I confirm your posterity

2 Sm 7:16

and establish your throne for all generations."

II

Pss 19:2; 97:16

6 The heavens proclaim your wonders, O Lord,

Pss 34:10; 111:1

and your faithfulness, in the assembly of the holy ones.

7 For who in the skies can rank with the Lord?

Pss 8:6; 58:1; 82:1

Who is like the Lord among the sons of God?

Ex 15:11; Zech 14:5 Pss 84:8; 86:8

8 God is terrible in the council of the holy ones;

he is great and awesome beyond all round about him.

Pss 24:10; 35:10

9 O Lord, God of hosts, who is like you?

Mighty are you, O Lord, and your faithfulness
surrounds you.

Jb 7:12

10 You rule over the surging of the sea;

you still the swelling of its waves.

Is 30:7; 51:9; Jb 26:12 Nm 10:35f; Ps 68:2ff Ps 24:1

11 You have crushed Rahab with a mortal blow;

with your strong arm you have scattered your enemies.

12 Yours are the heavens, and yours is the earth;

the world and its fullness you have founded;

13 North and south you created;

Thabor and Hermon rejoice at your name.

Ps 21:14

14 Yours is a mighty arm;

strong is your hand, exalted your right hand.

Pss 9:8; 74:12; 93:2 Pss 25:10; 115:1; 138:2

15 Justice and judgment are the foundations of your throne;

kindness and truth go before you.

16 Happy the people who know the joyful shout;

Is 60:19; Ps 80:4		in the light of your countenance, O Lord, they walk.
Pss 75:10; 92: 5	17	At your name they rejoice all the day,
		and through your justice they are exalted.
	18	For you are the splendor of their strength,
Ps 75:5		and by your favor our horn is exalted.
	19	For to the Lord belongs our shield,
Is 6:3; Ps 78: 41		and to the Holy One of Israel, our king.
		III
2 Sm 7:4ff	20	Once you spoke in a vision,
		and to your faithful one you said:
1 Chr 17:7		"Of a stripling I have made a champion;
		over the people I have set a youth.
Is 42:1; Ps 18: 51	21	I have found David, my servant;
Acts 13:22; 1 Sm 2:10		with my holy oil I have anointed him,
	22	That my hand may be always with him,
		and that my arm may make him strong.
	23	"No enemy shall deceive him,
		nor shall the wicked afflict him.
1 Chr 17:8	24	But I will crush his foes before him
		and those who hate him I will smite.
Ex 34:6; Pss 57:4· 98:3	25	My faithfulness and my kindness shall be with him,
		and through my name shall his horn be exalted.
	26	I will set his hand upon the sea,
		his right hand upon the rivers.
1 Chr 17:13f; Ps 2:7 Pss 78:35; 92: 16	27	"He shall say of me, 'you are my father,
		my God, the Rock, my savior.'
	28	And I will make him the first-born,
Rev 1:5		highest of the kings of the earth.
	29	Forever I will maintain my kindness toward him,
Is 55:3; Ps 132:11f		and my covenant with him stands firm.
	30	I will make his posterity endure forever
Ps 72:5		and his throne as the days of heaven.
Lv 26:14-33	31	"If his sons forsake my law
Pss 81:12; 95: 8ff		and walk not according to my ordinances,
Dt 4:25ff	32	If they violate my statutes
		and keep not my commands
	33	I will punish their crime with a rod
		and their guilt with stripes.

34 Yet my kindness I will not take from him,

Ez 16:60
nor will I belie my faithfulness.

Is 61:8; Sir 47:22
35 "I will not violate my covenant;
the promise of my lips I will not alter.

Am 4:2
36 Once, by my holiness, have I sworn;

Is 55:3; Jer 33:20f
I will not be false to David.

37 His posterity shall continue forever,
and his throne shall be like the sun before me;

Sir 43:6; Ps 72:7
38 Like the moon, which remains forever —
a faithful witness in the sky."

IV

Ps 44:10:25
39 Yet you have rejected and spurned

Ps 85:6
and been enraged at your anointed.

40 You have renounced the covenant with your servant,
and defiled his crown in the dust.

41 You have broken down all his walls;
you have laid his strongholds in ruins;

42 All who pass by the way have plundered him;

Ps 79:4
he is made the reproach of his neighbors.

43 You have exalted the right hands of his foes,
you have gladdened all his enemies.

44 You have turned back his sharp sword
and have not sustained him in battle.

45 You have deprived him of his luster
and hurled his throne to the ground.

Hos 11:1; Jer 2:2
46 You have shortened the days of his youth;

Is 46:3
you have covered him with shame.

V

Pss 6:4; 13:2ff
47 How long, O Lord? Will you hide yourself forever?
Will your wrath burn like fire?

Jb 7:7
48 Remember how short my life is;

Pss 39:5; 62: 10; 94:3
how frail you created all the children of men!

49 What man shall live, and not see death,
but deliver himself from the power of the nether world?

50 Where are your ancient favors, O Lord,
which you pledged to David by your faithfulness?

51 Remember, O Lord, the insults to your servants:
I bear in my bosom all the accusations of the nations

52 With which your enemies have reviled, O Lord,
with which they have reviled your anointed on his way!

* * *

Pss 72:17ff;
103:1

53 Blessed be the Lord forever.

Amen, and amen!

The three sections of the psalm (vv 6-19; 20-38; 39-46) are preceded by an introduction (vv 2-5) which announces the themes of the second and third sections: the hymnic praise of the Lord (vv 6-19) and the divine promise to the royal Davidic succession (vv 20-38). A supplication (vv 47-52) at the end of the psalm follows the fourth section (39-46), which, in the form of a national lament, describes the present disastrous situation, setting a sharp contrast with the divine promises. The references supplied indicate the main allusions to other biblical material (for the New Testament quotations, see also §16a). If it is assumed, with most commentators, that the national and royal calamity described in verses 39-46 alludes to the destruction of Jerusalem in 586, then the psalm as a whole is not pre-exilic, although preexisting material, like the theophany themes (vv 10-15; cf. Ps 18:8-16) could have been used in the composition.

It seems likely to A. Weiser that Ps 89 "was used in times of a grave national disaster (possibly pre-exilic) and was recited in the cult when the accession to the throne of both the heavenly King and the earthly king were (sic) celebrated together at the Covenant Festival." A cultic tradition also lies behind the prophecy of Nathan (2 Sm 7). According to Mowinckel (I, p. 63), the enthronement or anointment oracles, as recorded in Pss 2 and 110 or alluded to in Ps 89:20-22, have furnished "the material which the tradition used, when in the legend of Nathan, it makes Nathan pronounce such promises to David." It is not explained why what this author calls the "legend of Nathan" could not have provided the material to the oracles (see on *Ps 132:11f). In Weiser's setting, the various parts of the psalm appear as follows: a short hymn sung by a priest revealing God's character and providential rule (vv 2-5); jubilant response intonated by "the chorus of God's celestial attendants" (vv 6-8) and continued by the congregation (9-19); the king's answer (20-38); the community lament and supplication (vv 39-52). The psalmist could only express "the riddle of *Heilsgeschichte*" and hope for a solution. The solution seems to be that the Nathan prophecy was conditional and providential as regards the temporal Israelite monarchy, while the Davidic succession would endure through the Messianic King (cf. Lk 1:32f). Thus also the absolute promises made to Abraham were fulfilled in the new and eternal covenant: Jr 31:31; Ez 16:60; 38:26; Is 54:10; 55: 3; 61:8 (cf. Rm 4:16f; Lk 22:20). E. Lipiński believes that the primitive royal psalm consisted of vv 2-5 and 20b-35, composed by Ethan the Ezrahite towards the end of the tenth century.

For Mowinckel (I, p. 70), Ps 89 is a lament, attributed to the king (v 39) on a day of penance and prayer, after lost battles. The lament is directed at Yahweh himself, who has allowed such calamities to happen. Doubt, however, remains as to whether the psalm must be dated from pre-exilic times (I, p. 118). In his very exhaustive study G. W. Ahlström classifies Ps 89 as a *maśkîl,* a psalm belonging to the annual renewal-of-life ritual. J. J. de Vault (*Theol. Stud.,* 1960, p. 281) has clearly summarized Ahlström's views. "As a *maśkîl,* the Psalm belongs to those rites in which joy over the renewal of life is expressed, but to which are to be added also rites which represent suffering and death, dramatizing the (temporary) victory of the forces of chaos and the humiliation of the king. It is in this last significant ceremonial that the complaining words of the Psalmist are now heard (vv 39-46), words which ring out all the more clearly against the background of the earlier verses, in which Yahweh's victory over chaos and His great creative acts are hymned (vv 1-19), and in which the king is proclaimed Yahweh's song, supreme over the kings of the earth, and the great pact between Yahweh and David's house is concluded (vv 20-38). Verses 1-38, therefore, belong to the exultant ideology of the annual festival, and it is only with verses 39ff that the destructive activity of the enemy of God becomes apparent, so that the king's role turns to that of a suffering messiah whose task it is to assure the renewal of life through necessary suffering, portrayed as part of the cult ritual. In the closing verses the king in the first person turns to prayer, and the Psalm ends on a dark and somber note. It is at this point, says Ahlström, just as the Psalm ends, that a new phase of the ritual began, a phase opening with a sacrifice and concluding with the ritualistic saving of the king from his (and God's) enemies and his resurrection from Sheol."

As an erudite attempt to understand the psalm, Ahlström's study had to be mentioned. It follows the general tendency of the "extremists of the divine-kingship school" (including Engnell and Widengren), who assert that "the king represented the dying and rising nature deity in this cultic renewal ceremony." Others, adds J. M. Ward (*VT* 1961, p. 327), deny the currency in Israel of the dying-god myth while affirming the ritual humiliation of the king (e.g., Bentzen, Ringgren, A. R. Johnson). Still others deny the theory of ritual humiliation while assigning the royal psalms to pre-exilic ritual celebrations of the kingship (H. Schmidt, S. Mowinckel). Ward finally concludes (p. 336): "Without external controls against which to check the theory of a ritual humiliation, whether in the narrative portions of the OT or in the royal psalms, we are thrown back upon Ps 89 itself for an answer to the question of its liturgical background. And there is no ground in the psalm for supposing that the crisis is a mere sham, a dramatic device and nothing more. This is not to say that Ps 89 was not employed repeatedly in the national cultus, but rather to assert that the determining factor in bringing the ritual about was not the intention merely to demonstrate the king's humble dependence upon God, but an actual political experience, or series of experiences, of the nation." This seems to dispose of Ahlström's radical theory.

PSALM 101 (100)

Norm of Life for Rulers

1   *A psalm of David.*
    Of kindness and judgment I will sing;
      to you, O Lord, I will sing praise.

1 Kgs 9:4   2   I will persevere in the way of integrity;

Pss 50:3; Ex 20:24   when will you come to me?
Prv 20:7; Ps 26:11   I will walk in the integrity of my heart,
      within my house;

3   I will not set before my eyes

Is 33:15   any base thing.
    I hate him who does perversely;

Pss 28:3; 84:11   he shall not remain with me.
Prv 11:20; 17:20   4   A crooked heart shall be far from me;
      evil I will not know."

	5	Whoever slanders his neighbor in secret,
Ps 94:23		him will I destroy.
Prv 2:14		The man of haughty eyes and puffed-up heart
		I will not endure.
Ps 33:18	6	My eyes are upon the faithful of the land,
		that they may dwell with me.
1 Kgs 9:4; Prv 20:7		He who walks in the way of integrity
		shall be in my service.
	7	He shall not dwell within my house
		who practices deceit.
		He who speaks falsehood shall not stand
		before my eyes.
2 Sm 15:2; Jer 21:12	8	Each morning I will destroy
Zeph 3:5; Ps 94:23		the wicked of the land,
		And uproot from the city of the Lord
Prv 20:26; 25:5		all evildoers.

In this psalm a king of Judah reads a declaration, probably during a liturgical festival. His language is in part sapiential. The phrase, "when will you come to me?" (v 2; cf. Ex 20:24) could suggest that the Ark of the Covenant has not yet been transferred to Jerusalem (*BJ*). The "house" (vv 2, 7) of the king can be taken literally to mean his dwelling or figuratively, as in 2 Sm 7:11-16, to mean the Davidic lineage. In that case the psalm would represent the "charter" or the "speech from the throne" of the Davidic kings, in which on the day of their enthronement or even annually, they would proclaim their resolution to rule according to the statutes of the covenant (cf. 1 Kgs 23:3). The expression of this resolution shows affinities with so-called "negative confessions" known in Egypt. In the 125th chapter of the *Book of the Dead,* for example, a deceased individual makes a long "protestation of guiltlessness," upon "reaching the Broad-Hall of the Two Justices . . . ." A short extract illustrates the genre (*ANET*, p. 34).

I have not committed evil against men.
I have not committed sin in the place of truth.
I have not blasphemed a god.
I have not *done violence* to a poor man.

I have not done that which the gods abominate.
I have not defamed a slave to his superior.
I have not made (anyone) weep.
I have not killed.
I have not caused anyone suffering.
I have neither increased nor diminished the grain-measure.
I have not added to the weight of the balance.
I have not taken milk from the mouths of children.
I have not driven cattle away from their pasturage.
I have not built a dam against running water.
I have not stopped a god on his procession.

On the other hand, there exists no real proof that the king's declaration reflects the Babylonian enthronement ceremony at the New Year festival, when the king, by way of a confession before the god, would account for the way he had ruled his kingdom. H.-J. Kraus proposes to call the psalm *Loyalitätsgelübde des Königs* or *Reinheitsgelübde des Regenten* (see also K. Galling and F. Mand). Elements of such oaths of loyalty or of innocence are also found elsewhere (cf. Ps 18:21-27). It has been noted (cf. *Ps 31:7) that in certain contexts Dahood considers the term *śānē'tî*, "I hate," to be a *terminus technicus* employed in the formula of repudiation of false gods when one was accused of idolatry. Accordingly he would read in Ps 101:3: "I hate the making of images; may it never cling to me" (on Ps 5:6).

PSALM 110 (109)

The Messiah: King, Priest and Conqueror

1 *A psalm of David.*

I

<table>
<tr><td>1 Kgs 2:19; 1
Pt 3:22
Mt 22:44;
Acts 2:34f
1 Cor 15:25;
Heb 1:13</td><td>The Lord said to my Lord: "Sit at my right hand
    till I make your enemies your footstool."
2 The scepter of your power the Lord will stretch forth
        from Zion

"Rule in the midst of your enemies.</td></tr>
<tr><td>Pss 22:10; 71:
6</td><td>3 Yours is princely power in the day of your birth,
        in your splendor;</td></tr>
</table>

Pss 2:7; 89:27   before the daystar, like the dew, I have begotten you."

II

4 The Lord has sworn, and he will not repent:

Gn 14:18; Heb
5:6; 7:21   "You are a priest forever, according to the order of
Melchizedek."

III

5 The Lord is at your right hand;

Ps 2:9   he will crush kings on the day of his wrath.

6 He will do judgment on the nations, heaping up corpses;

Hb 3:13; Ps
68:22   he will crush heads over the wide earth.

7 From the brook by the wayside he will drink;

Is 8:6; Ps 3:4   therefore will he lift up his head.

An ever increasing periodical literature is devoted to this important Messianic psalm. The best relevant material will here be exposed or alluded to. Subdivisions are introduced for clarity's sake.

a) *An enthronement*

Probably this psalm also was connected with the religious festival of the king's enthronement. Mowinckel thinks "it evidently belongs to the moment when the king is led forth to ascend his throne" (I, p. 63). He then explains that in the East the king's throne was looked upon as a symbol of the throne of the deity. Enough can be found within the biblical tradition itself to explain adequately the various elements of the psalm. E. Podechard's interpretation rests on the assumption that Ps 110 was composed to honor David, when the sacred Ark was transferred to Zion (2 Sm 6), or soon afterwards. Melchizedek, king at Salem, the Jebusite city, was priest of *'ēl-'elyôn* (God-Most-High: Gn 14:18), worshipped by the Phoenicians and the Canaanites. In a way David installed Yahweh in Zion, to replace the former divinity. In return (cf. Ps 2:6) Yahweh proclaimed David king and priest according to the order of Melchizedek (Ps 110:4) and made with his family an eternal covenant (cf. also Pss 89:4, 5, 29, 30, 37; 132:11ff).

The invitation of the oracle, "Sit at my right hand" (110:1), could refer, adds Podechard, to the location of the palace in relation to the Tent of the Ark (2 Sm 6:17; 7:18). It is also possible that for the enthronement the king sat on a throne beside the Ark, seat of God's invisible presence (Kraus, p. 757). Parallels in the coronation ceremony in Egypt and to the following biblical text may serve to illustrate some aspects of both Ps 101 and Ps 110: "And the king (Josias) stood by the pillar and made a covenant before the Lord, to walk after the Lord and to keep his commandments and his testimonies and his statutes, with all his heart and all his soul, to perform the words of this covenant that were written in this book; and all the people joined in the covenant" (1 Kgs 23:3; cf. 2 Kgs 11:14; 2 Chr 23:13; 34:31; for Ps 110, cf. A. Barucq, *L'expression* . . . , p. 493ff). The king, it seems, had a special place "by the pillar" in the temple, perhaps at "the right hand" of the Ark. Figuratively David was the first king to sit at the right hand of the Lord since he was also first to come into close relationship with the Ark (on enemies as "footstools," v 1, see below).

b) *Divine adoption*

The first oracle (vv 1-3), presumably proclaimed by a temple prophet, certainly refers to the king's divine adoption (see on *Ps 2), although the text of verse 3 is obscure and poorly preserved. According to Mowinckel (I, p. 64) and G. Widengren, the "holy splendor" (*haderē qōdesh*) could refer to the royal robe of the enthronement ceremony ("*Ps 110* . . . ," *Uppsala Univ. Arsbok,* 1941, 7, 1). In connection with verse 3 J. de Savignac has been looking for Egyptian parallels. Among the closest he found are the following extracts (*ANET,* p. 374) from the "hymn of victory of Thut-mose III (1490-1436): "Words spoken by Amon-Re, Lord of the Thrones of the Two lands . . . I cause thy opponents to fall beneath thy sandals . . . They come, bearing tribute upon their backs, bowing down to thy majesty, as I decree . . . I have come that I may cause thee to trample down the great ones of Djáhi; I spread them out under thy feet throughout their countries. I cause them to see thy majesty as the lord of radiance, so that thou shinest into their faces as my likeness. I have come that I may cause thee to trample down those who are in Asia . . . I cause them to see thy majesty as a *shooting* star, sowing its fire in a flame, as it gives off its *steam"* (others understand "dew"). The results of the inquiry are rather disappointing (cf. Barucq, *ibid*).

The metaphor of verse 1, "till I make your enemies your footstool," occurs elsewhere also in the psalms: "Upon Edom I will set my shoe" (60:10); "Under God we shall do valiantly; it is he who will tread down our foes" (108:14; cf. 44:6). There exists several illustrations from the ancient world of enemies used as footstools. On a stela from Susa (now in the Louvre), Sargon's son, Naram-Sin of Agade, victor of the Lullubians, places his left foot upon the prostrate bodies of two enemies (cf. *ANEP*, n. 309 or H. Gressmann, *Altorientalische Bilden zum A.T.*, Tafel XVIII). On the sculptured rock of Zohab (Bagdad region) is an inscribed relief celebrating the victory of Anubanini, king of the Lullubians. In the middle of the upper register stands Inanna or Ishtar, vegetation and war goddess, with her left foot on the body of a prisoner (cf. *ANEP*, n. 524 and H. Gressman, Taf. CVIII; on the Lord's footstool, see on *Ps 99:5).

Turning to the biblical text itself of verse 3, J. Coppens wonders if *min*, "from," in *mērehem*, "from the womb," could not be taken "au sens privatif," to mean: "without the help of a womb." Thus the second part of the verse could read:

> By wombless birth,
> like the dew from the daystar,
> I have begotten thee.

The whole verse Coppens translates:

> A toi la principauté
> Au jour de ta naissance
> Dans l'enceinte sacrée.
> Du sein, de l'aurore,
> Sors comme la rosée:
> Je t'ai engendré.

Thus verse 3 would be a sort of poetic commentary of Ps 2:7: "You are my son; this day I have begotten you." As for *behaderê-qōdeš*, "in holy splendor" of the same verse, it is closely related to a similar expression in *Ps 29:2. In his article "In splendoribus sanctorum," A. Caquot writes about Ps 110:3: *"Behadrēy-qōdäš* (ou plutôt *behadrī-qōdäš*) *merāhäm* could be translated: "(tu es revêtu) de Majesté sainte dès le ventre (de ta mère)." The meaning would be: "You are clothed with holy Majesty from your mother's womb," that is, "chosen from your mother's womb," like so many outstanding biblical figures: cf. Jgs 16:17; Is 49:1; Jer 1:5; Pss 71:6; 139:13; Lk 1:15; Gal 1:15.

c) *The order of Melchizedek*

Perhaps the main messianic significance of the psalm depends on the interpretation of verse 4: "The Lord has sworn, and he will not repent: You are a priest forever, according to the order of Melchizedek" (cf. Heb 5:6; 7:21). In connection with this verse, H. H. Rowley would place the original setting of Ps 110 in David's time, when Gn 14 still had significance as an "aetiological story" legitimating for Israel Zadok's (formerly Jebusite) priesthood. "If the psalm is read in the light of this situation, it carries a clear meaning and the reference to Melchizedek is significant. In the opening verses Zadok addresses David, acknowledging that David's God had enabled him to conquer the city, and extolling the power of both God and king, and promising him the loyalty of the conquered but spared city. The phraseology with all its reminiscences of the cultic vocabulary of Ugarit, is precisely what would be expected in such circumstances .... In the first three verses the king is addressed by Zadok; in the fourth, Zadok is addressed by the king, who confirms Zadok in the priesthood" (p. 469f). If this is true, then we cannot say, with J. A. Fitzmyer (*CBQ* 1963, p. 308), quoting prevailing opinion: "Ps 110:4 thus presents the king as the heir of Melchizedek, succeeding him as priest forever." In fact the concept itself of priest-king would not be mentioned in the psalm.

On the other hand, J. W. Bowker admits, with Treves, that Ps 110 does not *necessarily* refer to a king and that David could hardly have been called a priest. Yet it is conceivable, he adds, that the king did act as priest on great occasions or in exceptional circumstances and this is perhaps precisely what Ps 110 envisages. For this reason also R. de Vaux questioned Rowley's solution in regard to verse 4. "The text, he writes, can be explained otherwise: it could mean that the king was a priest, but in the only way in which an Israelite king could be .... He was a priest in the same way as Melchizedek, who, it was thought, had been king and priest in that same Jerusalem where the new king was being enthroned" (*Ancient Israel ...*, p. 114). Bowker concludes: "On general grounds, therefore, there is no reason why the Psalm cannot be understood as an attempt to justify the special sense in which David might be called 'priest' " (*VT* 17, 1967, p. 36).

The origin of the Genesis story (14:18-20) about Melchizedek has been investigated anew by R. H. Smith. Summarizing some of his conclusions, he writes (p. 137): "Thus far we have found that the situation to which Gn 14:18-20 alludes so laconically seems to be this: Abram comes to Melchizedek's city with an army and encamps threateningly. To avoid siege and possible destruction of his city, Melchizedek capitulates to Abram, coming out with bread and wine as tokens of hospitality for Abram and his men, making a speech of conditional surrender, and offering Abram a fixed tribute from the city if he will depart. Abram presumably agrees and departs with the tribute, leaving Melchizedek's city inviolate." The presuppositions, it is explained, of the Melchizedek's story are so similar to those of the Keret [Ugaritic] legend that the stories may be said to have approximately the same cultural milieu and have circulated between 1600 and 1200 B.C. For it is quite possible that the Melchizedek story originally concerned some figure other than Abram. Which was Melchizedek's city we cannot know with certainty: Jerusalem, Shechem, Hebron, Bethel, "The fact is, writes Smith, that by its very nature the Melchizedek story could have happened at almost any Canaanite city" (p. 152).

Equally if not more hypothetical is the deletion from the psalm of any mention of Melchizedek. M. Dahood reads in verse 4 *malkī ṣedeq*, "his legitimate king" (on Ps 18:18). In 1937 already, T. H. Gaster had rendered verse 4: "Thou art a priest forever, A king rightfully appointed, In accordance with Mine order." Rowley, who reports this translation (p. 466, note 6), comments: "Gaster holds that the formula is of high antiquity, antedating the Israelite régime, since it harmonizes with the earliest usage of the priest-king, which is not in accord with Israelite custom. While I am doubtful whether any idea of a priest-king is rightly to be found in either Gn 14 or Ps 110, there is evidence that Israelite kings did on occasion exercise the priestly function, though later thought condemned such a practice (cf. 2 Chr 26: 16ff)."

Two scholars conclude in the following manner their study of a Qumran scroll concerned with a Melchizedek: "The function of Melchizedek as heavenly deliverer who protects the faithful people of God and as chief of the heavenly hosts runs parallel with that of the archangel Michael in the Dead Sea Scrolls, and in late Jewish and early Christian literature. Michael and Melchizedek are, however, not identified explicitly in the Qumran texts at our disposal. This identification is only found in certain medieval Jewish texts . . . . Melchizedek was a priest of the Most High God (Gn 14:18; Ps 110:4). In some Jewish sources he is called high-priest. In the Babylonian Talmud a heavenly high-priesthood is assigned to Michael. The question whether *11Q Melch* provides any explicit or implicit references to Melchizedek's (high-) priesthood can only be answered with difficulty" (M. de Jonge and A. S. van der Woude, "11Q Melchizedek and the New Testament," *New Test. Stud.* 12 [1966], p. 305).

The traditional interpretation of the phrase "according to the order of Melchizedek" is faithfully represented by the *CV* commentary: It means "in the same way as Melchizedek was a priest. There are three main points of resemblance between Melchizedek, the prophetic type and Christ who fulfilled this prophecy: both are kings as well as priests, both offer bread and wine to God, and both have their priesthood directly from God and not through Aaron, since neither belongs to the tribe of Levi. Cf. Gn 14:18; Heb 7." This can be completed by a note of *The Jerusalem Bible*: "The prerogatives of the Messiah, worldwide sovereignty and perpetual priesthood (cf. 2 Sm 7:1ff; Zech 6:12f), are no more conferred by earthly investiture than were those of the mysterious Melchizedek (Gn 14:18ff)" (for a detailed list of the N.T. quotations of Ps 110, see §16a).

d) *The last verse*

In connection with the third oracular utterance (vv 5-7), and its belligerent tone (cf. Ps 2:9), *JB* remarks: "As the text stands, this is addressed to the Messiah: the Lord (Yahweh) is to be at his right hand. Possibly the original text attributed the following act of judgment to the Messiah himself, and we should read 'At his (Yahweh's) right hand the Lord (the Messiah, as in v 1).' This text may have been corrected in order to reserve the functions of eschatological judge as described in the following lines. However this may be, Jesus, the Messiah and Son of God, claimed this right to judge as his own, Mt 24:30; 26:64; Jn 5:22; cf. Acts 7:56; 10:42; 17:31."

Perhaps the most difficult problem raised by Ps 110 is the meaning of the last verse: "De torrente in via bibet: propterea exaltabit caput" (*Vulg.*). Some of the solutions proposed are mentioned in a *BJ* note: Rather than to a brook of blood (cf. Nm 23:24; Ez 32:6; 39:17f; Is 34:

7; Zech 9:15), the Messiah would drink from the torrent of trials (cf. Pss 18:5; 32:6; 66:12) or of divine favors (Pss 36:9; 46:5; Jer 31: 9, 12). This last meaning does suit the context. God sustains his Messiah and makes certain his victory over the enemies, the pagans, in the last days. In the allegorical sense the text would describe the zeal of the Messiah, who, certain of victory, pursues his enemies (cf. Jgs 7:5; 15:18; 1 Sm 30:9; 1 Kgs 17:4). Hence the application to Christ, suffering and glorious (Phil 2:7-11).

Instead of *MT minnaḥal,* "from the brook," C. Schedl reads in verse 7a *manḥil,* "*Erbvollstrecker*" (executor of a testator's will), the one entrusted with allocating (land) inheritance (*naḥalâh:* cf. Ps 78:55). Instead of *MT yišteh,* "he will drink," he reads *yᵉšîtēhû,* "he will place him." Assuming besides that *derek,* "way," has "*ein heilsgeschichtlicher Begriff*" (a saving history meaning), the verse could mean that Yahweh entrusts the Messiah with a mission broader in scope and yet similar to that of Joshuah: "Be strong and of good courage; for you shall cause this people to inherit (*'attâh tanḥîl*) the land which I swore to their fathers to give them" (1:6; cf. Ps 2:8). This new Joshuah, a royal figure, is on the way to take over the empire of the nations. The enemies have their heads down (v 1) but God will raise the head of the Messiah (v 7). Noting that in Ugaritic *drkt* means (religious) "rule" or "dominion," in parallel with "kingdom," P. Nober, in 1948 already, had "anticipated" part of Schedl's solution and proposed the Latin translation: "Distributorem dominii constituet eum et ideo Yahweh extollet caput ejus": [God will] entrust to him the apportioning of his domain; therefore his head he will raise. C. Schedl's translation would presumably run more or less as follows: "On the way he constitutes him to apportion (the land); therefore his head He will raise."

There is little doubt that *drk* (*CV:* "wayside") does in some biblical texts connote the meaning of "power" or "authority": cf. Nm 24:17; Hos 10:13; Jer 3:13; Jb 26:14; Prv 19:16; Ps 138:5. Yet H. Zirker (*BZ* 1958, p. 293) does not believe that this notion of *drk* can be applied to Ps 110:7. Not particularly impressed by his reasoning, Dahood proposes for verse 7a: "He has set him as ruler upon the throne." The semantic transition, he explains, from "dominion" (*drk*) to the place where dominion is exercised can be illustrated by *mišpāt,* "justice, right," but also "court of judgment" (on Ps 1:1).

e) *Additional remarks*

Rowley and other authors would propose an early date for Ps 110. We have seen their reasons for doing so. At the other extreme M. Treves has recently proposed that Ps 110, like *Ps 2, is an acrostic, and that the only person "who fits the data of our Psalm" is Simon (143-134), the first civil ruler to become also high-priest. The acrostic would read: "Simon is terrible." The rehatched proposal will not likely gain more supporters than the original one made, almost a century ago, by G. Bickel and others. J. W. Bowker qualifies the acrostic theory as "extremely weak" and shows also the weakness of the other arguments presented by Treves. "Abstraction faite de ses multiples re-lectures" Tournay wrote (*RB* 1960, p. 38), Ps 110 seems to have been redacted about the time of Chronicles or Qoheleth, most probably before the rule of Antiochus III (223-187). His motives for assigning such a late date to the psalm cannot be discussed here, although they do call the reader's attention (e.g.,: that period was one in which the claims of the priestly power were exceptionally great).

The claims of the psalm to be called messianic are self-evident and the more prominent aspects have been pointed out. Not all authors will, however, admit that the psalm is directly or in the strict sense messianic. True, Coppens notes (p. 22), royal messianism is expressed in this psalm, yet not messianism in its strict sense, because eschatology is not explicitly stated. This monarch, besides, rules by force, the ideal of his kingship has not reached beyond the lower levels of typical messianism. His kingdom is still in this world.

PSALM 132 (131)

The Pact between David and the Lord

1   *A song of ascents.*

A

I

Remember, O Lord, for David

2 Sm 7:1ff; 1 Kgs 8:17   all his anxious care:

2   How he swore to the Lord,

Gn 49:24; Ps 94:7   vowed to the Mighty One of Jacob:

3   "I will not enter the house I live in,

2 Sm 7:1f   nor lie on the couch where I sleep;

4   I will give my eyes no sleep
         my eyelids no rest,

5   Till I find a place for the Lord,

Is 49:26; 60:   a dwelling for the Mighty One of Jacob."
16
                              II

Ru 4:11   6   Behold, we heard of it in Ephratha;

1 Sm 7:1   we found it in the fields of Jaar.

7   Let us enter into his dwelling,

Ps 99:5   let us worship at his footstool.

Nm 10:35; 2   8   Advance, O Lord, to your resting place
Par 6:41
Pss 68:25; 74:   you and the ark of your majesty.
2
9   May your priests be clothed with justice;

Pss 116:15;   let your faithful ones shout merrily for joy.
145:10
10   For the sake of David your servant,

Pss 2:2; 89:21;   reject not the plea of your anointed.
132:10
                              B
         I

2 Sm 7:12ff   11   The Lord swore to David

Ps 110:4   a firm promise from which he will not withdraw:
                 "Your own offspring

Ps 89:20   I will set upon your throne;

Ps 111:5   12   If your sons keep my covenant
                 and the decrees which I shall teach them,

Ps 89:31ff   Their sons, too, forever
                 shall sit upon your throne."

13   For the Lord has chosen Zion;

Pss 68:17; 74:   he prefers her for his dwelling.
2; 76:3
                              II

14   "Zion is my resting place forever;
         in her will I dwell, for I prefer her.

15   I will bless her with abundant provision,

Pss 68:6; 146:   her poor I will fill with bread.
9; 147:6
2 Chr 6:41; Is 16   Her priest I will clothe with salvation,
61:10
Jer 31:14; Ez   and her faithful ones shall shout merrily for joy.
29:21
Jer 23:5; 33:   17   In her will I make a horn to sprout forth for David;
15; Zech 3:8
1 Kgs 11:36;   I will place a lamp for my anointed.
2 Kgs 8:19
Ps 119:78   18   His enemies I will clothe with shame,
         but upon him my crown shall shine."

The transfer of the sacred Ark to Jerusalem (2 Sm 6; cf. §13b), alluded to in other royal psalms, is a central feature of Ps 132. Traditions related to the event belong to the essential background of this category of psalms. As Mowinckel puts it (I, p. 48), "in Ps 132 we meet the king as the leader of a religious festival play in remembrance of the time when David brought Yahweh's holy shrine up to Zion, and the king is here playing the part of David." Ps 132, would, he adds (I, p. 174), give us the "text" of a dramatic procession with Yahweh's ark. In 2 Chr 6:41f, Ps 132:8-11 forms the conclusion of the prayer offered on the occasion of the dedication of the temple. The annual commemoration of this event and the festival of the enthronement, Weiser assumes, coincided with the "Covenant festival of Yahweh" (cf. Ps 132:12, 15) celebrated in autumn (cf. §13c). The festival of the temple consecration, Mowinckel believes (I, p. 175), was at the same time the festival of the institution of the cult of Yahweh on Zion under David. The mention in this context of "the Mighty One of Jacob" (v 5) possibly reflects an attempt to merge Northern (cf. Gn 49:24) and Southern cultic traditions.

Verse 6 also alludes to the "changing fortunes" of the Ark of the Covenant: "Behold, we heard of it in Ephrata; we found it in the fields of Jaar." Ephrata may refer to Bethlehem, David's birthplace (cf. Ru 4:11; Mi 5:1), or Shiloh (cf. Jgs 21:19), the sanctuary in Ephraim (1 Sm 1:1 = Ephratha), where the Ark was stationed (cf. 1 Sm 2:12-17 and 1 Sm 3-4). Upon its return from Philistine territory the Ark passed from Bethshemesh to the house of Abinadab in *qiryat-yeʿārîm* (1 Sm 6:21; cf. 1 Chr 2:50). Nearby, "in the fields of *yāʿar*," the Ark *was found* (Ps 132:6). The cultic search for the Ark in Israel would correspond, Mowinckel suggests (I, p. 176), to a feature of the Babylonian New Year and enthronement drama: in Babylonia the other gods would go along with the king and the priests ... in a cultic procession to search for and deliver the lost, dead or imprisoned god (cf. also W. Frankfort, *Kingship of the Gods,* Chicago, 1948, p. 321ff). More to the point is the fact that Ps 132 is primarily "the *hieros logos* of the dedication of the Temple," including "a recital of the establishment of the sanctuary" (A. Weiser; cp. with §13b). Ps 132, Wolverton remarks, presents "a thoroughly mythological interpretation" of the election of Zion and of the line of David. It has been explained (cf. §13b) that in Wolverton's view to "mythologize" is to interpret a human action as of divine action. Not the reenactment of the transfer of the Ark, Weiser believes, but the appearing of God from Sinai or from heaven (cf. §13d) is dramatized in verse 8: "Advance, O Lord, to your resting place, you and the ark of your majesty" (cf. Pss 18:8-16; 68:17, 25; Nm 10:35ff; Jgs 5:4f; 1 Kgs 8:10f; Is 6:1-5).

The two fundamental ideas of the psalm concern the prophecy of Nathan and the election of Zion as God's dwelling-place. They feature together also in 2 Sm 8 and in Ps 78:67-71. In Ps 132, however, God's promises (cf. 1 Kgs 8:25; Ps 89:20f) are presented as the answer to an oath of David, not reported elsewhere. *The Oxford Annotated Bible* (p. 383) has this to say about 2 Sm 7:1-29: "This chapter is the only serious interruption of the Early Source in the entire book. Like 1 Sm 2:27-36, it is a late theological commentary inserted into an early historical source, seeking to explain why David was not chosen to build the temple. It seems to have been based to some extent on Ps 89 (compare Ps 132:11f). Nathan the prophet (vv 2, 3, 4, 17) is used as a mouthpiece of the author, though the historical Nathan does not appear in the Early Source until 12:1. Verses 4-17 are often referred to as The Prophecy of Nathan and verses 18-29 as The Prayer of David. In verse 6 the writer ignores the temple of Shiloh" (1 Sm 1:7; 3:3).

God's promise to the Davidic lineage was fulfilled with the advent of the messianic king (cf. Lk 1:32f; see §15c and *Ps 89:31-38). The "anointed" of Ps 132:10 is probably a reigning king of Judah, contemporaneous with the psalmist, although perhaps a post-exilic descendant of David, like Zerubbabel (cf. Ps 80:18) could be meant. To Zerubbabel's name that of Josue was substituted in Zech 6:11 (cf. Hag 1:1f). It is upon Zerubbabel, called "Sprout," "Shoot" or "Branch" (cf. Jer 23:5; 33:15) that the crown is to be placed (Zech 3:8; 6:11f). The same messianic theme occurs in Ps 132:17 (cf. Lk 1:69). In this verse 17, the expression 'rk nr, "set a lamp," is used, perhaps as an allusion to the lamp kept burning perpetually in the sanctuary (cf. Ex 27:20f; Lv 24:2ff). "My anointed" would be David himself (cf. Ps 18:50) rather than his successors. The phraseology of verse 18, writes Kirkpatrick, "seems intended to suggest that David's representative will have high-priestly as well as royal dignity." The Hebrew word *nezer*, "crown," is also used for the high-priest's diadem (Ex 29:6) and the verb used for "shine" is cognate to the noun *ṣîṣ*, which denotes in Ex 28:36 the plate of pure gold worn by the High-priest "upon the mitre" (Ex 28:37). On the plate were engraved the words: "Holiness to the Lord" (*ibid.*). The messianic connotations associated with the "lamp" theme have been investigated by F. Asensio, for both Testaments. The promise to David of a lamp is reported in the Book of Kings (1 Kgs 11:36; 15:4; 2 Kgs 8:19). A lightless house is deserted (cf. Jer 25:10; Jb 18:5). As for the Messiah he will be "a light for the nation" (Is 42:6; 49:6; Lk 2:32; cf. *BJ*).

PSALM 144 (143)

Prayer for Victory and Prosperity

1 *Of David.*

I

Pss 18:47; 95:1
Ps 18:35

  Blessed be the Lord, my rock,
    who trains my hands for battle, my fingers for war;

2 My refuge and my fortress,

Pss 18:2f; 28:1; 94:22
Ps 3:4

    my stronghold, my deliverer,
  My shield, in whom I trust,
    who subdues peoples under me.

II

Ps 8:5

3 Lord, what is man, that you notice him;
    the son of man, that you take thought of him?

4 Man is like a breath;

Jb 14:2; Pss 39:6; 78:39
Is 63:19; Ps 18:10
Ps 104:32

    his days, like a passing shadow.

5 Incline your heavens, O Lord, and come down;
    touch the mountains, and they shall smoke;

Pss 18:15; 77:19

6 Flash forth lightning, and put them to flight,
    shoot your arrows, and rout them;

7 Reach out your hand from on high —

Pss 18:5, 17:45; 69:15

    Deliver me and rescue me from many waters,
    from the hands of aliens.

8 Whose mouths swear false promises
    while their right hands are raised in perjury.

III

Pss 98:1; 149:1
Pss 33:2; 98:5; 149:3
Ps 18:51

9 O God, I will sing a new song to you;
    with a ten-stringed lyre I will chant your praise,

10 You who give victory to kings,

Pss 78:70; 132:10

    and deliver David, your servant.

11 From the evil sword deliver me;

and rescue me from the hands of aliens,
Whose mouths swear false promises
    while their right hands are raised in perjury.
IV
12 May our sons be like plants
        well-nurtured in their youth,

Sir 26:18   Our daughters like wrought columns
Ps 128:3   such as stand at the corners of the temple.

13 May our garners be full,
        affording every kind of store;
    May our sheep be in the thousands,

Dt 7:13   and increase to myriads in our meadows;
14   may our oxen be well laden.
    May there be no breach in the walls, no exile,

Is 65:19   no outcry in our streets.

15 Happy the people for whom things are thus;
    happy the people whose God is the Lord.

The first part of this psalm (vv 1-10) probably featured in a royal liturgy which included hymnic elements (vv 1-2; 9-11) and a supplication (3-8). Its literary affinities with Ps 18 and other psalms are to be accounted for, Weiser thinks, by "a common and fixed liturgical tradition" rather than by direct borrowings from other sources. The second part (12-15) could constitute the "new song" announced in verse 9. It is an original composition which presents an idyllic picture of the messianic era (*BJ*), or reflects the grateful reaction of the cult community to the blessings of the "grace of kingship" (Weiser).

CHAPTER EIGHT

DIDACTIC PSALMS

In this family of psalms different categories join in a sort of unity based on a common interest, that of *teaching* in a variety of forms: sapiential reflections, lessons of history, prophetic exhortations, liturgical instructions. They follow no common literary pattern but they do reflect a tone inspired by their common purpose.

§29. THE WISDOM PSALMS

(a) *General character*

The notion of "didactic psalms" applies first and best to the wisdom psalms. As *BJ* notes, the "spiritual guides" of Israel used the Psalms' literary genre to express their teaching or *tôrâ*. The scribes were both sages and poets. The "wise words of their teaching" they set down in rhythmical compositions (cf. Sir 44:4f). The forms of expression and the thought patterns of wisdom literature are reflected in many psalms. Pss 127 and 133, for example, have preserved the proverbial form (cf. Ps 78:2). Admonitions and exhortative instructions, typical of sapiential and didactic poetry, are also represented in the Pss 34: 12ff; 78:1-8; 81:9 (cf. Prv 8:4f). In the following passage some

important characteristics of the wisdom psalm find expression (note
the direct form of address: cp. Prv 22:17):

> Hear this, all you peoples;
>> hearken, all who dwell in the world,
> Of lowly birth or high degree,
>> rich and poor alike.
> My mouth shall speak wisdom;
>> prudence shall be the utterance of my heart.
> My ear is intent upon a proverb;
>> I will set forth my riddle to the music of the harp
>>>>> (Ps 49:2-5).

In wisdom poetry there exists a general tendency to substitute reflection
to prayer and to insist on a *practical* wisdom of life: a religious basis
is given for the practice of human virtues.

Several more common *themes* of the wisdom psalms can be pointed
out. God's faithful willingly meditate on the *Law* (Pss 1:2; 37:31;
119:15), with love (1:2; 119:47), for the Law is an inexhaustible
source of benefits (Ps 119). The morality maxim, "turn from evil and
do good" (Ps 37:27), is continually recalled in various ways. The
ways and the final destiny of the wicked run contrary to that of the
just (Pss 1, 37, 112). The happiness of the righteous (37:3f; 112:1),
the domestic joys of the faithful (Pss 127, 128, 133) are emphasized.
They will "possess the land" (37:9, 22, 29, 34), while the wicked,
threatened by God's judgment (1:4) are heading for ruin (Ps 37).
The just man reflects and understands (3:16f); the wicked is senseless
and foolish (49:21). Yahweh knows (1:6; 91:14; 139:1, 13ff, 23)
and protects the just (Ps 91), who trusts entirely in him (37:5ff).

Retribution is a pressing problem for the sage. Its many aspects
are featured in the wisdom psalms (cf. G. R. Castellino, *Libro . . .* ,
p. 729ff; see on "retribution": §14d). The testimony of experience
is produced:

> Neither in my youth, nor now that I am old,
>> have I seen a just man forsaken
>> nor his descendants begging bread.
> All the day he is kindly and lends,
>> and his descendants shall be blessed (37:25f).

On retribution the psalms reflect generally the traditional views: the righteous enjoy prosperity and happiness, the wicked harvest adversity and calamity (cf. Pss 1, 91, 112, 119, 127, 128). But the data of experience seemed to confirm the obvious shortcomings of temporal retribution. Some psalmists, faced with the prosperity of the wicked, profess to be scandalized and offended (cf. Pss 73:2-16; 139:19; cp. Eccl 8:14). The idea that a different destiny awaits the just and the wicked in the other world was formulated only gradually. Insights and hopes involving extratemporal values appear in a few statements: death is the shepherd of the worldly-minded, their dwelling is Sheol (49:15); the just, on the other hand, hope to be redeemed from the power of the nether world (49:16) and be received in glory (73:24), like Enoch (Gn 5:24) or Elijah (2 Kgs 2:1-11).

The wisdom psalms do not follow a strict *literary pattern.* Three are alphabetical compositions (Pss 37, 112, 119; cf. §6d). The *mashal,* "proverb," "saying" or "sentence," represents the oldest and simplest mode of expression in wisdom literature (cf. A. R. Johnson in *SVT,* III, 1955, pp. 162-169; H.-J. Kraus, *Psalmen,* p. 889; A. Bentzen, *Introduction . . .* I, p. 167ff). The form of the *mashal* is either short (Prv 10:29) or elaborate (Prv 1-9). The word appears in Ps 49:5 and the "proverbial" form is not rare in the Psalter (cf. Ps 62:12; cp. Prv 6:16), no more than certain typical expressions like "Happy the man . . ." (Ps 1:1; cp. Jb 5:17). Another peculiar feature of the wisdom psalmists is their more than usual recourse to the so-called "anthological style," characterized by the re-use of words or expressions belonging to previous scriptures (see on *Pss 33 and 119).

Introducing his lecture on "Psalms and Wisdom" (*SVT,* III, pp. 205-224), S. Mowinckel restated his conviction that "perhaps more than 140 of the 150 [psalms] of the Psalter, have not only been used as cult-poems, but have also been composed for that purpose" (p. 205: cf. §8a). The problem, in psalm exegesis, he said, is not the cultic psalms, but the non-cultic ones, which seem to belong to "learned psalmography," originated in the circles of the "wise men," the learned leaders of the "wisdom schools" (p. 206; cf. II, pp. 104-125). Five wisdom psalms (1, 37, 49, 112, 127) figure among Mowinckel's "non-cultic psalms" (the others: 19B, 34, 78, 105, 106, 111; cf. II, p. 111). In the latest psalmography, not related to definite cultic occasions, the learned writers try to adhere to the old rules of composition, but without much success and this would have brought "a dissolution of the style": the different modes and motives get mixed up ("Psalms and Wisdom," p. 213). This is particularly marked, Mowinckel noted, "in what Jewish opinion held most skillful, viz., alphabetic psalms" (*ibid.*).

(b) The wisdom psalms are the following: Pss 1, 37, 49, (73), (91), 112, 119, 127, 128, 133, (139).

PSALM 1

True happiness

I

Pss 112:1; 119:1	1	Happy the man who follows not the counsel of the wicked Nor walks in the way of sinners, nor sits in the company of the insolent,
Pss 63:7; 77: 13; 106.3 Jos 1:8; Sir 6: 37	2	But delights in the law of the Lord and meditates on his law day and night.
Jer 17:7; Is 58:11 Jb 29:19; Ez 47:12 Pss 52:10; 92: 13 Prv 11:28; Wis 5:14	3	He is like a tree planted near running water, That yields its fruit in due season, and whose leaves never fade. [Whatever he does, prospers.]

II

Ps 35:5	4	Not so the wicked, not so; they are like chaff which the wind drives away.
Jb 21:18; Hos 13:3	5	Therefore in judgment the wicked shall not stand, nor shall sinners, in the assembly of the just.
Pss 16:11; 37: 18 Dt 30:15f; Prv 4:18f Jer 21:8; Mt 7:13	6	For the Lord watches over the way of the just, but the way of the wicked vanishes.

Pss 1 and 2 form a sort of preface to the whole Psalter and bring out some of its moral and messianic ideas (see on *Ps 2). Ps 1 begins with a beatitude ('*ašrē*). This literary and religious category express-ing a praise, a salutation, or a wish was adopted by the wisdom litera-ture. It differs from the priestly blessing (*b*e*rākâh*), the counterpart of the curse. Yet Mowinckel suggests (II, p. 52) that the style pattern of the blessing and curse used in the "cultic rituals" has been imitated by the wisdom poetry, introduced in the prophetic admonitions, taken

Enter by the narrow gate sincere

up by the "learned psalmography" and finally adopted by "private psalmography" (Pss 1 and 112) in the form of statements on "the two ways," the way of piety and the way of ungodliness, leading to life or to death (cf. Mt 7:13f). These number among Mowinckel's "non-cultic poems" (see §8a and 29a). A. Weiser though notes that the practical and educational wisdom proposed in Ps 1 and elsewhere "is based on a firm religious foundation the roots of which are firmly embedded *in the tradition of public worship.*" He remarks also that in contrast to some of Paul's views (cf. Rm 3:20; Gal 4:21-31; 1 Cor 15:56) the law in Ps 1 is not regarded as an irksome burden but as a source of joy (cf. Pss 19:8-11; 119:92; Dt 30:11). It is the *God revealing law* that Jesus has come not to abolish but to fulfill (Mt 5:17). The psalmist sees it as the expression of divine will, affording guidance under God's providential rule. In God's verdict, at the hour of judgment (vv 5, 6), the final issue of the two ways will confirm the pattern of retribution (cf. §14d). Ps 112 also ends with a pronouncement on the ruin of the wicked.

It has been observed by Kirkpatrick that the three clauses of verse one "denote successive steps in a career of evil, and form a climax: (1) adoption of the principles of the wicked as a rule of life; (2) persistence in the practices of notorious offenders; (3) deliberate association with those who openly mock at religion." Dahood believes that in verse 3 the final destiny of the just is alluded to: "So shall he be like a tree transplanted near streams of water," transplanted, that is, "to the Elysian Fields," the abode of the blessed after death (see on *Ps 36:10). As for the wicked they "shall not stand in the place of judgment" (v 5; cf. Dt 25:1). Dahood comments: "As the final judgment will take place in the heavenly council, to which the wicked will not be admitted, they will be condemned *in absentia*" (cf. Ps 82:1).

According to E. P. Arbez "the psalm gives a consistent solution of the problem of retribution." Without excluding eschatology, the thoughts expressed in verses 2-3 can very well apply to the temporal life of the man who is nourished by the word of God: "As a tree is nourished by constant supplies of water, without which under the burning Eastern sun it would wither and die, so the life of the godly man is maintained by the supplies of grace drawn from constant communion with God through his relevation": cf. Pss 52:8; 92:12; 128:3 (Kirkpatrick). Attentive as always to the "sacral king" motif (cf. §8d), I. Engnell characterized Ps 1 as a "word of blessing" connected with a literary type called "mirror of the prince" or *"ṣᵉdakā*-table," a "table of righteousness." This author also quotes rather unimpressing parallels which would associate the Tammuz god, the king, and the tree of life. Such explanations seem unduly *recherchées* and unnecessary, in view of the obvious clarity of the text.

Written for those "who fear God and walk in his ways," the inscriptions of the Petosiris tomb in Egypt (end of the fourth century *BC;* cf. *BJ,* p. 51f and *RB* 1922, pp. 481-488) can be quoted in connection with this psalm: "I shall lead you to the way of life, the good way of he who obeys God; happy is he whose heart guides him to it. He who walks with a firm heart on the way of life is firmly established on earth. He who fears God greatly is very happy on earth" (Inscr. 62). In the "Instruction of Egyptian Amen-em-opet" (probably seventh-sixth cent. B.C.), can be read the following (*ANET,* p. 422):

> As for the heated man of a temple,
> He is like a tree growing in the open.
> In the completion of a moment (comes) its
> loss of foilage . . .
> (But) the truly silent man holds himself apart.
> He is like a tree growing in a garden.
> It flourishes and doubles its yield;
> It (stands) before its lord. [cp. Jr 17:5ff]

To conclude, a note on the metre of the psalm. Its peculiar character brings S. Bullough to suggest "that Psalm 1 is not in metre at all, but is plain rhythmic prose. Of course the metre is 'uncertain' (Kittel, *Bibl. Hebr.*), because it is more than the free pattern of well-written prose" (*VT* 1967, see B.'s prose translation, p. 49).

PSALM 37

The Fate of Sinners and the Reward of the Just

1 *Of David.*

Prv 3:31; 23:17
Mal 2:17; 3:14; Ps 73:3ff
Pss 34:22; 55:24
Is 40:7f

> Be not vexed over evildoers,
>   nor jealous of those who do wrong;
> 2 For like grass they quickly wither,
>   and like green herbs they wilt.

Pss 25:13; Dt
16:20
Is 14:30; Heb
11:9ff

3 Trust in the Lord and do good,
  that you may dwell in the land and enjoy security.
4 Take delight in the Lord,

Ps 20:6; Prv
10:24
Prv 3:5f

  and he will grant you your heart's requests.
5 Commit to the Lord your way;
  trust in him, and he will act.

Is 60:19; Wis
5:6

6 He will make justice dawn for you like the light;
  bright as the noonday shall be your vindication.
7 Leave it to the Lord,
  and wait for him;
  Be not vexed at the successful path
  of the man who does malicious deeds.
8 Give up your anger, and forsake wrath;
  be not vexed, it will only harm you.
9 For evildoers shall be cut off,

Is 57:13; Prv
2:21

  but those who wait for the Lord shall possess the land.
10 Yet a little while, and the wicked man shall be no more;
  though you mark his place he will not be there.

Mt 5:4
Ps 35:20

11 But the meek shall possess the land,
  they shall delight in abounding peace.

Ps 71:10

12 The wicked man plots against the just
  and gnashes his teeth at them;

Wis 4:18; Pss
2:4; 59:9

13 But the Lord laughs at him,
  for he sees that his day is coming.

Ps 11:2

14 A sword the wicked draw; they bend their bow
  to bring down the afflicted and the poor,
  to slaughter those whose path is right.
15 But their swords shall pierce their own hearts,

Pss 35:8; 57:7
Ps 49:7ff
Prv 15:16; 16:8

  and their bows shall be broken.
16 Better is the scanty store of the just
  than the great wealth of the wicked,
17 For the power of the wicked shall be broken,
  but the Lord supports the just.

Pss 1:6; 32:10
Pss 16:6; 34:8, 21

18 The Lord watches over the lives of the wholehearted;
  their inheritance lasts forever.
19 They are not put to shame in an evil time;
  in days of famine they have plenty.

Ps 32:10

20 But the wicked perish,

and the enemies of the Lord, like the beauty of the
meadows,
vanish; like smoke they vanish.

Hos 13:3; Wis
5:14   21   The wicked man borrows and does not repay;
Prv 2:9; Ps
112:9   the just man is kindly and gives,
Is 57:13; Mt
5:4   22   But those whom he blesses shall possess the land,
while those he curses shall be cut off.

Prv 20:24   23   By the Lord are the steps of a man made firm,
Pss 40:3; 94:
18   and he approves his way.
24   Though he fall, he does not lie postrate,
for the hand of the Lord sustains him.

Sir 2:10; Jb
4:7   25   Neither in my youth, nor now that I am old,
have I seen a just man forsaken
Pss 32:10; 34:
21   nor his descendants begging bread.
Ps 112:5   26   All the day he is kindly and lends,
and his descendants shall be blessed.

Ps 34:15; Am
5:14   27   Turn from evil and do good,
that you may abide forever;
28   For the Lord loves what is right,
Pss 32:6; 50:5   and forsakes not his faithful ones.
Pss 34:17; 92:
9   Criminals are destroyed,
Jb 18:19   and the posterity of the wicked is cut off.
Pss 27:13;   29   The just shall possess the land
116:9
Dt 30:16   and dwell in it forever.

Prv 10:31   30   The mouth of the just man tells of wisdom
and his tongue utters what is right.
Is 51:7; Dt 6:
6   31   The law of his God is in his heart,
Jr 31:33   and his steps do not falter.
32   The wicked man spies on the just,
and seeks to slay him.
33   The Lord will not leave him in his power
nor let him be condemned when he is on trial.

Ps 119:166   34   Wait for the Lord,
and keep his way;
He will promote you to ownership of the land;
when the wicked are destroyed, you shall look on.

Pss 10:3; 73:
4-12   35   I saw a wicked man, fierce,
Ez 31:10-14;
Jb 20:6f   and stalwart as a flourishing, age-old tree.

36 Yet as I passed by, lo! he was no more;

Is 14:16 I sought him, but he could not be found.

37 Watch the wholehearted man, and mark the upright;

Prv 23:18;
24:14 for there is a future for the man of peace.

38 Sinners shall all alike be destroyed;

Ps 34:17 the future of the wicked shall be cut off.

Pss 9:9; 31:2;
46:2
Is 25:4 39 The salvation of the just is from the Lord;

he is their refuge in time of distress.

40 And the Lord helps them and delivers them;

he delivers them from the wicked and saves them,

because they take refuge in him.

In this collection of maxims loosely joined to form an alphabetic psalm (cf. §6d), a wise old man (v 25) repeats to the godly that in putting their trust in God they have chosen the right path. To those who become impatient about the ways of the Lord he says: "Wait and see!" (v 34) To the frail, exposed to temptation because the wicked are prosperous, he recalls the traditional doctrine of retribution (cf. §14d): "Criminals are destroyed, and the posterity of the wicked is cut off" (v 28). In this "non-cultic poem" (Mowinckel; cf. *Ps 1), A. Weiser discovers various "references to elements of the tradition of the cult of the covenant": blessing and curse (v 22), (re) distribution of land (cf. *Ps 142), judgment and salvation (10f, 34, 37f). These references would allow the view that the psalm was composed and used in pre-exilic times. The *land,* so often mentioned in the psalm (vv 3, 9, 11, 22, 29, 34) is the Promised Land, Palestine (cf. Dt 11:1-32), later considered as a type or figure of heaven (cf. Heb 11:9-16), or of the kingdom of heaven (cf. Mt 5:4).

It is a teaching frequently but diversely expressed in the psalms (cf. Ps 35:8 + §12e), that the wicked perish by their own device: "Their swords shall pierce their own hearts" (v 15). It is an application of a more general religious truth that "sin is already in itself judgment" (Weiser). By divine disposition the sinner's sphere of life is bound to decay and ruin (cf. Hos 5:12; Jr 2:19; 5:25; 6:21, 30; 13:23; 18:17). For the just, adversity is medicinal and temporary. With God's assistance he will recover and lead a normal life (vv 23ff).

Some of the latest psalms, writes Mowinckel (I, p. 213), such as Pss 37, 49 and 73, present the more Jewish than Israelite conception of "the wicked": they are mainly "apostates," disregarding Yahweh's law and the claims of the covenant, and thus incurring "the chastising interference of Yahweh." The same author does not seem too particular about literary categories. Ps 37, for example, he lists both among the "personal thanksgiving psalms" (II, p. 114) and among "the wisdom psalms" (II, p. 138).

PSALM 49 (48)

The Vanity of Wordly Riches

1 *For the leader. A psalm of the sons of Core.*

Mi 1:2; Lam 1:18
Is 34:1; Prv 22:17

2 Hear this, all you peoples;
    hearken, all who dwell in the world,
3 Of lowly birth or high degree,

Prv 8:4f; Jb 34:19
Jb 33:2f; Ps 78:2

    rich and poor alike.
4 My mouth shall speak wisdom;
    prudence shall be the utterance of my heart.
5 My ear is intent upon a porverb;

Sir 44:4f

    I will set forth my riddle to the music of the harp.

I

6 Why should I fear in evil days
    when my wicked ensnarers ring me round?

Pss 37:16; 52:9
Prv 10:15; 11:28; Jer 9:22
Jb 31:25; Ps 19:15

7 They trust in their wealth;
    the abundance of their riches is their boast.
8 Yet in no way can a man redeem himself,
    or pay his own ransom to God;

Ex 21:30; Ez 7:19

9 Too high is the price to redeem one's life; he would never
                                              have enough

Prv 11:4; Jb 33:24

10   to remain alive always and not see destruction.
11 For he can see that wise men die,

Eccl 3:18f

    and likewise the senseless and the stupid pass away,

Eccl 2:14ff; 12:5

    leaving to others their wealth.
12 Tombs are their homes forever,
    their dwellings through all generations,
    though they have called lands by their names.
13 Thus man, for all his splendor, does not abide;

Pss 32:9; 39:5ff; 53:1

    he resembles the beasts that perish.

II

14 This is the way of those whose trust is folly,
the end of those contented with their lot:

Is 5:14; Prv 7:22, 27
Hos 13:14; Jer 12:13
Ps 44:23

15 Like sheep they are herded into the nether world;
death is their shepherd, and the upright rule over them.
Quickly their form is consumed;
the nether world is their palace.

Pss 16:10f; 36: 10; 44:27
Pss 73:24; 86: 13; 116:8

16 But God will redeem me
from the power of the nether world by receiving me.

III

17 Fear not when a man grows rich,
when the wealth of his house becomes great,

Ps 73:12

1 Tm 6:7; Jb 1:21
Eccl 5:15f; Sir 11:19f

18 For when he dies, he shall take none of it;
his wealth shall not follow him down.

19 Though in his lifetime he counted himself blessed,
"They will praise you for doing well for yourself,"

20 He shall join the circle of his forebears

Jb 10:21

who shall never more see light.

21 Man, for all his splendor, if he have not prudence,

Eccl 3:18f

resembles the beasts that perish.

The traditional wisdom doctrine on retribution (cf. Pss 37 and 73 + §14d) is applied here to a specific problem: the riches of the wicked. Himself a potential victim of hostile wealth (vv 6-7), the psalmist has not let envy prevail in his heart (cf. Ps 73:2f), but by objective analysis he has carefully examined the riddle of the prosperity of the wicked. He presents his solution in proverbial form (*māshāl,* v 5): wealth cannot save from death (vv 8-10), decreed for all men (11-13); the wicked perish hopelessly but the just will be redeemed from the power of the nether world (14-16), because trust in God can overcome even death. The problem discussed being universal in scope, the sapiential consideration is addressed to all who dwell in the world. Yet it will be more beneficial to the poor, to those of lowly birth (v 3), as an encouragement in their distress and a protection against temptation. The psalm concludes with an exhortation (vv 17-21) which again stresses the vanity of riches and repeats the maxim: "Man, for all his splendor, if he have not prudence (i.e., sapiential understanding) resembles the beasts that perish" (v 21: cf. v 13).

The beginning of verse 9 is a *crux interpretum.* The root *yqr* usually denotes the idea of "costly." In some Palmyrene funerary inscriptions, P. Joüon (*Syria* 1938, p. 99f) attributed to *yqr'* the meaning "monument d'honneur." From this and other indications Dahood conjectures that somehow *yqr* in verses 9 and 13 must mean "Mansion," "another of the thirty-odd names of the nether world heretofore recognized in biblical poetry." Thus these verses would read:

> But the Mansion shall be the redemption of his soul,
>   and he shall cease forever.
> For man in the Mansion will sleep indeed,
>   become like beasts that cease to be.

Verses 14-15 which also involve difficulties, are rendered thus by R. Pautrel:

> 14   Haec est via eorum qui sperant in se
>   et finis eorum qui ore suo delectantur.
> 15A Sicut oves in praedam ponunt,
>   mors pascet eos et dominabitur eis.
> 15B Dociles in gregem includet,
>   superesse inferno gloriantes.

Attention to the emphasizing particle *ki,* attested in Ugaritic texts, has brought about an improved translation of important verse 16: "But God will ransom me, from the hand of Sheol will he surely snatch me." Dahood adds the following comment: "What the psalmist is professing is his firm conviction that God will take him to himself, just as he took Enoch and Elijah; in other words, he is stating his belief in 'assumption.' Most commentators find this meaning in the psalmist's words . . . . The verb *lqh* is precisely that used in Gn 5:24; 2 Kgs 2:3; 5:9; Sir 42:15; 48:9; as well as in Ps 73:24" (*lqh* is, however, a very common verb!). The minimizing interpretations could be represented by *OABA*: "This might express the psalmist's assurance of his own immortality, but is perhaps better understood merely as confidence that he will be delivered from present trouble." Perhaps this is suggested by the three following parallel texts: "Great has been your kindness toward me; you have rescued me from the depths of the nether world" (Ps 86:13); "What man shall live, and not see death, but deliver himself from the power of the nether world?"; "Shall

I deliver them from the power of the nether world? shall I redeem them from death?" Preservation from death rather than rescue from Sheol after death seems to be intended. It is hard to deny that Ps 49:16 expresses the belief that the just can hope for immortality (Pss 16:10f and 73:23ff are not clear). J. van der Ploeg thinks that the affirmation of the verse goes beyond a mere hope of being preserved from a premature death. He would not exclude that the psalmist had in mind the immortality of the person or, even more probably, bodily resurrection (p. 172). In contrast to the destiny of the just is that of the wicked "who shall never more see light" (v 20), i.e., enjoy immortality (see on *Ps 36:10). "The light of God's face in the fields of life will be denied those who put their trust in riches and boast of financial success" (Dahood; on Ps 49:16, cf. also *RB* 1949, p. 493ff).

PSALM 73 (72)

The False Happiness of the Wicked

	1 A *psalm of Asaph.*
Pss 26:3; 85: 8; 86:5 Mt 5:8; Jer 12:3	How good God is to the upright; the Lord, to those who are clean of heart!
	2 But, as for me, I almost lost my balance; my feet all but slipped,
Ps 37:2; Prv 23:17 Jer 12:1; Jb 21:7 Mal 3:15; Eccl 7:15; 8:14 Jb 21:13ff; Ps 37:35	3 Because I was envious of the arrogant when I saw them prosper though they were wicked.
	4 For they are in no pain; their bodies are sound and sleek;
	5 They are free from the burden of mortals, and are not afflicted like the rest of men.
	6 So pride adorns them as a necklace; as a robe violence enwraps them.
Jer 5:28; Jb 15:27	7 Out of their crassness comes iniquity; their fancies overflow their hearts.
Pss 10:5; 17:10	8 They scoff and speak evil; outrage from on high they threaten.
Jb 22:13	9 They set their mouthings in place of heaven, and their pronouncements roam the earth:
Jer 12:7ff	10 "So he brings his people to such a pass

that they have not even water!"

Ex 8:12; Ps 10:11
Is 29:15

11 And they say, "How does God know?"
And, "Is there any knowledge in the Most High?"

12 Such, then, are the wicked;

Ps 49:17

always carefree, while they increase in wealth.

II

Mal 3:14 √

13 Is it but in vain I have kept my heart clean

Ps 26:6; Jb 21:15

and washed my hands as an innocent man?

14 For I suffer affliction day after day
and chastisement with each new dawn.

15 Had I thought, "I will speak as they do,"

Ex 4:22; Hos 11:1; Is 63:16
Is 55:9; Jb 42:3
Eccl 8:17

I had been false to the fellowship of your children.

16 Though I tried to understand this
it seemed to me too difficult,

Ex 21:7; Sg 2:22
Pss 92:9; 119: 130

17 Till I entered the sanctuary of God
and considered their final destiny.

III

Pss 66:9; 121: 3
Wis 4:19f

18 You set them, indeed, on a slippery road;
you hurl them down to ruin.

Jb 20:8; 21: 16ff

19 How suddenly they are made desolate!
They are completely wasted away amid horrors.

Is 29:7f; 51:9

20 As though they were the dream of one who had awakened,
O Lord,

Pss 68:2; 74: 22; 78:65

so will you, when you arise, set at nought these phantoms.

21 Because my heart was embittered
and my soul was pierced,

22 I was stupid and understood not;

Jb 18:3

I was like a brute beast in your presence.

IV

Pss 55:23; 112:1ff
Is 41:13; 42:6; 45:1
Pss 48:15; 78: 72
Gn 5:24; Jb 19:9
Is 58:8; Jb 5: 1

23 Yet with you I shall always be;
you have hold of my right hand;

24 With your counsel you guide me,
and in the end you will receive me in glory.

25 Whom else have I in heaven?
And when I am with you, the earth delights me not.

26 Though my flesh and my heart waste away,

Lam 3:24; Pss 11:6; 16:5

God is the rock of my heart and my portion forever.

27 For indeed, they who withdraw from you perish;

Hos 9:1; Jer 13:27

you destroy everyone who is unfaithful to you.

Ex 20:30; Ps   28   But for me, to be near God is my good;
25:3
Is 58:2; Pss   to make the Lord God my refuge.
71:7; 142:6
                     I shall declare all your works
                     in the gates of the daughter of Zion.

How can faith in God survive against the background of the prosperity of the wicked? The psalmist himself had to resist the scandal and refrain the impulse of envy (vv 2-3). After having described the well-being, the apparent happiness and the arrogance of the wicked (vv 4-12), he compares their fortunate lot to the distressing state of the just, like himself. He was tempted to imitate the wicked but then a divine revelation showed him in a new light their final destiny (13-17). He suddenly understood that the prosperous sinner is really on the verge of ruin because his apparent security has no real foundation (18-22). In contrast, the psalmist's future rests on the firm basis of trust in God, the effects of which endure beyond death's frontier (23-28). If Luther's translation of verse 25 is correct, "as long as I have thee, I wish for nothing else in heaven or on earth," then communion with God, whether in heaven or on earth, is for the psalmist the supreme and, in a way, the only good (see §12f). This psalmist has expressed his views in the relation of a personal experience available for a general application.

Taking as starting-point the statement, "till I entered the sanctuary of God," recent authors link Ps 73 with the cult. The central character, representing Israel (v 1), would be the king (E. Würthwein), and the psalm has probably featured in the mythologizing New Year festival (H. Ringgren). H. Gressmann discovered a royal rite in the affirmation: "You have hold of my right hand" (73:23; cf. Is 45:1). For H. Schmidt the psalm is the thanksgiving of an individual recited at a *Gelübdedankgottesdienst*. Mowinckel (II, p. 36) holds a similar view and describes the man's calamity as distress made more bitter by "travail of mind." There is much to be said in favor of these suggestions, some of which, however, depend too heavily on preconceived extraneous patterns of interpretation.

We read in verses 9-10:

They set their mouthings in place of heaven,
    and their pronouncements roam the earth:
So he brings his people to such a pass
    that they have not even water!

It is curious to read in this connection a text from the Ras Shamra tablets (cf. §9d), which states, Ringgren explains, "that some mythological beings, who obviously have some connection with chaos and death, put one lip to the sky and the other to the earth and drain the water in abundance" (*The Faith* . . . , p. 44f; cf. *VT* 1953, p. 265ff). The parallel is more apparent if the translation keeps closer to the Hebrew: "They set their mouths against the heavens, and their tongue struts through the earth" (*RSV*: Ps 73:9a). Other Ugaritic parallels are cited by R. T. O'Callaghan: "In the poem of the Gracious and Beautiful Gods, evidently of cosmognic character, Dawn and Dusk are begotten by El and their ravenous appetites soon after birth are described: 'One lip is (stretched down) to earth, one lip (upward) to the sky . . .' (t. 52:61f; Gordon, p. 175). It is not impossible that the Psalmist used the wording of an early cosmogonic myth as a striking figure of speech to mark the colossal insolence of the impious. In keeping with the voracious appetite of Dawn and Dusk we find a more forceful application of the same phrase to the god Môt into whose ravenous maw Baal will descend in the season of declining vegetation: 'One lip to earth and one lip to heaven, [He stretches his tongue to the stars], Baal enters within him, he descends into his maw' (t. 67, II, 2ff; Gordon, p. 178). Here the closest parallel is the biblical application to the extended gullet and insatiable hunger of Sheol, the most striking example being found perhaps in Is 5:14; cf. Hb 2:5; Prv 1:12; Ps 141:7" (*VT*, 1954, p. 169).

H. Birkeland's views on the "evildoing enemies" in the Psalms is known (cf. §12g). "Some revision of my exposition in *Die Feinde* . . . , he writes, will be found implied in the following attempt at a solution of the chief problems of Ps 73:17ff." The identification of the *reša'îm* with the *gôyîm* is directly required in Ps 73:1, where it is said, in Birkeland's view, "that God is good towards Israel" (cf. v 10). The "I" of the psalm, he explains, is a representative of Israel. What solved the psalmist's doubt, Birkeland claims, was no divine revelation, but a visit to "the illegitimate places of worship," to the *miqdᵉšē-ēl*, mentioned in verse 17. This interpretation presupposes the centralization of the cult in one sanctuary, that of Jerusalem (cf. Dt 12:5ff; 2 Kgs 22-23). "When the author came to (the remnants of) the illegitimate sanctuaries, which were destroyed, they became to him demonstrations of the fate of paganism and pagans, i.e., of gentile idolatry and the gentiles themselves: they flourished for a time, but were then demolished.

And it was Yahweh who had destroyed them, so that they fell into ruins . . . . The devastated sanctuaries have made him realize the uselessness of idols and the eternal value of his own communion with Yahweh; he and his people are safeguarded under the protection of God." *JB* translates verse 17, "Until the day I pierced the mystery . . ." and comments: "Lit. 'the sanctuaries of God.' The psalmist is not referring to the Temple where God may have enlightened him, nor to divine mysteries (Wis 2:22), revealed to him, but to the teaching contained in the scriptures, dwelling place of wisdom (Prv 9:1f; Sir 14:21f) and staple of Jewish piety (Sir 39:1)."

As for verse 24, the text, in Birkeland's view, "simply contains the following meaning: Yahweh takes, i.e., leads, the author on a path on which he is always after *kābōd* ("glory," "honor"), just as, for example, the shepherd is after the flock." The *kābōd,* in this case, consists "in real goods, for the time being communion with God, later on the restoration of the people." It is probably more true to say that the psalmist's intimate fellowship with God on earth has instructed him also on some secrets of the world to come. In accordance with parallel biblical passages (see on *Ps 49:16), Dahood would translate the verse: "Into your council lead me and with glory assume me." It is not easy to prove that he is wrong. The meaning of "glory" is thus explained by *JB*: "Probably not a reference to heavenly glory (Enoch, Gn 5: 24; Elijah, 2 Kgs 2:3). The versions translate 'with glory,' giving the word its usual sense when used of men; this interpretation suggests that God preserves the just man from an early and shameful death and will vindicate him, even though the upright man dies while the wicked survive. Moreover, as in 16:9f, the psalmist yearns for unbreakable union with God; this is a milestone on the road to a formulated belief in resurrection and eternal life."

In verse 26 the psalmist affirms that God is his portion forever (see on *Ps 142:6). The apportioning of the inheritance (see on *Ps 110:7) can be generally related to the allocating of the land under Joshuah, who "had given the Levites no inheritance among the tribes" (14:3f); "Yahweh the God of Israel was their inheritance, as he had told them" (Jos 13:4). Yahweh had explained to Aaron: "You shall have no inheritance in their land, no portion of it among them shall be yours. It is I who will be *your portion* and your inheritance among the sons of Israel" (Nm 18:20; cf. Dt 10:9).

PSALM 91 (90)

Security under God's Protection

I

<table>
<tr><td>Pss 7:18; 92:2</td><td>1</td><td>You who dwell in the shelter of the Most High,
who abide in the shadow of the Almighty,</td></tr>
<tr><td>1 Kgs 20:23;
Ps 68:15
2 Sm 22:3;
Prv 18:10</td><td>2</td><td>Say to the Lord, "My refuge and my fortress,
my God, in whom I trust."</td></tr>
<tr><td>Hos 9:8; Pss
31:5; 124.73</td><td>3</td><td>For he will rescue you from the snare of the fowler,
from the destroying pestilence.</td></tr>
<tr><td>Ex 19:4; Dt
32:11
Is 31:5; Mt
23:37
Pss 17:8; 63:8</td><td>4</td><td>With his pinions he will cover you,
and under his wings you shall take refuge;
his faithfulness is a buckler and a shield.</td></tr>
<tr><td>Prv 3:25</td><td>5</td><td>You shall not fear the terror of the night
nor the arrow that flies by day;</td></tr>
<tr><td>Dt 32:24; Hb
3:5
Jer 15:8; Sir
34:16</td><td>6</td><td>Not the pestilence that roams in darkness
nor the devastating plague at noon.</td></tr>
<tr><td></td><td>7</td><td>Though a thousand fall at your side,
ten thousand at your right side,
near you it shall not come.</td></tr>
<tr><td></td><td>8</td><td>Rather with your eyes shall you behold
and see the requital of the wicked,</td></tr>
<tr><td></td><td>9</td><td>Because you have the Lord for your refuge;</td></tr>
<tr><td>Pss 84:10; 91:
2</td><td></td><td>you have made the Most High your stronghold.</td></tr>
<tr><td>Prv 12:21; Dt
7:15</td><td>10</td><td>No evil shall befall you,
nor shall affliction come near your tent,</td></tr>
<tr><td>Ps 103:20f;
Heb 1:14
Gn 24:7; Ex
23:20
Ps 34:8</td><td>11</td><td>For to his angels he has given command about you,
that they guard you in all your ways.</td></tr>
<tr><td>Prv 3:23; Lk
4:9ff
Is 11:8; Mk
16:18
Lk 10:19; Ez
34:25
Jb 5:22</td><td>12</td><td>Upon their hands they bear you up,
lest you dash your foot against a stone.</td></tr>
<tr><td></td><td>13</td><td>You shall tread upon the asp and the viper;
you shall trample down the lion and the dragon.</td></tr>
</table>

II

<table>
<tr><td>Jer 33:3</td><td>14</td><td>Because he clings to me, I will deliver him;
I will set him on high because he acknowledges my name.</td></tr>
<tr><td>Pss 62:5; 66:9</td><td>15</td><td>He shall call upon me, and I will answer him;
I will be with him in distress;</td></tr>
</table>

Ps 50:15   I will deliver him and glorify him;
Prv 3:2; Dt   16   with length of days I will gratify him
4:40
Ps 50:23   and will show him my salvation.

In Ps 46 the cult community expressed its unreserved trust in God
"against the whole wide background of the *Heilsgeschichte* and of
eschatology." In Ps 91, "springing from the same cultic source" (Weiser), it is a "personal and intimate relationship of trust in God" which
is expressed and powerfully illustrated by various poetical metaphors.
The first part of the psalm (1-13) was perhaps pronounced by a priest
as an exhortation to the temple worshippers. Some authors (cf. G.
Pidoux, p. 145) suggest that Ps 91 consists of liturgical fragments;
others (cf. H. Schmidt) think it is one of the threshold dialogues
(*Pfortengespräche*), like Pss 15 and 24A. It is perhaps easier to assume,
with H.-J. Kraus, that the psalm was recited by a man who had taken
refuge in the sanctuary. His thanksgiving takes the form of a confession
(cf. Ps 34:12), in which the blessing of trust in God is impressed upon
the listener(s) by the teaching of personal experience.

The mention in verse 1 of the divine names, "Most High," "Almighty," Caquot writes, could reflect the probable fact that the Israelite
Yahweh replaced at a given time and place (Jerusalem) *'elyôn-šadday,*
the divinity of pre-davidic Zion (cf. v 9 and §13b). The central character meant throughout the psalm under the anonymity of the 3rd and
2nd persons could be the just *par excellence,* the Messiah himself, J.
Magne thinks. This would be in a way confirmed by the gospel narrative: Satan quoted verses 11-12 when he tempted Christ to presump-
tion against God's providence (Mt 4:6).

Various ancient versions, including the Vulgate (*"daemonium meridianum"*) read an allusion to "the noonday devil" in verse 6 (Hebr.:
yāšûd, "devastate"), influenced, it seems, by the ancient Oriental
representation of pestilence as a demon especially active during the
night and the noon siesta. J. De Fraine has shown from biblical
and non-biblical sources that a personal demonic power is meant even
in the *MT.* Verses 5-6, he pointed out, refer to four manifestations of
demonic power: during the night, in the morning, in the evening and
at noon, embracing the whole day. Consequently divine protection is
understood to accompany the just constantly. A. F. Kirkpatrick, on the
other hand, would consider Pss 90, 91, 92 as a group, and conclude:

"If now Ps 90 is the plea of Israel in exile, and Ps 92 its thanksgiving for deliverance, may not Ps 91 be the voice of faith assuring Israel that it will be safe in the midst of the calamities which are about to fall upon Babylon?"

The reading of "asp" in verse 13 follows the Greek, Syriac and Latin versions, but the Hebrew word *šaḥal* means "lion." What the psalmist has in mind, writes Weiser, is probably "the idea, widespread in the ancient Orient and handed down in the cultic myth, of the god killing a dragon and as a sign of victory over the monster putting his foot on its neck. And whereas the popular belief in Egypt led to the manufacturing of amulets with the picture of a god treading on a lion, and by its magic power giving protection against wild animals, in the Old Testament it is faith itself which supplies man with super-human, divine strength to overcome every kind of danger."

PSALM 112 (111)

The Blessings of the Just Man

1 Alleluia

Pss 1:1f; 128:1

   Happy the man who fears the Lord,
      who greatly delights in his commands.

Prv 20:7

2 His posterity shall be mighty upon the earth;
      the upright generation shall be blessed.

3 Wealth and riches shall be in his house;

Ps 111:3

      his generosity shall endure forever.

Is 58:10; Ps 37:6
Pss 97:11; 111:4; Ex 34:6
Dt 15:8; Ps 37:26

4 He dawns through the darkness, a light for the upright;
      he is gracious and merciful and just

5 Well for the man who is gracious and lends,
      who conducts his affairs with justice;

Pss 21:8; 73:23; 125:1
Wis 8:13; Prv 10:7
Sir 34:16

6 He shall never be moved;
      the just man shall be in everlasting remembrance.

7 An evil report he shall not fear;
      his heart is firm; trusting in the Lord.

8 His heart is steadfast; he shall not fear
      till he looks down upon his foes.

Prv 22:9

9 Lavishly he gives to the poor;
      his generosity shall endure forever;

2 Cor 9:9; Ps 18:3

      his horn shall be exalted in glory.

10 The wicked man shall see it and be vexed;
he shall gnash his teeth and pine away;

Prv 10:28 the desire of the wicked shall perish.

Not only the opening words but the rest of the psalm as well show similarities with Ps 1 in subject-matter. In form and language Ps 112 can be compared to Ps 111, another alphabetic psalm, perhaps written by the same author. Besides, some expressions said of God in Ps 111 are applied in Ps 112 to the just. Divine attributes are reflected in the works of the upright. Like God (cf. Pss 18:29; 27:1) the just man is a shining light (v 4; cf. Prv 13:9; Mt 5:16). The *ṣedeq* of both will endure forever (Pss 111:3; 112:3). In contrast there will be no other answer to the evil man's desire but powerless envy (v 10).

PSALM 119 (118)

Praise of God's Law

Aleph

Pss 1:1; 112:1 1 Happy are they whose way is blameless,
who walk in the law of the Lord.

2 Happy are they who observe his decrees,
Dt 4:29; 2 Chr who seek him with all their heart,
31:21

3 And do no wrong,
but walk in his ways.

4 You have commanded that your precepts
Prv 3:1 be diligently kept.

5 Oh, that I might be firm in the ways
of keeping your statutes!

6 Then should I not be put to shame
when I beheld all your commands.

7 I will give you thanks with an upright heart,
when I have learned your just ordinances.

8 I will keep your statutes;
do not utterly forsake me.

Beth

Eccl 12:1 9 How shall a young man be faultless in his way?
By keeping to your words.

10 With all my heart I seek you;

let me not stray from your commands.

11 Within my heart I treasure your promise,
that I may not sin against you.

Tb 4:19

Ps 143:10

12 Blessed are you, O Lord;
teach me your statutes.

13 With my lips I declare
all the ordinances of your mouth.

14 In the way of your decrees I rejoice,
as much as in all riches.

Ps 1:2

15 I will meditate on your precepts
and consider your ways.

16 In your statutes I will delight;
I will not forget your words.

Gimel

Ps 19:12

Dt 17:19

17 Be good to your servant, that I may live
and keep your words.

18 Open my eyes, that I may consider
the wonders of your law.

Gn 47:9; Ps
39:13

19 I am a wayfarer of earth;
hide not your commands from me.

20 My soul is consumed with longing
for your ordinances at all times.

Dt 27:26; Jer
11:3

21 You rebuke the accursed proud,
who turn away from your commands.

22 Take away from me reproach and contempt,
for I observe your decrees.

23 Though princes meet and talk against me,
your servant meditates on your statutes.

24 Yes, your decrees are my delight;
they are my counselors.

Daleth

Pss 7:6; 44:26

Dt 17:19

25 I lie postrate in the dust;
give me life according to your word.

26 I declared my ways, and you answered me;
teach me your statutes.

27 Make me understand the way of your precepts,
and I will meditate on your wondrous deeds.

Ps 77:3

28 My soul weeps for sorrow;
strengthen me according to your words.

29 Remove from me the way of falsehood,
    and favor me with your law.
30 The way of truth I have chosen;
    I have set your ordinances before me.
31 I cling to your decrees;
    O Lord, let me not be put to shame.
32 I will run the way of your commands
    when you give me a docile heart.

He

33 Instruct me, O Lord, in the way of your statutes,

Ps 19:12   that I may exactly observe them.

34 Give me discernment, that I may observe your law
    and keep it with all my heart.

Ps 25:4   35 Lead me in the path of your commands,
    for in it I delight.
36 Incline my heart to your decrees
    and not to gain.
37 Turn away my eyes from seeing what is vain;
    by your way give me life.

Ps 31:17   38 Fulfill for your servant
Is 66:2   your promise to those who fear you.

39 Turn away from me the reproach which I dread,
    for your ordinances are good.
40 Behold, I long for your precepts;
    in your justice give me life.

Vau

41 Let your kindness come to me, O Lord,
    your salvation according to your promise.
42 So shall I have an answer for those who reproach me,

Ps 130:5   for I trust in your words.

43 Take not the word of truth from my mouth,
    for in your ordinances is my hope;
44 And I will keep your law continually,
    forever and ever.
45 And I will walk at liberty,

Ezr 7:10   because I seek your precepts.

46 I will speak of your decrees before kings
    without being ashamed.
47 And I will delight in your commands,

which I love.

48 And I will lift up my hands to your commands
and meditate on your statutes.

Zain

Ps 34:23   49 Remember your word to your servant
since you have given me hope.

50 My comfort in my affliction is
that your promise gives me life.

51 Though the proud scoff bitterly at me,
Dt 17:11   I turn not away from your law.

Ps 77:7   52 I remember your ordinances of old, O Lord,
and I am comforted.

53 Indignation seizes me because of the wicked
who forsake your law.

54 Your statutes are the theme of my song
in the place of my exile.

Pss 1:2; 63:7   55 By night I remember your name, O Lord,
and I will keep your law.

56 This has been mine,
that I have observed your precepts.

Heth

57 I have said, O Lord, that my part
is to keep your words.

58 I entreat you with all my heart,
have pity on me according to your promise.

59 I considered my ways
and turned my feet to your decrees.

60 I was prompt and did not hesitate
in keeping your commands.

61 Though the snares of the wicked are twined about me,
your law I have not forgotten.

Ps 77:3   62 At midnight I rise to give you thanks
because of your just ordinances.

63 I am the companion of all who fear you
and keep your precepts.

Ps 33:5   64 Of your kindness, O Lord, the earth is full;
teach me your statutes.

Teth

Ps 69:37   65 You have done good to your servant,

Ps 106:12   O Lord, according to your word.

66   Teach me wisdom and knowledge,
for in your commands I trust.

67   Before I was afflicted I went astray,
but now I hold to your promise.

Pss 26:3; 86:5   68 You are good and bountiful;
teach me your statutes.

69 Though the proud forge lies against me,

Ps 40:9   with all my heart I will observe your precepts.

Pss 17:10; 73:7   70 Their heart has become gross and fat;
as for me, your law is my delight.

71 It is good for me that I have been afflicted,

Ps 94:12   that I may learn your statutes.

72 The law of your mouth is to me more precious
than thousands of gold and silver pieces.

Yod

Jb 10:8; Dt 32:6   73 Your hands have made me and fashioned me;
give me discernment that I may learn your commands.

74 Those who fear you shall see me and be glad,

Ps 130:5   because I hope in your word.

75 I know, O Lord, that your ordinances are just,
and in your faithfulness you have afflicted me.

76 Let your kindness comfort me

Ps 79:2   according to your promise to your servants.

77 Let your compassion come to me that I may live,
for your law is my delight.

Pss 40:15; 109:28   78 Let the proud be put to shame for oppressing me unjustly;
I will meditate on your precepts.

79 Let those turn to me who fear you
and acknowledge your decrees.

Ps 24:4   80 Let my heart be perfect in your statutes,
that I be not put to shame.

Caph

81 My soul pines for your salvation;

Ps 130:5   I hope in your word.

Ps 123:2   82 My eyes strain after your promise;

Ps 101:2   when will you comfort me?

Jb 30:30   83 Though I am shriveled like a leathern flask in the smoke,
I have not forgotten your statutes.

Ps 19:12
Ps 7:2

84 How many are the days of your servant?
       When will you do judgment on my persecutors?
85 The proud have dug pits for me;
       this is against your law.
86 All your commands are steadfast;

Ps 31:16

       they persecute me wrongfully; help me!
87 They have all but put an end to me on the earth,
       but I have not forsaken your precepts.
88 In your kindness give me life,
       that I may keep the decrees of your mouth.

Lamed

89 Your word, O Lord, endures forever;

Is 40:8

       it is firm as the heavens.
90 Through all generations your truth endures;
       you have established the earth, and it stands firm.
91 According to your ordinances they still stand firm:
       all things serve you.
92 Had not your law been my delight,
       I should have perished in my affliction.
93 Never will I forget your precepts,
       for through them you give me life.
94 I am yours; save me,
       for I have sought your precepts.
95 Sinners wait to destroy me,
       but I pay heed to your decrees.
96 I see that all fulfillment has its limits;
       broad indeed is your command.

Mem

Ps 40:9

97 How I love your law, O Lord!
       it is my meditation all the day.
98 Your command has made me wiser than my enemies,
       for it is ever with me.
99 I have more understanding than all my teachers
       when your decrees are my meditation.

Jb 32:6; Wis
4:9

100 I have more discernment than the elders,
       because I observe your precepts.
101 From every evil way I withhold my feet,
       that I may keep your words.
102 From your ordinances I turn not away,

for you have instructed me.

103 How sweet to my palate are your promises,

Ps 19:11; Jer 15:16
sweeter than honey to my mouth!

104 Through your precepts I gain discernment;
therefore I hate every false way.

Nun

Pss 18:29; 19: 8
Prv 6:23
105 A lamp to my feet is your word,
a light to my path.

106 I resolve and swear
to keep your just ordinances.

107 I am very much afflicted;
O Lord, give me life according to your word.

Heb 13:15; Ps 50:14
108 Accept, O Lord, the free homage of my mouth,
and teach me your decrees.

109 Though constantly I take my life in my hands,
Ps 40:9
yet I forget not your law.

Pss 64:6; 140: 6
110 The wicked have laid a snare for me,
but from your precepts I have not strayed.

111 Your decrees are my inheritance forever;
the joy of my heart they are.

112 I intend in my heart to fulfill your statutes
always, to the letter.

Samech

1 Kgs 18:21
113 I hate men of divided heart,
but I love your law.

114 You are my refuge and my shield;
in your word I hope.

Pss 6:9; 139: 19
115 Depart from me, you wrongdoers,
and I will observe the commands of my God.

116 Sustain me as you have promised, that I may live;
disappoint me not in my hope.

117 Help me, that I may be safe
and ever delight in your statutes.

118 You despise all who stray from your statutes,
for their deceitfulness is in vain.

Ez 22:18-22
119 You account all the wicked of the earth as dross;
therefore I love your decrees.

Jb 4:14f; Ps 88:17
120 My flesh shudders with dread of you,
and I fear your ordinances.

Ain

121 I have fulfilled just ordinances;
leave me not to my oppressors.

Ps 34:23   122 Be surety for the welfare of your servant;
let not the proud oppress me.

123 My eyes strain after your salvation
and your just promise.

Ps 80:5   124 Deal with your servant according to your kindness,
and teach me your statutes.

125 I am your servant; give me discernment
that I may know your decrees.

126 It is time for the Lord to act:
they have broken your law.

127 For I love your command
Ps 19:11   more than gold, however fine.

128 For in all your precepts I go forward;
every false way I hate.

Phe

129 Wonderful are your decrees;
therefore I observe them.

Pss 19:9; 73:   130 The revelation of your words sheds light,
17   giving understanding to the simple.

131 I gasp with open mouth
Ps 42:2   in my yearning for your commands.

132 Turn to me in pity
Pss 5:12; 25:   as you turn to those who love your name.
16
Ps 17:5   133 Steady my footsteps according to your promise,
and let no iniquity rule over me.

134 Redeem me from the oppression of men,
Ps 125:3   that I may keep your precepts.

Nm 6:25; Pss   135 Let your countenance shine upon your servant,
67:2; 80:4   and teach me your statutes.

136 My eyes shed streams of tears
Ezr 9:3f   because your law has not been kept.

Sade

137 You are just, O Lord,
and your ordinance is right.

138 You have pronounced your decrees in justice

and in perfect faithfulness.

Ps 69:10 139 My zeal consumes me,
because my foes forget your words.

Pss 12:7; 86:2 140 Your promise is very sure,
and your servant loves it.

141 I am mean and contemptible,
but your precepts I have not forgotten.

Pss 112:4;
143:11 142 Your justice is everlasting justice,
and your law is permanent.

143 Though distress and anguish have come upon me,
your commands are my delight.

144 Your decrees are forever just;
give me discernment that I may live.

Coph

145 I call out with all my heart; answer me, O Lord;
I will observe your statutes.

146 I call upon you; save me,
and I will keep your decrees.

147 Before dawn I come and cry out;
I hope in your words.

Pss 24:15; 63:
7; 77:3f 148 My eyes greet the night watches
in meditation on your promise.

149 Hear my voice according to your kindness, O Lord;
according to your ordinance give me life.

150 I am attacked by malicious persecutors
who are far from your law.

151 You, O Lord, are near,
and all your commands are permanent.

152 Of old I know from your decrees,
that you have established them forever.

Reš

153 Behold my affliction, and rescue me,
for I have not forgotten your law.

154 Plead my cause, and redeem me;
for the sake of your promise give me life.

155 Far from sinners is salvation,
because they seek not your statutes.

156 Your compassion is great, O Lord;

according to your ordinances give me life.

Ps 44:17   157 Though my persecutors and my foes are many,
I turn not away from your decrees.

Pss 15:4; 139:   158 I beheld the apostates with loathing,
21
because they kept not to your promise.

159 See how I love your precepts, O Lord;
in your kindness give me life.

160 Permanence is your word's chief trait;
each of your just ordinances is everlasting.

Sin

Pss 35:12ff;   161 Princes persecute me without cause
38:20f
but my heart stands in awe of your word.

162 I rejoice at your promise,
as one who has found rich spoil.

163 Falsehood I hate and abhor;

Ps 40:9   your law I love.

164 Seven times a day I praise you
for your just ordinances.

Ps 37:11   165 Those who love your law have great peace,
and for them there is no stumbling block.

Ps 37:34   166 I wait for your salvation, O Lord,
and your commands I fulfill.

167 I keep your decrees
and love them deeply.

168 I keep your precepts and your decrees,
Prv 5:21   for all my ways are before you.

Thau

Pss 88:3; 100:   169 Let my cry come before you, O Lord;
2; 102:1
in keeping with your word, give me discernment.

170 Let my supplication reach you;
rescue me according to your promise.

171 My lips pour forth your praise,
because you teach me your statutes.

172 May my tongue sing of your promise,
for all your commands are just.

173 Let your hand be ready to help me,
for I have chosen your precepts.

174 I long for your salvation, O Lord,

Ps 69:33   and your law is my delight.

Is 38:19   175 Let my soul live to praise you,

                     and may your ordinances help me.

Is 53:6; Jer 176 I have gone astray [like a lost sheep]; seek your servant,
50:6

                     because your commands I do not forget.

The longest psalm of the Psalter comprises twenty-two stanzas of eight lines, each of which begins with the same Hebrew letter, assigned alphabetically to every strophe. Tedious repetitions, poor thought-sequence, apparent lack of inspiration reflect the artificiality of the composition. Mowinckel (II, p. 78) believes that the long poem is a non-cultic individual psalm of lamentation (cf. vv 8, 61, 85, 95, 107, 110, 115, 150-154, 161) and that the numerous references to the author's own faithfulness with respect to the Law are intended as motivations of the supplication. The psalm can also be described as a hymn to the Law, mentioned under eight synonymns: law, statutes, commands, ordinances, decrees, precepts, words, and promises. The Law praised in the psalm should be understood as referring generally to divine revelation made known by the prophets and the messengers of God.

This great "Psalm of the Law," writes Kirkpatrick, "is based upon the prophetic (Ezra 9:11) presentation of the Law in the Book of Deuteronomy, with the spirit and language of which its author's mind was saturated. It represents the religious ideas of Deuteronomy developed in the communion of a devout soul with God .... The 'Law of God' which the psalmist describes ... is not the law in the narrower sense of the Mosaic legislation or the Pentateuch. The Hebrew word tōrāh has a wider range of meaning, and here, as in Pss 1 and 19, it must be understood to mean all Divine revelation as the guide of life. This it is which kindles the psalmist's enthusiasm and demands his allegiance. It is no rigid code of commands and prohibitions, but a body of teaching, the full meaning of which can only be realized gradually and by the help of Divine instruction." In his detailed study of Ps 119, A. Deissler has stressed the author's intelligent use of previous scriptures (anthological style, cf. *Ps 33). He also maintains that the psalm's subject-matter seems to be deuteronomic tōrāh. To consider the "Word of God" as almost personified (v 89) helps to understand that it is a source of life (v 93). The psalm is later then Proverbs and Malachias but was written before Sirach and Machabees, in the third and second century B.C. (on the "meditation" of the law, see §12f).

Additional views bring out the rich variety of the psalm's teaching in contrast with the apparent monotony of the expression. J. Enciso considers Ps 119 as a *Salmo-prologo* (see on *Ps 137) introducing the "Songs of ascents" (120-134; cf. §3c). He finds that many verses of the psalm reflect the context of a pilgrim's trip to Jerusalem. Some would allude to vexations endured when, coming from the North, the pilgrim passed through the territory of hostile Samaritans (cf. the *Caph* stanza: vv 81-88). The *Lamed* stanza (vv 89-96) is a kind of thanksgiving, marking the end (v 96) of the long trip. The following stanzas would describe the psalmist's state of soul durnig his stay in the Holy City, where he heard so much about the Law. Before leaving Jerusalem he prays God to "steady his footsteps" (v 133). During the return trip he suffers again in "distress and anguish" (v 143), is attacked by "persecutors" (vv 150, 157). The last two stanzas (vv 161-176) express the peace of mind and the gratitude of the pilgrim safely back in his country.

For H. Duesberg, on the other hand, Ps 119 has no concrete *Sitz im Leben*. This "mirror of the faithful," he believes, is a product of professional psalmography (see also Mowinckel II, pp. 104-125 and §29a); it could be a repertoire of pious sentences, collected for the spiritual training of the young scribes. M.-F. Lacan's view is that Ps 119 teaches us the alphabet of prayer, not in definitions, but in a prayerful dialogue with God. In the course of the dialogue several themes recur: the need of divine instruction to understand the mysterious Word of God (vv 12, 19, 66, 68); need of guidance (vv 28, 36, 37, 39, 59, 67); need of light (18, 34, 73, 105, 125, 144, 169); the lessons of trial (vv 67-71); prayer for fidelity (vv 5, 10, 44) in the face of wrongdoers (23, 46, 50, 53, 118f, 136, 158) and in the community of the just (1, 2, 38, 63); joy and satisfaction in the observance of the Law (14, 24, 35, 54, 92, 111, 131, 140, 143, 163, 167). As a result of the dialogue the attributes of God are revealed to the worshipper: his kindness (vv 41, 64, 76, 124), his fidelity (89ff, 140), his life-giving justice (40, 137f, 142, 144), the permanence of his Word (v 160), his salvation (vv 41, 81, 174). During prayer God lets his face shine upon the faithful (v 135), who reaps liberty, strength, joy, light, wisdom, docility, humility and life (vv 32, 45-47, 88, 130, 141, 154). Did the psalmist exaggerate when he wrote: "I have more understanding than all my teachers when your decrees are my meditation"? (v 99)

PSALM 127 (126)

The Need of God's Blessing: His Gift of Sons

1 A *song of ascents. Of Solomon.*

I

Unless the Lord build the house,
 they labor in vain who build it.
Unless the Lord guard the city,
 in vain does the guard keep vigil.
2 It is vain for you to rise early,
 or put off your rest,
You that eat hard-earned bread,
 for he gives to his beloved in sleep.

II

3 Behold, sons are a gift from the Lord;
 the fruit of the womb is a reward.
4 Like arrows in the hand of a warrior
 are the sons of one's youth.
5 Happy the man whose quiver is filled with them;
 they shall not be put to shame when they contend
 with enemies at the gate.

Dt 8:18; Prv 10:22

Prv 3:24

Eccl 2:24f; Ps 22:27

Dt 28:11

Ps 128:3

Prv 17:6

Prv 31:23

It is generally admitted that this is a unified psalm consisting originally of two expanded proverbial sayings. The "title" attributes the psalm to Solomon, for various possible reasons: he built the temple, he wrote proverbs (cf. 1 Kgs 4:32), he is called *y^edîdyâh,* "God's beloved" (2 Sm 12:25), and in his sleep God appeared to him (1 Kgs 3:5). Verses 1-2 present, clothed in imagery, a general truth expressed more concisely elsewhere:

It is the Lord's blessing that brings wealth,
and no effort can substitute for it (Prv 10:22).

Work is not condemned, but a godless attitude to work is, for "without God's blessing all human endeavor is futile" (*CV*). Trust in God's loving Providence was also insisted upon by Jesus (Mt 6:25-34). According to Prv 31:23, the husband of the "ideal wife" is prominent at the city gates as he sits with the elders of the land." His influence will be the greater if he has a large family. Like arrows in the hand of a warrior, sons defend the father. Human justice will not easily be denied to a large family protected by a row of robust and devoted sons. This is more clearly asserted in Dahood's translation of verse 5b: "They will not be humiliated but will drive their foes from the gate" (on Ps 2:5). In Amarna letter 76:38-41, Rib-Addi writes to the Pharaoh: "Send a large number of archers so that they might drive out the enemies of the king from the midst of his country." The meaning "drive out" of Akkadian *dubburu* seems preserved in the *yᵉdabbᵉrû* of Ps 127:5. In the same article (*TS* 1953, p. 85ff) Dahood proposed an emendation by which the last part of verse 2 would read: "Thus he gives to his beloved rich nourishment (*dōšen*: Mishnic Hebrew)," expressing a thought mentioned elsewhere: "He has given food to those who fear him" (Ps 111:5).

PSALM 128 (127)

The Happy Home of the Just Man

1   *A song of ascents.*

I

Happy are you who fear the Lord,
    who walk in his ways!

Pss 94:12; 112:1ff

2 For you shall eat the fruit of your handiwork;
    happy shall you be, and favored.

Ps 37:3ff

3 Your wife shall be like a fruitful vine
    in the recesses of your home;
  Your children like olive plants
    around your table.

Prv 31:10ff; Ps 92:14; Pss 144:12

Jb 29:5; Pss 52:10; 127:4

4 Behold, thus is the man blessed
    who fears the Lord.

II

5 The Lord bless you from Zion:
    may you see the prosperity of Jerusalem
    all the days of your life;

Pss 20:3; 45: 3; 134:3

6 May you see your children's children.
    Peace be upon Israel!

Gn 50:23; Jb 42:16
Ps 125:5

The blessings of family life are also celebrated in this psalm, which may owe its origin to a liturgical benediction. Man is taught to acknowledge God's splendid gifts in the domestic joys and riches. Elsewhere the just himself is compared to "a green olive tree in the house of God" (Ps 52:10; cf. Ps 92:14). In line with the general tendency of wisdom teaching "the psalm deliberately confines itself to a strictly limited field of devout conduct in everyday life and should be understood within these limits" (A. Weiser). The final blessing (vv 5-6) is, however, broader in scope, and suggests that the prosperity of the nation itself rests on the foundation of a sound family life (see on *Ps 134:3).

PSALM 133 (132)

The Benefits of Brotherly Concord

1 *A song of ascents. Of David.*
  Behold, how good it is, and how pleasant,
    where brethren dwell as one!

Ps 23:5   2 It is as when the precious ointment upon the head
Ex 30:22-33   runs down over the beard, the beard of Aaron,
           till it runs down upon the collar of his robe.

Gn 27:27ff; Ps 48:3 3 It is a dew like that of Hermon,
Hos 14:6; Jl 4:17f   which comes down upon the mountains of Zion;
          For there the Lord has pronounced his blessing,
Dt 28:8; 30:20   life forever.

This also is a song of ascents (cf. §3c) and, as in Pss 127 and 128, the poet extols the values of brotherhood, which perhaps are understood here in the broader national context. The psalm probably reflects a period when these values were in peril. In oriental taste scented oil dripping down to the collar through a long flowing beard is a telling expression of blessing, here the charm, beauty and internal value of brotherhood. After the daytime heat the refreshing dew of the night (Dt 5:2; Hos 14:6) is a special blessing. Mount Zion covered with Hermon dew is an expressive although idyllic metaphor (see on *Ps 48:3). Divine blessing assures long life on earth (Dt 30:20) and the inseparable union with God, source of life (Ps 36:10) and heritage of the just (Ps 73:26).

These three psalms of blessing (127, 128, 133) Kirkpatrick would assign to the Restoration period, when Nehemiah was trying to rebuild the Jewish community on a sound religious and civic basis, especially in Jerusalem (cf. Neh 11:1f). He also notes that "the running down upon the collar of his robe" can refer to the beard of Aaron, instead of the oil. In that same verse 3 seems to be recalled the scene of the consecration of Aaron himself (Lv 8), since sacred oil was not used in the time of the Second Temple. As for "dew," writes Kirkpatrick, it is "a symbol for what is refreshing, quickening, invigorating; and the psalmist compares the influence of brotherly unity upon the nation to the effect of the dew upon vegetation."

Instead of *ṣiyyôn* (v 3) some authors (Power, Zorell, Pascual) would read *śi'ôn*, mentioned in Dt 4:48: "Mount Zion, which is Hermon." As Power puts it: "Just as the sacred ointment descends from the head to the beard . . . so the heavenly dew descends from the highest summit to the lower peaks of the same mountain range." Less *recherchée* is the explanation that the psalmist follows popular belief: in some way the amount of dew falling on the Zion hills depends on Mount Hermon.

PSALM 139 (138)

The All-knowing and Ever-present God

1 *For the leader. A psalm of David.*

I

Ps 7:10; Jer 12:3

O Lord, you have probed me and you know me;

2   you know when I sit and when I stand;

Sir 42:18ff

you understand my thoughts from afar.

3 My journeys and my rest you scrutinize,

2 Kgs 19:27; Jb 31:4

with all my ways you are familiar.

4 Even before a word is on my tongue,

Am 4:13; Ps 44:22

behold, O Lord, you know the whole of it.

5 Behind me and before, you hem me in

Ps 16:8, 11

and rest your hand upon me.

6 Such knowledge is too wonderful for me;

too lofty for me to attain.

II

7 Where can I go from your spirit?

<table>
<tr><td>Jer 23:24</td><td></td><td>from your presence where can I flee?</td></tr>
</table>

Jer 23:24   from your presence where can I flee?

Am 9:2ff   8 If I go up to the heavens, you are there;

Prv 15:11; Jb 11:8f   if I sink to the nether world, you are present there.

9 If I take the wings of the dawn,
  if I settle at the farthest limits of the sea,

Ps 16:11   10 Even there your hand shall guide me,
  and your right hand hold me fast.

11 If I say, "Surely the darkness shall hide me,
  and night shall be my light" —

Jb 12:22; 34:22
Dn 2:22   12 For you darkness itself is not dark,
  and night shines as the day.
  [Darkness and light are the same.]

III

13 Truly you have formed my inmost being;

Ps 22:10   you knit me in my mother's womb.

14 I give you thanks that I am fearfully, wonderfully made;

Pss 136:4; 145:5   wonderful are your works.
  My soul also you knew full well;

15 nor was my frame unknown to you

Jb 10:8f   When I was made in secret,
  when I was fashioned in the depths of the earth.

16 Your eyes have seen my actions;

Mal 3:16; Dn 7:10
Pss 56:9; 69:29; Jb 14:5   in your book they are all written;
  my days were limited before one of them existed.

17 How weighty are your designs, O God;

Jb 11:7; Rm 11:33
Ps 40:6   how vast the sum of them!

18 Were I to recount them, they would outnumber the sands;
  did I reach the end of them, I should still be with you.

IV

Ps 5:6f   19 If only you would destroy the wicked, O God,

Jb 21:14; Ps 119:115   and the men of blood were to depart from me!

20 Wickedly they invoke your name;

Ps 120:2   your foes swear faithless oaths.

21 Do I hate, O Lord, those who hate you?

Ps 119:158   Those who rise up against you do I not loathe?

22 With a deadly hatred I hate them;
  they are my enemies.

Pss 7:10; 17:3; 26:2   23 Probe me, O God, and know my heart;

                        try me, and know my thoughts;
            24   See if my way is crooked,
Jer 6:6; Ps 5:9   and lead me in the way of old.

This poem could, like Ps 90 with which it shows affinities, be classified as a supplication. Mowinckel (I, p. 24) believes that these two psalms really spring from a concrete situation, that of need; the reflection on God's eternity and omniscience (cf. §10c) would constitute a secondary accompaniment of divine intervention in the situation. The introductory section of both psalms is a hymn celebrating God's attributes. The most important part of Ps 139 is, in Mowinckel's opinion (II, p. 75), the prayer for the help of God against the "men of blood" (vv 19-24), perhaps "men of idols" (v 19; see on *Pss 5:7; 26:9). Yet this section could also reflect a rite of self-purification of the covenant community (separation from evildoers; cf. Pss 26:4; 31:7). Mowinckel admits (II, p. 131f) that "the profound consideration of God's omniscience and omnipresence in Ps 139 actually is a new form of the motif of innocence." In that respect also it is considered to be a "protective psalm" (see on *Ps 71).

In verse 24 *CV* reads "see if my way is crooked" (*'āqōb*). E. Würthwein, however, is for keeping the consonantal *MT* and for understanding *'ṣb* as referring to "idols" (cf. Is 48:5). As for *derek,* "way," it could mean *Kultübung,* "cult-practice" (cf. Am 8:14; Jer 2:23; 10:2; 12:16). Verse 24 then would be part of the psalmist's repudiation of idols: "See [O Lord] if I have taken part in idol worship"! In other words, a sort of "oath of exculpation" would be involved here as elsewhere (cf. *Pss 7 and 26). It is the Omniscient God described in verses 1-18 who is asked to "probe" the psalmist and testify to his innocence.

It has been noted (cf. *Ps 92) that the praise of divine knowledge can be related to a theme called *Gerichtsdoxologie,* whereby the judgments of God are declared just and infallible. Yet such varying motifs as found in Ps 139 seem cast in a didactic and sapiential mould (cf. Sir 42:18ff; Ps 94:8-11). It can be conceded to Castellino (p. 731) that in this psalm, as in Pss 17, 37, 49, 73, wisdom language tends to take a new tone, that of the religious meditation. In one of the El-Amarna letters (cf. §9d), a Babylonian named Tagi tells his (divinized) king: "Whether we go up to heaven or go down to the earth our head is in thy hands" (tr. Mercer, II, p. 677; letter 264), while the Hebrew psalmist confessed: "I go up to the heavens, you are there; if I sink to the nether world, you are present there" (139:5).

God knows everything (vv 1-6), he is present everywhere (7-12), he can do anything (12-16), his thoughts and designs defy human reason (vv 17f). If this is so, he can destroy the wicked (19-22) and provide guidance (23f). The divine attributes of omniscience, omnipresence and omnificence the poet does not express them in abstract philosophical terms but in terms of I-Thou relationship. The first verses especially, as Weiser points out, "express the astonishment of a man who discovers that in all his ways he is involved in relations which remain hidden from the natural eye; that he no longer belongs entirely to himself or lives his life exclusively for his own sake, because it points everywhere to those invisible bonds which unite him to the reality of God." Here, as elsewhere in the Psalter, God occupies the prominent place even in the construction of the sentences. The whole psalm is an authentic expression of true faith in God. "The consciousness of the intimate personal relation between God and man which is characteristic of the whole Psalter reaches its climax in Ps 139," writes Kirkpatrick. The ungodly the psalmist hates (vv 21f) because they are God's as well as his own enemies. He does not understand that divine forbearance extends even to the wicked (Mt 5:45). It is true that in biblical wisdom itself some problems concerning retribution remained unsolved for a long time (cf. §14d + 29a). Not all the sacred authors saw a clear distinction between evil and evildoers (on the idea of a "divine book," verse 16, see above §14d).

§30. THE HISTORICAL PSALMS

(a) General character

These psalms are hymnic narratives describing the significant events of *Heilsgeschichte* (saving history). They celebrate the *magnalia Dei,* mainly those traditionally preserved in what some call the "historical credo" (cf. Dt 6 and 26; see §13c). "It was above all in worship that Israel extolled Jahweh's acts in history. The hymns which take history as their subject obviously depend on a picture of the saving history which already possessed canonical validity at a very early time, and whose original form lies before us in the *Credo* of Dt 26:5ff or Jos

24:2ff. The simplest, and probably also the oldest, form of the hymn was the almost unconnected enumeration of the bare facts of creation and of the saving history which still lie before us as paradigms in Ps 136 (cf. Pss 77, 105, 114, 135). But in the course of an epic widening out of those facts, the poems did not confine themselves solely to enumerating and glorifying the acts of Jahweh, they also made Israel and her attitude, yes, and her failure as well, the object of their meditation (cf. Ps 106). In the process the hymn receives a somber tone, and in proportion as interest in the sin of Israel increased in them, their mood changed greatly, and they became somber confessions of Israel's failure and of Jahweh's judgment (Ps 78)" (G. von Rad, *Old Testament Theology*, I, p. 357).

In view of the importance of the historical tradition in Israel it is somewhat surprising that the Psalter does not contain a greater number of explicit references to the outstanding events of the Pentateuch. According to F. N. Jasper ("Early Israelite . . . ," p. 50f), only Pss 44, 47, 60, 68, 77, 78, 80, 81, 99, 105, 106, 108, 114, 135, 136 "afford a recognizable link with the traditions of Israel's origins as a people. It is true that with a knowledge of the Pentateuch we can construct a coherent narrative from these Psalms. The people of Israel, the offspring of Abraham and Jacob, (105:6) had gone down to Egypt by Joseph's invitation (105:16ff). God delivered them from oppression (77:15; 81:6) in Egypt (78:12; 81:10; 114:1; 136:11f) by Moses and Aaron (77:20; 99:6f; 105:26) after inflicting plagues upon their masters (78:44ff; 105:27ff; 135:8f; 136:10). He made a way for them through the Sea of Reeds in which the pursuers were drowned (77:16ff; 78:13, 53; 106:9ff; 114:3f; 136:13f). He guided and sustained them in the wilderness in spite of their rebellions (68:7f; 78:14ff, 52; 81:7; 105:39ff; 106:6f, 19ff, 28ff; 136:16). He gave them the land of Canaan as a heritage (44:2; 47:4; 60:7f; 78:54f; 80:8ff; 105:44; 135:10ff; 136:17ff), as he had promised the ancestors (105:9ff). But only in Pss 78, 105, 106, 135, and 136 is there an attempt to give a chronological record of the events. Jasper adds to his outline: "Apart from this, there are only occasional implicit references, which make no real historical contribution" (e.g., Pss 74:2, 12f; 91:6). Of the 15 "historical psalms" listed above he singles out five as "probably fairly late" in their present form: Pss 78, 105, 106, 135, 136: "earlier versions of them may have been used in pre-exilic times . . . but they now stand as the product of early Judaism," when the "separatist policy of Nehemiah and Ezra required that the traditions shared with the Samaritans" be not emphasized. The other ten psalms, however, belong to "the early, spontaneous group" which being already part of the established liturgy remained so, although the disappearance of the monarchy could have called for modifications (p. 59; on "The Psalms and History," cf. also S. du Toit).

A. Gelin has given striking expression to the biblical meaning of history. "The basic faith in Israel is that history is sustained by God, that it is an epiphany of God. God gives history its meaning because He is carrying out a design in it: God speaks through events . . . . The Bible calls the setbacks and disappointments of history God's 'angers' (see §11h)." Among the "signs" of God (see §12f) on earth figure the *mirabilia Dei* visible in some privileged events: "Renew your *signs, once more begin to work your wonders*" (Sir 36:5). "These wonders are the historical acts which launched the history of Israel: the exodus from Egypt, the desert of the Covenant, the entrance into the Promised Land . . . . But this history is not a lifeless fossil. History lives again in the present of worship, history is made eternal, history is a mystery . . . . The essential thing was to make the people understand that history is 're-actualized,' that it is not something past and gone, and that it is the liturgical 'today' which allows us to grasp history (cf. Ps 95:6-11) . . . . In worship we find history as a sign of God" (*The Psalms are our Prayers,* p. 28f; on the "actualizing" of history in the psalms, see also C. Westermann, "Vergegenwärtigung . . .").

S. Mowinckel calls Pss 78 and 105 "didactic hymns" (II, p. 112). Writing on "Psalms and Wisdom," he notes that "a didactic hymn may develop into a downright 'hymnal legend,' a synopsis of the holy history in the style of a hymn, as is the case with Pss 78 and 105 . . . . But history may also provide the material for a confession of sins and a prayer for restoration on the part of the congregation, and thus result in a *historical penitential psalm,* like Ps 106" (p. 214). Some authors would in fact list Ps 106 with the "historical psalms," while Pss 111, 114, 135, 136 are also considered by others for the same category. There are, however, sound objective reasons for limiting the group to two psalms.

(b) The historical psalms are Pss 78 and 105.

PSALM 78

God's Goodness despite Israel's Ingratitude

1 A *maśkîl* of Asaph.

Prv 8:4ff; Ps 81:9
Dt 32:1

Hearken, my people, to my teaching;
    incline your ears to the words of my mouth.

Ez 17:2; Mt 13:35
Ps 49:5

2 I will open my mouth in a parable,
    I will utter mysteries from of old.

3 What we have heard and know,

Pss 44:2; 95:9

    and what our fathers have declared to us,

Ps 22:31; Ex 10:2
Dt 4:9; Is 38:19

4 We will not hide from their sons;
    we will declare to the generation to come
The glorious deeds of the Lord and his strength
and the wonders that he wrought.

5 He set it up as a decree in Jacob,

Dt 33:4

    and established it as a law in Israel,
That what he commanded our fathers

Dt 6:7

    they should make known to their sons;

Pss 22:31; 71:18

6 So that the generation to come might know,
    their sons yet to be born,
That they too may rise and declare to their sons

7   that they should put their hope in God,
And not forget the deeds of God
    but keep his commands,

8 And not be like their fathers,

Ps 95:10

    a generation wayward and rebellious,

Ps 81:12

A generation that kept not its heart steadfast

Dt 31:27; Ez 20:18

    nor its spirit faithful toward God.

I

Hos 7:16; 12:15

9 The sons of Ephraim, ordered ranks of bowmen,
    retreated in the day of battle.

10 They kept not the covenant with God;
    according to his law they would not walk;

11 And they forgot his deeds,
    the wonders he had shown them.

12 Before their fathers he did wondrous things,

Nm 13 22; Is 19:11
Pss 77:20f; 106:9ff

    in the land of Egypt, in the plain of Soan.

13 He cleft the sea and brought them through,

Ex 14:21f; 15:8		and he made the waters stand as in a mound.
Pss 68:8f; 81:17	14	He led them with a cloud by day,
Ex 13:21; Wis 18:3		and all night with a glow of fire.
Ps 105:41	15	He cleft the rocks in the desert
Ex 17:6; Nm 20:11		and gave them water in copious floods.
Dt 8:15; Wis 11:4	16	He made streams flow from the crag
Ps 114:8		and brought the waters forth in rivers.

II

Dt 9:7	17	But they sinned yet more against him,
		rebelling against the Most High in the wasteland,
Ex 16:3; Nm 11:5f	18	And they tempted God in their hearts
Ps 106:14		by demanding the food they craved.
	19	Yes, they spoke against God, saying,
Pss 22:7; 23:5; 63:6		"Can God spread a table in the desert?
	20	For when he struck the rock, waters gushed forth,
Is 48:21		and the streams overflowed;
		Can he also give bread
		and provide meat for his people?"
Nm 11:1; Ez 20:13	21	Then the Lord heard and was enraged;
		and fire blazed up against Jacob,
		and anger rose against Israel,
	22	Because they believed not God
		nor trusted in his help.
	23	Yet he commanded the skies above
Mal 3:10		and the doors of heaven he opened;
	24	He rained manna upon them for food
Ex 16:4, 14f; Jn 6:31		and gave them heavenly bread.
Wis 16:20	25	The bread of the mighty was eaten by men;
		even a surfeit of provisions he sent them.
	26	He stirred up the east wind in the heavens,
Nm 11:31ff		and by his power brought on the south wind.
	27	And he rained meat upon them like dust,
		and, like the sand of the sea, winged fowl,
	28	Which fell in the midst of their camp
		round about their tents.
	29	So they ate and were wholly surfeited;
		he had brought them what they craved.
	30	They had not given over their cravings,
		and their food was still in their mouths,

31 When the anger of God rose against them
    and slew their best men,
    and laid low the young men of Israel.

III

32 Yet for all this they sinned still more
    and believed not in his wonders.

33 Therefore he quickly ended their days
    and their years with sudden destruction.

34 While he slew them they sought him

Is 26:16
    and inquired after God again,

Dt 32:4; Pss
75:6; 89:27
Is 41:14; Ps
77:16
35 Remembering that God was their Rock
    and the Most High God, their redeemer.

36 But they flattered him with their mouths

Is 29:13; Hos
8:2
    and lied to him with their tongues,

37 Though their hearts were not steadfast toward him,

Pss 74:20;
103:18
    nor were they faithful to his covenant.

38 Yet he, being merciful, forgave their sin
    and destroyed them not;
Often he turned back his anger

Is 48:9; Ez
20:22
    and let none of his wrath be roused.

39 He remembered that they were flesh,

Pss 39:6; 144:
4
    a passing breath that returns not.

IV

40 How often they rebelled against him in the desert
    and grieved him in the wilderness!

Pss 72:18; 89:
19
Is 41:14; Jer
50:29
41 Again and again they tempted God
    and provoked the Holy One of Israel.

42 They remembered not his hand
    nor the day he delivered them from the foe,

43 When he wrought his signs in Egypt

Ex 7-12; Ps
105:27ff
    and his marvels in the plain of Soan,

44 And changed into blood their streams —
    their running water, so that they could not drink;

45 He sent among them flies that devoured them
    and frogs that destroyed them.

46 He gave their harvest to the caterpillar,
    the fruits of their toil to the locust.

47 He killed their vines with hail

and their sycamores with frost.

48 He gave over to the hail their beasts
and their flocks to the lightning.

Pss 75:9; 79:6 49 He loosed against them his fierce anger,
wrath and fury and strife,

Ex 12:23; Dt 32:24 a detachment of messengers of doom.

50 When he measured the course of his anger
he spared them not from death,
he delivered their beasts to the plague.

Ex 12:29 51 He smote every first-born in Egypt,

Gn 49:3 the first fruits of manhood in the tents of Ham;

52 But his people he led forth like sheep

Ps 77:21 and guided them like a herd in the desert.

53 He led them on secure and unafraid,
while he covered their enemies with the sea.

Ps 114:2 54 And he brought them to his holy land,

Ex 15:17 to the mountains his right hand had won.

Pss 47:4; 118: 10ff 55 And he drove out nations before them;
he distributed their inheritance by lot,
and settled the tribes of Israel in their tents.

V

56 But they tempted and rebelled against God the Most High,
and kept not his decrees.

57 They turned back and were faithless like their fathers;

Hos 7:16 they recoiled like a treacherous bow.

58 They angered him with their high places

Lv 26:30 and with their idols roused his jealousy.

59 God heard and was enraged

Ps 95:11 and utterly rejected Israel.

Jos 18:1 60 And he forsook the tabernacle in Silo,

1 Sm 4:3ff; Jer 7:12ff Pss 105:4; 132:8 the tent where he dwelt among men.

61 And he surrendered his strength into captivity,

1 Sm 4:11; Ps 96.6 his glory into the hands of the foe.

62 He abandoned his people to the sword
and was enraged against his inheritance.

Dt 32:22 63 Fire consumed their young men,

Jer 7:34 and their maidens were not betrothed.

64 Their priests fell by the sword,

Jb 27:15 and their widows sang no dirges.

VI

Pss 73:20; 76:10; 80:2	65	Then the Lord awoke, as wakes from sleep a champion overcome with wine;
	66	And he put his foes to flight
1 Sm 5:6-9		and cast them into everlasting disgrace.
	67	And he rejected the tent of Joseph, and the tribe of Ephraim he chose not;
	68	But he chose the tribe of Judah, Mount Zion which he loved.
	69	And be built his shrine like heaven, like the earth which he founded forever.
2 Sm 7:8	70	And he chose David, his servant, and took him from the sheepfolds;
1 Sm 16:10ff	71	From following the ewes he brought him
2 Chr 6:6; Ez 34:23		to shepherd Jacob, his people,
Jer 10:16; 51:19		and Israel, his inheritance.
	72	And he tended them with a sincere heart,
Pss 73:24; 86:11; 95:7		and with skillful hands he guided them.

Other psalms contain some of the historical material offered here (cf. 105, 106, 114, 136). Yet Ps 78 is more interested in the interpretation of history than in its recital. The "mysteries (*ḥîdôt*, riddles) from of old" (v 2), the queer happenings of the past, follow the pattern "rebellion-punishment." The tribes of the North, Joseph/Ephraim, predecessors of the Samaritans, bear most of the blame. Verse 9 which seems to reflect a late antisamaritan trend did not necessarily belong to the primitive psalm. The favor of the Lord passed to the tribe of Judah and to David, who would preserve and perpetuate the sacred traditions. A. Weiser suggests that Ps 78, described as a *tôrâh* or *māshāl* (vv 1-2), could have been recited by a priest in connection with the covenant festival (cf. §13c). Its main thought-pattern reflects that of Deuteronomy, as expressed for example in ch 32:

The Rock — how faultless are his deeds,
how right all his ways!
A faithful God, without deceit,
how just and upright he is!
Yet basely has he been treated by his degenerate children,
a perverse and crooked race! (vv 4-5)

Think back on the days of old,
reflect on the years of age upon age.
Ask your father and he will inform you,
ask your elders and they will tell you . . ." (v 7)

Surely, the Lord shall do justice for his people;
on his servants he shall have pity.
When he sees their strength failing,
and their protected and unprotected alike disappearing (v 36).

There is no compelling ground, however, for supposing that Ps 78 is later than the late seventh century Deuteronomy, since any presumed dependence can be accounted for by a common, older deuteronomic tradition. The psalm is often described as pre-exilic because it does not even allude to the fall of Jerusalem. Ephraim's retreat "in the day of battle" (v 9) probably alludes to Saul's defeat at Gilboa and to the transfer of kingship from the tribes of Rachel to that of Judah. No clear mention is made of the downfall of the Northern Kingdom. No real conclusion, in fact, can be drawn, on the psalm's date, from the Davidic *terminus ad quem* of the historical schema, since it probably reflects theological interests. The scholars who assign the psalm to a late period read in it the Chronicler's Davidic ideology. C. Westermann has noted that "Deuteronomy 32 is the clearest example of how the historical Psalms pass over into eschatological Psalms" (*The Praise . . .*, p. 141). Ps 78 is also a "descriptive psalm of praise" (cf. §22), he adds, "but the introduction here is not an imperative call to praise; its place has been taken by an introduction in the style of wisdom literature."

The glorious deeds of the Lord must be proclaimed and a lesson drawn from history, states the psalmist (vv 1-8): the "sons of Ephraim" have been disloyal (9-11), like their forefathers, for whom God had worked wonders at the exodus (12-16) and in the wilderness (17-31). Their repeated rebellious acts were answered by new divine deeds intended to punish or to relieve the people (32-55), till finally God rejected the guilty tribes and turned to Judah, Mount Zion and the house of David (65-72). From the wilderness people's fate follows a lesson: God often grants extravagant requests but he will let their beneficiaries perish in the midst of the satisfaction of their inordinate desires, when his kindness does not lead to repentance but is followed by even greater avidity. Thus are the grace and the judgment of God related to each other (Weiser).

PSALM 105 (104)

God's Fidelity to His Promise

I

1 Chr 16:8-22	1 Give thanks to the Lord, invoke his name;
Pss 102:23; 117:1	make known among the nations his deeds.
	2 Sing to him, sing his praise,
Is 12:4; Ps 107:8	proclaim all his wondrous deeds.
	3 Glory in his holy name;
	rejoice, O hearts that seek the Lord!
Dt 4:29	4 Look to the lord in his strength;
Ps 27:8	seek to serve him constantly.
	5 Recall the wondrous deeds that he has wrought,
Sir 36:5	his portents, and the judgments he has uttered,
Gn 22:17	6 You descendants of Abraham, his servants,
Is 45:4; 65:9	sons of Jacob, his chosen ones!
	7 He, the Lord, is our God;
	throughout the earth his judgments prevail.

II

Pss 103:18; 106:45	8 He remembers forever his covenant
	which he made binding for a thousand generations —
	9 Which he entered into with Abraham
Gn 26:3	and by his oath to Isaac;
	10 Which he established for Jacob by statute,
	for Israel as an everlasting covenant,
	11 Saying, "To you will I give the land of Chanaan
Gn 12:7; 15:8; Ps 16:6	as your allotted inheritance."

III

	12 When they were a few in number,
Dt 26:5	a handful, and strangers there,
	13 Wandering from nation to nation
	and from one kingdom to another people,
	14 He let no man oppress them,
Gn 12:17; 20:6f	and for their sake he rebuked kings:
	15 "Touch not my anointed,
	and to my prophets do no harm."

IV

Lv 26:26	16 When he called down a famine on the land

Gn 41:57; Ez 5:16		and ruined the crop that sustained them,
	17	He sent a man before them,
Gn 37:28, 36		Joseph, sold as a slave;
	18	They had weighed him down with fetters,
Gn 39:20		and he was bound with chains,
	19	Till his prediction came to pass
Gn 40:21f		and the word of the Lord proved him true.
	20	The king sent and released him,
Gn 41:14		the ruler of the peoples set him free.
	21	He made him lord of his house
Gn 41:41; Acts 7:10		and ruler of all his possessions,
	22	That he might train his princes to be like him
		and teach his elders wisdom.
		V
	23	Then Israel came to Egypt,
Gn 46:6; Acts 7:15		and Jacob sojourned in the land of Ham.
	24	He greatly increased his people
Ex 1:7; Acts 7:17		and made them stronger than their foes,
		VI
	25	Whose hearts he changed, so that they hated his people,
Ex 1:8-14		and dealt deceitfully with his servants.
	26	He sent Moses his servant;
		Aaron, whom he had chosen.
Ex 7-12; Ps 78:43-51 Ps 135:8f	27	They wrought his signs among them,
		and wonders in the land of Ham.
		VII
	28	He sent the darkness; it grew dark,
		but they rebelled against his words.
	29	He turned their waters into blood
		and killed their fish.
	30	Their land swarmed with frogs,
		even in the chambers of their kings.
	31	He spoke and there came swarms of flies;
		gnats, throughout all their borders.
	32	For rain he gave them hail,
		with flashing fires throughout their land.
	33	He struck down their vines and their fig trees
		and shattered the trees throughout their borders.
	34	He spoke, and there came locusts

and grasshoppers without number;

35 And they devoured every plant throughout the land;
     they devoured the fruit of their soil.

36 Then he struck every first-born throughout their land;
     the first fruits of all their manhood.

Ex 12:35

37 And he led them forth laden with silver and gold,
     with not a weakling among their tribes.

38 Egypt rejoiced at their going,

Ex 12:33

     for the dread of them had fallen upon it.

VIII

39 He spread a cloud to cover them

Ex 13:21; Neh 9:12
Ps 78:24ff

     and fire to give them light by night.

40 They asked, and he brought them quail,

Ex 16:13ff; 17:1ff
Nm 11:31; Wis 16:20
Nm 20:11

     and with bread from heaven he satisfied them.

41 He cleft the rock, and the water gushed forth;
     it flowed through the dry lands like a stream,

42 For he remembered his holy word
     to his servant Abraham.

43 And he led forth his people with joy;
     with shouts of joy, his chosen ones.

IX

Dt 4:38

44 And he gave them the lands of the nations,
     and they took what the peoples had toiled for,

Dt 6:23f

45 That they might keep his statutes
     and observe his laws. Alleluia.

Like Ps 78, Ps 105 is a didactic hymn, a kind of synopsis of sacred history in the style of a hymn. Mowinckel (II, p. 112) speaks in this regard of "hymnal legends." They constitute, he explains, "a sort of Theodicy," in which God's judgment is vindicated. In Ps 105, however, no mention is made of God's disfavor toward Israel on account of its sins. At a certain date at least the psalm was used in the liturgy, as it appears from the opening verses (1-6), and from the fact that in 1 Chr 16:8-22 the first 15 verses of the psalm are quoted (see on *Ps 96) as a festal hymn in connection with the transfer of the sacred ark to Mount Zion. The origin of Ps 105, C. Westermann believes (*The Praise . . .*, p. 140), can be explained thus: the "historical report" has been separated from the total unit of the "descriptive Psalm of praise" (cf. §22) and has become an independent psalm.

The successive periods of early Israelite history are represented in this *Heilsgeschichte* account (cf. *Ps 66): the patriarchs (vv 8-15), the story of Joseph (16-23), the call of Moses (24-27), the (seven) plagues in Egypt (28-36), the exodus and wandering in the desert (37-43), and finally the entry into Canaan (44-45; cf. 9-11). The opening words of the psalm are similar to those with which begin Pss 106, 107, 118, 136. They call upon the members of the covenant community to sing hymns of praise and thanksgiving to God. The main theological theme of the psalm is that God keeps his promises and fulfills his salvific plans in spite of or in the course of the apparently adverse or purposeless human interference or activities.

Valuable reflections on the thought association of three psalms are offered by A. F. Kirkpatrick. "The two historical Psalms which stand at the end of Book IV are closely related. Ps 105 is a psalm of thanksgiving, recapitulating the marvelous works by which Jehovah demonstrated His faithfulness to the covenant which He made with Abraham. Ps 106 is a Psalm of penitence, reciting the history of Israel's faithlessness and disobedience. They present, so to speak, the obverse and reverse of Israel's history; the common prophetic theme of Jehovah's loving kindness and Israel's ingratitude. They have much in common with Ps 78, with which their author was evidently familiar; but that Psalm is distinguished by its didactic and monitory character, and it combines the two strands of thought which are here separated" (Introd. to Ps 105). Such a recital of the proofs of Jehovah's faithfulness as is contained in Ps 105, Kirkpatrick adds, was very suitable as an encouragement to the community of the Restoration . . . . The repeated call to "give thanks to Jehovah . . . to praise Yah" (cf. *Ps 11) corresponds exactly to the term in which the function of the Levites is described in the books of Ezra, Nehemiah, and Chronicles (Ezr 3:11; Neh 12:24; 1 Chr 16:4; see also *Ps 106).

G. von Rad reads in verse 15, "Touch not my anointed ones, and to my prophets do no harm," "the same reinterpretation in the collective sense" as the one apparent in Deutero-Isaiah, who did not "interpret Yahweh's promises concerning the throne of David and the anointed one of Israel in the traditional way, for he understands them to have been made not to David but to the whole nation" (*Theology* . . . II, p. 240).

§31. THE "PROPHETIC" EXHORTATIONS

(a) *General character*

Of the psalmists it is said that they prophesy (1 Chr 25:1; 2 Chr 20:14). Some of them certainly utilized the prophetic writings, mainly Isaiah, whose style they adapted for a didactic purpose (cf. *BJ,* p. 27). The psalms of the present category, "prophetic exhortations," have in common a tonality and some "prophetic" literary elements, as the oracle and the exhortative speech, which include promises and threats.

"In the earliest period in Israel the priest was not originally in the first instance sacrificer but, as with the old Arabs, custodian of the sanctuary, oracle priest, 'seer' and holder of the effectual future-creating and future-interpreting word of power, the blessing and the curse" (Mowinckel, II, p. 53). At a certain period at least the priest was a "giver of oracles" (cf. §8e). To admit the prophetic role of the priest is to question the supposed fundamental rivality between prophecy and priesthood (cf. *Exp.T.* 1950, pp. 3-9; *ZAW* 1951, pp. 157-182; *TLZ* 1956, p. 339ff). Biblical evidence does suggest the existence in ancient Israel of "cult oracles" and "cult prophets" (cf. §8e). F. N. Jasper notes that "the reformation under Hezekiah as recorded by the Chronicler mentions Asaph, 'the seer' " (2 Chr 29:30). This almost certainly means that the Asaphite guild was originally a group of cultic prophets in Jerusalem who were later relegated to the position of Temple singers. Even if some of the Asaphite Psalms as they now stand are post-exilic, their original form might well reflect the part taken by the cultic prophets in Israel's worship during the monarchy" ("Early . . .," p. 54; cf. §3b). Ps 81, an Asaphite oracular psalm, "seems to be linked with a regular cultic practice rather than a specific event" (*ibid.*) and its Deuteronomic tone could point to a Northern background.

The association of divine revelation with the offering of sacrifices appears in the story about Solomon's dream at Gibeon (1 Kgs 3:4ff). The deity's answer to a request could be obtained either by casting lots with the "Urim and Thummim" (cf. 1 Sm 14:41f) or by means of "looking for special signs in the sacrificial animal, and by interpreting them" (Mowinckel, II, p. 53f; cf. *Pss 5:4; 27:4; 86:17). At an undefined period of Israel's history prophetic inspiration became in a way institutionalized, that, is attached to a function rather than dependent on ecstatic experience or sudden revelations: "With the organized temple prophets, inspiration is rather what we should call an official, occupational inspiration, a permanent charismatic equipment belonging to the office itself . . . . Even at the time of Jesus, Judaism ascribed to the high priest an official prophetic inspiration" (id., p. 57; cf. Jn 11:51).

In preceding paragraphs (cf. §5c, 13a) another problem has been discussed: have psalms been composed in the style of prophetic predication or have the prophets taken over the psalmic way of expression? In any case, some psalms more than others deserve to be called "prophetic exhortations," as will be seen in the special introductions that follow.

(b) The "prophetic" exhortations are: Pss 14, 50, 52, 53, 75, 81, 95.

PSALM 14 (13)

A Lament over Widespread Corruption

1 *For the leader. Of David.*

I

Is 32:6; Ps 10:4
Jer 5:12; 32:9

The fool says in his heart,
    "There is no God."
Such are corrupt; they do abominable deeds;

Mi 7:2

    there is not one who does good.

2 The Lord looks down from heaven upon the children of men,

Zeph 1:12

    to see if there be one who is wise and seeks God.

Gn 6:5; Rm 3:12

3 All alike have gone astray; they have become perverse;
    there is not one who does good, not even one.

II

Pss 27:2; 28:3

4 Will all these evildoers never learn,

Is 9:11; Mi 3:3
Pss 57:5; 79:7

    they who eat up my people just as they eat bread?
They have not called upon the Lord;

Dt 28:67; 1 Sm 14:15

5   then they shall be in great fear,
    for God is with the just generation.

6 You would confound the plans of the afflicted,
    but the Lord is his refuge.

III

Pss 20:3; 85:2; 126:1
Dt 30:3; Am 9:14
Jer 29:14

7 Oh, that out of Sion would come the salvation of Israel!
    When the Lord restores the well-being of his people,
    then shall Jacob exult and Israel be glad.

This recension of the psalm seems to transmit more faithfully the original text than the other recension, Ps 53. Universal impiety (vv 2-3) is a theme known to the prophets:

Roam the streets of Jerusalem,
look about and observe,
Search through her public places,
to find even one
Who lives uprightly
and seeks to be faithful
and I will pardon her! (Jer 5:1; cf. 8:6; Is 64:6)

To prove by the Scriptures that Jews and Greeks alike are all under sin, St. Paul (Rm 3:10-18) combines various sources into one quotation: Pss 5:10; 140:4; 10:7; Prv 1:16; Is 59:7f; Ps 36:2). The Pauline text has been inserted in Ps 14 (after v 3) by the Vulgate and some Greek manuscripts. Micah (3:3) voiced complaints against the leaders of his time: "They eat the flesh of my people," and Habakkuk (1:13) writes: "The wicked man devours one more just than himself." The expression "devour my people" (cf. v 4) is also used about external enemies (cf. Is 9:11; Jer 10:25; see also below). Practical atheism (cf. §10a), more than metaphysical disbelief, is meant in the psalm (v 1), quite as in Jer 5:12: "They denied the Lord saying, Not he — No evil shall befall us, neither sword nor famine shall we see." It is also against the leading class of Israel that a prophetic threat is pronounced by the psalmist (vv 5-6), for these influential people know their duty, as Jeremiah would point out (5:5-6).

The meaning of the Hebrew phrase *bᵉšûb yhwh šᵉbût 'ammô* (v 7) has been discussed in connection with *Ps 85. It is understood by Mowinckel (I, p. 147) as a prayer of later times asking for the restoration of Israel's destiny, and Ps 14 would be, like Ps 85, a national supplication. More precisely, it is asserted, the phrase refers to a new "laying down of fate" to take place at God's enthronement on the New Year festival (cf. §13a). What the psalmist has in mind, Weiser believes, is probably the act of divine judgment firmly established in the ritual of the covenant cult at Jerusalem.

"Though commonly classified as a lament, writes Dahood, Ps 14 has many points of contact with Wisdom Literature and could, with equal validity, be put in the category of Wisdom psalms." His translation of verses 4-5 being notably different from the *CV* is given here, with biblical references to support the changes: "Don't they know all the evildoers, that they who devour his people, devour the grain of Yahweh (Nm 14:9) they did not harvest (*Ps 147:9; Prv 27:16). See how (Ps 66:6) they formed a cabal (Pss 64:2; 91:5), but God is in the assembly of the just." That its enemies devour (the people of) Israel (like bread) is a prophetic expression, notes *BJ*: cf. Is 9:11; Mi 3:3; Jer 10:25; 30:16; Hb 1:13 (cf. Pss 27:2; 79:7; Prv 30:14). Other commentators divide differently the *MT* and understand: "They eat the bread of God, but do not invoke his name."

The mention of the "assembly of the upright" in Ps 92:2 and of "the council of the upright" in Ps 111:1 would suggest that these two psalms have the same author as Ps 14. While the rest of Ps 14 is concerned with individuals, writes Eerdmans, the last verse refers to the people, to Israel. "Similar wishes for the restoration of the Jewish state occur at the end of other psalms. They are manifestly additions from a later period, when the psalms were recited in synagogical services" (*OTS* I, p. 260).

PSALM 50 (49)

The Acceptable Sacrifice

1 *A psalm of Asaph.*

I

Dt 10:17; Jos 22:22

    God the Lord has spoken and summoned the earth,
      from the rising of the sun to its setting.

Lam 2:15; Ps 48:13f

2 From Zion, perfect in beauty,
      God shines forth.

Is 63:19; Dt 5:22
Ex 16:18; 19: 16ff
Pss 68:3; 83: 16; 97:3
Dt 4:26; 31: 28; 32:1
Is 1:2; Mi 6: 1f
Ps 37:28

3 May our God come and not be deaf to us!
      Before him is a devouring fire;
      around him is a raging storm.

4 He summons the heavens from above,
      and the earth, to the trial of his people:

5 "Gather my faithful ones before me,
      those who have made a covenant with me by sacrifice."

Ex 24:5ff

Pss 19:2; 89: 6; 97:6

6 And the heavens proclaim his justice
      for God himself is the judge.

II

Dt 6:4; Jer 5: 21

7 "Hear, my people, and I will speak;

Israel, I will testify against you;

Ex 20:2; Dt 32:39
God, your God, am I.

Pss 40:7; 51: 18
8 Not for your sacrifices do I rebuke you,

Am 5:23; Hos 14:3
for your holocausts are before me always.

Is 1:11; Mi 6: 6f
9 I take from your house no bullock,

no goats out of your fold.

10 For mine are all the animals of the forests,

beasts by the thousand on my mountains.

11 I know all the birds of the air,

and whatever stirs in the plains, belongs to me.

12 If I were hungry, I should not tell you,

Ps 24:1
for mine are the world and its fullness.

13 Do I eat the flesh of the strong bulls,

or is the blood of goats my drink?

Pss 69:32; 107:22
14 Offer to God praise as your sacrifice

Pss 7:18; 57:3; 83:19
and fulfill your vows to the Most High;

15 Then call upon me in time of distress;

Ps 91:15
I will rescue you, and you shall glorify me."

III

16 But to the wicked man God says:

"Why do you recite my statutes,

Is 29:13; Mk 7:6f
and profess my covenant with your mouth

Prv 3:11; 5: 12
17 Though you hate discipline

and cast my words behind you?

18 When you see a thief, you keep pace with him,

and with adulterers you throw in your lot.

19 To your mouth you give free rein for evil,

you harness your tongue to deceit.

Lv 19:16
20 You sit speaking against your brother;

against your mother's son you spread rumors.

21 When you do these things, shall I be deaf to it?

Or think you that I am like yourself?

I will correct you by drawing them up before your eyes."

IV

Dt 32:15; Ps 9:18
22 "Consider this, you who forget God,

Dt 32:39
lest I rend you and there be no one to rescue you.

23 He that offers praise as a sacrifice glorifies me;

Ps 91:16
and to him that goes the right way I will show

the salvation of God."

It can well be that the setting of this instructive admonition by Yhwh was the festival of the renewal of the covenant (cf. Kraus, Beaucamp). According to E. Osty the psalm fits well in the category which R. G. Castellino calls *"Liturgia della fedeltà yahwistica"* (Pss 78, 81, 95, 105, 106). It is cast, writes Mowinckel (II, p. 70), in the mould of prophetic speech, with a hymnal description of the glory of the theophany for an introduction (vv 1-6). Its central theme is the powerful experience of man's encounter with God and the conclusion to be drawn therefrom (A. Weiser). Also in line with the "decalogical tradition" is the insistence on the commandments of the covenant. The "cult prophet" (cf. §8e and *Ps 95) blames the community mainly for tolerating in its midst three sins: theft, adultery and slander (or sorcery). This admonition (vv 16-21) is addressed to the "wicked" in the present text. It is, however, possible that the phrase, "But to the wicked man God says," was added later to shelter the faithful from the condemnation. For a similar reason, perhaps, verse 21c would have been shifted from verse 7, which read (cf. *JB*):

> Listen, my people, I am speaking;
> Israel, I am giving evidence against you!
> I charge, I indict you to your face,
> I, God, your God.

M. Dahood describes Ps 50 as "a prophetic liturgy of divine judgment. In the tradition of the prophets, the psalmist stresses the futility of sacrifice divorced from true morality." In verse 14 it is possible to understand, "offer God a sacrifice of thanksgiving" (cf. Pss 50:23; 107:22; 116:17, and R. Pautrel, p. 239). Sacrificial cult is not condemned, not even in Ps 51:18f, but it is sometimes recalled, as Aben Esra puts it, that sacrifices are not useful to God but to man (Ps 50: 9-13). The strong words of the pre-exilic prophets (cf. Is 1:11-17; Jer 6:20; 7:21f; Hos 6:6; Am 5:21-27; Mi 6:6ff) have been related to a literary form called "dialectical negation": an absolute negation that can be interpreted relatively (see on *Ps 51:18). The offence reproved is disrespect towards God, shown by considering the sacrificial cult as influencing God, as making Him dependent on man. A sacrifice of thanksgiving, on the other hand, expresses man's dependence on God. The purpose of the psalm is to confront the worshipper with God as He is, to destroy the other image of God, that produced by wishful thinking (on "sacrificium laudis," see also G. Bornkamm).

The first line of verse 1 is translated by Dahood: "The God of gods is Yahweh." The expression *'ēl 'elōhîm* recurs in Pss 62:2 and 77:2 (*bis*). It seems to be used as a superlative, like "the king of kings." In verse 4, Dahood explains, "heaven and earth are summoned by God to function as witnesses in his controversy with Israel. G. E. Wright, *The Old Testament against its Environment*, p. 36, has suggested that heaven and earth, invoked in the literary genus known as 'lawsuit,' can best be interpreted in the light of the divine assembly, the members of which constitute the host of heaven and earth." From some Ugaritic texts it can in fact be inferred that for the Canaanites Earth and Heaven were deities who formed part of the divine assembly. The term *'elôah,* a poetic designation of God, is used in verse 22. It occurs normally in ancient poems (Dt 32:15, 17; Ps 18:32) and as a archaism in other texts, mainly in Job (41 times) but also in Pss 114: 7; 139:19; Prv 30:5; Is 44:8; Hb 3:3; Neh 9:17; Dn 11:38.

PSALM 52 (51)

The Deceitful Tongue

1 Sm 21:1-8; 22:6ff	1 *For the leader. A maśkîl of David, when Doeg the Edomite*
	2 *went and told Saul, "David went to the house of Ahimelech."*
	I
	3 Why do you glory in evil
Pss 4:3; 58:2	you champion of infamy?
	4 All the day you plot harm;
Pss 31:21; 59:13; 140:4	your tongue is like a sharpened razor,
	you practiced deceiver!
	5 You love evil rather than good,
	falsehood rather than honest speech.
	6 You love all that means ruin,
Jer 9:4	you of the deceitful tongue!
	II
	7 God himself shall demolish you;
	forever he shall break you;
Jb 18:14	He shall pluck you from your tent,
Prv 2:22	and uproot you from the land of the living.
	III
	8 The just shall look on with awe;

then they shall laugh at him:

9 "This is the man who made not
   God the source of his strength,

Jb 31:25; Prv
11:28
Pss 49:7; 62:4

But put his trust in his great wealth,
and his strength in harmful plots."

Jer 11:16;
Zech 4:11
Pss 1:3; 92:
14; 128:3

10 But I, like a green olive tree
   in the house of God,
   Trust in the kindness of God
   forever and ever.

11 I will thank you always for what you have done,
   and proclaim the goodness of your name

Pss 50:5; 79:2

before your faithful ones.

The historical circumstance (1 Sm 21:1-8; 22:6-19) proposed for this psalm by the "title" cannot be maintained. Doeg cannot be branded as a liar, since he told Saul the objective truth. Furthermore the psalm alludes to the temple (v 10), inexistent in Saul's time. A possible parallel would be Isaiah's threat against "Sobna, master of the palace" (Is 22:15-19), elsewhere called the "scribe" (36:3; 2 Kgs 18:18). It is, however, doubtful that the "champion of infamy" refers to a specific character (see below). As in Ps 28, the original setting of Ps 52 could be the ritual expulsion of the evildoers by means of a curse pronounced by the covenant community. Yet the psalm quite clearly contains a prophetic judgment which exposes the crimes of the wicked and predicts their approaching doom (cf. Is 14 and 22). Deceit and lie are also the sins severely denounced by Jeremiah:

They ready their tongues like a drawn bow;
with lying, and not with truth,
they hold forth in the land . . .

Each one deceives the other
no one speaks the truth.
They have accustomed their tongues to lying,
and are perverse, and cannot repent (9:2, 4).

The translation of verse 3, "Why do you glory in evil, you champion of infamy?" follows the Latin and Greek versions. The Hebrew text is rendered in various ways:

Why do you boast of your malice, O mighty man?
The grace of God endures forever (A. Weiser).

Why do you boast, O mighty man,
of mischief done against the godly?
All the day you are plotting destruction (*RSV*).

Strength, vitality and durability characterize the just who worship in the temple and trust in God. These attributes are symbolized by solidly rooted and healthy trees (Pss 1:3; 52:10; 92:14).

Why was the Doeg episode given as heading to the psalm? A "champion" is mentioned in verse 3. The same Hebrew word, *gibbôr*, is used for members of Saul's personal guard (1 Sm 14:52), to which Doeg in a way belonged (1 Sm 21:7). So when David, the presumed author of the psalm, complains of a *gibbôr*, it must have been Doeg! (cf. Mowinckel, II, p. 101) A powerful curse is pronounced against this *gibbôr*. According to A. M. Scharf's reading and translation of verse 7 it would cover three generations: "May God demolish you forever: make you fatherless (*yᵉhattēk*), pluck you from your tent and render you childless (*šērēš*) in the land of the living" (on "the land of the living," cf. *Ps 142).

PSALM 53 (52)

Lament over Widespead Corruption

Ps 88:1	1 *For the leader; according to Mahalath. A maśkîl of David.*
	I
	2 The fool says in his heart,
Pss 49:13; 76: 6; 115:2	"There is no God."
	Such are corrupt; they do abominable deeds;
	there is not one who does good.
	3 God looks down from heaven upon the children of men
	to see if there be one who is wise and seeks God.
	4 All alike have gone astray; they have become perverse;
Rm 3:12	there is not one who does good, not even one.
	II
Ps 59:3	5 Will all these evildoers never learn,

they who eat up my people just as they eat bread,
who call not upon God?

6 There they were in great fear,
where no fear was,

2 Kgs 19:35   For God has scattered the bones of your besiegers;

Pss 40:15; 70:   they are put to shame, because God has rejected them.
3

III

7 Oh, that out of Sion would come the salvation of Israel!
When God restores the well-being of his people,
then shall Jacob exult and Israel be glad.

Ps 53 differs from Ps 14 mainly in that it substitutes the divine name *'elōhîm* to the sacred tetragram. Some scholars conclude that Ps 53 is an Elohistic edition of an older Yahwistic song. H. Schmidt assigns the substitution to the Persian period and believes it anticipates the later Jewish tendency of not pronouncing the name of Yahweh. Eerdmans, however, has doubts about the existence of a collection of Elohim-psalms and notes that Ecclesiastes excepted the name "Yahweh" found in all proto-canonical books, even in the latest. More significant, he says, is verse 6, which would result from a deliberate alteration: He proposes the following translation:

Ps 14:5f There they are in great fear,
for Elohim acts righteously in the generation.
The counsel of the poor was:
Ye will put to shame, because Jahu was his refuge.

Ps 53:5f There they are in great fear.
It is no fear if Elohim scattereth the bones of him,
that encampeth within thee;
thou putteth to shame if Elohim rejecteth them.

"To have his bones scattered" means to be tired to death, as in Ps 141:7: "Our bones are scattered at the mouth of Sheol, like one, who has been digging and cleaving the soil." This verse reflects the oriental dislike of strenuous toil. In Ps 53:6 "he that encampeth within thee" is *spiritus malignus* (Lk 8:2): "Fever and illnesses were supposed to be caused by evil spirits which had penetrated into the body. Numerous amulets were worn to keep them off, and at a sick-bed sacred texts

were recited to expel them." Verse 6 then "asserts that if Elohim has
exhausted that evil power (has scattered his bones) there will be no
fear. Then the sick man will be cured." Considering [all] these facts,
Eerdmans concludes, we find no reason to attach importance to the
use of the term "Elohim" in Ps 53. But Ps 53:1-6 reflects an adaptation of Ps 14:1-6 for the purpose of medical incantation. "To these
psalms a final verse was added when they were recited for the sake
of a restoration of the people, after Israel and Judah had been deported
by the kings of Assyria in the last part of the eighth century B.C."
(*OTS*, I, pp. 258-267).

PSALM 75 (74)

God the Just Judge of the Wicked

1 *For the leader. (Do not destroy!) A psalm of Asaph; a song.*

I

2 We give you thanks, O God, we give thanks,
> and we invoke your name; we declare your wondrous
>> deeds.

II

3 "When I seize the appointed time,
> I will judge with equity.
4 Though the earth and all who dwell in it quake,
> I have set firm its pillars.
5 I say to the boastful: Boast not;
> and to the wicked: Lift not up your horns."
6 Lift not up your horns against the Most High;
> speak not haughtily against the Rock.
7 For neither from the east nor from the west,
> neither from the desert nor from the mountains —
8 But God is the judge;
> one he brings low; another he lifts up.
9 For a cup is in the Lord's hand,
> full of spiced and foaming wine,
> And he pours out from it; even to the dregs they
>> shall drain it;
> all the wicked of the earth shall drink.

Margin references:

Pss 72:18; 78:14

Pss 9:9; 96:10, 13

1 Sm 2:8; Jb 9:6; 38:6
Pss 18:3; 24:2

Dt 33:17;
Zech 2:1-4
Lam 2:3; Jb 15:25
1 Sm 2:3; Pss 18:3; 71:3

Jer 3:23

1 Sm 2:7; Jb 5:11
Hb 2:16; Ps 11:6
Jer 25:15ff; Ex 23:31ff
Is 51:17, 22

Ps 60:5

III

Pss 70:5; 89:17   10   But as for me, I will exult forever;
                          I will sing praise to the God of Jacob.
Zech 2:4   11   And I will break off the horns of all the wicked;
Pss 68:31; 112:9   the horns of the just shall be lifted up.

A prophetic judgment is also the central feature of this psalm, in which the oracle is set in a hymnal invocation and thanksgiving. The oracle, Mowinckel points out (II, p. 64), announces the coming of Yahweh to judge the pagan world and its unrighteous gods, under whose oppression Israel is now sighing and suffering. The judgment will come as an answer to the cult community's prayer for the reestablishment of Israel (cf. §14c). In these respects Ps 75 can be likened to Ps 82 and also to Pss 46, 48, 76 (cf. M., I, p. 151). More likely perhaps, what is announced is the proximity of a judgment against all the presumptuous evildoers (v 9) who dare oppose divine order and rule in this world. The judgment will surely come and at God's appointed time, as it becomes divine sovereignty. The "cup" (v 9) as symbolizing God's judgment is a metaphor frequently used by the prophets (cf. Is 51:17; Jer 25:15). In Ps 11:16, as in Ps 75:9, it is served to the wicked (cf. Ps 60:5). Hannah's song of praise speaks of God's free judgment in much the same way as Ps 75:

The bows of the mighty are broken,
but the feeble gird in strength . . .
The Lord kills and brings to life;
he brings down to Sheol and raises up.
The Lord makes poor and makes rich;
he brings low, he also exalts (1 Sm 2:1-7).

The psalm could be post-exilic since it seems to reflect Zech 2:1-14 and Hannah's canticle, inserted later in the historical account (cf. RB 1958, p. 322).

In the last verses the psalmist "exults" over God's judgment revealed by the oracle and considers himself instrumental in its proclamation or execution. But Dahood finds no "exult forever" in verse 10, which constitutes for him a good example of ancient faulty reading. "An imperfect knowledge," he writes, "of archaic divine appellatives will explain the repeated confusion between 'ēl, 'ēlī, 'the Most High,' and the prepositions *'al and 'ālay,* respectively: cf. Pss 7:9, 11; 16:6; 57: 3; 68:30, 35; 106:7. From this imperfect knowledge stems the erroneous division of consonants in Ps 75:10, where *MT* reads grammatically incongruent *'aggîd le'ôlām* for *'agaddēl 'ôlām,* 'I shall extol the Eternal,' parallel to 'I shall sing to the God of Jacob.' In other words, the real parallelism intended by the psalmist is between the God of Abraham, who in Gn 21:33 is called *'el 'ôlām,* 'El the Eternal,' and the God of Jacob (cf. *Ps 24:6). The Masoretes missed the historical allusion. The LXX experienced difficulty with the consonantal division and read *'āgîl,* 'I shall rejoice'; many modern versions have opted, ill-advisedly in my judgment, for the *LXX* emendation" (*Psalms* I, p. 23).

PSALM 81 (80)

Festive Song with an Admonition to Fidelity

Ps 8:1	1	For the leader; "upon the gittith." Of Asaph.
		A
	2	Sing joyfully to God our strength;
Pss 76:7; 84:9		acclaim the God of Jacob.
Jdt 16:2	3	Take up a melody, and sound the timbrel,
		the pleasant harp and the lyre.
Lv 23:24; Nm 29:1	4	Blow the trumpet at the new moon,
Am 8:5; Hos 2:13		at the full moon, on our solemn feast;
	5	For it is a statute in Israel,
		an ordinance of the God of Jacob,
	6	Who made it a decree for Joseph
		when he came forth from the land of Egypt.
		I
		An unfamiliar speech I hear:
	7	"I relieved his shoulder of the burden;
Ex 1:14; 19:16		his hands were freed from the basket.
	8	In distress you called, and I rescued you;
		Unseen, I answered you in thunder;
Nm 20:13; Ps 95:8		I tested you at the waters of Meriba
Prv 8:4ff; Ps 78:1	9	Hear, my people, and I will admonish you;
Ex 15:26; Is 55:2		O Israel, will you not hear me?
Ps 95:7	10	There shall be no strange gods among you

Ex 20:2f; Dt 5:6f   nor shall you worship any alien god.

Ps 50:7; Dt 5:6, 9   11 I, the Lord, am your God

Dt 20:1   who led you forth from the land of Egypt;

         open wide your mouth, and I will fill it.

      II

   12 But my people heard not my voice,

Pss 78:8ff; 89:31f   and Israel obeyed me not;

Jer 3:17   13 So I gave them up to the hardness of their hearts;

         they walked according to their own counsels.

   14 If only my people would hear me,

Dt 5:33; 10:12   and Israel walk in my ways,

   15 quickly would I humble their enemies;

Lv 26:8; Is 48:18   against their foes I would turn my hand.

   16 Those who hated the Lord would seek to flatter me,

         but their fate would endure forever,

Pss 78:14ff; 99:7f   17 While Israel I would feed with the best of wheat,

Ps 147:14; cf. Dt 32:13f   and with honey from the rock I would fill them."

The trumpet blast (cf. v 4) marked the beginning of the New Year according to Lv 23:24 and Nm 29:1. The festival of Harvest and New Year, celebrated in autumn (beginning of Tishri = October) became, writes Mowinckel (I, p. 157), the festival of the renewal of the historical covenant (cf. §13a). Ps 81 would reflect the central theme of the festival: God's epiphany in the cult accompanies the renewal of the covenant and reaffirms the covenant's foundation, the keeping of the commandments (v 9). Verse 11 carries the ancient "formula of epiphany": "I, the Lord, am your God who led you forth from the land of Egypt." In the midst of a joyous feast a prophet would come forth to proclaim the requirements of "God present," using the covenant formula: 'ānōkî yhwh 'elōhêkā, "I, the Lord, am your God" (v 11; cf. Dt 5:6, 9).

Pss 81 and 95 reflect, like Ps 50, the "decalogical tradition," but what they emphasize is the fundamental commandment, to worship Yahweh only. The "Meriba tradition," attested in the psalm (v 8; cf. 95:8), belongs to the Yahwist source and is seemingly pre-prophetic. This conclusion is also supported by the North Israelite basis of Ps 81, suggested by the use of "Jacob" and "Joseph" to designate the people. Mowinckel believes that the "prophetic element" in these psalms (50, 81, 95) belongs rather to the presuppositions of the "prophetic judgment" than to its consequences (II, p. 72). Yet the original compositions have been most likely "re-modeled" later in Jerusalem, in the Deuteronomic tradition (as regards Ps 81).

As in the so-called Deuteronomic writings of the Old Testament (Deuteronomy, Joshua, Judges, Samuel, Kings), Ps 81, writes H. Ringgren, "stresses the interaction of the people's religious attitude and their destiny: sin call for punishment; repentance is the way to restoration. The essential point is that history is, so to speak, God's workshop. The history of Israel is a series of divine acts which began with the deliverance from Egypt, when God's victorious power was supremely manifested" (*The Faith of the Psalmists*, p. 99).

PSALM 95 (94)

A Call to Praise and Obedience

I

Ex 17:1f; Dt 32:15 Ps 94:22; 2 Sm 24:18	1	Come, let us sing joyfully to the Lord; let us acclaim the Rock of our salvation.
	2	Let us greet him with thanksgiving; let us joyfully sing psalms to him
Pss 89:9; 96:4	3	For the Lord is a great God,
Dn 2:47; Pss 84:8; 86:8		and a great king above all gods;
Pss 86:13; 130:1	4	In his hands are the depths of the earth, and the tops of the mountains are his.
	5	His is the sea, for he has made it,
Pss 74:16f; 100:3		and the dry land, which his hands have formed.

II

	6	Come, let us bow down in worship; let us kneel before the Lord who made us.
Dt 27:9; Mi 7:14	7	For he is our God,
Jer 23:1f; Ez 34:11f		and we are the people he shepherds, the flock he guides.

III

Heb 3:7-11; 4:3ff	8	Oh, that today you would hear his voice
Ps 106:6ff; Ex 19:5		"Harden not your hearts as at Meriba,
Ex 17:7; Nm 20:13		as in the day of Massa in the desert,
Pss 78:3; 106: 14	9	Where your fathers tempted me;
Nm 14:22		they tested me though they had seen my works.

10 Forty years I loathed that generation,

Dt 32:5; Ps 78:8

and I said: They are a people of erring heart,

Jb 21:14

and they know not my ways.

Ex 20:15; Ps 78:59

11 Therefore I swore in my anger:

Nm 14:30; Dt 12:9

They shall not enter into my rest."

This psalm opens the daily Divine Office of the Church. It consists of two parts: a hymn of praise (vv 1-7c) and a divine oracle (7d-11). Their setting was a liturgy which introduced the congregation into God's presence. The bowing down, or *proskynesis* (v 6) followed the acclamation of the King (v 3). Then an oracle, proclaimed by an authorized interpreter of the covenant, reminded the worshippers of their duties, mainly fidelity to the covenant. The prophetic element appears mainly in the second part, comminatory in tone (vv 7d-11). Was it a "cult prophet," as some authors suggest, who intervened in the liturgical festivals reflected by Pss 50 and 95? H.-J. Kraus prefers to speak of a special "covenant mediator" (p. 374). This procession hymn (comp. Pss 24, 68, 132) ends, *BJ* notes, with a divine exhortation to fidelity (cf. Pss 60 and 81), recited perhaps on the feast of the tabernacles (Dt 31:10f).

"Every year perhaps," writes A. Gelin, "Israel celebrates a feast of the covenant; or, more simply, every important feast has this significance: to relive, to actualize the event of Sinai, as in Christianity we reactualize Christmas. In this way the mysteries of the Old Testament are eternalized. In these feasts there is the grace of the recall, the grace of a new beginning. For the temptation of the people is to settle down in their possession, in their victories, in their institutions" (*The Psalms are our Prayers,* p. 41). Ps 95 would belong to one of these revivals, in which the believers experience anew the great events of the past. If verses 8-10 depend on the "Priestly" account of Nm 20: 1-13 the psalm is post-exilic. But it must also be reckoned with older traditions reflected in Ex 17:1-7.

Mowinckel sees in the first part of Ps 95 an "enthronement hymn": "The king, Yahweh, creator of the world and of Israel, has come to take his seat on his throne and receive the homage of his people; in the second part of the psalm it is as a king renewing the covenant — through the mouth of the cultic prophet — that he recalls the first making of the covenant and the faithlessness of the people at Meriba and Massa, and warns against breaking the commandments of the covenant" (I, p. 156f). Leaving aside the "enthronement idea," one will readily view the setting of the psalm as an encounter between God and his people, in which "the ancient tradition of *Heilsgeschichte* regarding creation, election and the making of the covenant at Sinai is here renewed as a present sacral event" (A. Weiser; cf. the "today" in v 7, Deuteronomic expression, as in Dt 4:4; 5:3). To the divine power and the divine grace revealed and released in the liturgical festival must correspond on the part of the faithful the decision, to be made "today," in regard to the observance of the commandments. In verse 7b the literal translation of *ṣ'ōn yādô,* "the sheep of his hand" (*RSV, BJ* and Latin Psalter) should perhaps be kept (cf. Ps 78:72): the expression makes a good parallel with "his voice" (7a), and evokes the "hands" of creation (v 5), as well as the tradition of "the hand of God": Ps 78:42; Ex 14:31; Dt 11:2; Jer 16:21.

§32. LITURGIES

(a) *General character*

Liturgical fragments can be found scattered throughout the Psalter (see §8). Yet in three psalms the liturgical element is important enough to justify their classification as "liturgies." H. Gunkel described Pss 15 and 24 as *Tora-Liturgien* (cf. *Einleitung . . . §11:14*). "Another liturgy of an exceptionally brief but not altogether unrelated character may be found in Ps 134, which Gunkel explained as a combination of hymn and priestly blessing appropriate to the close of worship at one of Israel's festivals" (A. R. Johnson, "The Psalms," p. 178).

An important subject of priestly oracles, notes A. Bentzen, has been the treatment of the problems of cultic life (*Introduction . . .* p. 188f): "Especially must many people have asked for divine guidance concerning conditions excluding from the service in the temple." The solution of moral problems was also expected from the priests. A corpus of traditions allowed them to find appropriate answers. Unusual problems could require that the oracle be consulted (cf. 2 Sm 21: 1ff; Ag 2:11-14; Zech 7:1-14). The *tôrâh-liturgies* are better understood against this background: in them are proclaimed the conditions for access to the sanctuary. They are also called "*tôrôt* of entry" and echoes of them can be found in the prophets (cf. Jer 7:1-10):

With what shall I come before the Lord,
   and bow before God most high?
Shall I come before him with holocausts,
   with calves a year old?
Will the Lord be pleased with thousands of rams,
   with myriad streams of oil?
Shall I give my first-born for my crime,
   the fruit of my body for the sin of my soul?

                        (Mi 6:6f)

He who practices virtue and speaks honestly,
   who spurns what is gained by oppression,
Brushing his hands free of contact with a bribe,
   stopping his ears lest he hear of bloodshed,
   closing his eyes lest he look on evil —
He shall dwell on the heights,
   his stronghold shall be the rocky fastness,
   his food and drink in steady supply.

                        (Is 33:15f)

But the typical *Tora-Liturgien* are Pss 15 and 24 (see also *Ps 26). Related to these liturgies is the "Protestation of Guiltlessness" or the "Negative Confession," of which a good example is found in chapter 125 of the Egyptian *Book of the Dead* (see on *Ps 101). Lists of faults against the covenant rules were known and recalled (cf. also Ez 18:5-9). Sometimes the confession is a very general one: "I have not transgressed any of thy commandments, neither have I forgotten them" (Dt 26:13; cf. Jb 31:5ff); "From every evil way I withhold my feet, that I may keep your words" (Ps 119:101; cf. Ps 17:4f).

The decalogical tradition of Sinai expressed itself then also in a new form, that which belongs to the ancient custom of announcing the "sacred laws" of the sanctuary. These were not unknown among ancient Israel's neighbors. An inscription of an Egyptian temple warned: "He who enters here must be pure; purify yourself fittingly at the entrance of the great god's temple" (cf. A. Erman, *Die Religion der Ägypter,* p. 90). In Babylonia a man confessed: "I have always entered into the temple in a state of impurity; what displeases you most I have always done it" (cf. A. Falkenstein and W. von Soden, *Sumerische . . . ,* p. 273; on the "Liturgies" see also the studies of K. Koch,

K. Galling and J. Morgenstern, "The Gates . . ."). The *Tora-Liturgien* merit to take place among the *didactic* psalms, since in their own way they also teach the faithful the law of God.

(b) The "liturgies" are Pss 15, 24, 134.

PSALM 15 (14)

The Guest of God

1   *A psalm of David.*

I

    O Lord, who shall sojourn in your tent?

Ps 24:3   Who shall dwell on your holy mountain?

II

Prv 28:18; Mi 6:8   2   He who walks blamelessly and does justice;

Pss 26:11; 101:6   who thinks the truth in his heart

3   and slanders not with his tongue;

    Who harms not his fellow man,

Ps 24:4   nor takes up a reproach against his neighbor;

Ps 119:158   4   By whom the reprobate is despised,

Pss 61:6; 115:11   while he honors those who fear the Lord;

    Who, though it be to his loss, changes not his pledged word;

Ex 22:24; 23:8; Mi 3:11   5   who lends not his money at usury

Is 1:23; 33:15   and accepts no bribe against the innocent.

III

Is 26:4; Ps 26:12   He who does these things

    shall never be disturbed.

The first verse clearly identifies this psalm as a "liturgy of entry," in which the conditions for admission to the sanctuary are set forth, like "a moral catechism." The influence of the "decalogical tradition," Mowinckel notes (I, p. 158), is especially noticeable in Ps 15, in which *ten* "laws of entrance" are listed (vv 2-5). In the original cultic act perhaps the candidates for admittance clarified their status in regard to these laws. A more general response, "He who does these things shall never be disturbed" (v 5), would have been introduced later, when the psalm came to be used apart from its primitive setting. Dissociated from the cult the whole psalm, interpreted figuratively, refers to the spiritual relationship of the faithful with God. It is remarkable, as Weiser notes, that moral and social, not ritual, requirements are stressed. This reflects the prophetic attitude of disengagement from the sacrificial institution (cf. *Ps 51:18) and the gradual spiritualization of religion. "By attributing the 'perfection' of man's conduct and the 'righteousness' of his actions to the inward truthfulness of his conviction (v 2), Weiser notes, the psalmist has arrived at a conception of the moral law which is not very different from the basic moral truths taught in the Sermon on the Mount." As concerns the mention of the "reprobate" in verse 4, Weiser adds: "We shall have to understand this viewpoint of the psalmist as meaning that, where God has turned against a man, it does not befit the godly to go beyond that divine decision."

PSALM 24 (23)

The Lord's Solemn Entry into Zion

1 A psalm of David.

I

Dt 10:14; 1 Cor 10:26
Pss 50:12; 89:12
Pss 33:7; 75:4; 82:5

The Lord's are the earth and its fullness;
    The world and those who dwell in it.
2 For he founded it upon the seas
    and established it upon the rivers.

II

Ps 15:1; 2 Sm 6:12
Is 33:15f; Mi 6:6f
Jer 7:1-10

3 Who can ascend the mountain of the Lord?
    or who may stand in his holy place?
4 He whose hands are sinless, whose heart is clean,
    who desires not what is vain,

Ps 15:3

    nor swears deceitfully to his neighbor.
5 He shall receive a blessing from the Lord,
    a reward from God his savior.
6 Such is the race that seeks for him,

Is 41:21; Pss 11:7; 27:8

    that seeks the face of the God of Jacob.

III

Ez 44:2; Ps 118:19

7 Lift up, O gates, your lintels;
    reach up, you ancient portals,

Mal 3:1

    that the king of glory may come in!

Ex 24:16; 1 Cor 2:8

8 Who is this king of glory?

The Lord, strong and mighty,
the Lord, mighty in battle.

9 Lift up, O gates, your lintels;
reach up, you ancient portals,
that the king of glory may come in!

Ps 46:8, 12   10 Who is this king of glory?

1 Sm 4:4; Am
4:13
The Lord of hosts; he is the king of glory.

The middle section of this psalm (vv 3-6) is a *Tor(a)-Liturgie* which has much in common with Ps 15. Here also ethical, not ritual conditions are set. The *leges sacrae* regulating admittance to the sanctuary have been in part preserved in the *tôrâh* liturgies (see §32a), also called sometimes *Torliturgien,* "Gateliturgies." The first expression concerns the conditions of entry, the second one alludes to the place where the "liturgy" was performed (cf. G. Pidoux, *Du Portique à l'Autel,* p. 20).

In Ps 24, as elsewhere in the Old Testament (cf. 1 Sm 2:8; Pss 74:16f; 89:11f; 95:4f), creation is considered as the basis of God's universal sovereignty (cf. vv 1-2). An allusion to the victory of God on "the hostile powers of chaos" can be read in verse 8 if the third stanza (vv 7-10) is interpreted as referring to God's theophany in the sanctuary. More obviously these verses describe, as in Ps 118, the entry in the temple of the ark of the covenant, which bears the name of Yahweh Sabaoth (2 Sm 6:2; 1 Par 13:6;), the God of Hosts or Armies (cf. "mighty in battle," v 8). The "king of glory" is called "Yahweh Sabaoth" in verse 10, as in the following passage: "So the people went to Shiloh, and brought from there the ark of the covenant of the Lord of hosts, who is enthroned on the cherubim" (1 Sm 4:4). The association of "Yahweh Sabaoth" with the ark (cf. §13c) could reflect an attempt to "demythicize" the ancient title of "Yahweh Sabaoth" (cf. H.-J. Kraus, *Psalmen,* p. 201), originally connected perhaps with the mysterious powers of nature religions. W. Schmidt (*Königtum . . .* pp. 76-79) has studied the hypothesis of a Canaanite origin for the title "Yahweh Sabaoth."

Some psalms, mainly 24, 68, 118, 132, could be understood only in the setting of a festal procession, Mowinckel believes (I, p. 5). The three stanzas of Ps 24, he explains, were successively used on the way to the temple, before the gates and as the procession filed through the gates. Ps 132, on the other hand, describes "the beginning of the day's procession, as it started from a place outside the temple citadel, corresponding to the house of Obed-Edom, where the ark had stood for three months (2 Sm 6:10f). H. Vilar's view is that Ps 24 was composed for the liturgy of the second temple, more precisely for the feast of Tabernacles (see on *Ps 118), when the return of the Glory of God was commemorated. In "The Gates of Righteousness" (p. 34) J. Morgenstern also mentions the $k^e b \hat{o} d$ $Yhwh$ passing through the "eastern gate" (cf. Ez 10:19; 11:1).

Psalm 24:2 is translated by Dahood: "For he based it upon the seas, established it upon the ocean currents," that is, "the pillars upon which the earth rests have been sunk into the subterranean ocean" (cf. Jb 38:6; 1 Sm 2:8; Ps 75:4 and §14d). The meaning "ocean currents" is attested in a Ugaritic text (t. 68:12ff; cf. C. H. Gordon, p. 180) and would recur in Pss 46:5; 89:26; Is 44:27; Jon 2:4. In verse 4 $nap\check{s}\hat{\imath}$ can be retained, with the meaning of $nap\check{s}\hat{o}$, "his mind" (CV: "who desires"), since Phoenician usage (cf. $JNES$ 1951, p. 228ff) reveals the existence of a third-person suffix - y (See a full listing of the biblical examples in Dahood's commentary of Ps 2:6). Then Ps 24:4 should read: "The clean of hands and pure of heart; who has not raised his mind to an idol, nor sworn by a fraud" (cf. Pss 5:7; 16:4). This rendition could perhaps be related to the passages which call "virgins" those who have not worshipped the Beast of Idolatry (Rev 14:9; 20:4; cf. Hos 1:2). The divine name "Eternal" occupies a prominent place in Dahood's translation of Ps 24. In verse 6, as in *Ps 75:10, it occurs in parallel with the "God of Jacob": "The One of Eternity seek, O you who search for the Presence of Jacob" (cf. $Harv.Th.Rev.$, 1962, p. 238f). Then twice (vv 7 and 9) an acclamation goes to the "gates of the Eternal" (CV: "ancient portals").

In connection with the belief of the descent of Christ to the underworld (cf. 1 Pt 3:19; 4:6), writes A. Cabaniss, the early Christians are likely to have been struck by some words of Ps 24: "gates," "glory," "princes" (v 9; LXX: $archontes$), "king of glory." Mention can be made here of Col 2:15: "Disarming the Principalities and Powers, he displayed them openly, leading them away in triumph by force of it." Then, continues Cabaniss, "we may venture to assume, even without literary evidence and long before the preparation of the $descensus$-section of the Gospel of Nicodemus [fourth cent. apocryphal], that the early Christian Church was using the 24th psalm liturgically to commemorate the Lord's victorious conquest of Hades and death." A possible illustration of ceremonial use of Ps 24 could be, he adds, the well-known letter of Pliny the Younger to emperor Trajan, written in A.D. 113. The relevant section of it we quote here from D. M. Stanley's article, "Carmenque Christo quasi Deo dicere . . .":

> They [the Christians] insisted however that their whole crime or error came to this: they had the custom of meeting on a certain fixed day, before daybreak, to sing a hymn, alternating among themselves, to Christ as God; and to bind themselves solemnly by an oath, not with any criminal intent, but to avoid all fraud, theft, adultery, unfaithfulness to their promises, or denial of "the deposit" (cf. 1 Tm 6:20) if summoned to do so. After dispatching this business, it was their habit to disband, reassembling once more to take food, which is however of an ordinary and innocent kind . . . (*CBQ* 1958, p. 176).

The antiphonal hymn mentioned in this text applies well also to Ps 24 which has a dialogue structure and was probably sung by alternating choirs. The innocence motif is also found in both texts.

PSALM 134 (133)

Exhortation to the Night Watch to Bless the Lord

	1 *A song of ascents.*
Pss 115:18; 135:1f	Come, bless the Lord,
Dt 10:8; Dn 3:84f	all you servants of the Lord
	Who stand in the house of the Lord
1 Chr 9:33; 23:30	during the hours of night
Ps 141:2	2 Lift up your hands toward the sanctuary,
	and bless the Lord.
Nb 6:24	3 May the Lord bless you from Zion,
Pss 3:9; 118: 26; 128:5	the maker of heaven and earth.

The last of the "Pilgrim Songs" preserves the remains of a night liturgy. It ends with a priestly blessing (v 3; cf. §3c). The first two verses are hymnic in character and could represent the answer of the congregation to the thanksgiving of an individual. Possibly also they are addressed to priests or pilgrims who participated in a vigil of prayers. Kissane observes, however, that the term "servants of Yahweh" includes all Israel (cf. Ps 135:1, 19f), and the phrase "who stand in the house of Yahweh" is not the equivalent of "who stand before Yahweh" as His ministers (cf. Dt 10:8), but merely "who are present in the temple" (Ps 122:2). The mention of "the night" is linked by LXX (and *Vulg.*), perhaps correctly, with verse 2: "Every night lift up your hands . . ." and "can refer to prayers offered outside the Temple by pilgrims who turn towards the Temple in prayer" (Kissane). The allusion in verse 3 to the divine title "Creator" stresses the validity and power of God's blessing (cf. Pss 24:1f; 121:2; 124:8).

In his "Notes on Pss 68 and 134," Albright has called attention to the fact that a Canaanite text published by R. A. Bowman (*JNES* 1944, pp. 219-231) contains an exact parallel to Ps 134:3. It reads: "Baal from the North will bless you." In the same article he brings to notice the evidence (cf. *JBL* 1944, p. 4ff) of the ancient Canaanite divine title: "El, Creator of the Earth." This is reflected also in Ps 134:3. Albright concludes that verse 3 of Ps 134 "brings together two characteristic cola from pagan Canaanite literature, with slight modification to adapt them to monotheism and exilic or early postexilic age" (p. 6). Similar reflections could be applied to Ps 128:5 (also a "Song of Ascents"), "The Lord bless you from Zion," and to Ps 118:26: "Blessed is he who comes in the name of the Lord; we bless you from the house of the Lord."

APPENDICES

§33. LIST OF THE PSALMS: LOGICAL ORDER

(The symbols used in the numerical list are given here between brackets):

I. Hymns:
   a) The hymns proper (H): 8, 19, 29, 33, 100, 103, 104, 111, 113, 114, 117, 135, 136, 145, 146, 147, 148, 149, 150.
   b) The Psalms of Yahweh's Kingship (YK): 47, 93, 96, 97, 98, 99.
   c) The Canticles of Zion (CZ): 46, 48, 76, 84, 87, 122.

II. Laments, psalms of confidence, and thanksgivings: of the Individual:
   a) Laments of the individual (LI): 5, 6, 7, 13, 17, 22, 25, 26, 28, 31, 35, 36, 38, 39, 42/43, 51, 54, 55, 56, 57, 59, 61, 63, 64, 69, 70, 71, 86, 88, 102, 109, 120, 130, 140, 141, 142, 143.
   b) Psalms of confidence of the individual (CI): 3, 4, 11, 16, 23, 27, 62, 121, 131.
   c) Thanksgivings of the individual (TI): 9/10, 30, 32, 34, 40 (vv 2-12), 41, 92, 107, 116, 138.

III. Laments, psalms of confidence, and thanksgivings: of the Community:
   a) Laments of the community (LC): 12, 44, 58, 60, 74, 77, 79, 80, 82, 83, 85, 90, 94, 106, 108, 123, 126, 137.
   b) Psalms of confidence of the community (CC): 115, 125, 129.
   c) Thanksgivings of the community (TC): 65, 66, 67, 68, 118, 124.

IV. Royal psalms (R): 2, 18, 20, 21, 45, 72, 89, 101, 110, 132, 144.

V. Didactic psalms:
   a) The wisdom psalms (W): 1, 37, 49, 73, 91, 112, 119, 127, 128, 133, 139.

b) The historical psalms (Hi): 78, 105.
c) The prophetic Exhortations (Ex): 14, 50, 52, 53, 75, 81, 95.
d) Liturgies (L): 15, 24, 134.

§34. LIST OF THE PSALMS: NUMERICAL ORDER

(The number within brackets is that of the Septuagint and the Latin Psalter; the symbols give the category; the page indicates the beginning of the "text and introduction" to the psalm).

Pages of vol. 2 are set in **heavy type.**

1	(1) p.	**260**	W	35	(34) p.	**32**	LI	68	(67) p.	196	TC
2	(2) p.	**212**	R	36	(35) p.	**35**	LI	69	(68) p.	**64**	LI
3	(3) p.	91	CI	37	(36) p.	262	W	70	(69) p.	**68**	LI
4	(4) p.	92	CI	38	(37) p.	**38**	LI	71	(70) p.	**69**	LI
5	(5) p.	5	LI	39	(38) p.	**40**	LI	72	(71) p.	**232**	R
6	(6) p.	8	LI	40	(39) p.	**124**	TI	73	(72) p.	**269**	W
7	(7) p.	9	LI	41	(40) p.	**127**	TI	74	(73) p.	**151**	LC
8	(8) p.	182	H	42	(41) p.	**42**	LI	75	(74) p.	**318**	Ex
9/10	(9) p.	**112**	TI	43	(42) p.	**43**	LI	76	(75) p.	236	CZ
11	(10) p.	94	CI	44	(43) p.	145	LC	77	(76) p.	**155**	LC
12	(11) p.	143	LC	45	(44) p.	**229**	R	78	(77) p.	**298**	Hi
13	(12) p.	12	LI	46	(45) p.	**231**	CZ	79	(78) p.	**157**	LC
14	(13) p.	309	Ex	47	(46) p.	**217**	YK	80	(79) p.	**159**	LC
15	(14) p.	**326**	L	48	(47) p.	**234**	CZ	81	(80) p.	**320**	Ex
16	(15) p.	96	CI	49	(48) p.	**266**	W	82	(81) p.	**162**	LC
17	(16) p.	14	LI	50	(49) p.	**311**	Ex	83	(82) p.	**164**	LC
18	(17) p.	217	R	51	(50) p.	**45**	LI	84	(83) p.	238	CZ
19	(18) p.	184	H	52	(51) p.	314	Ex	85	(84) p.	**165**	LC
20	(19) p.	**225**	R	53	(52) p.	316	Ex	86	(85) p.	71	LI
21	(20) p.	**227**	R	54	(53) p.	**51**	LI	87	(86) p.	240	CZ
22	(21) p.	17	LI	55	(54) p.	**52**	LI	88	(87) p.	**73**	LI
23	(22) p.	99	CI	56	(55) p.	**54**	LI	89	(88) p.	**236**	R
24	(23) p.	**327**	L	57	(56) p.	**56**	LI	90	(89) p.	**168**	LC
25	(24) p.	22	LI	58	(57) p.	148	LC	91	(90) p.	**274**	W
26	(25) p.	25	LI	59	(58) p.	**58**	LI	92	(91) p.	**130**	TI
27	(26) p.	102	CI	60	(59) p.	149	LC	93	(92) p.	220	YK
28	(27) p.	27	LI	61	(60) p.	**60**	LI	94	(93) p.	**170**	LC
29	(28) p.	186	H	62	(61) p.	**105**	CI	95	(94) p.	**322**	Ex
30	(29) p.	**117**	TI	63	(62) p.	**62**	LI	96	(95) p.	222	YK
31	(30) p.	29	LI	64	(63) p.	**63**	LI	97	(96) p.	224	YK
32	(31) p.	**119**	TI	65	(64) p.	**190**	TC	98	(97) p.	226	YK
33	(32) p.	189	H	66	(65) p.	**192**	TC	99	(98) p.	227	YK
34	(33) p.	**121**	TI	67	(66) p.	**195**	TC	100	(99) p.	191	H

101 (100) p. **241** R
102 (101) p. **75** LI
103 (102) p. 192 H
104 (103) p. 194 H
105 (104) p. **304** Hi
106 (105) p. **174** LC
107 (106) p. **133** TI
108 (107) p. **178** LC
109 (108) p. **78** LI
110 (109) p. **243** R
111 (110) p. 199 H
112 (111) p. **276** W
113 (112) p. 200 H
114/115 (113) p. 202,
    185 H:CC
116 (114/115) p. **137** TI
117 (116) p. 203 H

118 (117) p. **203** TC
119 (118) p. **277** W
120 (119) p. **80** LI
121 (120) p. **107** CI
122 (121) p. 242 CZ
123 (122) p. **179** LC
124 (123) p. **207** TC
125 (124) p. **187** CC
126 (125) p. **180** LC
127 (126) p. **289** W
128 (127) p. **290** W
129 (128) p. **188** CC
130 (129) p. **82** LI
131 (130) p. **108** CI
132 (131) p. **251** R
133 (132) p. **291** W
134 (133) p. **330** L

135 (134) p. 203 H
136 (135) p. 205 H
137 (136) p. **182** LC
138 (137) p. **138** TI
139 (138) p. **292** W
140 (139) p. **83** LI
141 (140) p. **84** LI
142 (141) p. **86** LI
143 (142) p. **87** LI
144 (143) p. **255** R
145 (144) p. 207 H
146 (145) p. 209 H
147 (146/147) p. 210
    H
148 (148) p. 212 H
149 (149) p. 214 H
150 (150) p. 215 H

BIBLIOGRAPHY

Abrahams, I., "E. G. King on the Influence of the Triennial Cycle upon the Psalter," *JQR* 16 (1904), pp. 579-583.

Ackroyd, P. R., "Some Notes on the Psalms," *JTS* 17 (1966), pp. 392-399. [about Ps 74:4; 93:1; *hadrat qōdeš*, Ps 118 at Qumrân]

Ackroyd, P.R. - Knibb, M.A., "Translating the Psalms," *The Bible Translator* 17 (1966) pp. 148-162.

Ahern, B. M., "Can the Psalms again be popular Prayers?" *Proceedings of the National Liturgical Week* (Esberry, Mo. 1954), pp. 117-125. [cf. §16d]

Ahlström, G. W., *Psalm 89. Eine Liturgie aus dem Ritual des leidenden Königs* (Lund, 1959). [Uppsala School viewpoint; cf. *JBL* 1960, p. 68f + §7b]

A la rencontre de Dieu. Mémorial Albert Gelin (Le Puy, 1961). [cf. E. Beaucamp, P. E. Bonnard, H. Cazelles, R. Pautrel]

Albright, W. F., "A Catalogue of early Hebrew Lyric poems (Psalm LXVIII)," *HUCA* 23, 1 (1950f), pp. 1-40.

Id., "Baal-Zephon," *Festschrift für Alfred Bertholet* (Tübingen 1950), pp. 1-14.

Id., "Notes on Psalms 68 and 134," *Interpretationes ad Vetus Testamentum pertinentes Sigmundo Mowinckel Septuagenario missae* (Oslo 1955), pp. 1-12. [see also §9d, 10g]

Aldama, J. A. de, "La naissance du Seigneur dans l'exégèse patristique du Psaume 21:10a," *RSR* 51 (1963), pp. 5-29.

Allegro, J. M., "A newly-discovered Fragment of a Commentary on Psalm 37 from Qumrân," *PEQ* 86 (1954), pp. 69-75.

Allgeier, A., *Die altlateinischen Psalterien* (Freiburg 1928).

Id., *Die Psalmen der Vulgata. Ihre Eigenart, sprachliche Grundlage und geschichtliche Stellung* (Paderborn 1940).

Id., "Psalm 93 (94):20. Ein auslegungs - und bedeutungsgeschichtlicher Beitrag," *Fs. A. Bertholet* (Tübingen 1950), pp. 15-28.

Alonso Schökel, L., *Estudios de Poética Hebrea* (Barcelona 1963). [cf. §6e]

Id., *Salmos* (Madrid 1966).

Id., "Psalmus 136 (135)," *VD* 45 (1967), pp. 129-138.

Anderson, G. W., *Enemies and Evildoers in the Book of Psalms* (Manchester 1965). [from *BJRL* 48, 1, 1965, pp. 18-29]

Ap-Thomas, D. R., "An Appreciation of Sigmund Mowinckel's Contribution to Biblical Studies," *JBL* 85 (1966), pp. 315-325.

Arbesmann, R., "The Daemonium meridianum (Ps 91:6) and Greek and Latin Exegesis," *Tradition* 14 (1958), pp. 17-31.

Arbez, E. P., "A Study of Psalm 1," *CBQ* 7 (1945), pp. 398-404.

Arconada, R., "La escatología mesiánica en los Salmos ante dos objeciones recientes," *Bib* 17 (1936), pp. 202-229; 294-326; 461-478.

Arens, A., *Die Psalmen im Gottesdienst des Alten Bundes. Eine Untersuchung zur Vorgeschichte des christlichen Psalmengesanges* (Trier 1961). [cf. *CBQ* 1962, p. 209f + §8c]

Id., "Hat der Psalter seinen 'Sitz im Leben' in der Synagogalen Leseordnung des Pentateuch?" *Le Psautier* [cf. R. De Langhe], pp. 107-131.

Arnaldich, L., "Carácter mesiánico del Salmo 16 (Vulg. 15)," *Verdad y Vida* 1 (1943), pp. 251-286; 688-706; 2 (1944), pp. 24-65.

Asensio, F., "Salmos Mesiánicos o Salmos Nacionales?" *Greg* 33 (1952), pp. 219-260; 566-611. [Pss 2, 72, 22, 16]

Id., "Sugerencias del Salmista 'Peregrino y extranjero' (Salm. 39:13)," *Greg* 34 (1953), pp. 421-426.

Id., "En torno al 'Sol-héroe' del Salmo 19," *Greg* 35 (1954), pp. 649-655.

Id., "El *despertar* del justo en el Salm. 17:15," *Greg* 36 (1955), pp. 669-675.

Id., "El Salmo 132 y la 'Lámpara' de David," *Greg* 38 (1957), pp. 310-316.

Id., "Entrecruce de símbolos y realidades en el Salmo 23," *Bib* 40 (1959), pp. 237-247.

Id., "Salmo 36. Su avance hacia la plenitud Luz-Vida," *EstE* 34 (1960), pp. 633-643.

Id., "Teología Bíblica de un tríptico: Salmos 61, 62 y 63," *EstBib* 21 (1962), pp. 111-125.

Id., "El *Yahweh mālak* de los 'Salmos del Reino' en la historia de la 'Salvación,'" *EstBib* 25 (1966), pp. 299-315.

Auvray, P., "Le Psaume I. Notes de grammaire et d'exégèse," *RB* 53 (1946), pp. 365-371.

Ayuso Maraguela, T., *La Vetus Latina Hispana. V, El Salterio* (Madrid 1962), vols. I-III.

Baillet, M., "Psaumes, hymnes, cantiques et prières dans les manuscrits de Qumrân," *Le Psautier* [cf. R. De Langhe], pp. 389-405.

Balla, E., *Das Ich der Psalmen*, FRLANT 16 (Göttingen 1912). [cf. *Ps 129]

Barth, C., *Die Errettung vom Tode in den individuellen Klage-und Dankliedern des Alten Testaments* (Zürich 1947). [Pss 17:15; 18:17; 49:16; 73:23; cf. *RB* 1948]

Id., *Introduction to the Psalms* (New York 1966). [Tr. of the German edition, 1961; cf. *CBQ* 1964, p. 140f]

Bartina, S., "Alabar, no 'Confessar' [en el Nuevo Salterio Latino]," *EstE* 30 (1956), pp. 37-66.

Barucq, A., "La lode divina nei Salmi," *BibOr* 1, 3 (1959), pp. 66-77.

Id., *L'expression de la louange divine et de la prière dans la Bible et en Égypte* (Le Caire, 1962).

Bauer, J. B., "Incedam in via immaculata, quando venias ad me (Ps 100 [101]:2)," *VD* 30 (1952), pp. 219-224.

Id., "Theologie der Psalmen," *BiLit* 20 (1952f); 21 (1953f); 22 (1954f). [several articles]

Id., "L'aiuto divino al mattino," *RBibIt* 2 (1954), pp. 43-47. [cf. *Ps 5]

Baumann, E., "Struckter-Untersuchungen im Psalter," *ZAW* 61 (1945-48) 115-176; 62 (1949f) 115-152. [Pss 4, 8, 13, 18, 26, 32, 36, 39, 40, 50, 56, 57, 59, 60, 72, 73, 84, 85, 110, 126, 135, 144]

Baumgärtel, F., "Der 109. Psalm in der Verkündigung," *Monatschrift f. Past. Theol.* 42 (1953), pp. 244-253.

Id., "Zur Frage der theologischen Deutung der messianischen Psalmen," *BZAW* 105 (1967), pp. 19-25.

Bea, A., "The New Psalter: its Origin and Spirit," *CBQ* 8 (1946), pp. 1-35.
Id., "I primi dieci anni del nuovo Salterio latino," *Bib* 36 (1955), pp. 161-181. [cf. *Liber Psalmorum . . .*]
Beaucamp, E., "Psaume 47. Verset 10A," *Bib* 38 (1957), pp. 457-460.
Id., "La théophanie du Psaume 50 (49)," *NRT* 81 (1959), pp. 897-915.
Id., "Le Psaume 21 (20), psaume messianique," *ColBibLat* 13 (1959), pp. 35-66.
Id., "Justice divine et pardon (Ps 51:6b)," *A la rencontre . . .* pp. 129-144.
Id., "Le problème du Psaume 87," *Liber Annuus* 13 (1962f), pp. 53-75.
Id., "Des justices plein ta main, de redoutables exploits plein ta droite (Ps 45:5c)," *Bib* 47 (1966), pp. 110-112.
Id., [also] *Bible et Vie Chrétienne,* N. 22 (Ps 21), N. 24 (Ps 85), N. 28 (Ps 45), N. 29 (Ps 103), N. 63 (Ps 68), N. 65 (Ps 67), N. 66 (Ps 74).
Beauchamp, P., "Plainte et louange dans les Psaumes," *Christus* 13 (1967), pp. 65-82.
Becker, J., *Israel deutet seine Psalmen* (Stuttgart 1966).
Id., "Structures strophiques des Psaumes," *RSR* 56 (1968), pp. 199-223.
Beer, G., "Zur Erklärung des 22. Psalms," Fs K. Marti, *BZAW* 41 (1925), pp. 12-20.
Begrich, J., "Die Vertrauensäusserungen im israelitischen Klagenliede des Einzelnen und in seinem babylonischen Gegenstück," *ZAW* 46 (1928), pp. 221-260.
Id., "Das priesterliche Heilsorakel," *ZAW* 52 (1934), pp. 81-92.
Behler, G. M., "Der Herr als guter Hirt und milder Wirt (Ps 23)," *BiLit* 39 (1964f), pp. 254-287.
Id., "Der nahe und schwer zu fassende Gott. Eine biblische Besinnung über Ps 139 (138)," *Bib* 6 (1965), pp. 135-152.
Bentzen, A., "Der Tod des Beters in den Psalmen. Randbemerkungen zur Diskussion zwischen Mowinckel und Widengren," *Gottes ist der Orient, Fs. O. Eissfeldt* (Halle 1947), pp. 57-60.
Id., *King and Messiah* (London 1955). [cf. §8a]
Id., *Introduction to the Old Testament,* I-II (Copenhagen 1957).
Bernhardt, K.-H., *Das Problem der altaorientalischen Königsideologie im Alten Testament, unter besonderer Berücksichtigung der Geschichte der Psalmenexegese dargestellt und kritisch gewürdigt* (Leiden 1961). [rejects the "ritual pattern" theory and advocates an explanation of royal ideology based on the historical rejection of the kingship and on the traditions of the nomadic period. Cf. *RB* 1963, p. 633f]
Bernimont, E., "De l'inégale valeur des Psaumes," *NRT* 84 (1962), pp. 843-852.
Bernini, G., *Le preghiere penitenziali del Salterio* (Romae 1953), [especially Pss 19, 25, 32, 38-41, 51, 65, 69, 79, 85, 90, 103, 106, 130, 143].
Beyerlin, W., "Die *tôdā* der Heilsverkündigung in den Klageliedern des Einzelnen," *ZAW* 79 (1967), pp. 208-224.
Bickel, G., *Carmina Veteris Testamenti metrice* (Oeniponte 1882).
Bierberg, R. P., *Conserva me, Domine (Ps 16),* (Washington 1945). [cf. *CBQ* 1946, pp. 359-363]
Bileham, A., *El primer libro de los salmos* (Madrid 1966).
Bird T. E., "Some Queries on the New Psalter," *CBQ* 11-12 (1949f), a series of articles.

Birkeland, H., *'Ani und 'anaw in den Psalmen* (Oslo and Leipzig, 1933). [cf. §12a]

Id., *Die Feinde des Individuums in der israelitischen Psalmenliteratur* (Oslo 1933).

Id., *The Evildoers in the Book of Psalms* (Oslo 1955). [cf. *JBL* 1957, pp. 162 + §12g]

Id., "The Chief Problems of Ps 73:17ff," *ZAW* 67 (1955), pp. 99-103.

Blackman, A. M., "The Psalms in the Light of Egyptian Research," *The Psalmists* [cf. D. C. Simpson], pp. 177-197. [cf. §9c]

Blenkinsopp, J., "Can we pray the Cursing Psalms?" *Clergy Review* 50 (1965), pp. 534-538.

Blidstein, G. J., "Nature in Psalms," *Judaism* 13, 1964, pp. 29-36.

Bloch, J., "The New Latin Version of the Psalter," *JQR* 38 (1947f), pp. 267-288.

Boling, R. G., "Synonymous Parallelism in the Psalms," *JSS* 5 (1960), pp. 221-255.

Bollegui, J. M., *Los Salmos. Oraciones inventadas por Dios para los hombres* (Barcelona 1967).

Bonkamp, B., *Die Psalmen nach dem hebräischen Urtext übersetzt* (Freiburg i.B., 1952). [is in part an attempt to study the Psalter with the contribution of Assyriological material; cf. *VT* 1953, pp. 202-208]

Bonnard, P. E., "Le vocabulaire du *Miserere*," *A la rencontre* ... pp. 145-156.

Id., *Le psautier selon Jérémie* (Paris 1960). [see pp. §5d + *Ps 6]

Bonnes, J. P., *David et les Psaumes* (Paris 1957). [cf. *RB* 1958]

Bornert, R., "Les Psaumes (Ps 97): Hymne pour la manifestation du Seigneur," *Assemblées du Seigneur* 17 (1962), pp. 7-20. [cf. §13a]

Bornkamm, G., "Lobpreis Bekenntnis und Opfer," in *Apophoreta*, BZNW 30 (Berlin 1964), pp. 43-63.

Botterweck, G. J., "Ein Leid vom glücklichen Menschen (Ps 1)," *Theologische Quartalschrift* 138 (1958), pp. 129-151.

Bouyer, L., "Les Psaumes dans la prière chrétienne traditionnelle," *BiViChr* 10 (1955), pp. 22-35.

Bowker, J. W., "Psalm CX," *VT* 17 (1967), pp. 31-41.

Breit, H., "Die Psalmen in der christlichen Kirche," *Klerus Blatt* 45 (1965), pp. 379-384.

Brekelmans, C., "Pronominal Suffixes in the Hebrew Book of Psalms," *JEOL* 17 (1964), pp. 202-206.

Brethes, C., *Mon âme, bénis le Seigneur! Commentaire et traduction en vers des Psaumes* (Paris 1965).

Briggs, C. A., *A Critical and Exegetical Commentary on the Book of Psalms*, I-II (Edinburgh 1906f).

Brinktrine, J., "Dominus regnavit a ligno," *BZ* 10 (1966) 105-107. [cf. *Ps 96: 10]

Brongers, H. A., "Die Rache-und Fluchpsalmen im Alten Testament," *OTS* 13 (1963), pp. 21-42.

Brownlee, W. H., "Le livre grec d'Esther et la royauté divine," *RB* 73 (1966), pp. 161-185. [cf. *Ps 13 + §26f]

Bückers, H., "Die Sündenvergebung in den Psalmen," *Divus Thomas Freib.* 29 (1951), pp. 188-210.

Id., "Zur Verwertung der Sinaitraditionen in den Psalmen," *Bib* 32 (1951), pp. 401-422.

Budde, K., "Zum Text der Psalmen," *ZAW* 35 (1915), pp. 175-195.

Bulcke, M., "Le Psaume 67 (68), psaume de Pentecôte," *Rev. Clergé Afr.* 9 (1954), pp. 569-582.

Bullough, S., "The question of metre in Psalm 1," *VT* 17 (1967), pp. 42-49.

Buss, M. J., "The Psalms of Asaph and Korah," *JBL* 82 (1963), pp. 382-392.

Buttenwieser, M., *The Psalms, chronologically treated, with a new Translation* (Chicago 1938).

Cabaniss, A., "The Harrowing of Hell. Psalm 24 and Pliny the Younger," *Vigiliae Christianae* 7 (1953), pp. 65-74.

Calès, J., *Le livre des Psaumes*, I-II (Paris 1936).

Callan, C. J., *The Psalms, translated from the Latin Psalter in the light of the Hebrew, of the Septuagint and Peshitta versions, and of the Psalterium juxta Hebraeos of St. Jerome with introductions, critical notes and spiritual reflections* (New York 1944). [cf. *CBQ* 1946, p. 247f]

Cambe, M., "L'interprétation symbolique du Psaume XXIX (XXVIII) par les Septante. Note sur le verset 6," *Rev. Thom.* 65 (1964), pp. 223-229.

Candole, H. de, *The Christian Use of the Psalms* (London 1955).

Caquot, A., "In splendoribus sanctorum," *Syria* 33 (1956), pp. 36-41. [Ps 29:2; 96:9; 1 Chr 16:29]

Id., "Remarques sur le Psaume CX," *Sem* 6 (1956), pp. 33-52.

Id., "Le Psaume XCI," *Sem* 8 (1958), pp. 21-37.

Id., "Le Psaume 47 et la royauté de Yahvé," *RHPhilRel* 39 (1959), pp. 311-337.

Id., "Purification et expiation selon le psaume LI," *RHR* 169 (1966), pp. 133-154.

Carmignac, J., "Précisions sur la forme poétique du Psaume 151," *RQum* 5 (1965), pp. 249-252. [cf. §3a]

Castellini, G. M., "I Salmi, preghiera cristiana," *EphLitg* 72 (1958), pp. 341-347.

Castellino, G. R., *Le lamentazioni individuali e gli inni in Babilonia e in Israele, raffronta riguardo alla forma e al contenuto* (Torino 1940).

Id., "Lamentazioni individuali Accadiche ed Ebraiche," *Salesianum* 10 (1948), pp. 145-162.

Id., *I Salmi* (Torino 1955).

Id., "Salmo 73:10," *Studi Orient. G. Levi della Vida* I (Romae 1956), pp. 141-150.

Cazelles, H., "La question du *lamed auctoris*," *RB* 56 (1949), pp. 93-101. [cf. §4f]

Id., "Une relecture du Psaume 29?" *A la rencontre* ... pp. 119-128.

Id., "L'expression hébraïque *šûb šebût* viendrait-elle de l'accadien d'Assarhaddon?" *Groupe Linguistique d'Etudes Chamito-Sémitiques* 9 (1961), pp. 57-60. [for Pss 14:7; 53:7; 85:2]

Id., "Note sur le Psaume 8," *Parole de Dieu et Sacerdoce, Hommage à J. J. Weber* (Paris 1962), pp. 79-91.

Charles, R. H., *The Apocrypha and Pseudepigrapha of the Old Testament*, I-II

(Oxford 1913).

Cheyne, T. K., *The Book of Psalms* (London 1888 and 1904).

Chouraqui, A., *Les Psaumes. Traduits et présentés* (Paris 1956).

Cilleruelo, P. Lope, "La mentalidad del salmo de Loanza," *Ciudad de Dios* 164 (1952), pp. 533-552. [the sacrifice of praise]

Clark, D. L.-Mastin, B. A., "*Venite exultemus Domino*: Some Reflections on the Interpretation of the Psalter," *ChQR* 167 (1966), pp. 413-424.

Clines, D. J. A., "Psalm Research since 1955:I. The Psalms and the Cult," *Tyndale Bulletin* 18 (1967), pp. 103-126.

Closen, G. E., "Gedanken zur Textkritik von Ps 2:11b + 12a," *Bib* 21 (1940), pp. 288-309.

Cohen, A., *The Psalms. Hebrew Text, English Translation and Commentary* (Hindhead 1945).

Colunga, L. A., "Jerusalén, la ciudad del Gran Rey. Exposición messiánica de algunos Salmos," *EstBib* 14 (1955), pp. 255-279. [Pss 46ff, 87, 122, 137]

Condamin, A., *Poèmes de la Bible* (Paris 1933).

Cooper, C. M., "The Revised Standard Version of Psalms," *JQR, Seventy-fifth Anniversary Volume* (Philadelphia 1967), pp. 137-148.

Coppens, J., "De torrente in via bibet (Ps 110:7), *ETL* 20 (1943), pp. 54-56.

Id., "Les parallèles du Psautier avec les textes de Ras Shamra," *Le Muséon* 59 (1946), pp. 113-142.

Id., "Trois parallèles ougaritiens du Psautier," *ETL* 23 (1947), pp. 173-177. [Pss 110:3, 6b; 82:7]

Id., "La portée messianique du Ps 110," *ETL* 32 (1956), pp. 5-23.

Id., *Het onsterfelijkheidsgeloof in het Psalmboek* (Brussel 1957). [Pss 16, 49, 73, including a summary, and a translation of these Pss in French]

Id., "Les psaumes des *ḥasidim*," *Mélanges bibliques* ... pp. 214-224. [cf. §12c]

Id., *Le Psautier et ses problèmes, Anal. Lovan.* 3, 19 (Louvain 1960).

Id., "Les Psaumes 6 et 41 dépendent-ils du livre de Jérémie?" *HUCA* 32 (1961), pp. 217-226.

Id., "Les études récentes sur le Psautier," *Le Psautier* [cf. R. De Langhe], pp. 1-71. [cf. §5e, 12cd]

Id., "Les Saints (*qedôšîm*) dans le Psautier," *ETL* 39 (1963), pp. 485-500.

Id., "La date des Psaumes de l'Intronisation et de la Royauté de Yahvé," *ETL* 43 (1967), pp. 192-197.

Couroyer, B., "L'arc d'airain," *RB* 72 (1965), pp. 508-514. [Ps 18:35]

Creager, H. L., "Note on Psalm 109," *JNES* 6 (1947), pp. 121-123.

Crim, K. R., *The Royal Psalms* (Richmond, Va. 1962).

Cross, F. M., "Notes on a Canaanite Psalm in the Old Testament (Ps 29)," *BASOR* 117 (1950), pp. 19-21.

Cross, F.M-Freedman, D. N., "A Royal Song of Thanksgiving: II Samuel 22 = Psalm 18a," *JBL* 72 (1953), pp. 15-34.

Culley, R. C., *Oral Formulaic Language in the Biblical Psalms* (Diss. Univ. of Toronto 1963), dact. [Obtainable from Ann Arbor, Univ. Microfilms: cf. *Biblica, elenchus*, 1967 n. 1805]

Dahood, M., *Psalms I* and *Psalms II* (The Anchor Bible, New York 1966 and 1968).

Id., "The root *GMR* in the Psalms," *TS* 14 (1953), pp. 595-597. [see on *Ps 51]

Id., "Philological Notes on the Psalms," *TS* 14 (1953), pp. 85-88.

Id., "The Divine Name '*ELI* in the Psalms," *TS* 14 (1953), pp. 452-57. [see on *Ps 51]

Id., "The Language and Date of Psalm 48," *CBQ* 16 (1954), pp. 15-19.

Id., "Enclitic *mem* and emphatic *lamedh* in Psalm 85," *Bib* 37 (1956), pp. 338-40.

Id., "Vocative *lamedh* in the Psalter," *VT* 16 (1966), pp. 299-311.

Id., "A New Metrical Pattern in Biblical Poetry," *CBQ* 29 (1967, pp. 574-79.

Daiches, S., *Studies in the Psalms* (Oxford 1930).

Id., "The Meaning of 'Sacrifices' in the Psalms," *Essays in Honour of the Very Rev Dr. J. H. Hertz* (London 1944), pp. 97-109.

Dalglish, E. R., *The Hebrew Penitential Psalms with Special Reference to Psalm 51* (New York 1951). [cf. §4e]

Id., *Psalm Fifty-One in the Light of Ancient Near Eastern Patternism* (Leiden 1962).

Daniélou, J., "Le Psaume 22 dans l'exégèse patristique," *ColBibLat* 13 (1959), pp. 189-211.

Davies, G. H., "The Ark in the Psalms," *Promise and Fulfilment. Essays presented to Prof. S. H. Hooke* (Edinburgh 1963), pp. 51-61. [cf. §13b]

Deaver, G. R., *An Exegetical Study of Psalm 24* (Dallas 1953).

De Boer, P. A. H., "Psalm CXXI:2," *VT* 16 (1966), pp. 287-292.

De Fraine, J., *L'aspect religieux de la royauté israélite* (Rome 1954).

Id., "Quel est le sens exact de la filiation divine dans Psaume 2:7?" *Bijdragen* 16 (1955), pp. 349-356.

Id., "Le démon du midi (Ps 91:6)," *Bib* 40 (1959), pp. 372-383.

Id., "*Entmythologisierung* dans les Psaumes," *Le Psautier* [cf. R. De Langhe], pp. 89-106.

Id., "Les nations païennes dans les Psaumes," *Studi G. Rinaldi* (Genova 1967), pp. 285-292.

Deissler, A., *Psalm 119 (118) und seine Theologie. Ein Beitrag zur Erforschung der anthologischen Stilgattung im Alten Testament* (München 1955). [cf. *VT* 1958, p. 441ff]

Id., "Der anthologische Charakter des Psalmes 33 (32)," *Mélanges Bibliques* ... pp. 225-233.

Id., "Der anthologische Charakter des Ps 48 (47)," *Sacra Pagina* I (Paris-Gembloux 1959), pp. 495-503.

Id., "Mensch und Schöpfung. Eine Auslegung des Ps 103 (104)," *Oberrheinisches Pastoralblatt* (Freiburg i.B), 61 (1960), pp. 15-22; 41-45.

Id., "Zur Datierung und Situierung der kosmischen Hymnen Pss 8, 19, 29," *Lex Tua Veritas, Fs. H. Junker* (Trier 1961), pp. 47-58.

Id., "Das lobpreisende Gottesvolk in den Psalmen," *Sentire Ecclesiam* ... *Fs. H. Rahner* (Freiburg 1961), pp. 17-49. [cf. §13e]

Id., *Die Psalmen* (Düsseldorf 1963ff). [cf. *ETL* 1965, p. 219f; also a French Edit]

Id., *Le livre des Psaumes.* 1-75 (Paris 1966).

De Langhe, R. (édit.), *Le Psautier. Ses origines, ses problèmes littéraires, son influence. Etudes présenteés aux XIIe Journées Bibliques* (Louvain 1962). [cf. J. Coppens, A. Descamps, J. De Fraine, A. Arens, E. Lipiński, P. Van den Berghe, A. Rose, J. Dupont, M. Baillet, M. Delcor]

Delcor, M., "Cinq nouveaux psaumes esséniens?" *RQum* I: 1 (1958), pp. 85-102.

Delekat, L., "Probleme der Psalmenüberschriften," *ZAW* 76 (1964), pp. 280-297. [cf. §4de]

Id., *Asylie und Schutzorakel am Zionheiligtum. Eine Untersuchung zu den Privatpsalmen* (Leiden 1967).

Del Páramo, S., "El fin de las parábolas de Cristo y el Salmo 77 (cf. Mt 13:10-17), *Sem. Bibl. Esp.* (Madrid 1954), pp. 341-364.

Id., "El género literario de los Salmos," *EstBib* 6 (1947), pp. 241-264; 450f.

De Pinto, B., "The Torah and the Psalms," *JBL* 86 (1967), pp. 154-174.

Dequeker, L., "Les *qedôšîm* du Psaume 89 à la lumière des croyances semitiques," *ETL* 39 (1963), pp. 469-484. [cf. §12d]

Descamps, A., "Pour un classement littéraire des Psaumes," *Mélanges bibliques . . .* pp. 187-196.

Id. "Les genres littéraires du Psautier; un état de la question," *Le Psautier* [cf. R. De Langhe], pp. 73-88.

Didier, M., "Le Psaume II dans l'Ancien Testament," *Rev. de Namur* 11 (1957), pp. 120-130.

Id., "Une lecture des psaumes du règne de Yahvé," *ibid.* 12 (1958), pp. 457-470.

Donner, H., "Ugaritismen in der Psalmenforschung," *ZAW* 79 (1967), pp. 322-350. [cf. §9d]

Drijvers, P., *The Psalms, their Structure and Meaning* (New York 1965).

Driver, G. R., "The Psalms in the Light of Babylonian Research," *The Psalmists* [cf. D. C. Simpson], pp. 109-176. [cf. §9b]

Id., "Textual and Linguistic Problems of the Book of Psalms," *Harv.Th.Rev.* 29 (1936), pp. 171-195.

Id., "Notes on the Psalms," *JTS* 43 (1942), pp. 149-160; 44 (1943), pp. 12-23.

Id., "The Resurrection of Marine and Terrestrial Creatures," *JSS* 7 (1962), pp. 12-22. [see on °Ps 104:24-30]

Id., "Psalm CX: its Form, Meaning, and Purpose," *Studies in the Bible presented to Prof. M. H. Segal* (Jerusalem 1964), pp. 17-31.

Duesberg, H., "Le miroir du fidèle: le Psaume 119 (118) et ses usages liturgiques," *BiViChr* 15 (1956), pp. 87-97.

Id., *Le psautier des malades* (Maredsous 1952).

Duhm, B., *Die Psalmen* (Tübingen 1899 and 1922).

Duplacy, J., "La lecture juive du Psaume 8," *BiViChr* 16 (1956), pp. 87-95.

Dupont, J., "Filius meus es tu. L'interprétation de Ps 2-7 dans le Nouveau Testament," *RSR* 35 (1948), pp. 522-543.

Id., "L'interprétation des Psaumes dans les Actes des Apôtres." *Le Psautier* [cf. R. De Langhe], pp. 357-388.

Dürr, L., "Zur Datierung von Ps 4," *Bib* 16 (1935), pp. 330-338.

Eaton, J., "Problems of Translation in Ps 23:3f," *BiTrans* 16 (1965), pp. 171-176.

Eaton, J. H., *Psalms. Introduction and Commentary.* Torch Bible Comm. (London 1967).

Ebel, B., "Das Bild des Guten Hirten im 22. Psalm nach Erklärungen der Kirchenväter," *Fs. A. Stohr,* I (Mainz 1960), pp. 48-57.

Eerdmans, B. D., *OTS* IV (Leiden 1947).

Id., "Essays on Masoretic Psalms," *OTS* I (Leiden 1942), pp. 105-296: "On the Road to Monotheism"; "Foreign Elements in pre-exilic Israel"; "The Songs of Ascents"; "Thora-Songs and Temple-Singers in the pre-exilic period"; "The Chasidim"; "Psalm XIV-LIII and the Elohim-psalms"; "Psalms XL, XLI, LV, LXVIII." [cf. §12c + °Pss 41, 118]

Ehrman, A., "What did Cain say to Abel?" *JQR* 53 (1962f), pp. 164-167. [cf. °Ps 4:5]

Eichrodt, W., *Theology of the Old Testament,* I (London 1961). [cf. °Ps 99]

Eissfeldt, O., "Psalm 80," *Geschichte und Altes Testament. Fs. A. Alt* (Tübingen 1953), pp. 65-78.

Id., "Psalm 76," *TLZ* 82 (1957), pp. 801-808.

Id., *Baal Zaphon, Zeus Kasios und der Durchzug der Israeliten durchs Meer* (Halle 1932).

Id., "Psalm 121," *Stat Crux, dum volvitur orbis. Fs. H. Lilje* (Berlin 1959), pp. 9-14. [also in *Kleine Schriften* III, pp. 494-500]

Id., "Mein Gott' im Alten Testament," *ZAW* 61 (1945-48), pp. 3-16. [in the Pss: pp. 10-16]

Id., "Jahwes Verhältnis zu 'Eljon und Schaddaj nach Psalm 91," *Die Welt des Orients,* II (1954-59), pp. 343-348.

Id., "Psalm 132," *ibid.,* pp. 480-484.

Id., "Ein Psalm aus Nord-Israel," *Z.d. Deutschen Morg. G.* 112 (1962), pp. 259-268. [cf. *ibid.* 115, 1965, pp. 14-22 = Mi 7:7-20]

Id., *Das Lied Moses Deut. 32:1-43 und das Lehrgedicht Asaphs Psalm 78 . . .* (Berlin 1958).

Elbogen, I., *Der judische Gottesdienst in seiner geschichtlichen Entwicklung* (Leipzig 1913).

Emerton, J. A., "Melchizedek and the Gods: Fresh Evidence for the Jewish Background of John X:34-36," *JTS* 17 (1966), p. 399ff. [concerns also Ps 82; cf. *ibid.* 11 (1960), pp. 329-332]

Id., "Spring and Torrent' in Psalm LXXIV:15," *Volume du Congrès, Genève 1965,* VTSuppl XV (Leiden 1966), pp. 122-133. [cf. §14d]

Emmanuel, *Commentaire juif des Psaumes* (Paris 1963). [cf. *RBiblt* 1964, p. 435f]

Enciso, J., "El salmo 67 (68)," *EstBib* 11 (1952), pp. 127-155.

Id., "Indicaciones musicales en los titulos de los Salmos," *Misc. Bibl. B. Ubach* (Montserrat, 1953), pp. 185-200.

Id., "Los titulos de los Salmos y la historia de la formación del Salterio," *EstBib* 13 (1954), pp. 135-166.

Id., "El Salmo 9-10," *EstBib* 19 (1960), pp. 201-214.

Id., "Los Salmos-prólogos," *EstE* 34 (1960), pp. 621-631.

346   THE PSALMS: *Their Origin and Meaning*

Id., "Como se formó la primera parte del libro de los Salmos," *Bib* 44 (1963), pp. 129-158. [cf. §4a + *Pss 2, 119, 137]

Engnell, I., *Studies in Divine Kingship in the Ancient Near East* (Uppsala, 1943 and 1967).

Id., "Planted by the Streams of Water'. Some remarks on the Problems of Interpretation of the Psalms, as illustrated by a detail in Psalm 1," *Studia Orient. Io. Pedersen* (Hauniae 1953), pp. 85-96. [cf. §8d]

Eybers, I. H., "The Stem S-P-T in the Psalms," *Studies on the Psalms*, pp. 58-63.

Falkenstein, A. and W. von Soden, *Sumerische und Akkadische Hymnen und Gebete* (Zurich-Stuttgart 1953).

Farndale, W. E., *The Psalms in new Light* (London 1956).

Feinberg, C. L., "Old-Hundreth-Psalm C," *Bibl. Sacra* 103 (1946), pp. 53-66.

Id., "Parallels to the Psalms in Near Eastern Literature," *Bibl. Sacra* 104 (1947), pp. 290-297.

Id., "Are there Maccabean Psalms in the Psalter?" *Bibl. Sacra* 105 (1948), pp. 44-55.

Id., "The Uses of the Psalter," *Bibl. Sacra* 105 (1948), pp. 154-169. [cf. §8f]

Fensham, F. C., "Ps 68:23 in the Light of recently discovered Ugaritic Tablets," *JNES* 19 (1960), p. 292f.

Id., "Widow, Orphan, and the Poor in Ancient Near Eastern Legal and Wisdom Literature," *JNES* 21 (1962), pp. 129-139.

Id., "Psalm 29 and Ugarit," *Studies on the Psalms*, pp. 84-99.

Id., "Psalm 21 - A Covenant Song?" *ZAW* 77 (1965), pp. 193-205.

Feuillet, A., "Le verset 7 du *Miserere* et le péché originel," *RSR* (1944), pp. 5-26.

Id., "Souffrance et confiance en Dieu. Commentaire du Psaume XXII," *NRT* 70 (1948), pp. 137-149.

Id., "Les psaumes eschatologiques du règne de Yahweh," *NRT* 83 (1951), pp. 244-260; 352-363.

Fichtner, J., "Vom Psalmenbeten. Ist das Beten aller Psalmen der christlichen Gemeinde möglich und heilsam?" *Wort und Dienst* 3 (1952), pp. 38-80.

Finkelstein, L., "The Origin of the Hallel (Pss 113-118)," *HUCA* 23, 2 (1950f), pp. 319-337.

Fischer, B., *Die Psalmenfrömmigkeit der Märtyrerkirche* (Freiburg 1949). [also: *La Maison-Dieu* 27 (1951), pp. 86-113]

Id., "Der Psalm *Qui habitat* in der *Quadragesima*," *ZfKatTh* 80 (1958), pp. 421-429. [Pss 90-91]

Fisher, L. R., "Betrayed by Friends. An Expository Study of Psalm 22," *Interpr* 18 (1964), pp. 20-38.

Fitzmyer, J. A., *The Aramaic Inscriptions of Sefire.* Biblica et Orientalia, 19 (Rome 1967). [cf. *Ps 126:1]

Flashar, M., "Exegetische Studien zum Septuagintapsalter," *ZAW* 32 (1912), pp. 81-116; 161-189; 241-268.

Forrester, W. F., "Sin and Repentance in the Psalms," *Clergy Rev.* 41 (1956), pp. 663-674. [cf. §12e]

Franken, H. J., *The Mystical Communion with JHWH in the Book of Psalms*

(Leiden 1954). [includes a general study and a special analysis of Pss 16, 18, 25, 27, 31, 36, 63; cf. §12f]

Frethsim, T. W., "Psalm 132: a Form-Critical Study," *JBL* 86 (1967), pp. 289-300.

Frost, S. B., "The Christian Interpretation of the Psalms," *CanJT* 5 (1959), pp. 25-34.

Id., "Psalm 118: an Exposition," *CanJT* 7 (1961), pp. 155-166.

Id., "Psalm 22: an Exposition," *CanJT* 8 (1962), pp. 102-115.

Füglister, N., *Das Psalmengebet* (München 1965). [cf. *VD* 1966, p. 110]

Galdos, R., "La estrófica de los Salmos y su utilidad en la critica textual y en la exégesis," *EstBib* 5 (1946), pp. 215-230.

Galling, K., "Der Beichtspiegel. Eine gattungsgeschichtliche Studie," *ZAW* 47 (1929), pp. 125-130.

Garcia Cordero, M., *Libros de los Salmos*, I (BAC, Madrid 1963).

Garrone, G., *How to pray the Psalms* (Notre-Dame, Ind. 1965).

Gasnier, M., *Les Psaumes, école de spiritualité* (Mulhouse 1957).

Gaster, T. H., "Psalm 29," *JQR* 37 (1946f), pp. 55-65.

Id., *Thespis, Ritual, Myth and Drama in the Ancient Near-East* (New York 1950). [cf. §8a]

Id., "Psalm 45," *JBL* 74 (1955), pp. 239-251.

Gelin, A., "Les quatre lectures du Psaume 22," *BiViChr* 1 (1953), pp. 31-39.

Id., "La prière du pèlerin au temple (Ps 84)," *BiViChr* 11 (1955), pp. 88-92.

Id., *L'âme d'Israël dans le Livre* (Paris 1958), pp. 46-68.

Id., "La question des 'relectures' bibliques a l'intérieur d'une tradition vivante," *Sacra Pagina* I, pp. 203-215. [Ps 47; Ps 22 and Is 53; Zach 3:9; Ps 78; Ps 110:3 *LXX*]

Id., *The Psalms are our Prayers* (Collegeville, Minn.).

Gelineau, J., "Marie dans la prière chrétienne des Psaumes," *Maison-Dieu*, 38 (1954), p. 56ff.

Gelli, M., "Il Salmo del sacerdozio di Cristo (109/110)," *Ambrosius* 39 (1963), pp. 197-212.

Gelston, A., "A Note on *Yhwh mlk*," *VT* 16 (1966), pp. 507-512.

Gemser, B., "Gesinnungsethik im Psalter," *OTS* 13 (Leiden 1963), pp. 1-20. [thought-morality in the Psalter]

George, A., "Jésus et les Psaumes," *A la rencontre* ... pp. 297-308.

Id., *Praying the Psalms. A guide for using the Psalms as Christian Prayer* (Notre-Dame, Indiana 1964).

Gese, H., "Zur Geschichte der Kultsänger am zweiten Tempel," *Fs. O. Michel* (1963), pp. 222-234. On Ps 22 see Id. in *ZTK* 1968, pp. 1-22.

Giavini, G., "La struttura letteraria del Salmo 86 (85)," *RBiblt* 14 (1966), pp. 455-458.

Giblet, J., "Les Psaumes et la prière d'Israël," *ColMech* 42 (1957), pp. 512-520.

Gierlich, A. M., *Der Lichtgedanke in den Psalmen. Eine terminologisch-exegetische Studie* (Freiburg i. Br. 1940).

Ginsberg, H. L., "A Phoenician Hymn in the Psalter," *Atti del XIX Congresso Internazionale degli Orientalisti* (Roma 1935), pp. 472-476. [Ps 29]

Id., "Psalms and Inscriptions of Petition and Acknowledgement," *L. Ginzberg Jubilee Volume* (New York 1945), pp. 159-171. [cf. §4b]

Id., "Some Emendations in the Psalms," *HUCA* 23, 1 (1950f), pp. 97-104.

Glombitza, O., "Betende Bewältigung der Gottesleugnung. Versuch einer existentialen Interpretation der drei Psalmen 59; 94; 137," *NedTTs* 14 (1959f), pp. 329-349.

Glueck, J. J., "Some Remarks on the Introductory Notes of the Psalms," *Studies on the Psalms,* pp. 30-39.

Goitein, S. D., "Ma'on - a Reminder of Sin" *JSS* 10 (1965), p. 52f.

Goldstain, J., *Le monde des Psaumes* (Paris 1964).

Gomes, M., *Salmo 18 (17). Unità, genere letterario e carattere messianico* (Romae 1956).

González, A., "El Salmo 75 y el Juicio escatológico," *EstBib* 21 (1962), pp. 5-22.

Id., "Le Psaume 82," *VT* 13 (1963), pp. 293-309.

Id., *El Libro de los Salmos. Introducción, versión y comentario* (Barcelona 1966).

González, Ruiz J. M., "Las teofanias en los Salmos," *EstBib* 13 (1954), pp. 267-287.

Goodwin, D. W., "A rare spelling, or a rare root, in Ps. LXVIII:10?" *VT* 14 (1964), p. 490f.

Gordis, R., "Psalm 9/10 — A textual and exegetical Study," *JQR* 48 (1957f), pp. 104-122.

Gordon, C. H., *Ugaritic Textbook* (Roma 1965). [cf. §9d]

Gössmann, W. E., "Der Wandel des Gottesbildes in den Übersetzungen des 23. Psalms," *Münchener Theol.Z.* 5 (1954), pp. 276-288. [the varying translations of Ps 23 reflect human ways of understanding God]

Goy, W. A., "Dieu a-t-il changé? Psaume 77," *Maqqél shâqédh . . . W. Vischer* (Montpellier 1960), pp. 56-62.

Grail Breviary Psalter. The Daily Psalms, Canticles and Antiphons in Modern English (London 1966).

Gray, G. B., "The References to the 'King' in the Psalter, in their Bearing on Questions of Date and Messianic Beliefs," *JQR* 7 (1894), p. 658ff.

Gray, J., "The Kingship of God in the Prophets and Psalms," *VT* 11 (1961), pp. 1-29.

Grelot, P., "*Hofši* (Ps LXXXVIII)," *VT* 14 (1964), pp. 256-263.

Gressmann, H., "The Development of Hebrew Psalmody," *The Psalmists* [cf. D. C. Simpson], pp. 1-22. [cf. §5c]

Grosmann, W., *Poetic Devices in the Book of Psalms* (New York 1954). [cf. *JBL* 1956, p. 160]

Gross, H., "Lässt sich in den Psalmen ein 'Thronbesteigungsfest Gottes' nachweisen?" *TrierTZ* 65 (1956), pp. 24-40. [cf. §13a]

Gruenthaner, M., "The Future Life in the Psalms," *CBQ* 2 (1940), pp. 57-63.

Gualandi, D., "Salmo 17 (16):13-14," *Bib* 37 (1956), pp. 199-208.

Id., "Salmo 29 (28)," *Bib* 39 (1958), pp. 478-485. [also *RBiblt* 1958, pp. 210-223: Pss 68, 141]

Guichou, P., *Les Psaumes commentés par la Bible,* I-III (Paris 1958f).

Id., "La prière de pèlerinage dans la Bible," *Rev. de Namur* 18 (1964), pp. 347-368.

Guilding, A., "Some Obscured Rubrics and Lectionary Allusions in the Psalter," *JTS* 3 (1952), pp. 41-55. [Pss 49:14b; 81:6; 32:6b; 110]

Id., "The Arrangement of the Pentateuch and Psalter," *The Fourth Gospel and Jewish Worship* (Oxford 1960), pp. 24-44. [cf. §8c]

Guillaume, A., "The Meaning of *tôlēl* in Psalm 137:3," *JBL* 75 (1956), p. 143f.

Id., *Prophecy and Divination among the Hebrews and other Semites* (London 1938), pp. 272-289.

Guillet, J., "L'entrée du juste dans la Glorie," *BiViChr* 9 (1955), pp. 58-70. [Ps 73:24]

Gunkel, R., *Schöpfung und Chaos in Urzeit und Endzeit* (Göttingen 1895).

Id., *Ausgewählte Psalmen* (4th ed.: Göttingen 1917).

Id., *Die Psalmen* (Göttingen 1926).

Id., "The Religion of the Psalms," in *What remains of the Old Testament and other essays*, transl. by A. K. Dallas (London 1938), pp. 69-114.

Gunkel, H. and J. Begrich, *Einleitung in die Psalmen. Die Gattungen der religiösen Lyrik Israels* (Göttingen 1933). [cf. §7a]

Gunn, G. S., *God in the Psalms* (Edinburgh 1956). [cf. §11b]

Guthrie, H. H., Jr., *Israel's Sacred Songs: a Study of Dominant Themes* (New York 1966). [cf. *CBQ* 1966, p. 505f]

Hall, B., "The Problem of Retribution in the Psalms," *Script.* 7 (1955), pp. 84-92.

Haller, M., "Ein Jahrzehnt Psalmforschung," *Theol. Rundschau* 1 (1929), pp. 377-402.

Hanel, A., *Die Erlösergestalt in ausgewählten Psalmen* (Wien 1962). [typescript]

Haran, M., "The Ark and the Cherubim: their Symbolic Significance in Biblical Ritual," *IEJ* 9 (1959), pp. 30-38; 89-94.

Hardy, E. R., "The date of Psalm 110," *JBL* 64 (1945), pp. 385-390.

Häring, P., "Gross ist der Herr in unserer Gottesstadt: Ps 47 (48)," *Erbe und Auftrag* 36 (1960), pp. 94-104.

Harvey, J., "La typologie de l'Exode dans les Psaumes," *ScEcc* 15 (1963), pp. 383-405. [cf. §5e, 14a]

Haspecker, J., "Ascendit Deus in jubilatione (Ps 46-47) und Himmelfahrt Christi," *GeistLeb* 28 (1955), pp. 87-95.

Hauret, C., "L'interprétation des Psaumes selon l'école Myth and Ritual," *Rev. Sc. Rel.* 33 (1959), pp. 321-346; 34 (1960), pp. 1-34.

Id., "Un problème insoluble? La chronologie des psaumes," *RSR* 35 (1961), pp. 225-256. [good survey of various opinions and methods in Psalm Chronology]

Id., *Notre Psautier* (Paris 1964).

Id., "Les ennemis-sorciers dans les supplications individuelles," *RechBib* 8 (Bruges-Paris 1967), pp. 129-137.

Id., "Les Psaumes, études recentes état de la question," in *Oú en sont les études bibliques?* (Paris 1968), pp. 67-84.

Heinemann, H., "The date of Psalm 80," *JQR* 40 (1949), pp. 297-302.

Hempel, J., "Mensch und König, Studie zu Psalm 8 und Hiob," *Forschungen und*

Fortschritte 35 (1961), pp. 119-123.

Herder's Commentary on the Psalms (Westminster, Md. 1961).

Hermission, H.-J., *Sprache und Ritus im altisraelitischen Kult. Zur "Spiritualisierung" der Kultbegriffe im Alten Testament* (Neukirchen-Vluyn 1965).

Herrmann, J., "Der 103. Psalm: Dienst unter dem Wort," *Festgabe . . . H. Schreiner* (Gütersloh (1953), pp. 82-93.

Hesse, F., "Zur Frage der Wertung und der Geltung alttestamentlicher Texte Ps 109)," *Fs. F. Baumgärtel* (Erlangen 1959), pp. 74-96.

Hjelt, A., "Sjukdomslidandet och fienderna i psalmerna," *Buhlfestskrift*, pp. 64-74. [cf. §12g]

Hofbauer, J., "Psalm 88 (89). Sein Aufbau, seine Herkunft und seine Stellung in der Theologie des AT," *Sacra Pagina* I, pp. 504-510.

The Holy Bible (CV), III: *The Sapiential Books* (New Jersey 1955). [cf. Foreword]

Hooke, S. H. (edit.), *Myth and Ritual. Essays on the Myth and Ritual of the Hebrews in Relation to the Cultic Pattern of the Ancient East* (Oxford 1933). [cf. §8d]

Id., (edit.), *The Labyrinth. Further Studies in the Relation between Myth and Ritual in the Ancient World* (London 1935).

Id., (edit.), *Myth, Ritual and Kingship. Essays on the Theory and Practice of Kingship in the Ancient Near East and in Israel* (Oxford 1958).

Hunt, I., "Recent Psalm Study," *Worship* 41 (1957), pp. 85-98.

Hyatt, C. M., *The Doctrine of Salvation in the Book of Psalms* (Fort Worth, Tex. 1952).

The Interpreter's Bible, IV, "Psalms, Proverbs" (New York 1955).

Iwry, S., "Notes on Psalm 68," *JBL* 71 (1952), pp. 161-165.

Jacob, E., *Theology of the Old Testament* (London 1958). [cf. §11a]

James, F., *Thirty Psalmists: Personalities of the Psalter* (New York 1965).

Jänicke, H., "Futurum exactum. Eine Bibelarbeit über Ps 13 . . ." *Evang. Theol.* 11 (1951f), pp. 471-478.

Jasper, F. N., "Early Israelite traditions and the Psalter," *VT* 17 (1967), pp. 50-59. [cf. §30]

Jefferson, H. G., "Psalm 93," *JBL* 71 (1952), pp. 155-160.

Id., "Is Psalm 110 Canaanite?," *JBL* 73 (1954), pp. 152-156.

Id., "Canaanite Literature and the Psalms," *The Personalist* 39, 4 (1958), pp. 356-360.

Id., "The Date of Psalm LXVII," *VT* 12 (1962), pp. 201-205.

Id., "Psalm LXXVII," *VT* 13 (1963), pp. 87-91.

Jellicoe, S., "A Note on 'al mût (Ps 48:15)," *JTS* 49 (1949), p. 52f.

Id., "The Interpretation of Ps 73:24," *ExpTim* 67 (1955f), p. 209f.

Jeremias, Jörg, *Theophanie. Die Geschichte einer alttestamenlichen Gattung* (Neukirchen-Vluyn 1965). [cf. §13d, 14b]

Jiménez Gómez, H., "Los Géneros Literarios en los Salmos," *Seminario Conciliar* 6 (1961), pp. 9-25.

Bibliography 351

Jirku, A., "Die Sprache der Gottheit in der Natur," *TLZ* 76 (1951), p. 631.
Johnson, A. R., *The Cultic Prophet in Ancient Israel* (Cardiff 1944 and 1962). [cf. §8d]
Id., "The Psalms," *The Old Testament and modern Study* (H. H. Rowley, edit., Oxford 1951), pp. 162-209.
Id., *Sacral Kingship in Ancient Israel* (Cardiff 1955).
Jones, G. H., "The decrees of Yahweh (Ps 2:7)," *VT* 15 (1965), pp. 336-344.
Junker, H., "Unité, composition et genre littéraire des Psaumes IX et X," *RB* 60 (1953), pp. 161-169.
Id., "Die Entstehungszeit des Ps. 78 und des Deuteronomiums," *Bib* 34 (1953), pp. 487-500.
Id., "Der Strom, dessen Arme die Stadt Gottes erfreuen (Ps 46:5)," *Bib* 43 (1962), pp. 197-201.
Id., "Salmos imprecatorios," *EncBib* VI (Barcelona 1965) p. 367ff.
Id., "Das theologische Problem der Fluchpsalmen," *Pastor Bonus* 5 (1940), pp. 65-74.

Kaiser, O., "Erwägungen zu Psalm 101," *ZAW* 74 (1962), pp. 195-205.
Kapelrud, A. S., "Nochmals *Jahwä mālāk*," *VT* 13 (1963), p. 229ff.
Id., "Scandinavian Research in the Psalms after Mowinckel," *Ann. Sw. Th. Inst.* 4 (1965), pp. 148-162.
Kasser, R. (ed.), *Papyrus Bodmer XXIV: Psaumes 17-118* (Cologny-Genève 1967).
Kaznowski, Z., "Autor Ps 110 (109)," *Roczniki Teologiczno-Kanoniczne* (Lublin), 7, 3 (1960), pp. 50-70.
Keel, O., *Die Schilderung der Feinde in den individuellen Klage-und Lobpsalmen* (Diss. Freiburg, Schw. 1967).
Keet, C. C., *A Liturgical Study of the Psalter* (London 1928).
King, E. G., "The Influence of the Triennial Cycle upon the Psalter," *JTS* 5 (1904), pp. 203-213. [cf. I. Abrahams]
King, P. J., *A Study of Psalm 45 (44)*, (Romae 1959).
Kirkpatrick, A. F., *The Book of the Psalms* I-III (Cambridge 1892-1903).
Kissane, E. J., *The Book of Psalms. Translated from a critically revised Hebrew Text with a Commentary* I, Ps 1-72 (Dublin 1953); II, Ps 73-150 (Dublin 1955).
Kleber, A., "Psalm 2, 9 in the Light of an Ancient Ceremony," *CBQ* 5 (1943), pp. 63-67.
Kleist, J. A., "Toward a more rhythmical Rendering of the Psalms," *CBQ* 11 (1949), pp. 66-75.
Knox, R., *The Psalms. A New Translation* (London 1947).
Koch, K., "Denn seine Güte währet ewiglich," *Evang. Theol.* 21 (1961), pp. 537-544. [Pss 100, 106, 107, 118, 136]
Id., "Tempeleinlassliturgien und Dekaloge," *Studien zur Theologie der Altest. Uberlieferungen. Fs. G. von Rad* (Neukirchen 1961), pp. 45-60. [Pss 15 + 24:4ff; Is 33:14ff; Mi 6:6ff; Ez 18:5ff; cf. §32]
Koehler, L., "Jahwäh mālāk," *VT* 3 (1953), p. 188f. [cf. Ps 93:1]
Id., "Psalm 23," *ZAW* 68 (1956), pp. 227-234.

König, E., *Die Psalmen eingeleitet, übersetzt und erklärt* (Gütersloh 1927).

Konus, W. J., *Dictionary of the New Latin Psalter of Pope Pius XII* (Westminster, Md. 1959).

Koole, J. L., "Psalm 15 - eine königliche Einzugsliturgie?" *OTS* 13 (1963), pp. 98-111.

Id., Psalmen (Neukirchen 1961). [cf. *RB* 1961, pp. 127-134]

Kraus, H.-J., Worship in Israel, tr. by G. Buswell (Oxford 1966). [cf. §7b, 13b]

Id., "Quelques remarques sur Psaume 139," *Studia biblica et semitica*: Fs. T. C. Vriezen (Vageningen 1.966), pp. 176-180.

Krinetzki, L., "Zur Poetik und Exegese von Psalm 48," *BZ* 4 (1960), pp. 70-97.

Id., "Psalm 110 (109). Eine Untersuchung seines dichterischen Stils," *Theol. Blätter* 51 (1961), pp. 110-121.

Id., "Psalm 30 (29) in stilistisch-exegetischer Betrachtung," *ZKatTh* 83 (1961), pp. 345-360.

Id., "Der anthologische Stil des 46. Psalms und seine Bedeutung für die Datierungsfrage," *MüTZ* 12 (1961), pp. 52-71.

Id., "Psalm 5. Eine Untersuchung seiner dichterischen Struktur und seines theologischen Gehaltes," *Tüb. Th. Qu.* 142 (1962), pp. 23-46.

Id., "Jahwe ist uns Zuflucht und Wehr. Eine stilistisch-theologische Auslegung von Ps 46 (45)," *BiLeb* 3 (1962), pp. 26-42.

Krings, H., *Der Mensch vor Gott. Die Daseinserfahrung in den Psalmen* (Würzburg 1952).

Kroeze, J. H., "Some remarks on recent trends in the exegesis of the Psalms," *Studies on the Psalms* . . . pp. 40-47.

Kruse, H., "Fluminis impetus laetificat Civitatem Dei (Ps 45-46:5)" *VD* 27 (1949), pp. 23-27.

Id., "Two hidden comparatives: Observations on Hebrew Style," *JSS* 5 (1960), pp. 333-347.

Id., "Archetypus Psalmi 104 (103)," *VD* 29 (1951), pp. 31-43.

Küchler, F., "Das priesterliche Orakel in Israel und Juda," *Fs. W. G. von Baudissin*, *BZAW* 33 (1918), pp. 285-301.

Kühlewein, J., *Das Reden von Geschichte in den Psalmen* (Diss. Heidelberg 1966).

Kuntz, J. K., *An Examination of Theophany in the Old Testament, with special reference to Theophanic contexts in the Psalter* (New York 1963). [microfilm]

Kunz, L., "Die formale Anklage des 95. Psalmes," *MüTZ* 4 (1953), pp. 349-356.

Id., "Die Gestalt des 84. Psalmes," *TGl* 45 (1955), pp. 22-34.

Id., "Selah, Titel und authentische Gliederung der Psalmen," *TGl* 46 (1956), pp. 363-369. [Ps 84]

Id., "Zur symmetrischen Struktur der Psalmen," *Misc. H. Anglés* I (Barcelona 1958-1961), pp. 453-464.

Id., "Zur Liedgestalt der ersten fünf Psalmen," *BZ* 7 (1963), pp. 261-270.

Labuschagne, C. J., "Some remarks on the Translation and Meaning of *'āmarti* in the Psalms," *OTW* 5 (1962), pp. 27-33. [cf. *Studies on the Psalms*]

Lacan, M. F., "Le mystère de la prière dans le Psaume 119," *Lumière et Vie* 23 (1955), pp. 125-142 [677-694].

Id., "Les Psaumes, prière de l'Église," *Vie Spir.* 112 (1965), pp. 519-530.

Lamb, J. A., *The Psalms in Christian Worship* (London 1962). [history of the Liturgical Use of the Psalms]

Lambert, W. G., "Three Literary Prayers of the Babylonians," *Archiv. f. Orientforschung* 19 (1959-60), pp. 47-66.

Lamparter, H., *Das Buch der Psalmen übersetzt und ausgelegt,* I-II (Stuttgart 1958f).

Id., *Das Psalmengebet in der Christengemeinde. Eine Einführung in das Gebetbuch der Bibel* (Stuttgart 1965).

Laridon, V., "Psalmorum doctrina de retributione," *Col. Brug.* 44 (1948), pp. 283-287.

Lattey, C., *The Psalter in the Westminster Version of the Sacred Scriptures* London 1945). [seeks to reconstruct the original metre: cf. §6]

Lauha, A., *Die Geschichtsmotive in den alttestamentlichen Psalmen. Acta Acad. Scient. Fennicae,* 56, 1 (1945).

Le Mat, L. A. F., *Textual Criticism and Exegesis of Psalm XXXVI. A Contribution to the Study of the Hebrew Book of Psalms* (Utrecht 1957). [also treats of the "titles" of the psalms and of the "evildoers"]

Leslie, E. A., *The Psalms. Translated and Interpreted in the Light of Hebrew Life and Worship* (New York 1949). [cf. *JBL* 1950, p. 184ff]

Leveen, J., "Psalm 10 (Vulg. 9:II): a Reconstruction," *JTS* 45 (1944), pp. 16-21.

Id., "A Note on Ps 10:17-18," *JBL* 67 (1948), p. 249f.

Id., "The textual problems of Psalm 17," *VT* 11 (1961), pp. 48-54.

Id., "The textual problems of Psalm VII," *VT* 16 (1966), pp. 439-445.

Liber Psalmorum cum Canticis Breviarii Romani, nova e textibus primigeniis interpretatio latina cum notis criticis et exegeticis cura Professorum Pontificii Instituti Biblici edita (Romae 1945). [cf. Foreword and A. Bea, J. Bloch, B. Steiert, T. E. Bird, J. C. M. Travers]

Liebreich, L. J., "The Songs of Ascents and the Priestly Blessing," *JBL* 74 (1955), pp. 33-36. [cf. §3c]

Id., "Pss 34 and 145 in the Light of their Key-Words," *HUCA* 27 (1956), pp. 181-192.

Id., "The Liturgical Use of Ps 78:38," *Studies A. A. Neumann* (Leiden 1962), pp. 365-374.

Lilly, J. L., "The Sacred Duty of Hating and Imprecating," *AmER* 115 (1946), pp. 271-277.

Lindblom, J., "Die Eschatologie des 49. Psalms," *Horae Soederblomianae,* I (1944), pp. 21-27.

Linton, O., "Interpretation of the Psalms in the Early Church," *SPatrist* 4 (Berlin 1961), pp. 143-156.

Lipiński, E., "Les Psaumes de la royauté de Yahvé dans l'exégèse moderne," *Le Psautier* [cf. R. De Langhe], pp. 133-272.

Id., "Yahweh mâlāk," *Bib* 44 (1963), pp. 405-460.

Id., "Les Psaumes du Règne: l'Intronisation royale de Dieu," *AssSeign* 9 (1964), pp. 7-22.

Id., *La royauté de Yahvé dans la poési et le culte de l'ancien Israël* (Bruxelles

1965). [cf. *JBL* 1966, p. 498f; *RB* 1966, pp. 420-25 and §18]

Id., "Juges 5:4-5 et Psaume 68:8-11," *Bib* 48 (1967), pp. 185-206.

Id., *Le poème royal du Psaume LXXXIX, 1-5. 20-38* (Paris 1967). [cf. *VD* 1967 pp. 366f.]

Lohfink, N., "Herausgeführt in der Freiheit," *GeistLeb* 38 (1965), pp. 81-84. [Ps 66:1-12]

Louis, C., *The Theology of Psalm VIII. A Study of the Traditions of the Text and the Theologcial Import* (Washington 1946). [the psalm is messianic, but not in the strict sense]

Lovitt, H. B., *A Critical and Exegetical Study of Ps 139* (Diss. Columbia Univ., N.Y. 1964. Ann Arbor 1964, Univ. Microfilms).

Lowth, R., *De sacra poësi Hebraeorum praelectiones academicae Oxonii habitae* (Oxford 1753).

Lubsczyk, H., "Einheit und heilsgeschichtliche Bedeutung von Ps 114/115 (113)," *BZ* 11 (1967), pp. 161-173.

Luger, A., *Der Messianismus der Psalmen* (Wien 1959). [typescript]

Lussier, A., "The New Latin Psalter: an exegetical Commentary," *CBQ* 9 (1947) to 12 (1950): a series of articles on Pss 1 to 33.

Luyten, J., "Het Zelfbeklag in de Psalmen," *ETL* 39 (1963), pp. 501-538.

Lyonnet, S., "La notion de justice de Dieu en Rom III:5 et l'exégèse paulinienne du Miserere," *Sacra Pagina* II, pp. 342-356.

MacKenzie, R. A. F., *The Book of Psalms*. O. T. Reading Guide, 23 (Collegeville 1967). [a selection]

Maertens, T., *Jérusalem, Cité de Dieu* (*Pss 120-128*), 2nd edit. (Bruges 1954).

Id., "La catéchèse des Psaumes," *Par. Lit.* 40 (1958), pp. 257-294.

Maggioni, B., "Osservazioni sul Salmo 29 (28): Afferte Domino," *BibOr* 7 (1965), pp. 245-251.

Magne, J., "Le texte du Psaume XXXV et l'hypothèse de sa transcription primitive sur deux colonnes," *RB* 54 (1947), pp. 42-53.

Id., "Répétitions de mots et exégèse dans quelques Psaumes et le Pater," *Bib* 39 (1958), pp. 177-197. [Pss 1, 29, 51, 91, 123, 137]

Id., "Le texte du Psaume XXII et sa restitution sur deux colonnes," *Sem* 11 (1961), pp. 29-41.

Maier, J., *Das altisraelitische Ladeheiligtum*, BZAW 93 (Berlin 1965).

Maillot, A.-A. Lelièvre, Les Psaumes, vols. I-II (Genève 1962 and 1966). [Pss 1-100]

Mand, F., "Die Eigenständigkeit der Danklieder des Psalters als Bekenntnislieder," *ZAW* 70 (1958), pp. 185-199.

Mannati, E. & E. de Solms, *Les Psaumes*, I-IV (Bruges 1966-68).

Martin-Achard, R., "La prière d'un malade: quelques remarques sur le Psaume 38," *Verbum Caro* 12 (1958), pp. 77-82.

Id., "Notes bibliques: Remarques sur le Psaume 22," *VerbC* 17 (1963), pp. 78-87.

Id., "La prière des malades dans le psautier," *Lumiere et Vie* 86 (1958), pp. 25-43.

Martindale, C. C., *Towards Loving the Psalms* (New York 1940).

May, H. G., "Some cosmic Connotations of *mayim rabbim*, many waters," *JBL* 74 (1955), pp. 9-21.

Mayer, H. H., *The Modern Reader's Book of Psalms* (New York 1944).

McClellan, W. H., "Obscurities in the Latin Psalter," *CBQ* 1 (1939) to 6 (1944): a series of articles.

McKeating, H., "Divine Forgiveness in the Psalms," *ScotJT* 18 (1965), pp. 69-83.

McKenzie, J. L., "A Note on Ps 73 (74):13-15," *TS* 11 (1950), pp. 275-282.

Id., "Royal Messianism," *CBQ* 19 (1957), pp. 25-52.

Id., "The Imprecations of the Psalter," *AmER* 111 (1944), pp. 81-96.

McNeill, J., *The Twenty-Third Psalm* (Westwood, N.J. 1965).

Meek, T. J., "The Metrical Structure of Psalm 23," *JBL* 67 (1948), pp. 233-235.

Mélanges bibliques rédigés en l'honneur de André Robert (Paris 1957). [cf. J. Coppens, A. Deissler, A. Descamps]

Mercati, J., *Psalterii Hexapli reliquiae cura et studio Ioh. Card. Mercati editae* - I, (Bibl. Vaticana 1958).

Merrill, A. L., "Psalm XXIII and the Jerusalem Tradition," *VT* 15 (1965), pp. 354-360.

Meysing, J., "A Text-Reconstruction of Ps CXVII (CXVIII):27," *VT* 10 (1960), pp. 130-137.

Michel, D., "Studien zu den sogenannten Thronbesteigungspsalmen," *VT* 6 (1956), pp. 40-68.

Id., *Tempora und Satzstellung in den Psalmen* (Bonn 1960).

Miller, A., "Gibt es direkt messianische Psalmen?" *Misc. Bibl. B. Ubach* (Montserrat 1953), pp. 201-209.

Id., "Die psalmen in christlicher Sicht," *BiLit* 24 (1956f), pp. 134-140.

Miller, P. D., "Two critical Notes on Psalm 68 and Deuteronomy 33," *HarvTR* 57 (1964), pp. 240-243.

Moeller, H. R., "Biblical Research and Old Testament Translation," *BiTrans* 13 (1962), pp. 16-22. [Ps 8:2]

Möller, H., "Strophenbau der Psalmen," *ZAW* 50 (1932), pp. 240-256.

Montagnini, F., "Illuminans te mirabiliter a montibus aeternis (Ps 76:5)," *VD* 40 (1962), pp. 258-263.

Montgomery, J. A., "Recent Developments in the Study of the Psalter," *AnglTR* 16 (1934), pp. 185-198.

Id., "Stanza-formation in Hebrew Poetry," *JBL* 64 (1945), pp. 379-384.

Moos, M. F., *Les Psaumes, prières chrétiennes* (Paris 1956).

Morag, S., "Light is sown (Ps 97:11)," *Tarbiz* 33 (1963), pp. 140-148.

Morant, P., *Das Psalmengebet. Neu übersetzt und für das Leben erklärt* (Schwyz 1948).

Moré, P., "Métaphores de la protection divine dans les Psaumes," *RClAfr* 10 (1955), pp. 577-584.

Moreton, M. J., "The Sacrifice of Praise," *Church Qu. Rev.* 165 (1964), pp. 481-494.

Morgenstern, J., "The Book of the Covenant," *HUCA* 5 (1928), 1-151. [the

greater part is devoted to the Ark]
Id., "Biblical Theophanies," *Z. f. Assyr.* 25 (1911), pp. 139-193 and 28 (1914), pp. 15-60.
Id., "The Gates of Righteousness," *HUCA* 6 (1929), pp. 1-37. [Pss 24 and 118]
Id., "The mythical Background of Psalm 82," *HUCA* 14 (1939), pp. 29-126.
Id., "Psalm 48," *HUCA* 16 (1941f), pp. 1-95. [cf. *JBL* 1945, p. 285f]
Id., "Psalms 8 and 19 A," *HUCA* 19 (1945f), pp. 491-523.
Id., "Psalm 23," *JBL* 65 (1946), pp. 13-24.
Id., "Psalm 11," *JBL* 69 (1950), pp. 221-231.
Id., "Psalm 126," *Homenaje a Millás Vallicrosa* II (Barcelona 1956), pp. 107-117.
Id., "The Cultic Setting of the Enthronement Psalms," *HUCA* 35 (1964), pp. 1-42.
Mowan, O., "Quatuor Montes Sacri in Ps 89:13?" *VD* 41 (1963), pp. 11-20.
Mowinckel, S., *Psalmenstudien* I-VI (Oslo 1921-1924).
Id., "Zum Problem der Hebräischen Metrik," *Fs. A. Bertholet* (Tübingen 1950), pp. 379-394.
Id., "Traditionalism and Personality in the Psalms," *HUCA* 22 (1950f), pp. 205-231.
Id., *Zum israelitischen Neujahr und zur Deutung der Thronbesteigungspsalmen* (Oslo 1952).
Id., "Metrischer Aufbau und Textkritik an Psalm 8 illustriert," *Studia Orientalia* I. Pedersen... (Hauniae 1953), pp. 250-262.
Id., *Der achtundsechzigste Psalm* (Oslo 1954). [cf. *RB* 1956, pp. 129-132]
Id., "Psalm Criticism between 1900 and 1935. Ugarit and Psalm Exegesis," *VT* 5 (1955), pp. 13-33.
Id., "Psalms and Wisdom," *Wisdom in Israel and in the ancient Near-East, Fs. H. H. Rowley, VTSuppl.* 3 (1955), pp. 204-224.
Id., *Real and Apparent Tricola in Hebrew Psalm Poetry* (Oslo 1958).
Id., *The Psalms in Israel's Worship,* I-II (Oxford 1962): a translation by D. R. Ap-Thomas of the fully revised text of *Offersang og Sangoffer,* Oslo 1951. [will be quoted as Mowinckel I or II; see II, p. 282f, for a complete list of M.'s works, and §5d, 7b, 8a, 13a, 14d on some of his views]
Muilenburg, J., "Psalm 47," *JBL* 63 (1944), pp. 235-256.
Id., "A Study in Hebrew rhetoric, repetition and style," *VTSuppl* I (Leyden 1953), pp. 128-149.
Munch, P. A., "Einige Bemerkungen zu den 'aniyyim und den resha'im in den Psalmen," *Le Monde Oriental* 30 (1936), pp. 13-26.
Id., "Das Problem des Reichtums in den Psalmen 37, 49, 73," *ZAW* 55 (1937), pp. 36-46.
Muntingh, L. M., "A few social concepts in the Psalms and their relation to the Canaanite residential area," *Studies on the Psalms,* pp. 48-57.
Murphy, R., *A Study of Psalm 72* (Washington 1948).
Id., "A New Classification of Literary Forms in the Psalms," *CBQ* 21 (1959), pp. 83-87.
Murphy, R. A. T., *A Commentary to the Psalms in the Little Office of the Blessed Virgin* (New York 1953).

Nácar, E., "Rey y sacerdote. Salmo 110," *EstBib* 5 (1946), pp. 281-302.

Nagel, G., "A propos des rapports du Psaume 104 avec les textes égyptiens," *Fs. für A. Bertholet* (Tübingen 1950), pp. 395-403.

Neusner, J., *The 89th Psalm; Paradigm of Israel's Faith* (London 1965).

Neuwirth, A., *"kis'akā 'elōhîm. Dein Thron, O Gott"* (Ps 45:7). *"Untersuchungen zum Gottkönigtum im Alten Orient und im Alten Testament"* (Diss. Graz 1963f).

Nicolsky, N., *Spuren magischer Formeln in den Psalmen,* BZAW 46 (Giessen 1927).

Nober, P., "De torrente in via bibet (Ps 110:7a)," *VD* 26 (1948), pp. 351-353.

Nogosek, R., *The Royal Psalms in Form Criticism* (Paris 1961). [typescript]

Nötscher, F., *Die Psalmen* (Würtzburg 1947). [cf. *ETL* 1966, p. 686f]

Obermann, J., "An Antiphonical Psalm from Ras Shamra," *JBL* 55 (1936), pp. 21-42.

O'Callaghan, R. T., "A Note on the Canaanite Background of Psalm 82," *CBQ* 15 (1953), pp. 311-314.

Id., "Echoes of Canaanite Literature in the Psalms," *VT* 4 (1954), pp. 164-176.

Oesterley, W. O. E., *A Fresh Approach to the Psalms* (London 1937).

Id., *The Psalms translated with textcritical and exegetical Notes,* I-II (London 1939 + 1954).

Ohlmeyer, A., *Reichtum der Psalmen. Erschlossen von Heiligen aller Christlicher Zeiten,* I-II (Frankfurt 1965).

Osty, E., *Les Psaumes. Traduction nouvelle avec introduction et notes* (Paris 1960).

Palmer, M., "The Cardinal Points in Psalm 48," *Bib* 46 (1965), p. 357f.

Pannier, E.-H. Renard, *Les Psaumes. La Sainte Bible, L. Pirot* (Paris 1950).

Páramo, S. del, *Libro de los Salmos, EncBib* VI (Barcelona 1965), pp. 269-285.

Pascual, B., "Las dos comparaciones del Salmo 133 y su transcendencia doctrinal," *EstBib* 17 (1958), pp. 189-197.

Paterson, J., *The Praises of Israel. Studies Literary and Religious in the Psalms* (New York 1950).

Patton, J. H., *Canaanite Parallels in the Book of Psalms* (Baltimore 1944). [cf. *CBQ* 1946, p. 104f]

Pautrel, R., "Si dormiatis inter medios cleros (Ps 68:14)," *RSR* 33 (1946), pp. 359-367.

Id., "Absorpti sunt juncti petrae judices eorum (Ps 141-140:6)," *RSR* 44 (1956), pp. 219-228.

Id., "Essai sur le Psaume 57 (58):8ss," *RSR* 44 (1956), pp. 566-572.

Id., "Immola Deo sacrificium laudis (Ps 50:14)," *Mélanges Bibliques ...* pp. 234-240.

Id., "Sur le texte de Ps 17 (16):14," *RSR* 46 (1958), pp. 78-84.

Id., "Le style de cour et le Psaume 72," *A la rencontre de Dieu ...* pp. 157-163.

Id., "La Mort est leur pasteur (sur le texte de Ps. 49-48:14, 15)," *RSR* 54 (1966), pp. 530-536.

Pax, E., "Studien zur Theologie von Ps 29," *BZ* 6 (1962), pp. 93-100.

Id., "Studien zum Vergeltunsproblem der Psalmen," *Liber Annuus* 11 (1960f), pp. 56-112.

Pedersen, J., *Israel, its Life and Culture*, I-II; III-IV (London-Copenhagen 1926 and 1940).

Peinador, M., "Los attributos 'misericordia,' 'justitia,' 'veritas' en los Salmos," *Virtud y Letras* 52 (1954), pp. 228-241.

Id., *Los Salmos, plegaría de la Iglesia y de los fieles* (Madrid 1957).

Peters, J. P., *The Psalms as Liturgies* (New York 1922).

Petuchowski, J. J., "*Hoshi'ah na* in Ps 118:25 — A Prayer for Rain," *VT* 5 (1955), pp. 266-271.

Pfeiffer, R. H., *Introduction to the Old Testament* (New York-London 1941, 1948). [cf. §5b]

Philonenko, M., "L'origine essénienne des cinq psaumes syriaques de David," *Sem* 9 (1959), pp. 35-48.

Piatti, T., *Il Libro dei Salmi. Versione omòfona dall'originale ebraico criticamente e metricamente ricostrutto, con introduzione critica sulla poesia e la metrica ebraica* (Roma 1954).

Pidoux, G., *Du portique à l'autel. Introduction aux Psaumes* (Neuchâtel 1959).

Pierik, M., *The Psalter in the Temple and the Church* (Washington 1957). [the musical adaptation of the Psalms]

Podechard, E., "Psaume LXVIII," *RB* 54 (1947), pp. 502-520.

Id., "Psaume 110," *Etudes de critique et d'histoire religieuse, volume offert à L. Vaganay* (Lyon 1948), pp. 7-24.

Id., *Le Psautier*, I: Pss 1-75. *Notes critiques. Traduction littérale et explication historique* (Lyon 1949). [also: Pss 95-100 + 110, Lyon 1954]

Porter, J. R., "The Interpretations of 2 Sam. VI and Psalm CXXXII," *JTS* 5 (1954), pp. 161-173.

Id., "Psalm XLV:7," *JTS* 12 (1961), pp. 51-53.

Porubčan, S., "Il Salmo *De Profundis* (Sal 130)," *Aloisiana* 1 (1960), pp. 3-17.

Power, E., "Sion or Si'on in Psalm 133 (Vulg 132)?" *Bib* 3 (1922), pp. 342-349.

Id., "The shepherd's two rods in modern Palestine and in some passages of the Old Testament (Ps 23:4; Zach 11:7ff; 1 Sam 17:43)," *Bib* 9 (1928), pp. 434-442.

Press, R., "Die eschatologische Ausrichtung des 51. Psalms," *TZBas* 11 (1955), pp. 241-249.

The Psalms: Fides Translation (Notre-Dame, Ind. 1963).

The Psalms, A Prayer Book, also the Canticles of the Roman Breviary (Benziger, New York 1945). [cf. *CBQ* 1946, pp. 355-359]

Puukko, A., "Der Feind in den Alttestamentlichen Psalmen" *OTS* VIII (1950), pp. 47-65.

Quell, G., *Das kultische Problem der Psalmen* (Berlin 1926). [cf. §8f]

Rabinowitz, L., "Does Midrash Tillim reflect the Triennial Cycle of Psalms?" *JQR* 26 (1935f), pp. 349-368.

Rabinowitz, I., "The Existence of a hitherto unknown Interpretation of Ps 107 among the Dead Sea Scrolls," *BA* 14 (1951), p. 50ff.

Rabinowitz, L. J., "The Psalms in Jewish Liturgy," *Historia Judaica* 6 (1944), pp. 109-122. [cf. *CBQ* 1945, p. 353]

Rad, G. von, "Erwägungen zu den Königspsalmen," *ZAW* 57 (1940-41), pp. 216-222.

Id., "Gerechtigkeit' und 'Leben' in der Kultsprache der Psalmen," *Fs. für A. Bertholet* (Tübingen 1950), pp. 418-437.

Id., "Hiob XXXVIII und die altägyptische Weishheit," *VTSuppl.* III (1955), pp. 293-301. [for Ps 148]

Id., *Old Testament Theology*, I-II (Edinburgh-London 1962, 1965).

Rahlfs, A., *'Ani und 'anaw in den Psalmen* (Göttingen 1892). [cf. §12a]

Ramlot, M. L., "Hymne à la gloire du Créateur, Psaume 104," *BiViChr* 31 (1960), pp. 39-47.

Ravanelli, V., *Psalmus 89 (88): Textus - Compositio - Doctrina* (Romae 1957).

Reinelt, H., *Die altorientalische und biblische Weisheit und ihr Einfluss auf den Psalter* (Diss., Freiburg i. Br. 1966).

Rees, W., "The New Latin Psalter," *Scripture*, 4 (1950), pp. 205-212.

Rendtorff, R., "El, Ba'al und Jahwe." Erwägungen zum Verhältnis von kanaanäischer und israelitischer Religion," *ZAW* 78 (1966), pp. 277-292.

Rengstorf, K. H., "Old and New Testament Traces of a Formula of the Judaean Royal Ritual," *NT* 5 (1962), pp. 229-244.

Rhodes, A. B., *Creation and Salvation in the Psalter* (Chicago 1952).

Richardson, R. D., "The Psalms as Christian Prayer and Praises," *AnglTR* 42 (1960), pp. 326-346.

Ricotti, A. L., "I Salmi nel Culto Giudaico," *BibOr* 3 (1961), pp. 161-174.

Ridderbos, N. H., *Psalmen en Cultus* (Kampen 1950).

Id., "Jahwäh malak," *VT* 4 (1954), pp. 87-89.

Id., *De "Werkers van Ongerechtigheid" in de individuelle Psalmen* (Kampen 1939).

Id., *De Psalmen*, I: Pss 1-41 (Kampen 1962).

Id., "The Psalms: Style-Figures and Structures (certain considerations, with special references to Pss 22, 25, 45)," *OTS* XIII (1963), pp. 43-76.

Id., "The Structure of Psalm 40," *OTS* XIV (1965), pp. 296-304.

Id., "Psalm 51:5-6," *Studia biblica et semitica: Fs. T. c. Vriezen* (Vageningen 1966), pp. 299-312.

Rinaldi, G., "Il Salmo 23 (Volg 22)," *BibOr* 3 (1961), pp. 81-85.

Id., "Synagoga deorum (Ps 82)," *BibOr* 7 (1965), pp. 9-11.

Id., "Al termine delle due vie (Salmo 1)," *BibOr* 9 (1967), pp. 69-75.

Ringgren, H., "Einige Bemerkungen zum LXXIII Psalm," *VT* 3 (1953), pp. 265-272.

Id., "Quelques traits essentiels de la piété des Psaumes," *Mélanges Bibliques* ... pp. 205-213.

Id., *The Faith of the Psalmists* (London 1963). [§8d, 12f]

Id., "Enthronement Festival or Covenant Renewal?," *Biblical Research*, 7 (1962), pp. 45-48.

Rios, R., "A Call to Worship (Ps 94, Vulg.)," *Scripture* 1 (1946), pp. 74-77.

Id., "Thirst for God (Psalms 41 and 42)," *Scripture* 2 (1947), pp. 34-38.

Robert, A., "Considérations sur le messianisme du Psaume 2," *RSR* 39 (1951), pp. 88-98. [see also above: *Mélanges Bibliques*...]

Id., "L'exégèse des Psaumes selon les méthodes de la 'Formgeschichte.' Exposé et critique," *Misc. Bibl. B. Ubach* (Montserrat 1953), pp. 211-225. [cf. J. Coppens in *Le Psautier*, R. De Langhe edit., p. 31ff + §7b]

Robinson, H. W., "The Inner life of the Psalmists," *The Psalmists* [cf. D. C. Simpson] pp. 45-66.

Id., "The Social Life of the Psalmists," *ibid.*, pp. 67-86.

Robinson, T. H., "The God of the Psalmists," *ibid.*, pp. 23-44. [cf. §8d]

Id., "The Eschatology of the Psalmists," *ibid.*, pp. 87-108.

Id., "Basic Principles of Hebrew poetic form," *Fs. A. Bertholet* (Tübingen 1950) pp. 438-450.

Robinson, W., "Psalm 118. A Liturgy for the Admission of a Proselyte," *Church Qu. Rev.* 144 (1947), pp. 179-183.

Rodd, C. S., *Psalms 73-150. Epworth's Preacher's Commentary* (London 1964).

Roifer, A., "Psalm 73," *Tarbiz* 32 (1963), pp. 109-113.

Rose, A., "L'influence des Psaumes sur les annonces et les récits de la Passion et de la Résurrection dans les Évangiles," *Le Psautier* [cf. R. De Langhe] pp. 297-356.

Id., "Le Psaume 44 (45). Son interprétation chrétienne," *QuLitPar* 36, 4 (1955), pp. 178-189.

Id., *Psaumes et prière chrétienne* (Bruges 1965).

Rosenberg, R. A., "Yahweh becomes King," *JBL* 85 (1966), pp. 297-307.

Rosenstock, E.-E. Huessy, "Vivit Deus," *In memoriam Ernst Lohmeyer* (Stuttgart 1951), pp. 250-260. [Ps 18:47]

Ross, J. P., "Yahweh Seba'ot in Samuel and Psalms," *VT* 17 (1967), pp. 76-92. [cf. §18a]

Rowley, H. H., "The Text and Structure of Psalm 2," *JTS* 42 (1941), pp. 143-154.

Id., "Melchizedek and Zadok (Gen 14 and Ps 110)," *Fs. für A. Bertholet* (Tübingen 1950), pp. 461-472.

Id., *Worship in Ancient Israel* (London 1967), pp. 173-212, "Psalmody and Music."

Sabbe, M., "Geborgenheid bij God, Ps 96," *ColBG* 7 (1961), pp. 68-85.

Sabourin, L., *Un classement littéraire des Psaumes* (Bruges 1964). [= *ScEcc* 1964, pp. 23-58]

Sainte-Marie, D. H. de, *S. Hieronymi Psalterium juxta Hebraeos. Édition critique* (Libr. Edit. Vaticana 1954).

Salguero, J., "Quien es el 'desamparado' del salmo 22?," *CiTom* 84 (1957), pp. 3-35.

Salmon, P., *Les tituli psalmorum des manuscrits latins* (Paris 1959). [cf. *TS* 1966, p. 94f]

San Pedro, E., "Problemata philologica Ps. XIV," *VD* 45 (1967), pp. 65-78.

Sanders, J. A., "The Scroll of Psalms (11QPss) from Cave 11," *BASOR* 165 (1962), pp. 11-15.

Id., "Ps. 151 in 11QPss," *ZAW* 75 (1963), pp. 73-86.

Id., *The Psalms Scroll of Qumrân Cave 11 (11Psᵃ), Discoveries in the Judaean Desert of Jordan.* IV (Oxford 1965).

Id., "*Variorum* in the Psalms Scroll (11QPsᵃ)," *HarvTR* 59 (1966), pp. 83-94.

Id., *The Dead Sea Psalms scroll* (Cornell Univ. Press, Ithica, N.Y.. 1967).

Sarna, N. M., "The Psalm for the Sabbath Day (Ps 92)," *JBL* 81 (1962), pp. 155-168.

Id., "Psalm 89: a Study in inner Biblical Exegesis," *P. W. Lown Institute, Brandeis Univ., Studies and Texts* 1 (1963), pp. 29-46.

Sauer, G., *Die strafende Gerechtigkeit Gottes in den Psalmen. Eine frömmigkeitsgeschichtliche Untersuchung* (Halle 1956).

Id., "I nemici nei Salmi," *Prot.* 13 (1958), pp. 201-207.

Id., "Erwägungen zum Alter des Psalmendichtung in Israel," *TZBas* 22 (1966), pp. 81-95.

Savignac, J. de, "Essai d'interprétation du Psaume CX à l'aide de la littérature égyptienne," *OTS* 9 (1951), pp. 107-135.

Id., "Théologie pharaonique et messianisme d'Israël," *VT* 7 (1957), pp. 82-90.

Scammon, J. H., *Living with the Psalms* (Valley Forge, Pa. 1967).

Scharf, A.ʼ M., "Quaedam commentationes in Ps 52:7," *VD* 38 (1960), pp. 213-222.

Schedl, C., "Aus dem Bache am Wege. Textkritische Bemerkungen zu Ps 110 (109):7," *ZAW* 73 (1961), pp. 290-297.

Id., "Die Pfade des Rechtsbrechers ʼorhôt-pārîṣ (Ps 17:4)," *BZ* 6 (1962), pp. 100-102.

Id., "Psalm 8 in ugaritischer Sicht," *Forschungen und Fortschritte* 38 (1964), pp. 183-185.

Id., "Die 'Heiligen' und die 'Herrlichen' in Ps 16:1-4," *ZAW* 76 (1964), pp. 171-175.

Id., "Neue Vorschläge zu Text und Deutung des Psalmes XLV," *VT* 14 (1964), pp. 310-318.

Scheele, P.-W., *Opfer des Wortes. Gebete der Heiden aus fünf Jahrtausenden* (Paderborn 1960).

Scheifler, J. R., "El Salmo 22 y la Crucifixión del Señor," *EstBib* 24 (1965), pp. 5-83.

Schildenberger, J., "Zur Textkritik von Ps 45 (44)," *BZ* 3 (1959), pp. 31-43.

Id., "Tod und Leben. Eine Auslegung von Ps 30 (29)," *BibKirche* 13 (1958), pp. 110-115.

Id., "Bemerkungen zum Strophenbau der Psalmen," *EstE* 34 (1960), pp. 673-687.

Id., "Psalm 78 (77) und die Pentateuchquellen," *Lex Tua Veritas, Fs. H. Junker* (Trier 1961), pp. 231-256.

Schilling, O., "Noch einmal die Fluchpsalmen," *TGl* 47 (1957), pp. 177-185.

Schmid, H. H., *Wesen und Geschichte der Weisheit. Eine Untersuchung zur Altorientalischen und Israelitischen Weisheitsliteratur, BZAW* 101 (Berlin 1966). [Wisdom in Israel: pp. 144-201; as personified: pp. 149-154]

Schmid, R., "Die Fluchpsalmen im christlichen Gebet," *Theologie im Wandel. Fs. Kath. Th. Fak. Tübingen* (München-Freiburg 1967).

Schmidt, H., *Das Gebet des Angeklagten im Alten Testament*, BZAW 49 (Giessen 1928). [cf. also in *Old Testament Essays*, London 1927, pp. 143-155 + §20a] Id., *Die Psalmen* (Tübingen 1934).

Schmidt, L. (ed.), *Die Psalmen*, I. Halbband (Stuttgart 1967).

Schmidt, W., *Königtum Gottes in Ugarit und Israel. Zur Herkunft der "Königsprädication" Jahwes*, BZAW, 80, 2nd ed. (Berlin 1966). [cf. pp. 80-97, "Das Königtum Gottes in Israel."]

Schmidt, W. H., "Gott und Mensch in Ps. 130. Formgeschichtliche Erwägungen," *TZBas*, 22 (1966), pp. 241-253.

Schmuttermayr, G., "Um Psalm 87 (86):5," *BZ* 7 (1963), pp. 104-110.

Id., *Studien zum Text der Ps 9-10 und 18. Probleme der Textkritik und Übersetzung und das Psalterium Pianum* (Diss. München 1966).

Schneider, H., "Die Psalterteilung in Fünfziger-und Zehnergruppen," *Universitas*, Fs. A. Stohr, I (Mainz 1960), pp. 36-47.

Schollmeyer, A., *Sumerisch-babylonische Hymnen und Gebete an Shamash* (Paderborn 1912).

Schönbächler, V., *Die Stellung der Psalmen zum alttestamentlichen Opferkultus* (Freiburg 1941).

Schreiner, J., *Sion-Jerusalem, Jahwes Königssitz. Theologie der Heiligen Stadt im Alten Testament* (München 1963).

Schulz, A., *Die Psalmen und die Cantica des Röm. Breviers verdeutscht* (Regensburg 1939).

Schwarzwäller, K., *Die Feinde des Individuums in den Psalmen* (Diss. Hamburg 1963). [typescript]

Scott, R. B. Y., *The Psalms as Christian Praise* (London 1958).

Seeligmann, I. L., "A psalm from the pre-regal times," *VT* 14 (1964), pp. 75-92. [Dt 33]

Segula, F., "Messias Rex in Psalmis," *VD* 32 (1954); pp. 23-33; 77-83; 142-154.

Sellers, O. R., "The Status and Prospects of Research concerning the Psalms," *Willoughby, The Study of the Bible Today and Tomorrow* (Chicago 1947), pp. 129-143.

Shenkel, J. D., "An Interpretation of Ps 93:5," *Bib* 46 (1965), pp. 401-416.

Sievers, E., *Metrische Studien I-III* (Berlin 1904-1907).

Simpson, D. C. (edit.), *The Psalmists* (Oxford 1926). [cf. H. Gressmann, T. H. Robinson, H. W. Robinson, G. R. Driver, A. M. Blackman + §5c]

Skehan, P. W., "Strophic Structure in Ps 72 (71)," *Bib* 40 (1959), pp. 302-308.

Id., "A Psalm Manuscript from Qumran (4QPsᵇ)," *CBQ* 26 (1964), pp. 313-322.

Id., "Borrowings from the Psalms in the Book of Wisdom," *CBQ* 10 (1948), pp. 384-397.

Smal, P. J. N., *Die universalisme in die Psalms* (Kampen 1956).

Smend, R., "Ueber das Ich der Psalmen," *ZAW* 8 (1888), p. 56ff.

Snaith, N. H., *Studies in the Psalter* (London 1934).

Id., *Hymns of the Temple* (London 1951).

Id., "Selah," *VT* 2 (1952), pp. 43-56.

Snijders, L. A., "Psaume 26 et l'innocence," *OTS* 13 (1963), pp. 112-130.

Soggin, J. A., "Appunti per l'esegesi cristiana della prima parte del Salmo 22,"

BibOr 7 (1965), pp. 105-116.

Sonne, I., "The second psalm," *HUCA* 19 (1945-46), pp. 43-55.

Id., "Psalm Eleven," *JBL* 68 (1949), pp. 241-245.

Sorg, R., *Hesed und Hasid in the Psalms* (St. Louis 1953). [cf. *CBQ* 1955, p. 520]

Sparks, H. F. D., "A Textual Note on Psalm 104:16," *JTS* 48 (1947), p. 57f.

Sperber, A., *A Historical Grammar of Biblical Hebrew* (Leiden 1966).

Stamm, J. J., "Ein Vierteljahrhundert Psalmenforschung," *Theol. Rundschau* 23 (1955), pp. 1-68. [complete bibliog.: 1929-1954]

Id., "Eine Bemerkung zum Anfang des achten Psalms," *TZBas* 13 (1957), pp. 470-478.

Id., "Erwägungen zu Ps 23," *BEvT* 44 (1966), pp. 120-128.

Steiert, B., "Einführung in die neue römische Psalmenversion," *Anal. S. Ord. Cist.* 7 (Roma 1951) pp. 91-166; 11 (Roma 1955), pp. 199-324. [cf. A. Bea, *VD* 1956, pp. 321-326]

Steinmann, J., *"Les Psaumes"* (Paris 1951).

Stoebe, H. J., *Gott sei mir Sünder gnädig. Eine Auslegung des 51. Psalms* (Neukirchen 1958).

Id., "Erwägungen zu Ps 110 auf dem Hintergrund von 1 Sam. 21," *Fs. F. Baumgärtel* (Erlangen 1959), pp. 175-191.

Strobel, A., "La conversion des gentils dans les psaumes" (Roma 1949). [typescript]

Strugnell, J., "A Note on Ps 126:1," *JTS* 7 (1956), pp. 239-243.

Id., "Notes on the Text and Transmission of the Apocryphal Psalms 151, 154 (= Syr. II) and 155 (= Syr. III)," *Harv. Th. Rev.* 59 (1966), pp. 257-281.

Studies on the Psalms: Papers read at the 6th Meeting of Die O. T. Werkgemeenskap in Suid-Afrika (Potchefstroom 1963). [cf. S. du Toit, J. J. Glueck, J. H. Kroeze, L. M. Muntingh, I. H. Eybers, A. H. Van Zyl, F. C. Fensham]

Stummer, F., "Die Psalmengattungen im Lichte der altorientalischen Hymnenlitteratur," *JSOR* 8 (1924), p. 123ff.

Id., *Sumerisch-akkadische Parallelen zum Aufbau alttestamentlicher Psalmen* (Paderborn 1922).

Sutcliffe, E. F., "A Note on Psalm CIV:8a," *VT* 2 (1952), pp. 177-179.

Szörenyi, A., "Quibus criteriis dignosci possit, qui Psalmi ad usum liturgicum compositi sint?" *Bib* 23 (1942), pp. 333-368.

Id., *Psalmen und Kult in Alten Testament. Zur Formgeschichte der Psalmen* (Budapest 1961). [rejects as a myth the existence of a special feast of Yahweh's enthronement; cf. §8f]

Teófilo de Orbiso, "El 'Reino de Dios' en los Salmos," *EstFranciscanos* (Barcelona) 49 (1948); pp. 13-35; 198-209.

Terrien, S., *The Psalms and their Meaning for Today* (New York 1952).

Id., "Creation, Cultus, and Faith in the Psalter," in *Horizons of Theological Education*, Fs. C. L. Taylor, edit. by J. B. Coburn (Dayton, Ohio 1966), pp. 116-128.

Thévenet, J., *La confiance en Dieu dans les Psaumes* (Paris 1965).

Thierry, G. J., "Remarks on various Passages of the Psalms," *OTS* 13 (1963), pp. 77-97. [Pss 7:15; 10:3; 22:10; 23:3f]

Thomas, D. Winton, "*niṣṣab* in Psalm XXXIX:16," *Studies in the Bible presented to Prof. M. H. Segal* (Jerusalem 1964), pp. 10-16.

Id., "Hebrew 'anî, Captivity," *JTS* 16 (1965), p. 444f.

Id., "Psalm XXXV:15f," *JTS* 12 (1961), p. 50f.

Toit, S. du, "Psalms and history," *Studies on the Psalms*, pp. 18-29.

Torczyner, H., *Die Bundeslade und die Anfänge der Religion Israels* (Berlin 1922).

Torrance, T. F., "The Last of the Hallel Psalms," *Evang. Theol.* 28 (1956), pp. 101-108.

Tournay, R., "Le psaume LXVIII," *Vivre et Penser* 2 (1942), pp. 227-245. [= *RB*]

Id., "Notes sur les psaumes," *Vivre et Penser* 3 (1945), pp. 214-237.

Id., "Les psaumes complexes," *RB* 54 (1947), pp. 521-542; 56 (1949), pp. 37-60.

Id., "L'eschatologie individuelle dans les Psaumes," *RB* 56 (1949), pp. 481-506.

Id., "Notules sur les Psaumes (Pss XIX:2-5; LXXI:15f)," *Alttestamentliche Studien F. Nötscher zum sechzigsten Geburtstage* . . . (Bonn 1950), pp. 271-280.

Id., "Sur quelques rubriques des Psaumes," *Mélanges Bibliques* . . . pp. 197-204.

Id., "Recherches sur la chronologie des Psaumes," *RB* 65 (1958), pp. 321-357; 66 (1959), pp. 161-190. [cf. §5e, 8b, 9a]

Id., "Le Psaume LXVIII et le livre des Juges," *RB* 66 (1959), pp. 358-368.

Id., "Le Psaume 141," *VT* 9 (1959), pp. 58-64.

Id., "Le Psaume CX," *RB* 67 (1960), pp. 5-41.

Id., "Le Psaume 72:16 et le réveil de Melqart," *Trav. Inst. Cath.* 10 (Paris 1964), pp. 97-104.

R. Tournay et R. Schwab, *Les Psaumes* (ed. 2, Paris 1955). [= *BJ*]

Travers, J. C.-M., "Le nouveau Psautier," *La Maison-Dieu*, n. 5 (1946), pp. 60-65. [also in the same number, on the New Latin Psalter: pp. 66-106, by various authors; see also *ibid.* n. 33 (1953), pp. 72-92]

Treves, M., "The Date of Ps XXIV," *VT* 10 (1960), pp. 428-434. [composed for the 25th day of Chisleu, 164 B.C.!]

Id., "Two acrostic Psalms," *VT* 15 (1965), pp. 81-90. [Pss 2 and 110, related to the Hasmoneans!]

Tsevat, M., *A Study of the Language of the Biblical Psalms* — *JBL Monogr.* series, vol. IX (Philadelphia 1955). [cf. §9d]

Tur-Sinai, H. H., "The Literary Character of the Book of Psalms," *OTS* 8 (1950), pp. 263-281. [cf. H. Torczyner]

Id., "On some obscure passages in the Book of Psalms," *Fs. A. H. Silver* (New York 1963), pp. 1-35.

Tuya, M. de, "El problema biblico de las 'imprecaciones,'" *CiTom* 78 (1951), pp. 171-192; 79 (1952), pp. 3-29.

Ubbelohde, H., *Fluchpsalmen und alttestamentliche Sittlichkeit* (Breslau 1938).

Vaccari, A., "Antica e nuova interpretazione del Salmo 16 (Volg. 15)," *Bib* 14 (1933), pp. 408-434.

Id., "Il Salmo della Risurrezione," *La Redenzione* (Roma 1934), pp. 165-190.

[Pss 16-15]

Id., "I salteri di S. Girolamo e di S. Agostino," *Scritti di erudizione e di filologia* (Roma 1952), pp. 207-255.

Id., *I Salmi tradotti dall'ebraico con a fronte la nuova versióne latina approvata da Pio XII. Seconda edizione completamente rifatta* (Torino 1953).

Id., "Il salmo 108 (109)," *RBibIt* 1 (1953), pp. 55-60.

Vagaggini, G., *Bibbia e spiritualità liturgica con particolare riferimento ai Salmi* (Roma 1964).

Vanbergen, P., "Le psaume 117 (118). Une Eucharistie qui éclaire l'Eucharistie de Jésus," *QLitPar* 45 (1964), pp. 65-81.

Vandenbroucke, F., "Le psautier, prophétie ou prière du Christ?" *QLitPar* 33 (1952), pp. 149-161; 201-213.

Id., *Les Psaumes et le Christ* (Louvain 1955).

Id., "Le Dieu des Psaumes," *Vie Spir.* 74 (1946), pp. 625-640.

Van den Berghe, P., " 'ani et 'anaw dans les Psaumes," *Le Psautier* [cf. R. De Langhe], pp. 272-296. [cf. §12a]

Van der Ploeg, J., *De Psalmen uit de grondtekst vertaald en van korte inleidingen en aantekeningen voorzien* (Roermond/Maaseik 1963).

Id., "Psalm XIX and some of its problems," *JEOL* 17 (1964), pp. 193-201.

Id., "Notes sur le Psaume XLIX," *OTS* 13 (1963), pp. 137-172.

Id., "Le Psaume XCI dans une recension de Qumrân," *RB* 72 (1965), pp. 210-217.

Id., "Réflexions sur les genres littéraires des Psaumes," *Studia Biblica et semitica*: *Fs. T. C. Vriezen* (Vageningen 1966), pp. 265-277.

Van der Weijden, A. H., *Die "Gerechtigkeit" in den Psalmen* (Nimwegen 1952).

Van der Woude, A. S., "Zwei alte Cruces im Psalter," *OTS* 13 (1963), pp. 131-136.

Van Imschoot, P., "De psalmis imprecatoriis," *ColGand* 27 (1944), pp. 89-93.

Van Zyl, A. H., "Psalm 23," *Studies on the Psalms*, pp. 64-83.

Vaux, R. de, "Les chérubins et l'arche d'alliance. Les sphinx gardiens et les trônes divins dans l'Ancient Orient," *Mél. Univ. St.-Joseph* 37 (1961), pp. 93-124 = *Bible et Orient* (Paris 1967), pp. 231-259.

Id., *Ancient Israel*, vol. I: *Social Institutions;* vol. II: *Religious Institutions* (New York 1965).

Vénard, L., "L'utilisation des Psaumes dans l'Epître aux Hébreux," *Mélanges E. Podechard* (Lyon 1945), pp. 253-264; cf. *SDB* II, cc 23-51.

Veugelers, P., "Le Psaume LXXII, poème messianique?" *ETL* 41 (1965), pp. 317-343.

Vilar, Hueso, "El Salmo 24: unidad literaria y ambiente histórico," *EstBib* 22 (1963), pp. 243-253.

Vogt, E., "The 'Place in Life' of Psalm 23," *Bib* 34 (1953), pp. 195-211.

Id., "Der Aufbau von Ps 29," *Bib* 41 (1960), pp. 17-24.

Id., "Ihr Tisch werde zur Falle (Ps 69:23)," *Bib* 43 (1962), pp. 79-82.

Id., "Psalm 26, ein Pilgergebet," *Bib* 43 (1962), pp. 328-337.

Id., "Gratiarum actio Psalmi 40," *VD* 43 (1965), pp. 181-190.

Id., "Die Himmel troffen (Ps 68:9)?," *Bib* 46 (1965), pp. 207-209.

Id., "Regen in Fülle (Psalm 68:10-11)," *Bib* 46 (1965), pp. 359-361.

Id., "Die Wagen Gottes, zehntausendfach, Tausende *šin'án* (Ps 68:18)," *Bib* 46 (1965), pp. 460-463.

Id., "Psalmus 44 et Tragoedia Ezechiae regis," *VD* 45 (1967), pp. 193-200.

Volz, P., "Psalm 49," *ZAW* 55 (1937), pp. 235-264.

Vos, J. G., "The Ethical Problem of the Imprecating Psalms," *Westm. Th. J.* 4, 2 (1942), pp. 123-138.

Vosté, J.-M., "Sur les titres des Psaumes dans la Pešittā surtout d'après la recension orientale," *Bib* 25 (1944), pp. 210-235.

Wächter, L., "Drei umstrittene Psalmstellen (Ps 26:1; 30:8; 90:4-6)," *ZAW* 78 (1966), pp. 61-68.

Wanke, G., *Die Zionstheologie der Korachiten in ihrem traditionsgeschichtlichen Zusammenhang*, BZAW, 97 (Berlin 1966). [Pss 46, 48, 84, 87 are post-exilic]

Ward, J. M., *A Literary and Exegetical Study of the 89th Psalm* (Ann Arbor 1958). [microfilm]

Id., "The Literary Form and the Liturgical Background of Psalm LXXXIX," *VT* 11 (1961), pp. 321-339.

Watts, J. D. W., "Yahweh Malāk Psalms," *TZBas* 21 (1965), pp. 341-348.

Weber, D. R., *Le Psautier Romain et les autres anciens Psautiers latins. Edition critique*, ColBibLat, X (1953).

Weber, J., *Le psautier du bréviaire romain. Texte et commentaire* (Paris 1937).

Weiser, A., "Zur Frage nach den Beziehungen der Psalmen zum Kult: die Darstellung der Theophanie in den Psalmen und im Festkult," *Fs. für Alfred Bertholet* (Tübingen 1950), pp. 513-532.

Id., *The Psalms* (London 1962). [cf. §13c]

Weiss, M., "Wege der neuen Dichtungswissenschaft in ihrer Anwendung auf die Psalmenforschung," *Bib* 42 (1961), pp. 255-302.

Welch, A. C., *The Psalter in Life, Worship and History* (Oxford 1926). [cf. §8f]

Werbeck, W., Art. "Psalmen" (Im AT), *RGG*, IV, 3rd. edit., cf. pp. 672-686. [with bibliogr.]

Westermann, C., "Struktur und Geschichte der Klage im Alten Testament," *ZAW* 66 (1954), pp. 44-80.

Id., *Gewendete Klage. Eine Auslegung des 22. Psalms* (Neukirchen 1955).

Id., "Zur Sammlung des Psalters," *Z. d. Morg. Ges.*, III (1961), p. 388f.

Id., "Vergegenwärtigung der Geschichte in den Psalmen," *Zwischenstation, Fs. K. Kupisch* (München 1963), pp. 253-280.

Id., *The Praise of God in the Psalms*, tr. by K. R. Crim (Richmond, Va. 1965). [cf. §7b, 13ad and 22]

Id., *Der Psalter. Bibl. Seminar im Calwer Verlag* (Stuttgart 1967).

Wevers, J. W., "A Study in the Form Criticism of Individual Complaint Psalms," *VT* 6 (1956), pp. 80-96.

Widengren, G., *The Accadian and Hebrew Psalms of Lamentation as religious Documents, a comparative Study* (Uppsala 1936). [new edit.: Stockholm 1937]

Id., *Sakrales Königtum im Alten Testament und im Judentum* (Stuttgart 1955).

Willesen, F., "The Cultic Situation of Psalm LXXIV," *VT* 2 (1952), pp. 289-

306.
William, P. R., *The Perfect Law of Liberty* (Ps 119), (London 1952).
Williams, W. G., "Liturgical Problems in Enthronement Psalms," *JBR* 25 (1957), pp. 118-122.
Wolff, H. W., "Der Aufruf zur Volksklage," *ZAW* 76 (1964), pp. 48-56.
Wolverton, W. I., "The Psalmists' Belief in God's Presence," *CanJT* 9 (1963), pp. 82-94.
Id., "The Meaning of the Psalms," *AnglTR* 47 (1965), pp. 16-33. [cf. §13b, 14c + on *Pss 46, 99] [on Pss 78, 105, 106 see also *idem* in *CanJT* 10, 1964, pp. 166-176]
Worden, T., *The Psalms are Christian Prayer* (London 1962). [Key patterns of Israelite thought and expression are explained; also two themes often recurring in the Psalms: "the Redemption of Israel," "Yahweh the Conqueror of Israel's Enemies"]
Wright, G. E., *The Old Testament against its Environment* (London 1950), pp. 30-41.
Würthwein, E., "Erwägungen zu Psalm 73," *Fs. für A. Bertholet* (Tübingen 1950), pp. 532-549.
Id., "Erwägungen zu Psalm CXXXIX," *VT* 7 (1957), pp. 165-182.

Young, E. J., *Psalm 139: a Study of the Omniscience of God* (London 1965).

Zandee, J., *Death as an Enemy according to Ancient Egyptian Conceptions* (Leiden 1960).
Id., "Hymnal Sayings addressed to the Sun-god by the High-priest of Amūn Nebwenenef, from his tomb in Thebes," *JEOL* 18 (1964), pp. 253-265.
Zbik, F., *De sensu filiationis divinae in Ps 2* (Romae 1951f).
Zeneboni, M. I., "Il Salterio e la gioia," *RAscMist* 27 (1957), pp. 374-389.
Ziegler, J., "Die Hilfe Gottes 'am Morgen,'" *Alttestamentliche Studien* (Fs. Fr. Nötscher: Bonn 1950), pp. 281-288. [see on *Ps 5:4]
Zink, J. K., "Uncleanness and sin. A Study of Job XIV, 4 and Psalm 51:7," *VT* 17 (1967), pp. 354-361.
Zirker, H., *Die kultische Vergegenwärtigung der Vergangenheit in den Psalmen* (Bonn 1964). [cf. *CBQ* 26, 1964, p. 518f]
Zolli, E., "In margine al *Miserere*," *Sefarad* 9 (1949), pp. 142-151.
Id., *Il Salterio* (Milano 1951).
Id., *I Salmi. Documenti di vita vissuta* (Milano 1953). [cf. *CBQ* 1954, p. 487f]
Zorell, F., "Einführung in die Metrik und Kunstform der hebräischen Psalmendichtung, (Münster 1914).
Id., *Psalterium ex Hebraeo Latinum* (Romae 1928).

SUBJECT INDEX

(Pages of vol. 2 are set in heavy type)